Thank you for picking up *Haikyu!!* volume 31! I've been attending the Spring Tournament for several years now for research purposes. They even let me go down onto the courts in between games to take pictures! I really appreciate it. To think that, one day, I would stand on Tokyo's Orange Court like this... Some things in life can be unexpected. But I kind of feel guilty about it.

Fried Egg

HARUICHI FURUDATE began his manga career when he was 25 years old with the one-shot *Ousama Kid* (King Kid), which won an honorable mention for the 14th Jump Treasure Newcomer Manga Prize. His first series, *Kiben Gakuha, Yotsuya Sensei no Kaidan* (Philosophy School, Yotsuya Sensei's Ghost Stories), was serialized in Weekly Shonen Jump in 2010. In 2012, he began serializing *Haikyu!!* in Weekly Shonen Jump, where i̶t̶ ̶became his most popular work to date.

HAIKYU!!
VOLUME 31
SHONEN JUMP Manga Edition

Story and Art by
HARUICHI FURUDATE

Translation ❶ **ADRIENNE BECK**
Touch-Up Art & Lettering ❷ **ERIKA TERRIQUEZ**
Design ❸ **JULIAN [JR] ROBINSON**
Editor ❹ **MARLENE FIRST**

HAIKYU!! © 2012 by Haruichi Furudate
All rights reserved.
First published in Japan in 2012 by SHUEISHA Inc., Tokyo.
English translation rights arranged by SHUEISHA Inc.

Printed in the U.S.A.

Published by VIZ Media, LLC
P.O. Box 77010
San Francisco, CA 94107

10 9 8 7 6 5 4 3 2 1
First printing, March 2019

VIZ MEDIA
viz.com

SHONEN **JUMP**
shonenjump.com

SHONEN JUMP MANGA

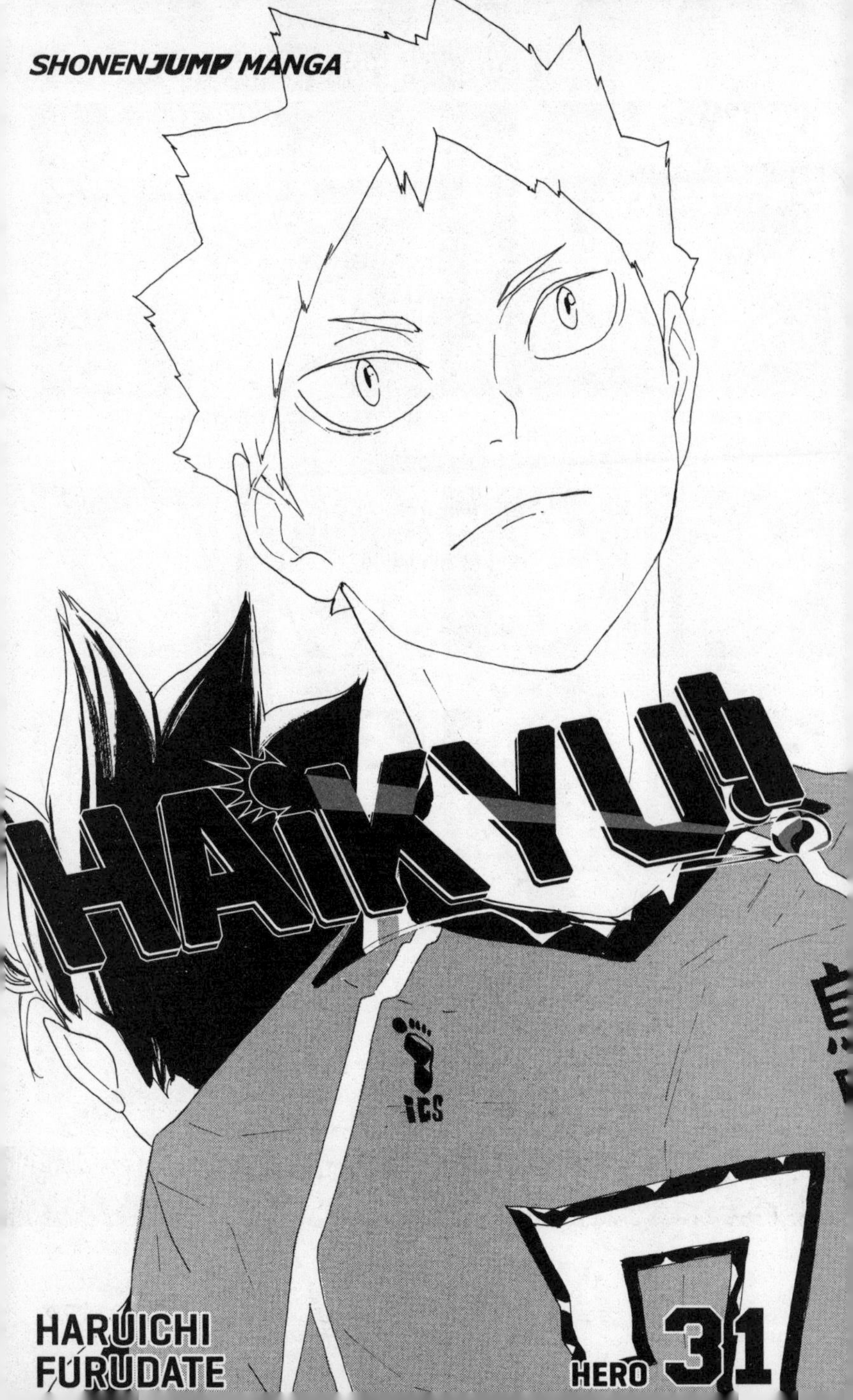

HAIKYU!!

HARUICHI FURUDATE

HERO 31

Karasuno High School Volleyball Club

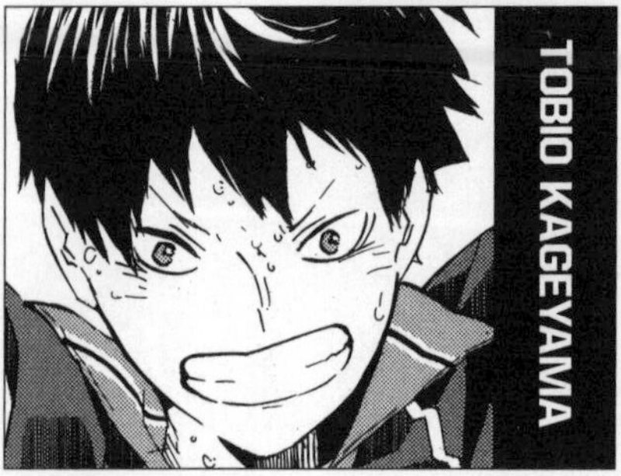
TOBIO KAGEYAMA

1ST YEAR / SETTER

His instincts and athletic talent are so good that he's like a "king" who rules the court. Demanding and egocentric.

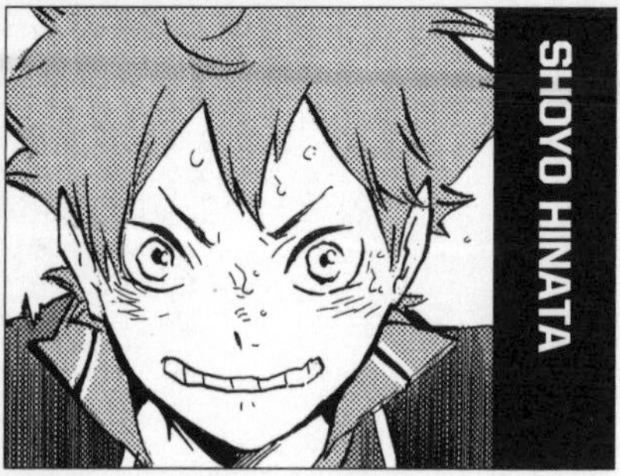
SHOYO HINATA

1ST YEAR / MIDDLE BLOCKER

Even though he doesn't have the best body type for volleyball, he is super athletic. Gets nervous easily.

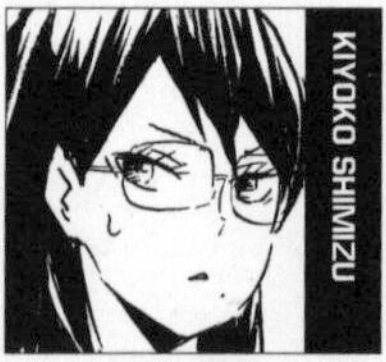
KIYOKO SHIMIZU

3RD YEAR
MANAGER

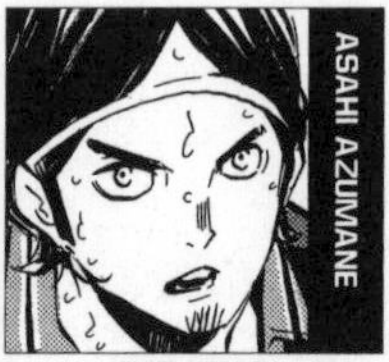
ASAHI AZUMANE

3RD YEAR
WING SPIKER

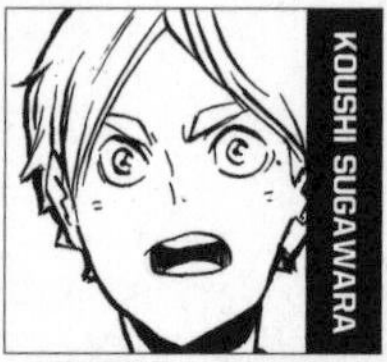
KOUSHI SUGAWARA

3RD YEAR (VICE CAPTAIN)
SETTER

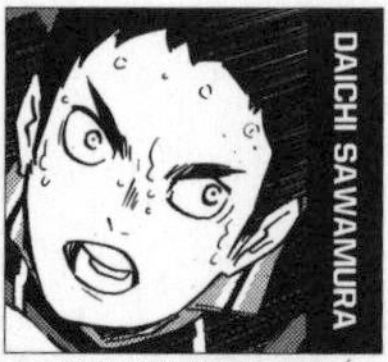
DAICHI SAWAMURA

3RD YEAR (CAPTAIN)
WING SPIKER

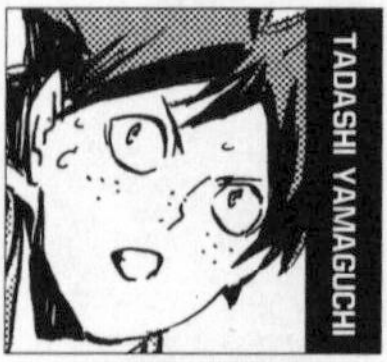
TADASHI YAMAGUCHI

1ST YEAR
MIDDLE BLOCKER

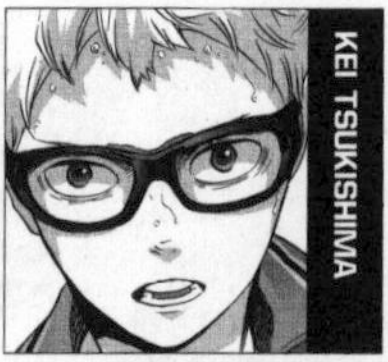
KEI TSUKISHIMA

1ST YEAR
MIDDLE BLOCKER

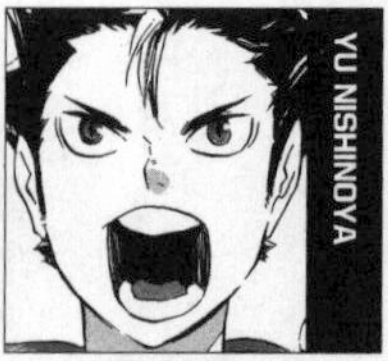
YU NISHINOYA

2ND YEAR
LIBERO

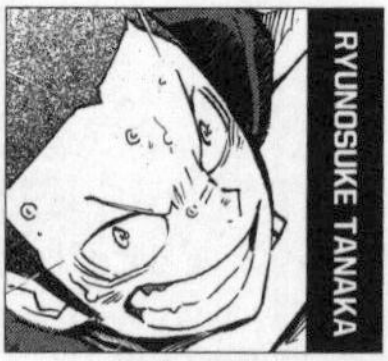
RYUNOSUKE TANAKA

2ND YEAR
WING SPIKER

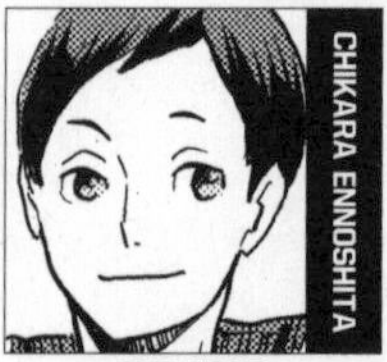
CHIKARA ENNOSHITA

2ND YEAR
WING SPIKER

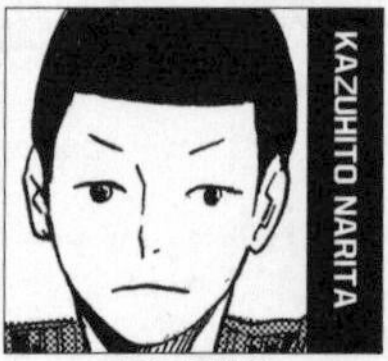
KAZUHITO NARITA

2ND YEAR
MIDDLE BLOCKER

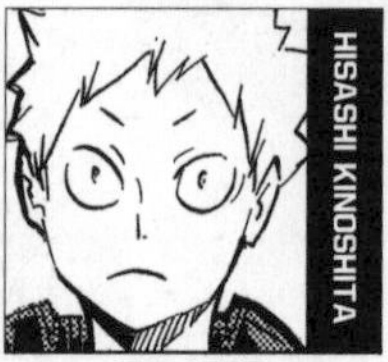
HISASHI KINOSHITA

2ND YEAR
WING SPIKER

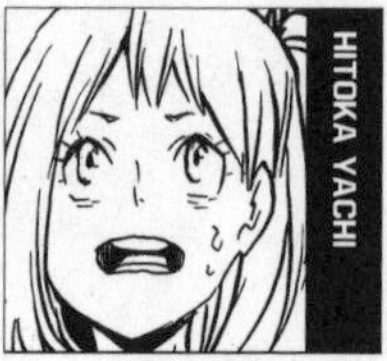
HITOKA YACHI

1ST YEAR
MANAGER

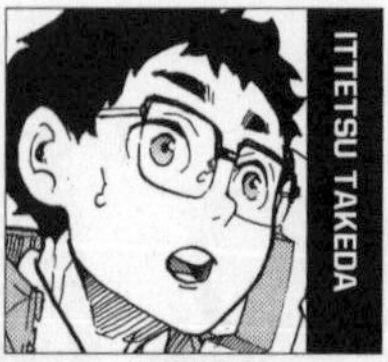
ITTETSU TAKEDA

ADVISER

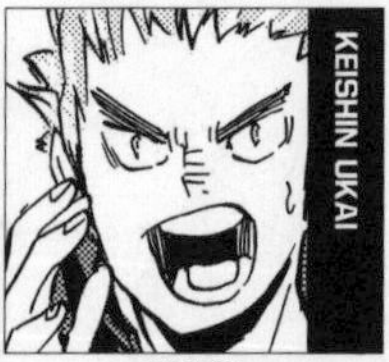
KEISHIN UKAI

COACH

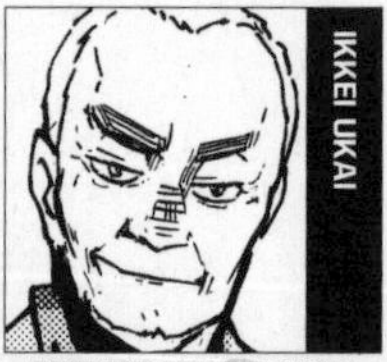
IKKEI UKAI

FORMER HEAD COACH

CHARACTERS

NATIONAL SPRING TOURNAMENT ARC

Inarizaki Volleyball Club

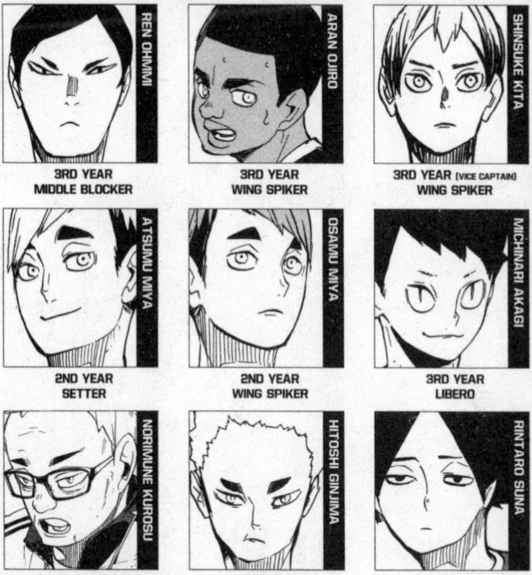

REN OHMI — 3RD YEAR, MIDDLE BLOCKER

ARAN OJIRO — 3RD YEAR, WING SPIKER

SHINSUKE KITA — 3RD YEAR (VICE CAPTAIN), WING SPIKER

ATSUMU MIYA — 2ND YEAR, SETTER

OSAMU MIYA — 2ND YEAR, WING SPIKER

MICHINARI AKAGI — 3RD YEAR, LIBERO

NORIMUNE KUROSU — HEAD COACH

HITOSHI GINJIMA — 2ND YEAR, WING SPIKER

RINTARO SUNA — 2ND YEAR, MIDDLE BLOCKER

Nekoma Volleyball Club

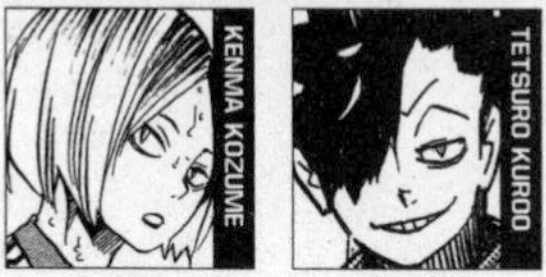

KENMA KOZUME — 2ND YEAR, SETTER

TETSURO KUROO — 3RD YEAR, MIDDLE BLOCKER

Karasuno Cheer Squad

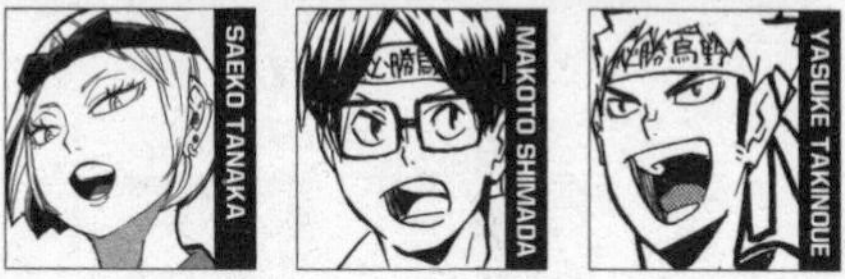

SAEKO TANAKA

MAKOTO SHIMADA

YASUKE TAKINOUE

Ever since he saw the legendary player known as "the Little Giant" compete at the national volleyball finals, Shoyo Hinata has been aiming to be the best volleyball player ever! He decides to join the volleyball club at his middle school and gets to play in an official tournament during his third year. His team is crushed by a team led by volleyball prodigy Tobio Kageyama, also known as "the King of the Court." Swearing revenge on Kageyama, Hinata graduates middle school and enters Karasuno High School, the school where the Little Giant played. However, upon joining the club, he finds out that Kageyama is there too! The two of them bicker constantly, but they bring out the best in each other's talents and become a powerful combo. The Spring Tournament begins! On the second day, Karasuno goes up against Inarizaki, the Greatest Contenders, and gets set point! Inarizaki fights back, targeting Tanaka, who has been in a slump all game. But Tanaka declares he has no time to be looking down and scores the winning point with his super cut shot! Meanwhile, Nekoma plays their round 2 game against Sarugawa. Sarugawa's plan is to exhaust Kenma, but he toughs it out, and after a long, hard-fought game, Nekoma wins! Back at Karasuno's game against Inarizaki, set 2 begins. Inarizaki is finding great success by aiming Atsumu Miya's jump floater serves at...Nishinoya?!

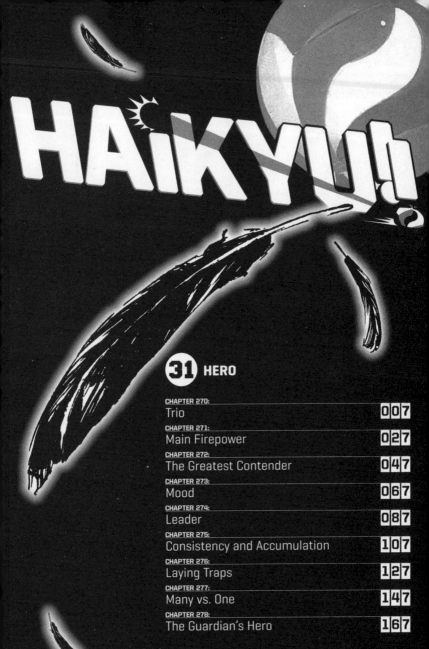

HAIKYU!!

31 HERO

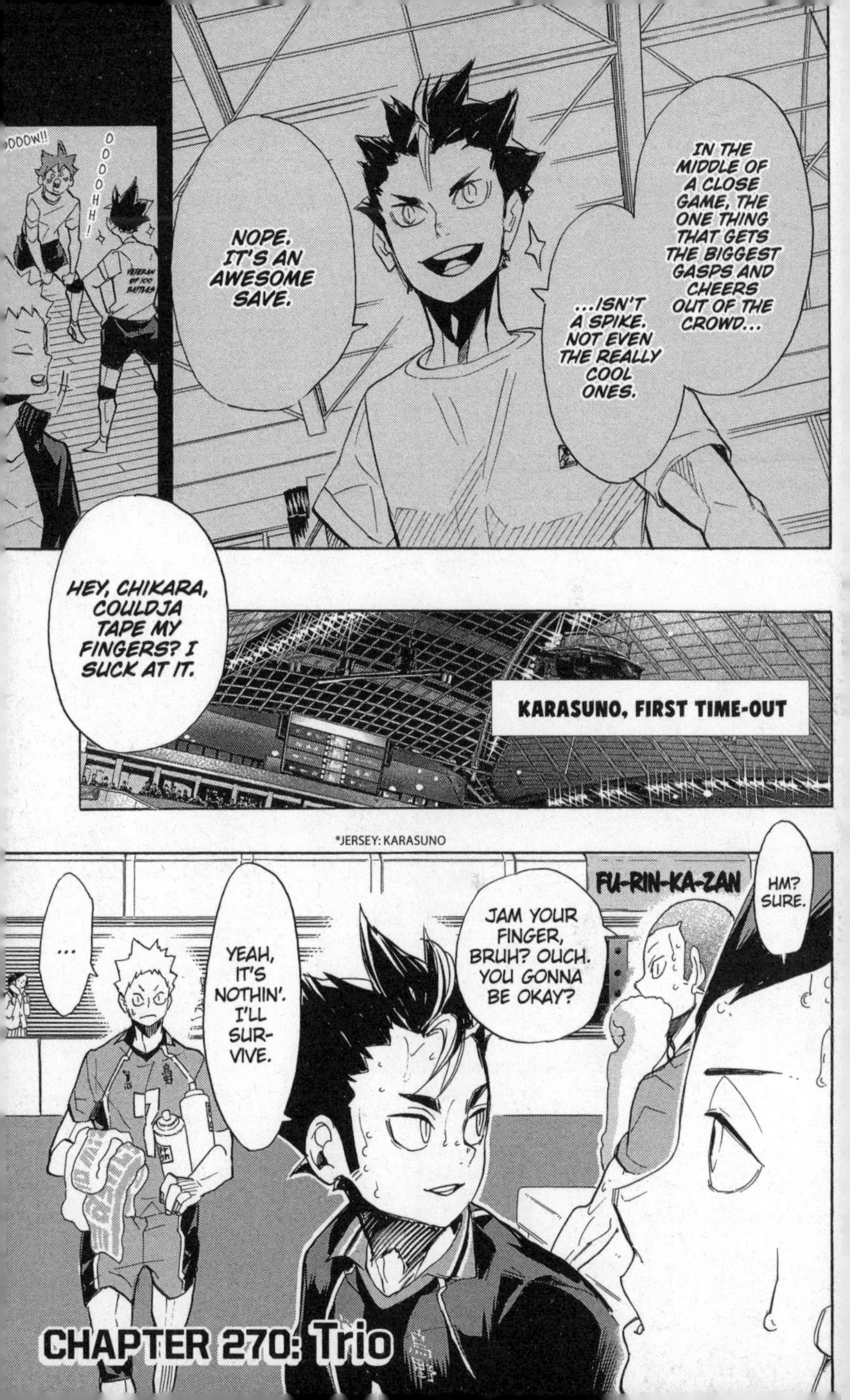
IN THE MIDDLE OF A CLOSE GAME, THE ONE THING THAT GETS THE BIGGEST GASPS AND CHEERS OUT OF THE CROWD...
...ISN'T A SPIKE. NOT EVEN THE REALLY COOL ONES.
NOPE. IT'S AN AWESOME SAVE.
OOOOHH!
OOOOW!!
VETERAN OF 100 BATTLES
KARASUNO, FIRST TIME-OUT
HEY, CHIKARA, COULDJA TAPE MY FINGERS? I SUCK AT IT.
*JERSEY: KARASUNO
HM? SURE.
FU-RIN-KA-ZAN
JAM YOUR FINGER, BRUH? OUCH. YOU GONNA BE OKAY?
YEAH, IT'S NOTHIN'. I'LL SURVIVE.
...

CHAPTER 270: Trio

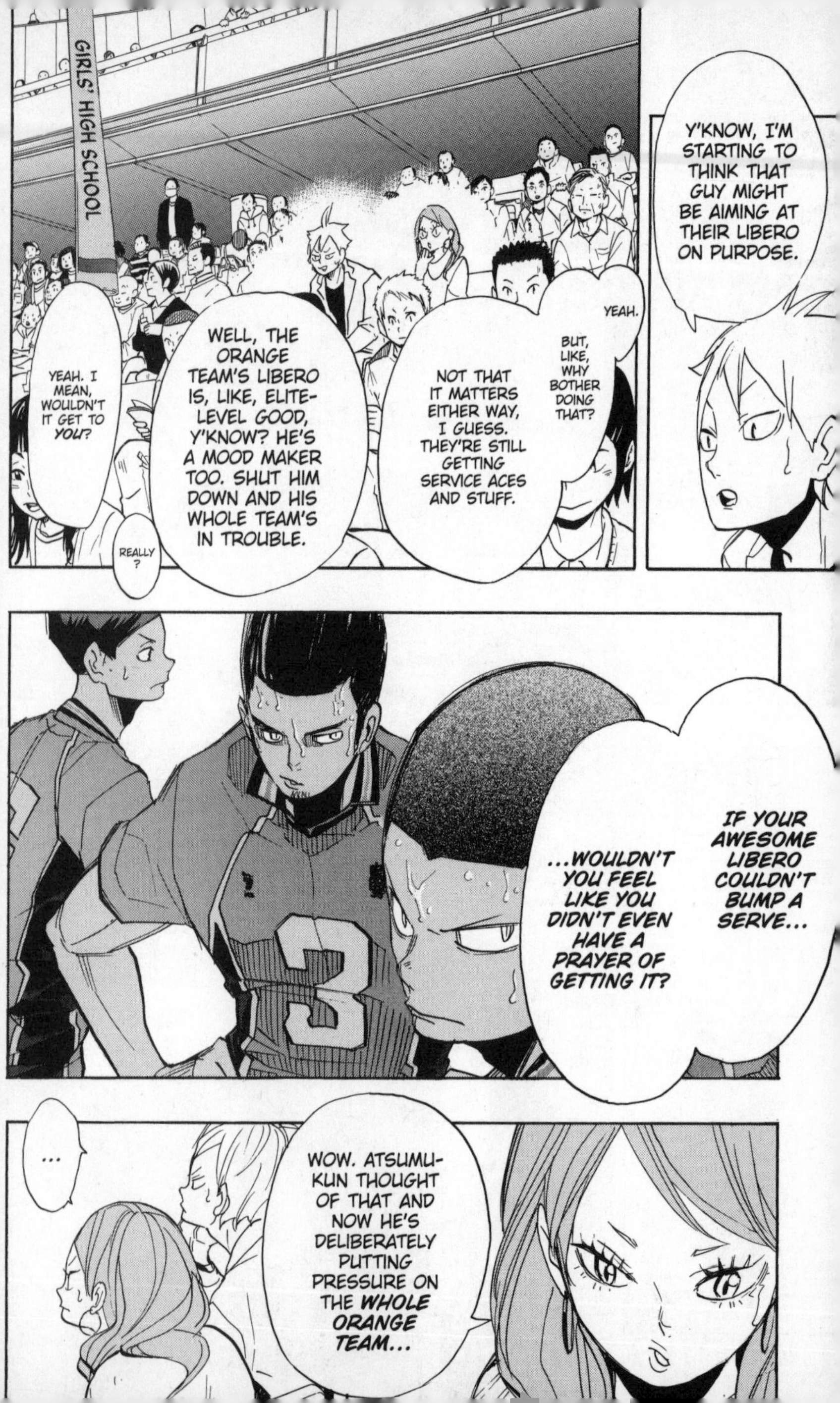
Y'KNOW, I'M STARTING TO THINK THAT GUY MIGHT BE AIMING AT THEIR LIBERO ON PURPOSE.
GIRLS' HIGH SCHOOL
YEAH.
BUT, LIKE, WHY BOTHER DOING THAT?
NOT THAT IT MATTERS EITHER WAY, I GUESS. THEY'RE STILL GETTING SERVICE ACES AND STUFF.
WELL, THE ORANGE TEAM'S LIBERO IS, LIKE, ELITE-LEVEL GOOD, Y'KNOW? HE'S A MOOD MAKER TOO. SHUT HIM DOWN AND HIS WHOLE TEAM'S IN TROUBLE.
REALLY?
YEAH. I MEAN, WOULDN'T IT GET TO *YOU*?
IF YOUR AWESOME LIBERO COULDN'T BUMP A SERVE...
...WOULDN'T YOU FEEL LIKE YOU DIDN'T EVEN HAVE A PRAYER OF GETTING IT?
WOW. ATSUMU-KUN THOUGHT OF THAT AND NOW HE'S DELIBERATELY PUTTING PRESSURE ON THE *WHOLE ORANGE TEAM...*
...

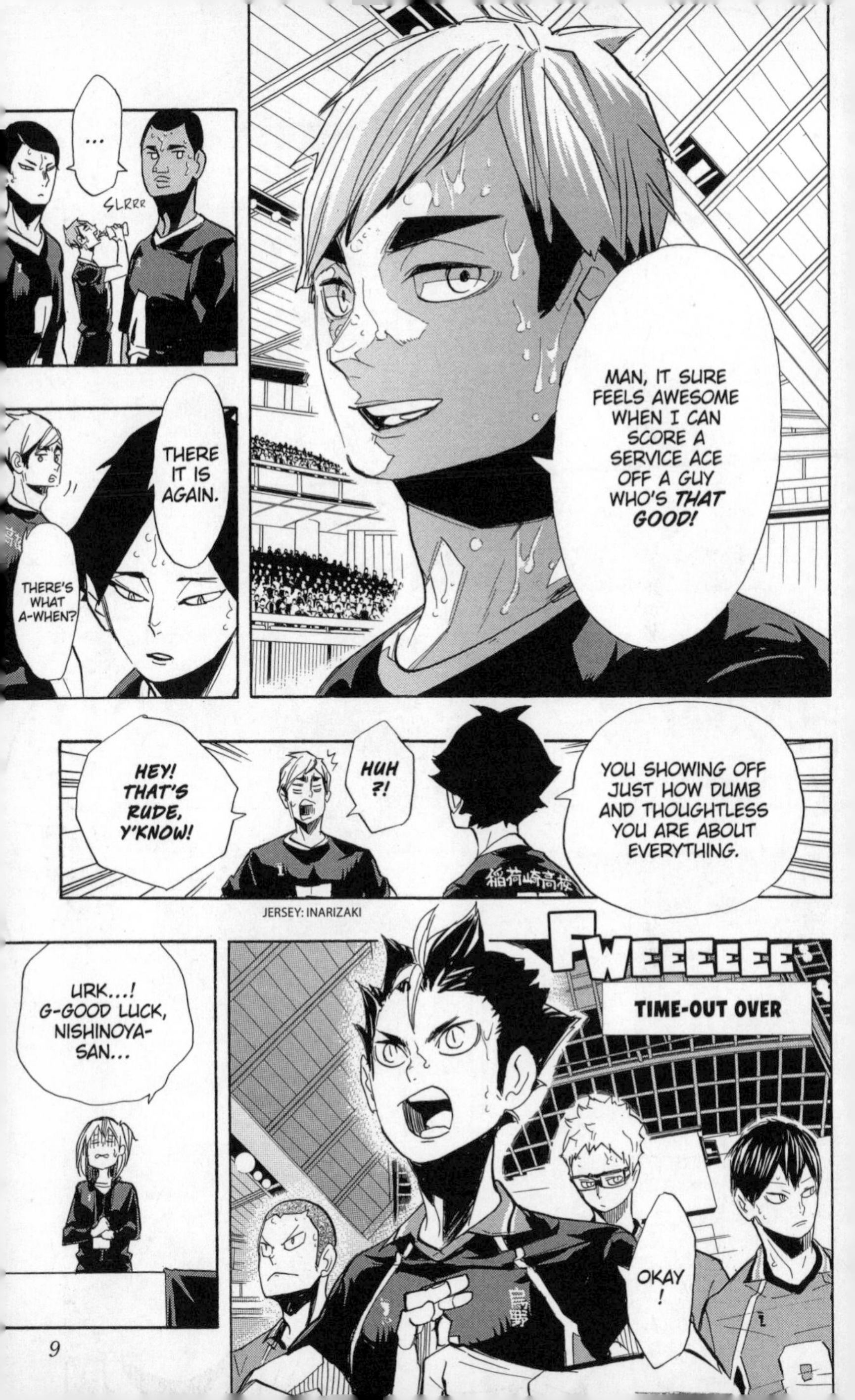
MAN, IT SURE FEELS AWESOME WHEN I CAN SCORE A SERVICE ACE OFF A GUY WHO'S *THAT GOOD!*
...
SLRRR
THERE IT IS AGAIN.
THERE'S WHAT A-WHEN?
YOU SHOWING OFF JUST HOW DUMB AND THOUGHTLESS YOU ARE ABOUT EVERYTHING.
HUH ?!
HEY! THAT'S RUDE, Y'KNOW!
稲荷崎高校
JERSEY: INARIZAKI
FWEEEEEE
TIME-OUT OVER
OKAY !
URK...! G-GOOD LUCK, NISHINOYA-SAN...

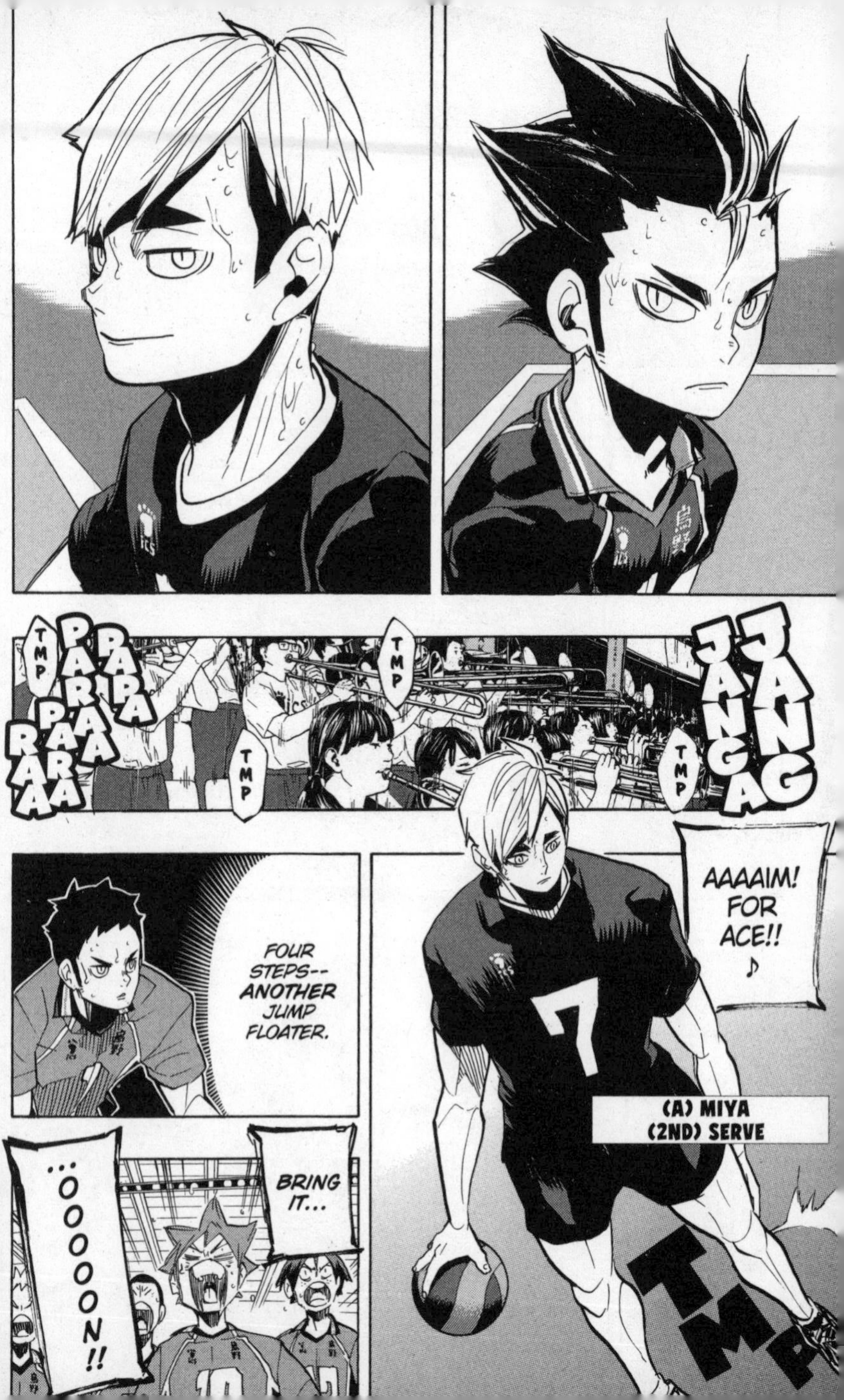

JANG JANGA
TMP
TMP
TMP
PAPA PARAA PARA RAA
TMP
AAAAIM! FOR ACE!! ♪
(A) MIYA (2ND) SERVE
TMP
FOUR STEPS-- ANOTHER JUMP FLOATER.
BRING IT...
...OOOOOON!!

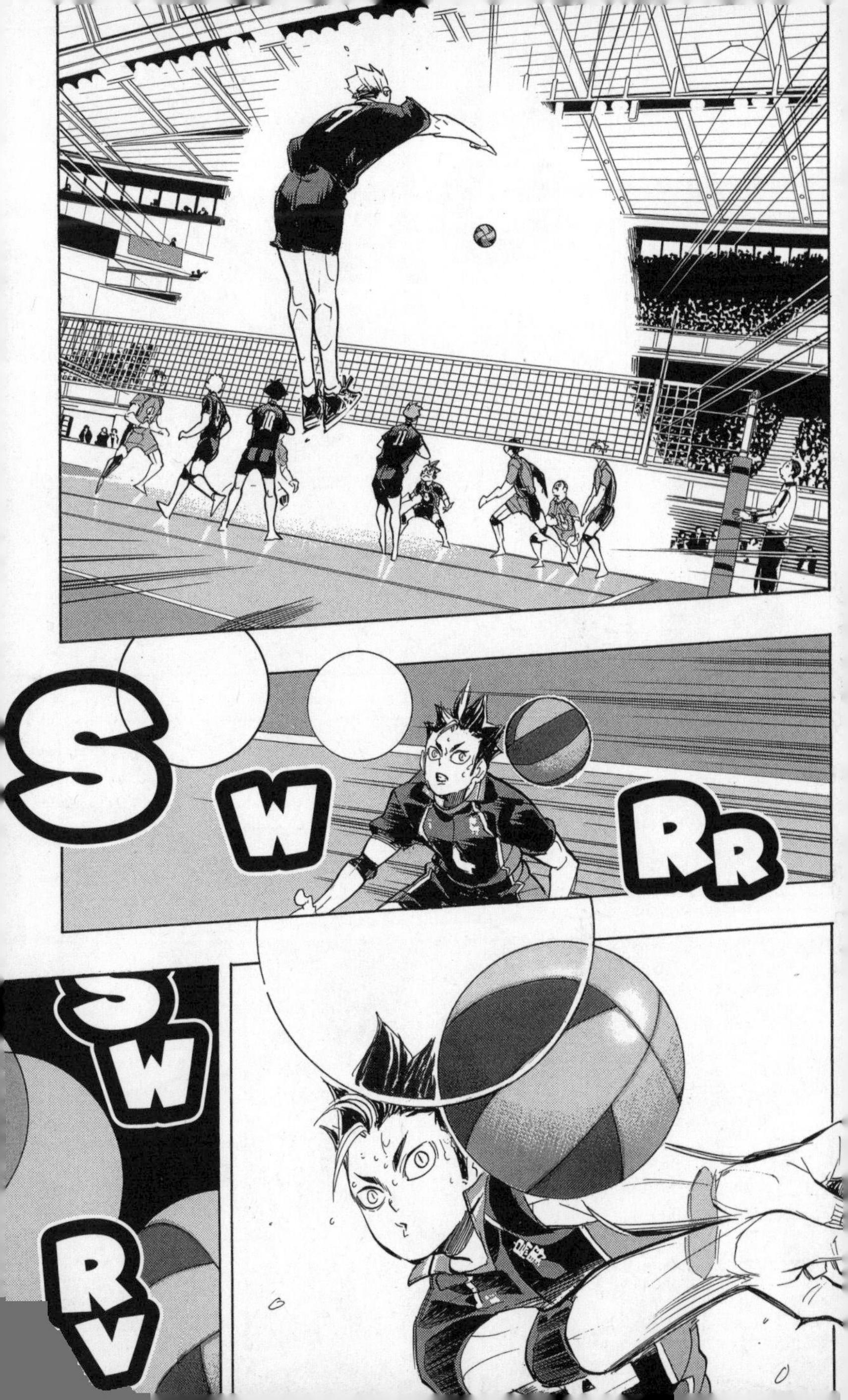
SWRR
SWRV

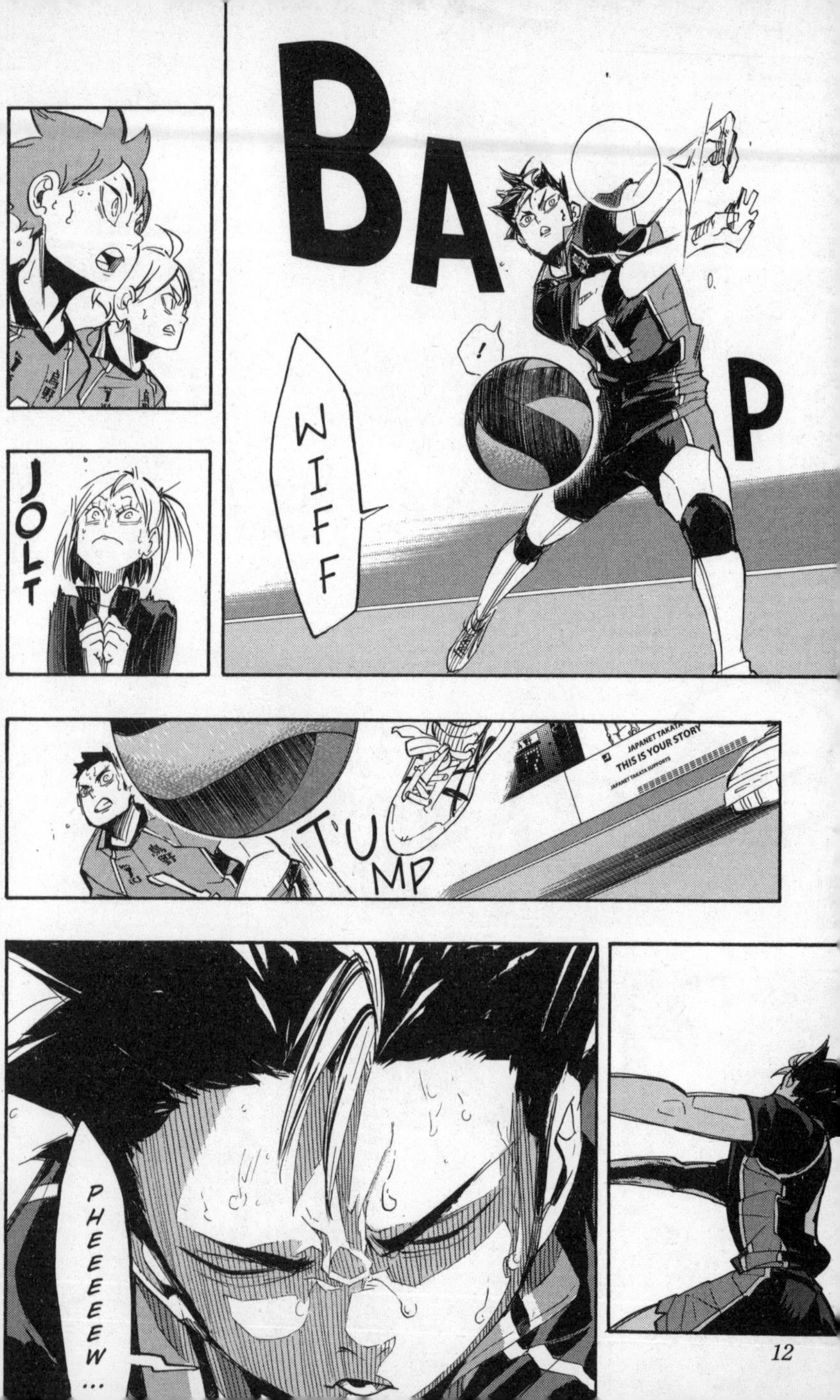
BA
P
!
WIFF
JOLT
TUMP
JAPANET TAKATA
THIS IS YOUR STORY
JAPANET TAKATA SUPPORTS
PHEEEEEW...

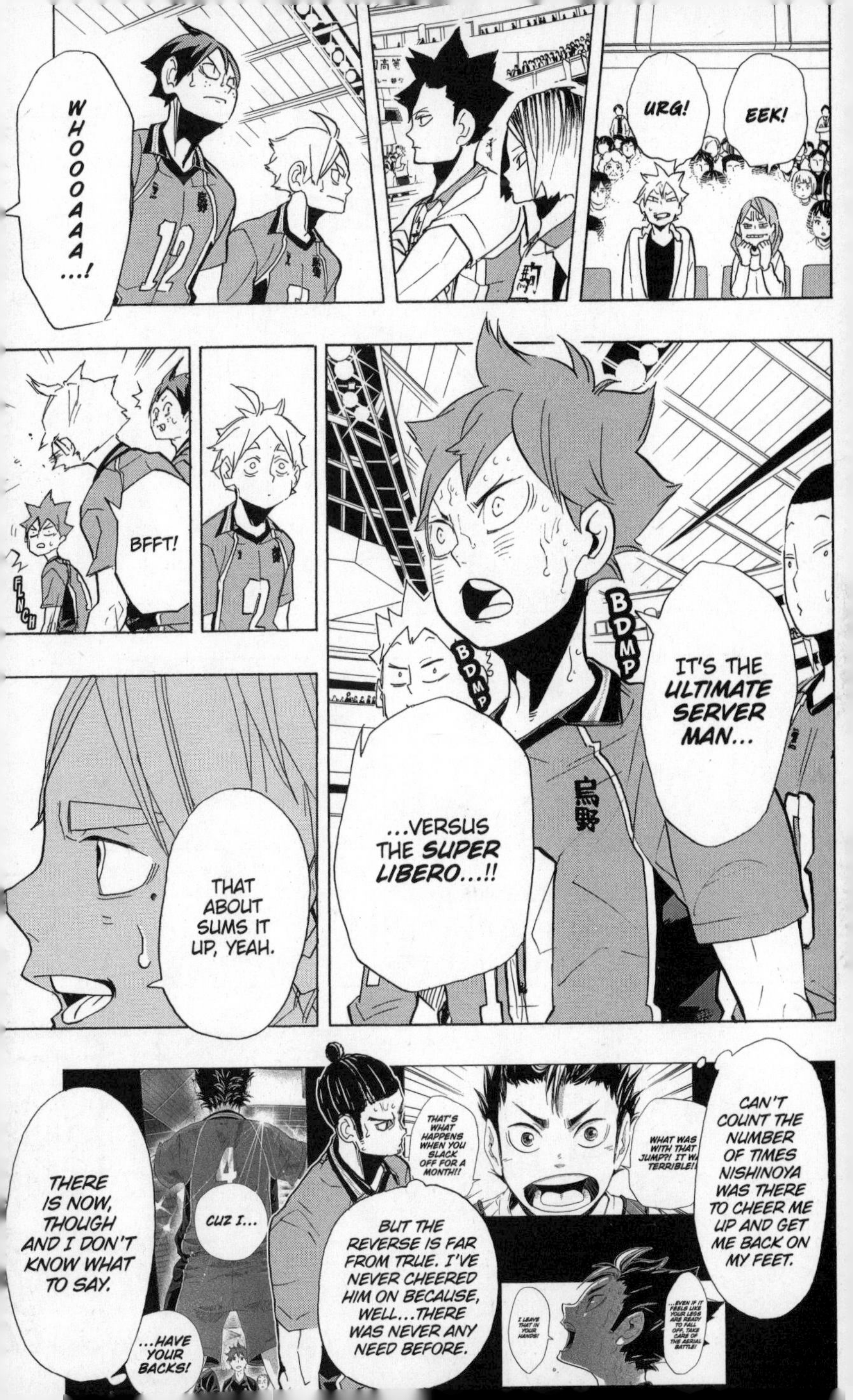
EEK!
URG!
WHOOOOAAA...!
BDMP
BDMP
IT'S THE ULTIMATE SERVER MAN...
...VERSUS THE SUPER LIBERO...!!
BFFT!
FLINCH
THAT ABOUT SUMS IT UP, YEAH.
CAN'T COUNT THE NUMBER OF TIMES NISHINOYA WAS THERE TO CHEER ME UP AND GET ME BACK ON MY FEET.
WHAT WAS WITH THAT JUMP?! IT WA TERRIBLE!!
THAT'S WHAT HAPPENS WHEN YOU SLACK OFF FOR A MONTH!!
...EVEN IF IT FEELS LIKE YOUR LEGS ARE READY TO FALL OFF, TAKE CARE OF THE AERIAL BATTLE!
I LEAVE THAT IN YOUR HANDS!
BUT THE REVERSE IS FAR FROM TRUE. I'VE NEVER CHEERED HIM ON BECAUSE, WELL...THERE WAS NEVER ANY NEED BEFORE.
CUZ I...
THERE IS NOW, THOUGH AND I DON'T KNOW WHAT TO SAY.
...HAVE YOUR BACKS!

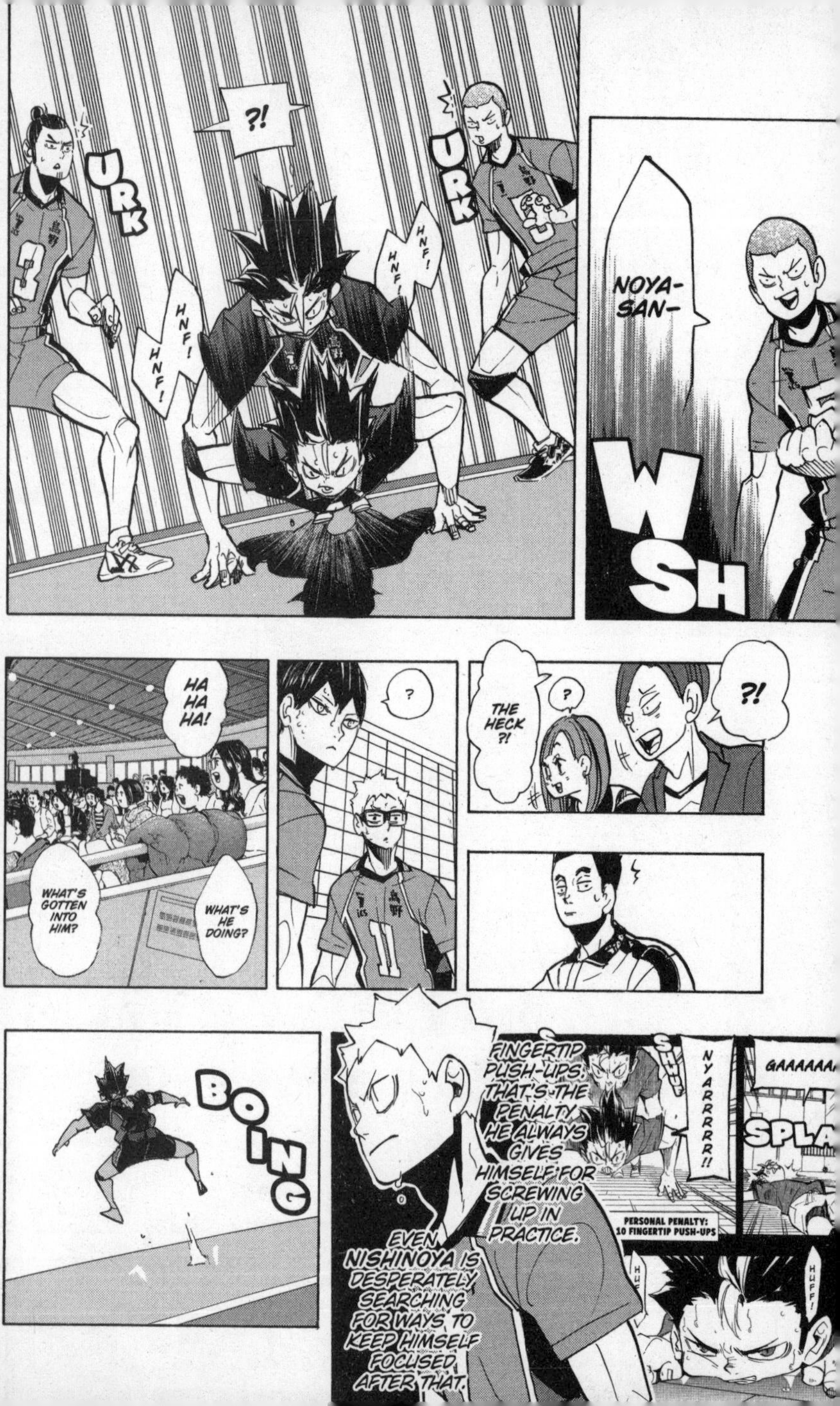

NOYA-SAN—
WSH
URK
?!
HNF! HNF!
URK
HNF! HNF!
?!
THE HECK?!
?
?
HA HA HA!
WHAT'S HE DOING?
WHAT'S GOTTEN INTO HIM?
GAAAAAA
SPLA
NYARRRRR!!
PERSONAL PENALTY: 10 FINGERTIP PUSH-UPS
HUFF!
HUFF
FINGERTIP PUSH-UPS. THAT'S THE PENALTY HE ALWAYS GIVES HIMSELF FOR SCREWING UP IN PRACTICE.
EVEN NISHINOYA IS DESPERATELY SEARCHING FOR WAYS TO KEEP HIMSELF FOCUSED AFTER THAT.
BOING

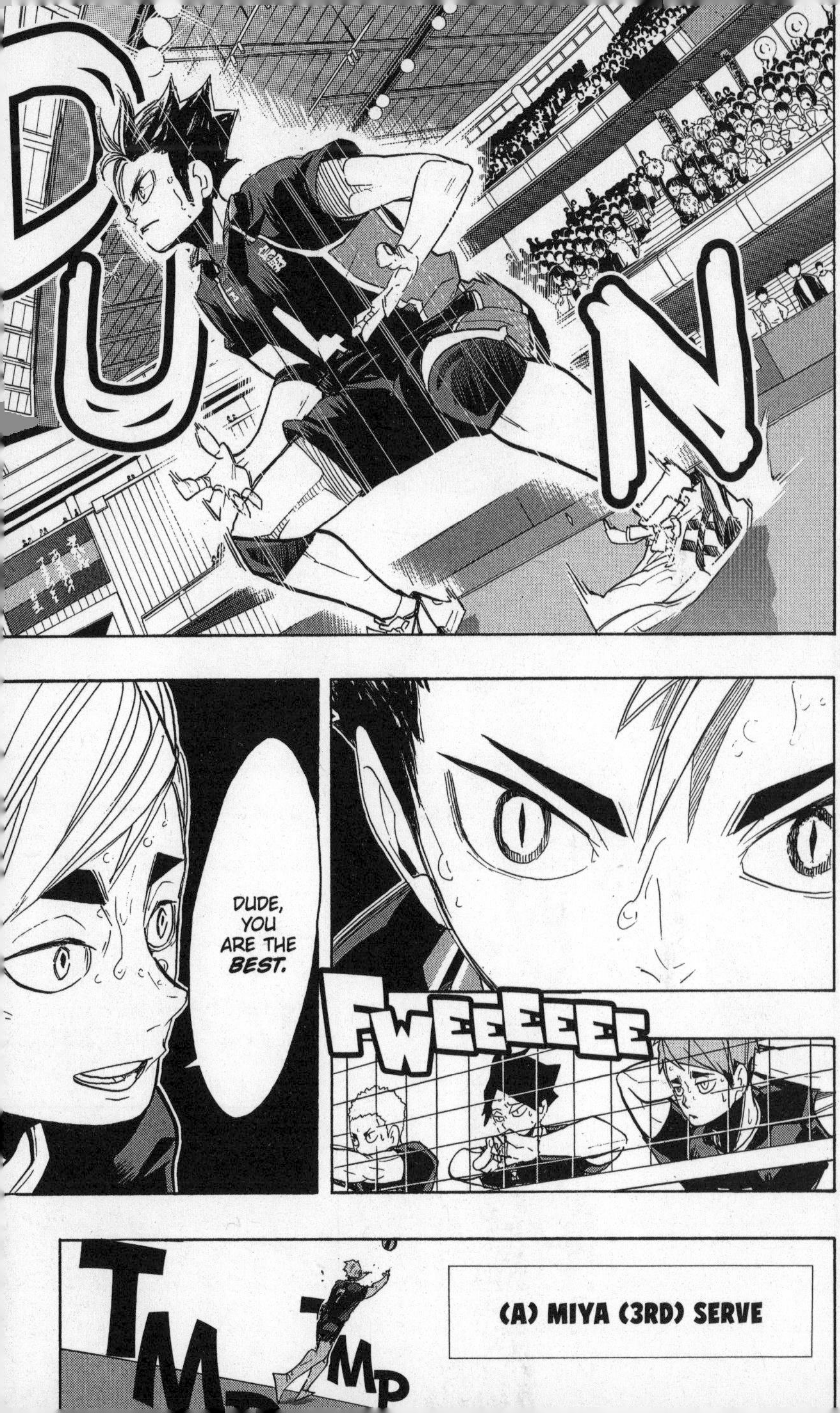
DUN
FWEEEEEE
DUDE, YOU ARE THE BEST.
(A) MIYA (3RD) SERVE
TMP TMP

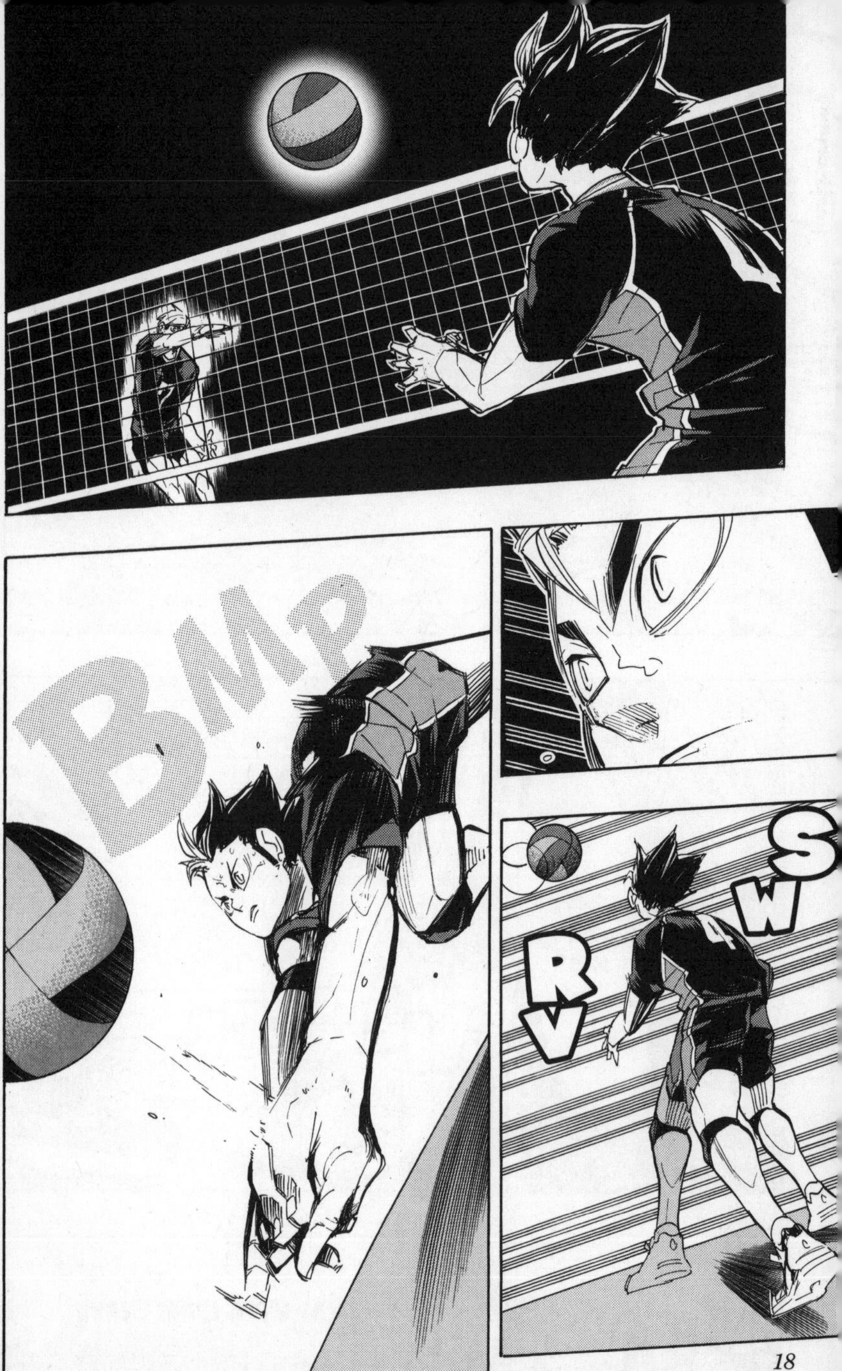
SWRV
BMP

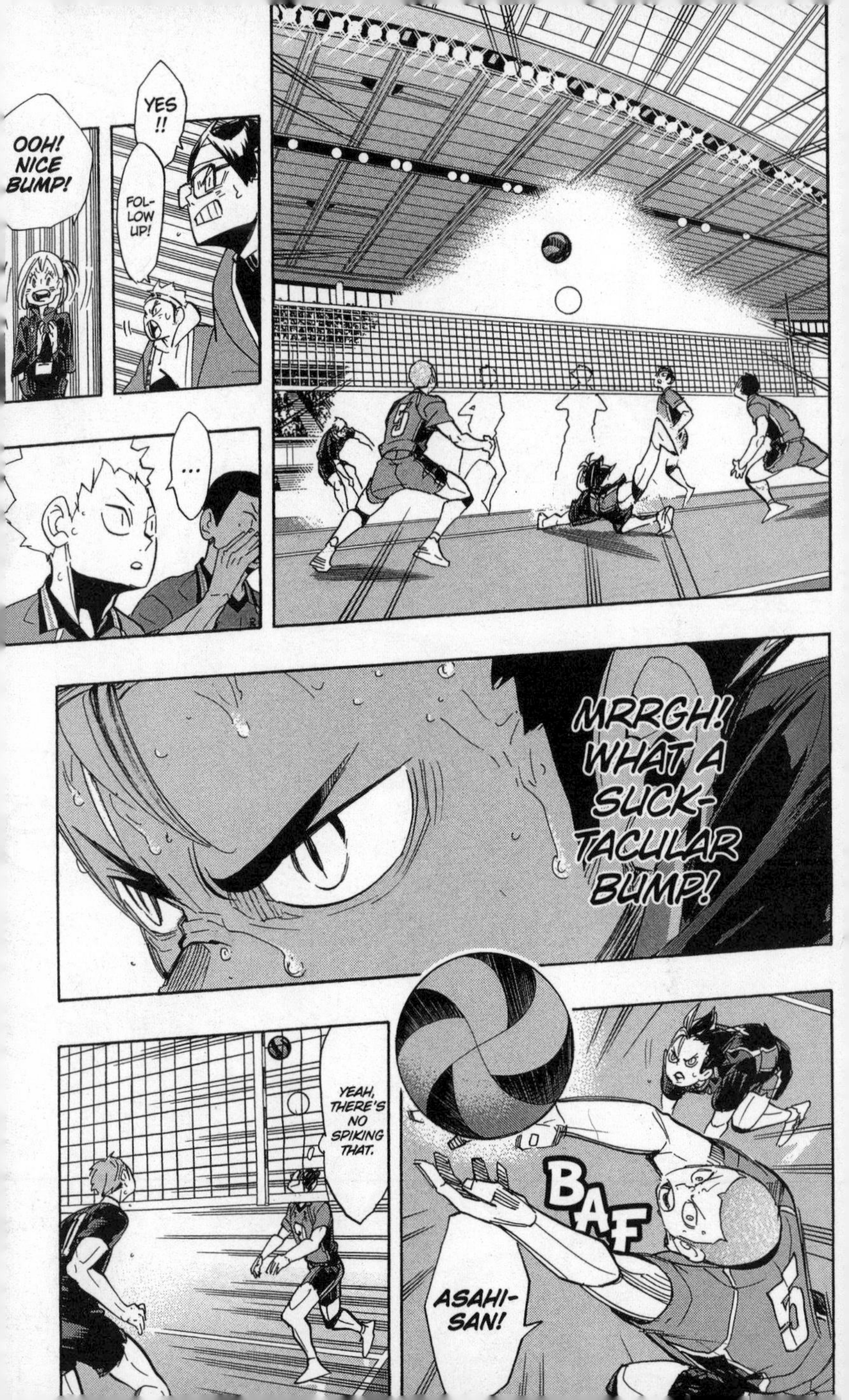
YES !!
FOL-LOW UP!
OOH! NICE BUMP!
...
MRRGH! WHAT A SUCK-TACULAR BUMP!
BAF
ASAHI-SAN!
YEAH, THERE'S NO SPIKING THAT.

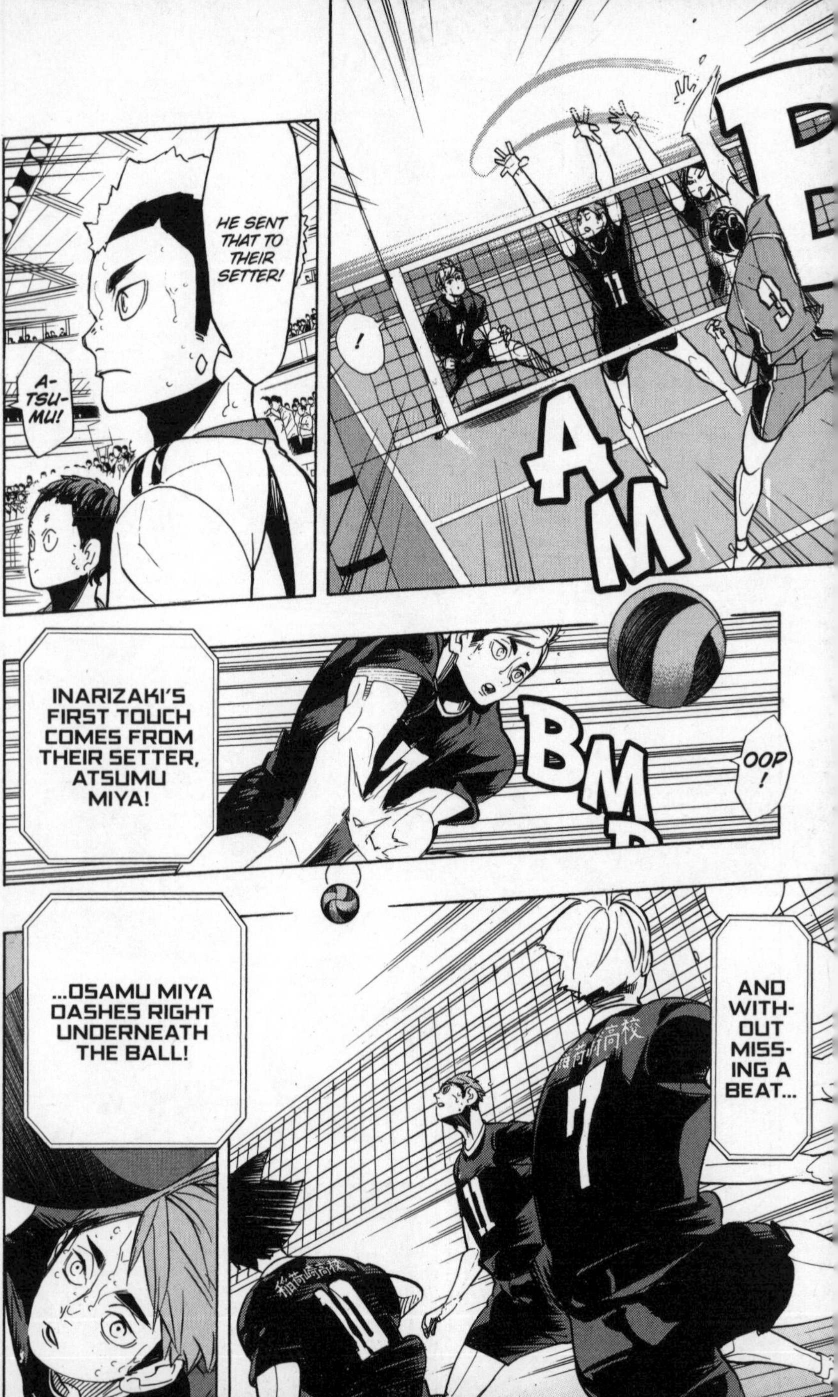
!
HE SENT THAT TO THEIR SETTER!
A-TSUMU!
OOP!
INARIZAKI'S FIRST TOUCH COMES FROM THEIR SETTER, ATSUMU MIYA!
AND WITH-OUT MISS-ING A BEAT...
...OSAMU MIYA DASHES RIGHT UNDERNEATH THE BALL!

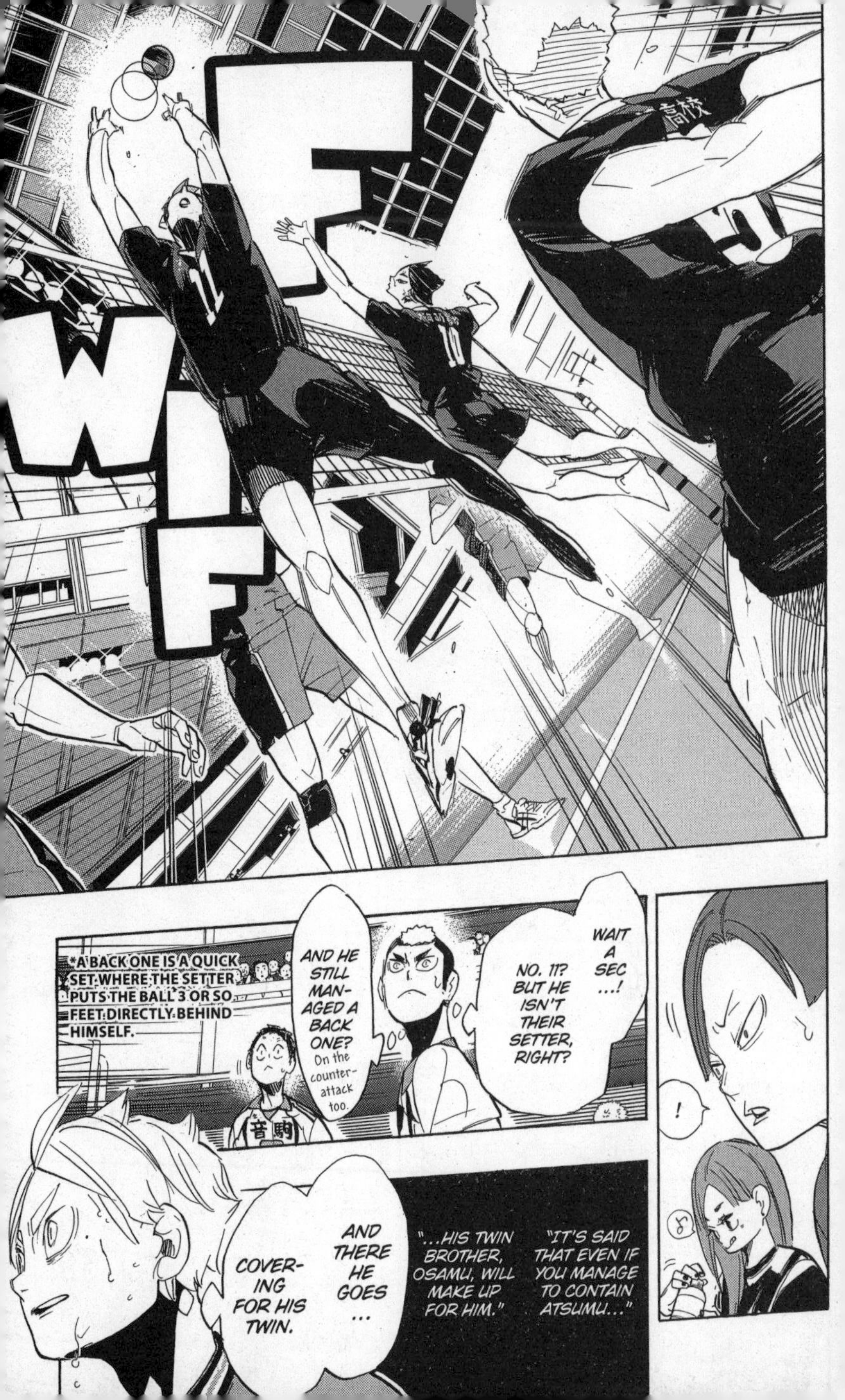
FWIF
!
♪
WAIT A SEC...!
NO. 11? BUT HE ISN'T THEIR SETTER, RIGHT?
AND HE STILL MANAGED A BACK ONE? On the counter-attack too.
*A BACK ONE IS A QUICK SET WHERE THE SETTER PUTS THE BALL 3 OR SO FEET DIRECTLY BEHIND HIMSELF.
"IT'S SAID THAT EVEN IF YOU MANAGE TO CONTAIN ATSUMU..."
"...HIS TWIN BROTHER, OSAMU, WILL MAKE UP FOR HIM."
AND THERE HE GOES...
COVERING FOR HIS TWIN.

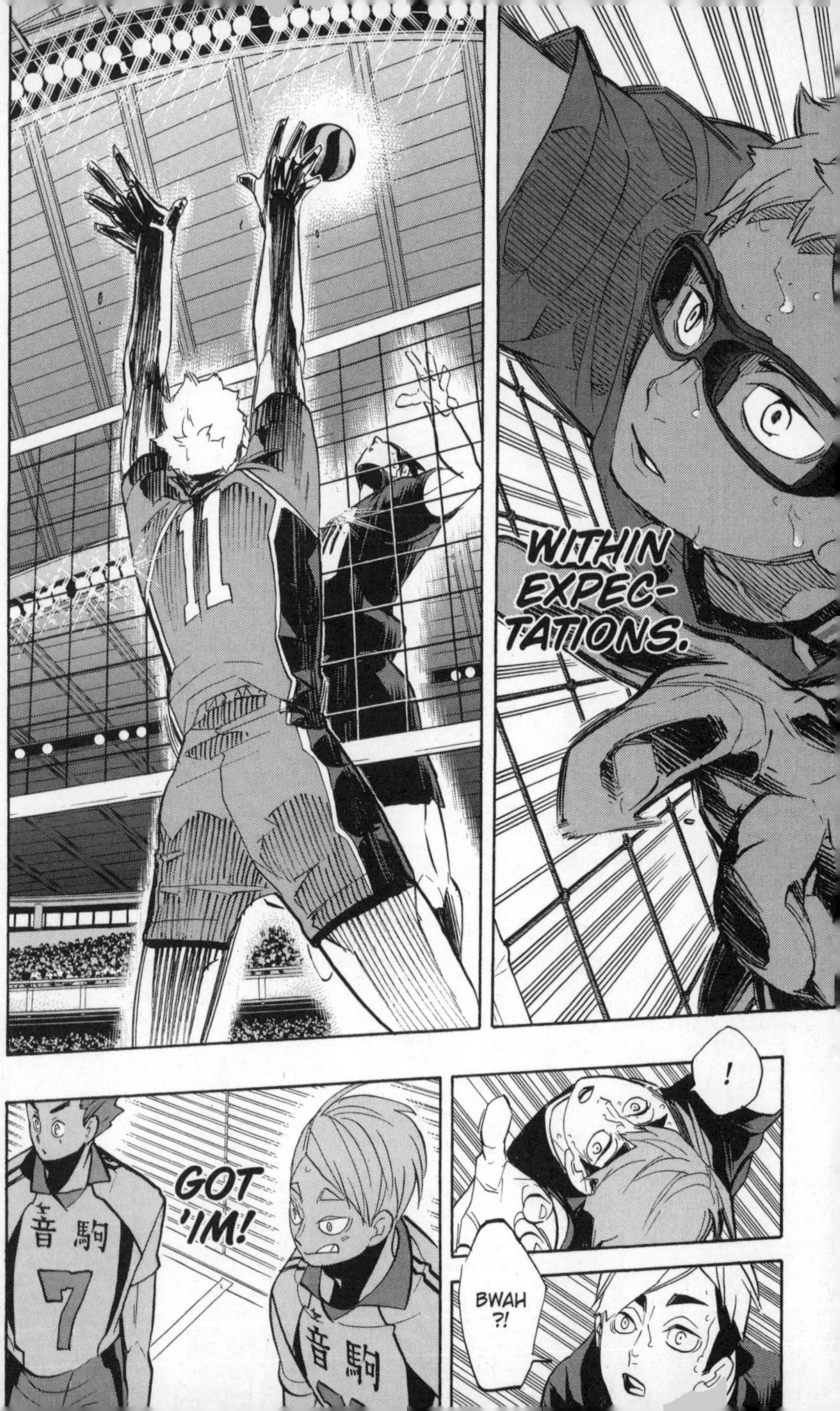
WITHIN EXPEC-TATIONS.
!
BWAH ?!
GOT 'IM!

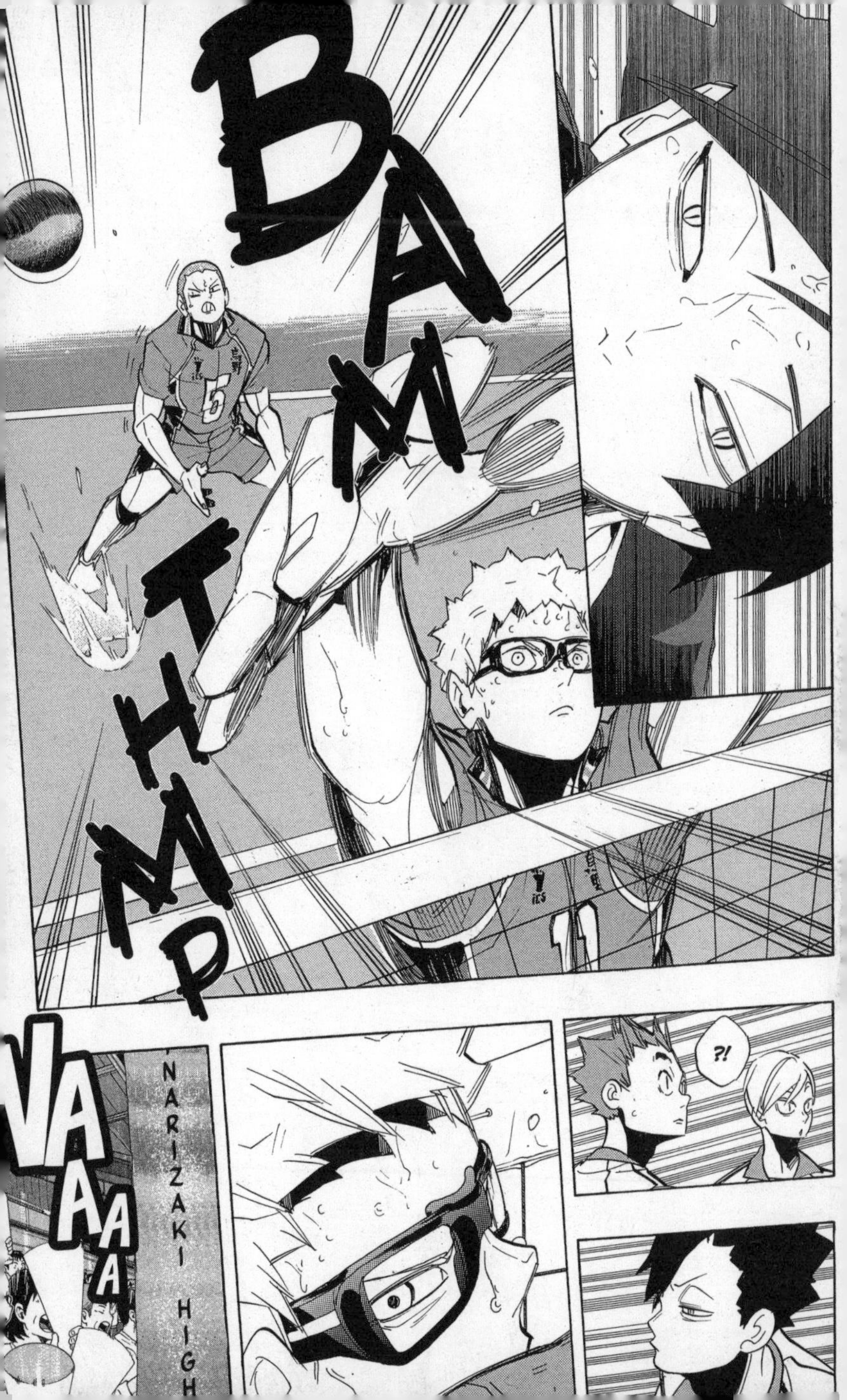
BAM
THMP
?!
VAAAAA
NARIZAKI HIGH

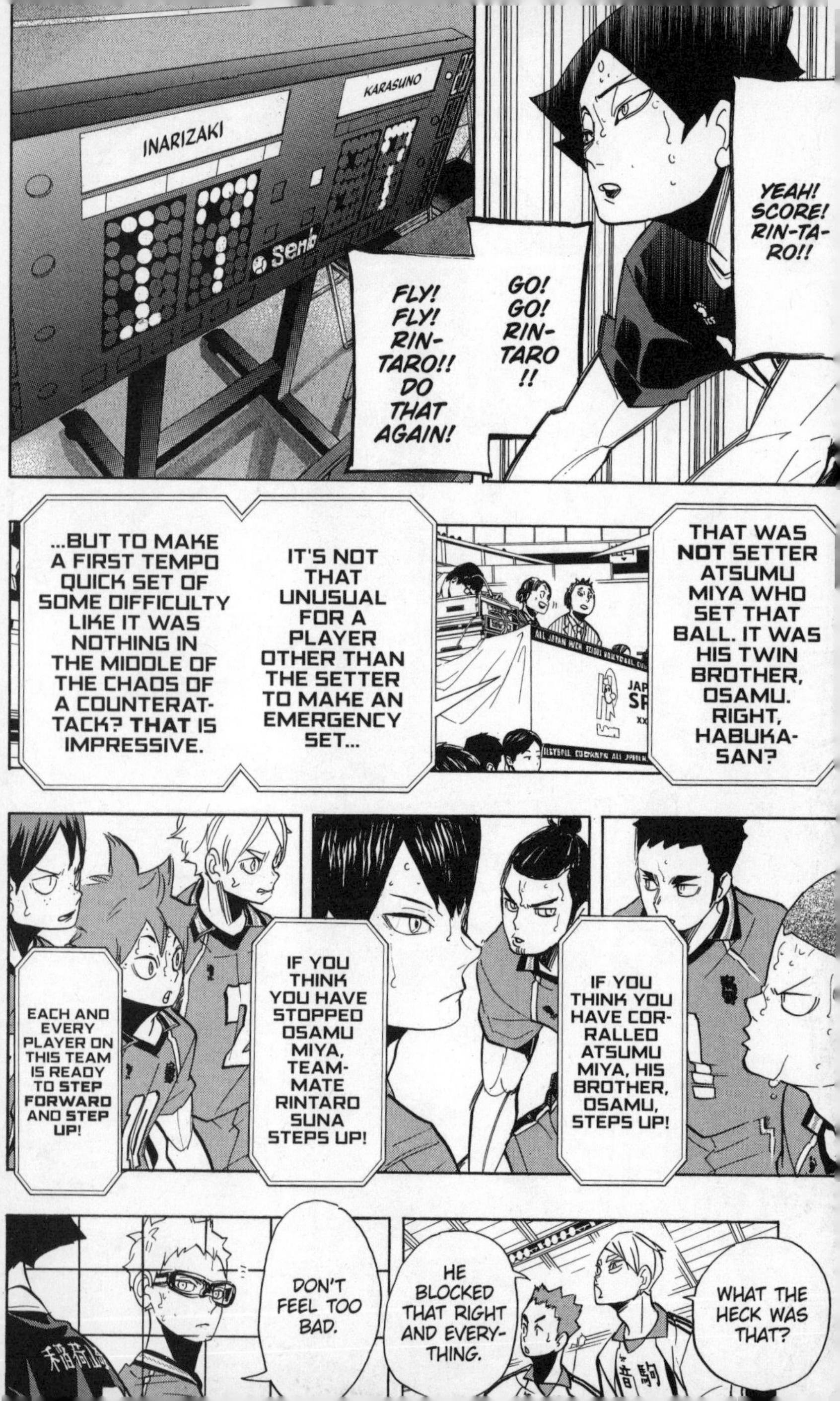

YEAH! SCORE! RIN-TARO!!
GO! GO! RIN-TARO!!
FLY! FLY! RIN-TARO!! DO THAT AGAIN!
KARASUNO
INARIZAKI
THAT WAS NOT SETTER ATSUMU MIYA WHO SET THAT BALL. IT WAS HIS TWIN BROTHER, OSAMU. RIGHT, HABUKA-SAN?
IT'S NOT THAT UNUSUAL FOR A PLAYER OTHER THAN THE SETTER TO MAKE AN EMERGENCY SET...
...BUT TO MAKE A FIRST TEMPO QUICK SET OF SOME DIFFICULTY LIKE IT WAS NOTHING IN THE MIDDLE OF THE CHAOS OF A COUNTERAT-TACK? THAT IS IMPRESSIVE.
IF YOU THINK YOU HAVE COR-RALLED ATSUMU MIYA, HIS BROTHER, OSAMU, STEPS UP!
IF YOU THINK YOU HAVE STOPPED OSAMU MIYA, TEAM-MATE RINTARO SUNA STEPS UP!
EACH AND EVERY PLAYER ON THIS TEAM IS READY TO STEP FORWARD AND STEP UP!
WHAT THE HECK WAS THAT?
HE BLOCKED THAT RIGHT AND EVERY-THING.
DON'T FEEL TOO BAD.

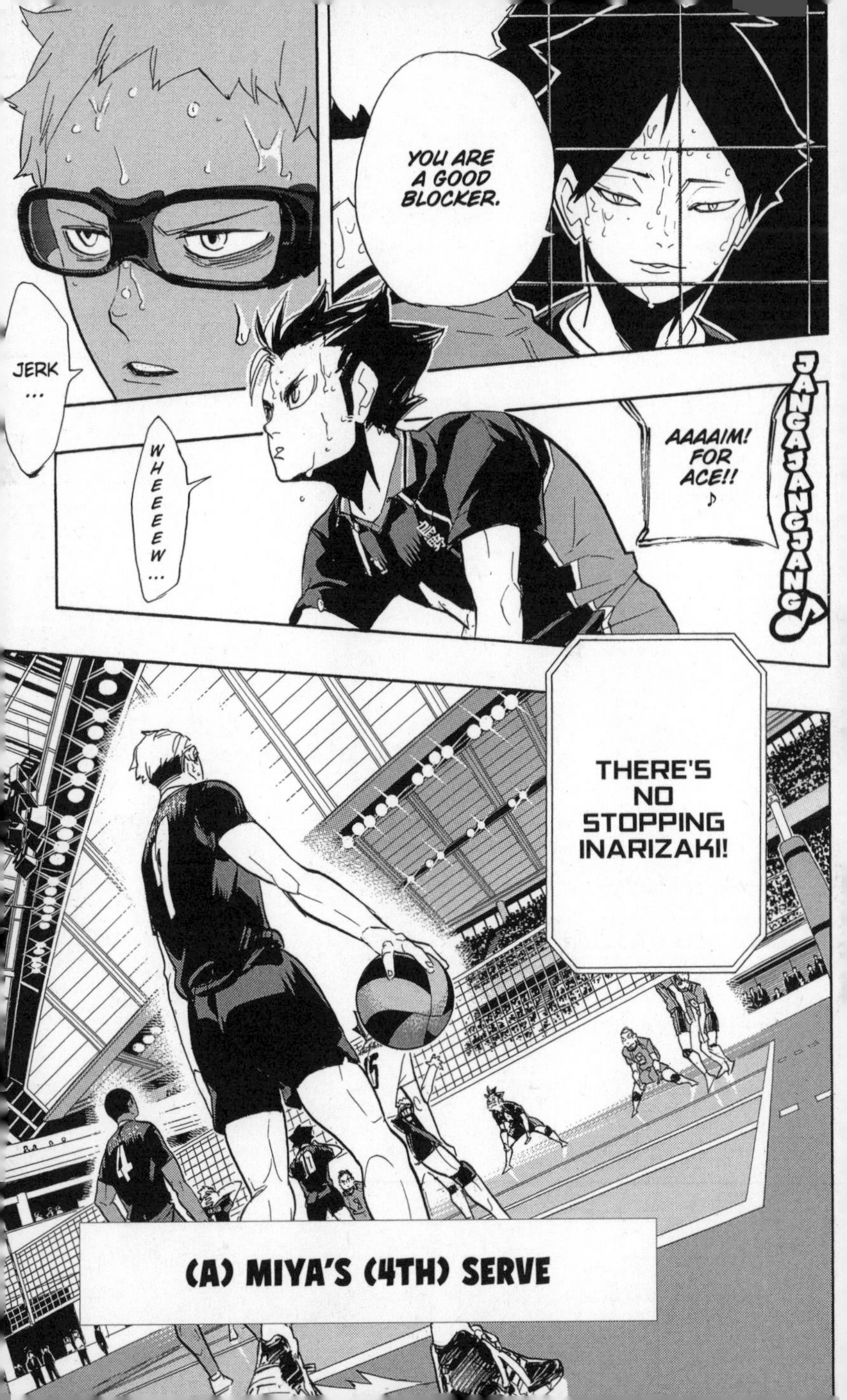
YOU ARE A GOOD BLOCKER.
JERK ...
JANGAJANGJANG♪
AAAAIM! FOR ACE!! ♪
WHEEEEEW ...
THERE'S NO STOPPING INARIZAKI!
(A) MIYA'S (4TH) SERVE

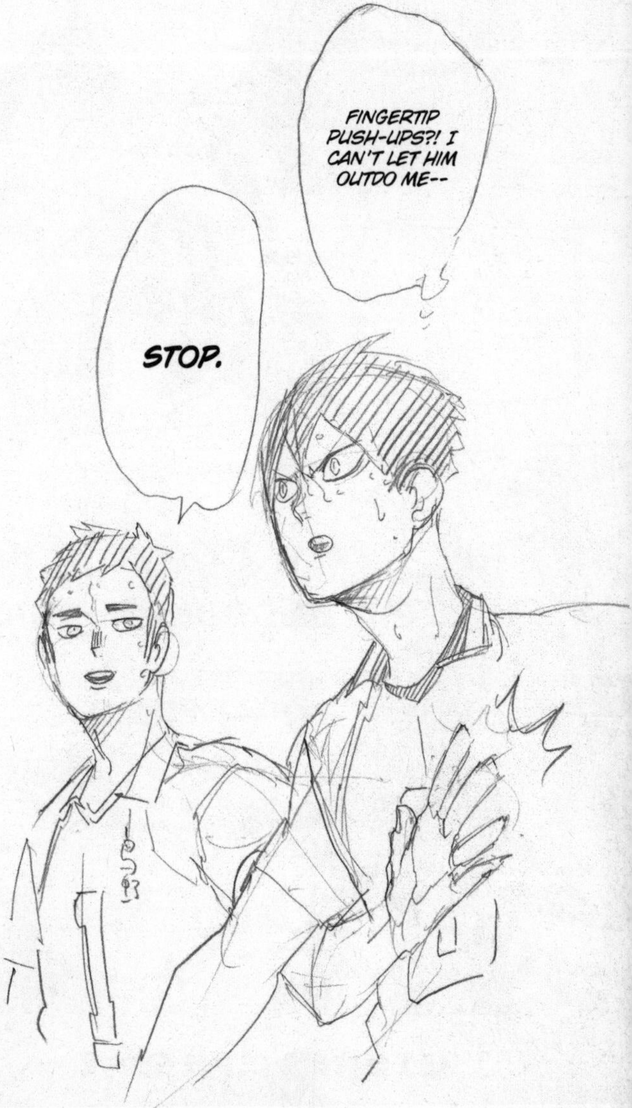
FINGERTIP PUSH-UPS?! I CAN'T LET HIM OUTDO ME--
STOP.

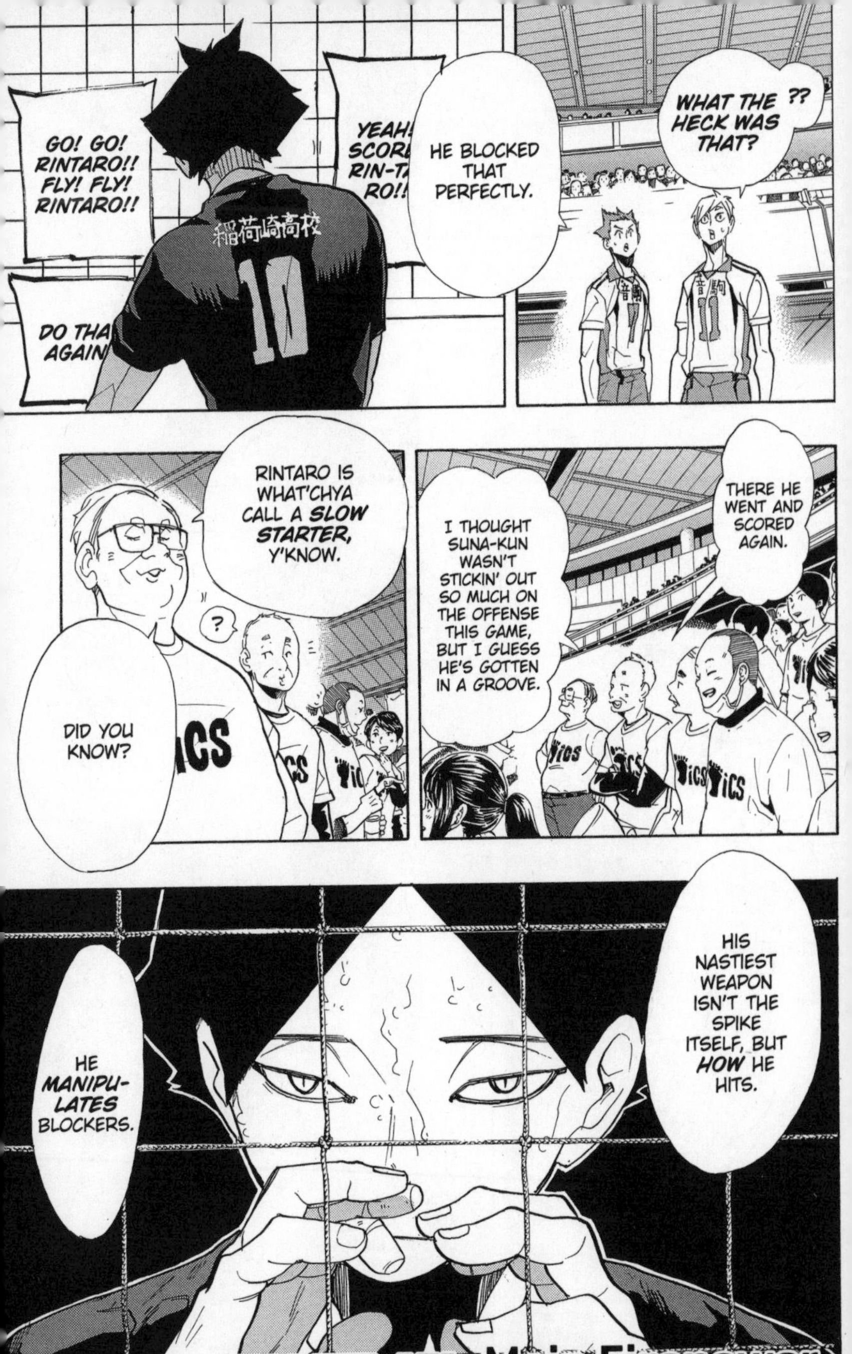
WHAT THE ?? HECK WAS THAT?
HE BLOCKED THAT PERFECTLY.
YEAH! SCOR RIN-TA RO!!
GO! GO! RINTARO!! FLY! FLY! RINTARO!!
DO THA AGAIN
THERE HE WENT AND SCORED AGAIN.
I THOUGHT SUNA-KUN WASN'T STICKIN' OUT SO MUCH ON THE OFFENSE THIS GAME, BUT I GUESS HE'S GOTTEN IN A GROOVE.
RINTARO IS WHAT'CHYA CALL A *SLOW STARTER*, Y'KNOW.
?
DID YOU KNOW?
HIS NASTIEST WEAPON ISN'T THE SPIKE ITSELF, BUT *HOW* HE HITS.
HE *MANIPULATES* BLOCKERS.

CHAPTER 271: Main Firepower

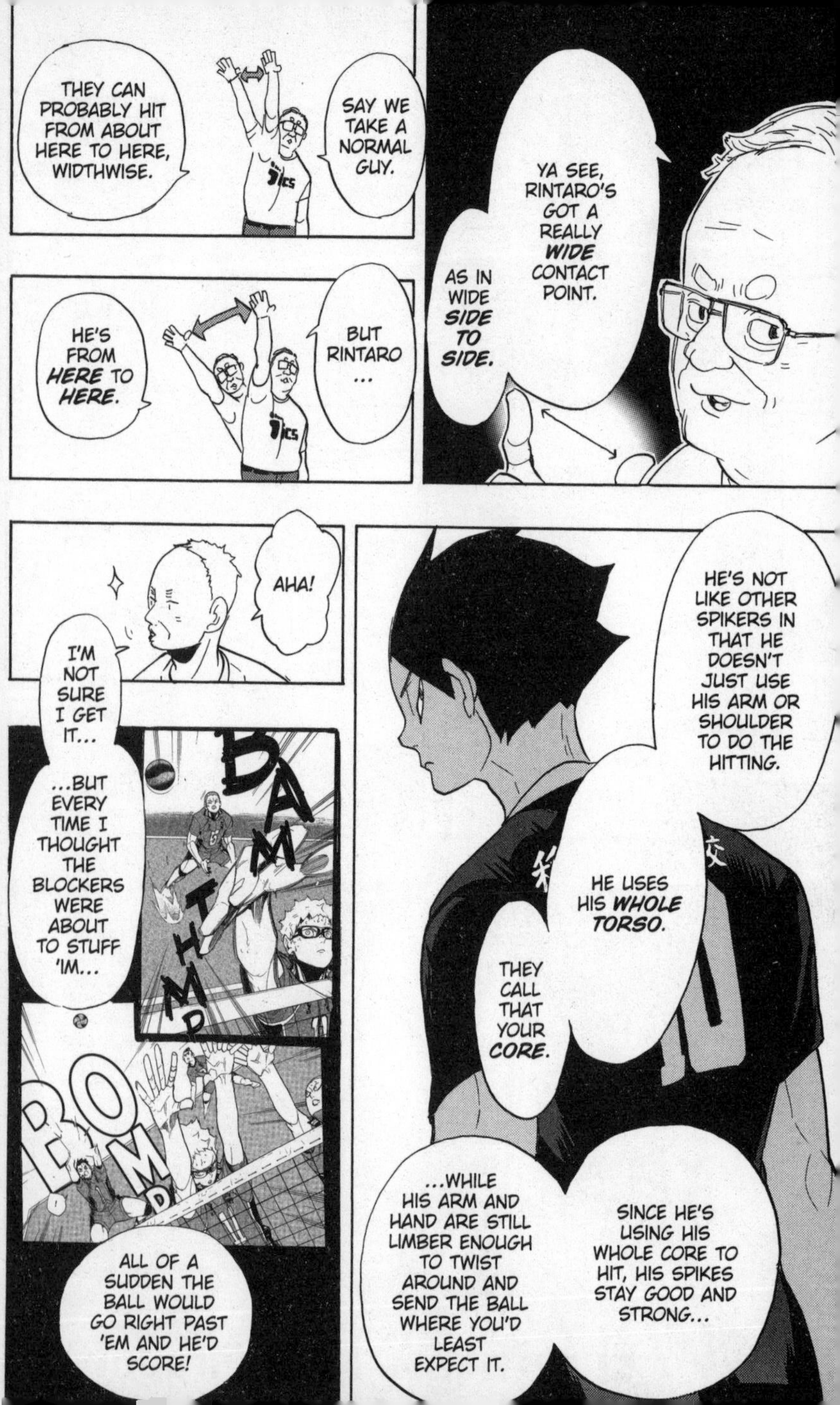
YA SEE, RINTARO'S GOT A REALLY WIDE CONTACT POINT.
AS IN WIDE SIDE TO SIDE.
SAY WE TAKE A NORMAL GUY.
THEY CAN PROBABLY HIT FROM ABOUT HERE TO HERE, WIDTHWISE.
BUT RINTARO...
HE'S FROM HERE TO HERE.
HE'S NOT LIKE OTHER SPIKERS IN THAT HE DOESN'T JUST USE HIS ARM OR SHOULDER TO DO THE HITTING.
HE USES HIS WHOLE TORSO.
THEY CALL THAT YOUR CORE.
SINCE HE'S USING HIS WHOLE CORE TO HIT, HIS SPIKES STAY GOOD AND STRONG...
...WHILE HIS ARM AND HAND ARE STILL LIMBER ENOUGH TO TWIST AROUND AND SEND THE BALL WHERE YOU'D LEAST EXPECT IT.
AHA!
I'M NOT SURE I GET IT...
...BUT EVERY TIME I THOUGHT THE BLOCKERS WERE ABOUT TO STUFF 'IM...
BAM
THMP
ALL OF A SUDDEN THE BALL WOULD GO RIGHT PAST 'EM AND HE'D SCORE!

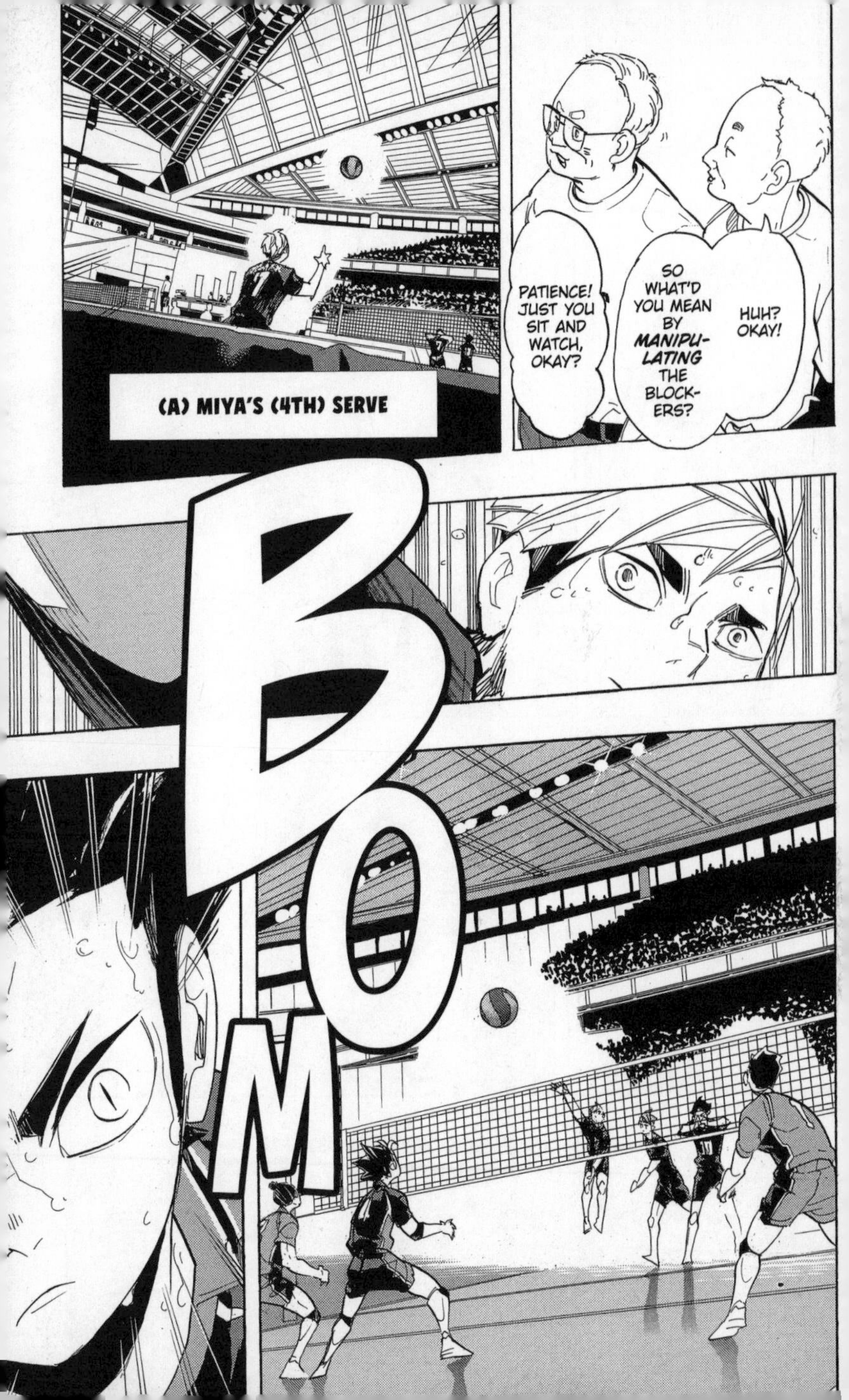

SO WHAT'D YOU MEAN BY *MANIPULATING* THE BLOCKERS?
PATIENCE! JUST YOU SIT AND WATCH, OKAY?
HUH? OKAY!
(A) MIYA'S (4TH) SERVE
BOOM

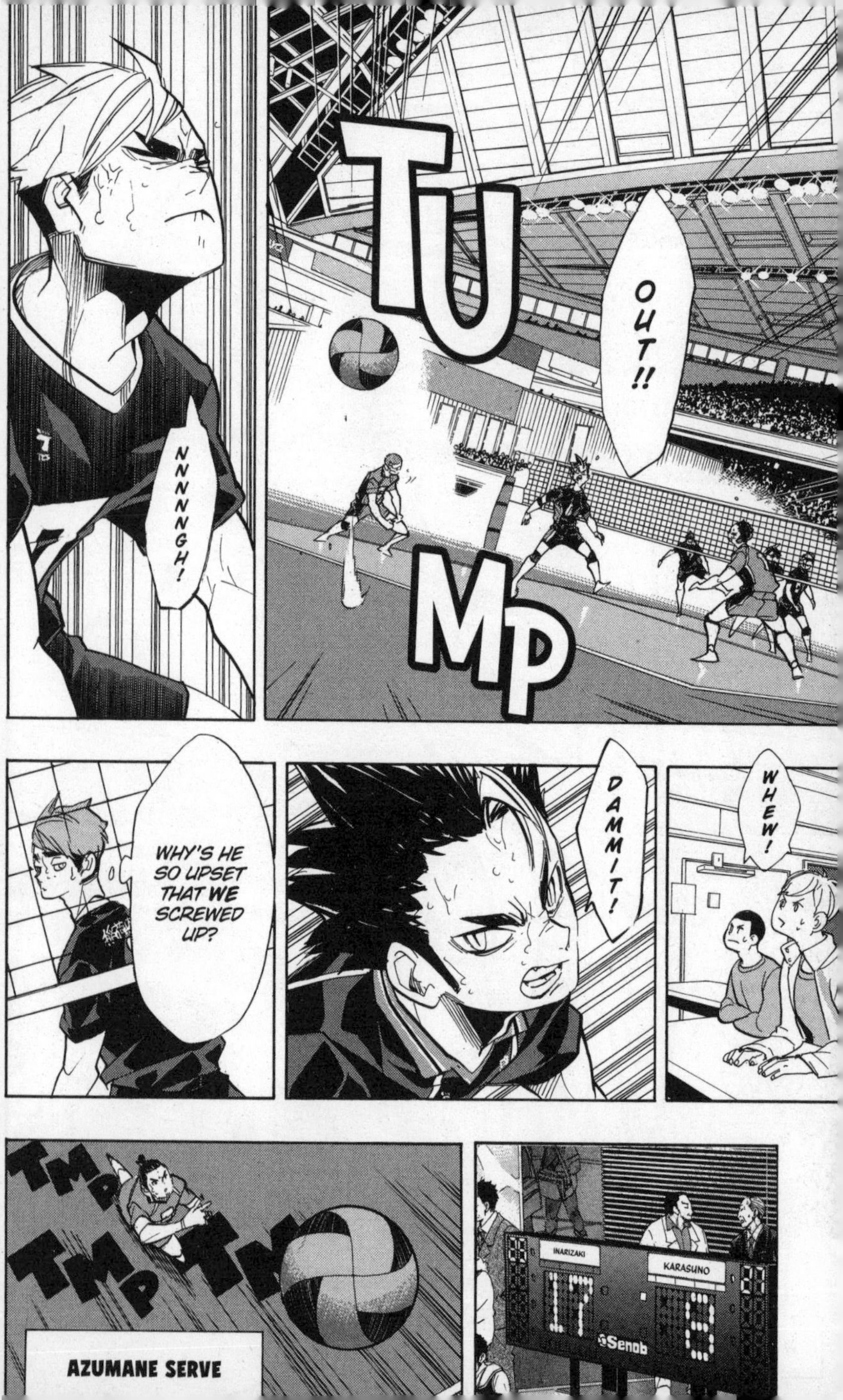
TUMP
OUT!!
NNNNNGH!
WHEW!
DAMMIT!
WHY'S HE SO UPSET THAT WE SCREWED UP?
INARIZAKI
KARASUNO
17
Senob
TMP TMP TMP
AZUMANE SERVE

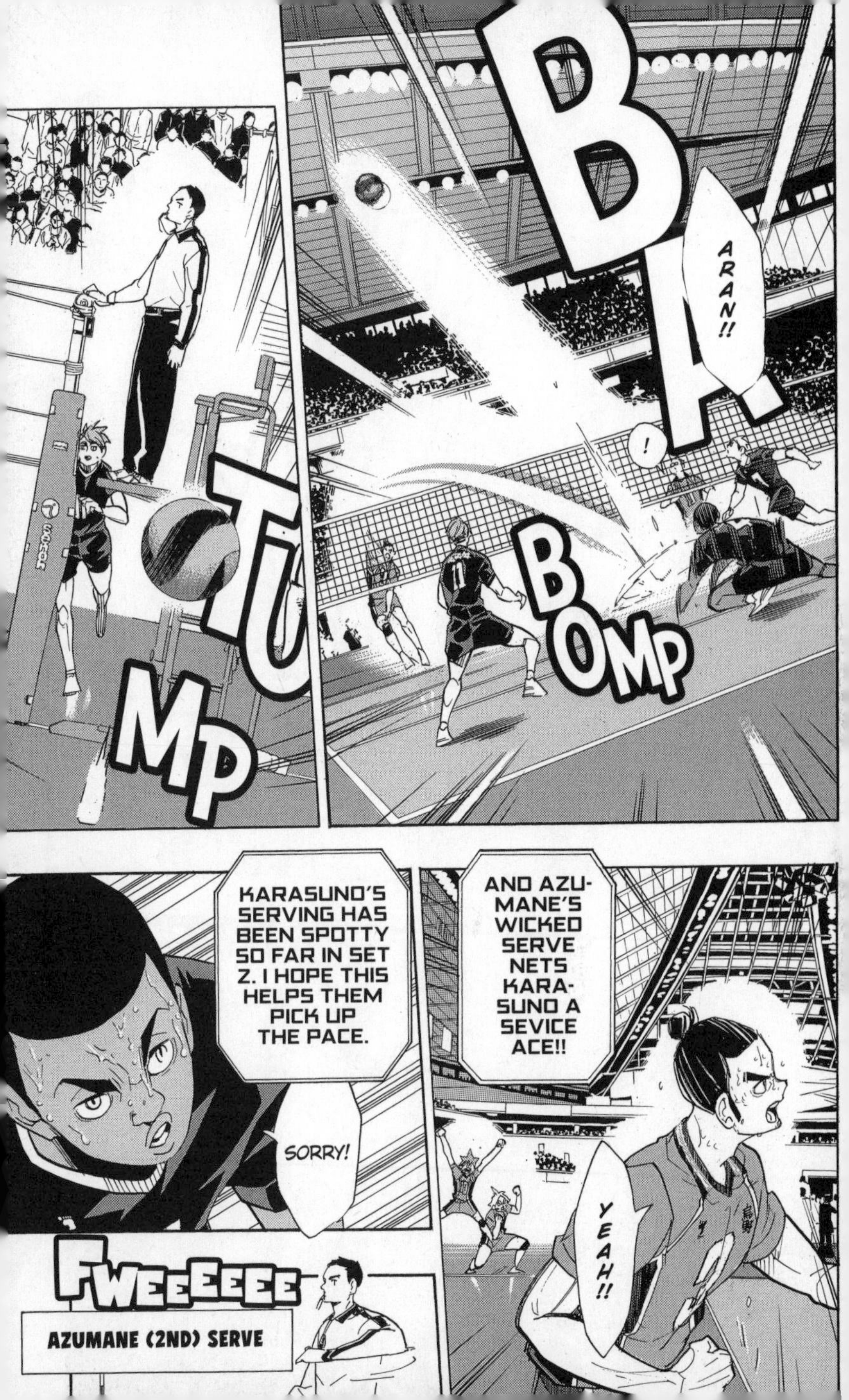
BA
ARAN!!
!
BOMP
TUMP
AND AZUMANE'S WICKED SERVE NETS KARASUNO A SEVICE ACE!!
YEAH!!
KARASUNO'S SERVING HAS BEEN SPOTTY SO FAR IN SET 2. I HOPE THIS HELPS THEM PICK UP THE PACE.
SORRY!
FWEEEEEE
AZUMANE (2ND) SERVE

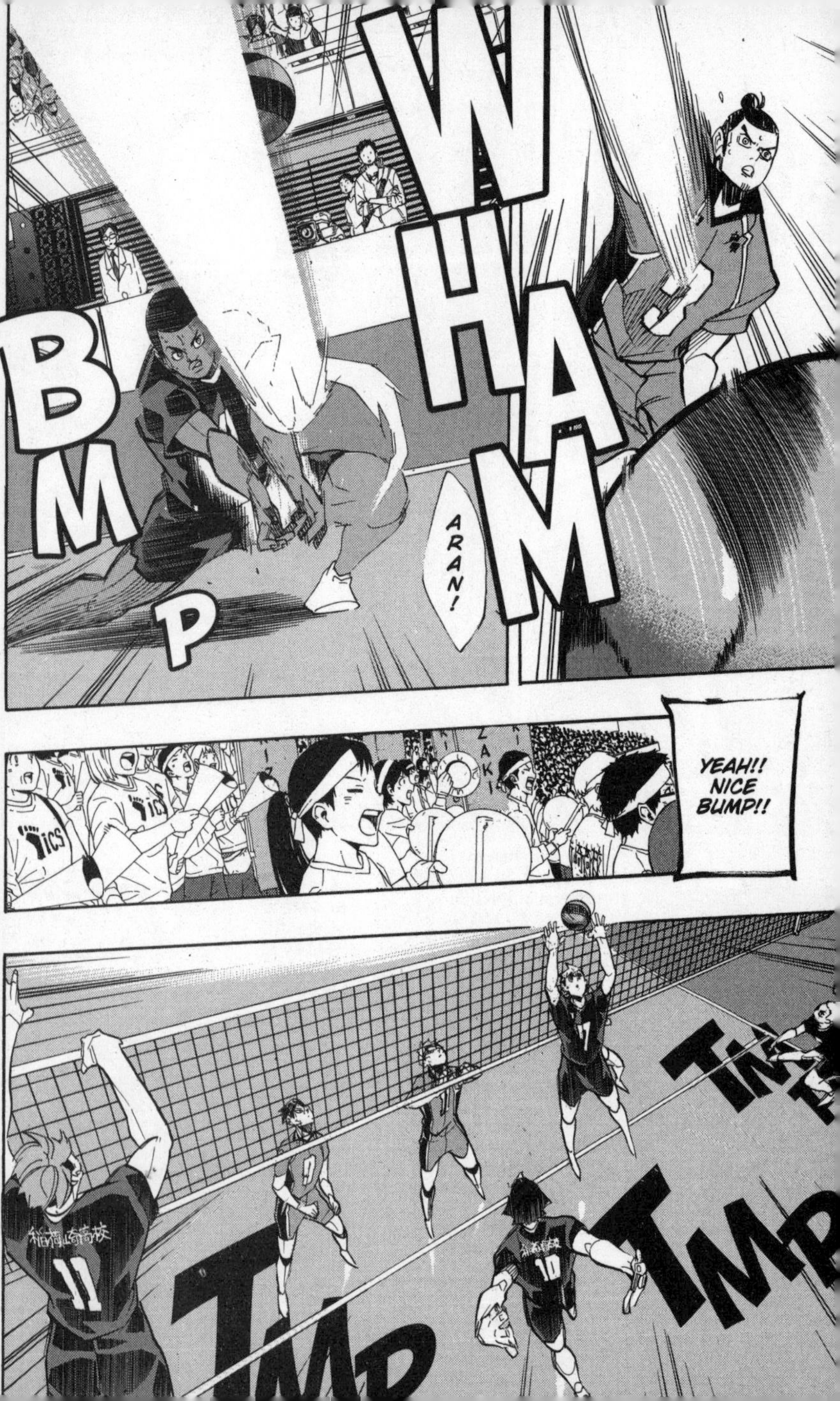
WHAM
BUMP
ARAN!
YEAH!! NICE BUMP!!
TMP
TMP

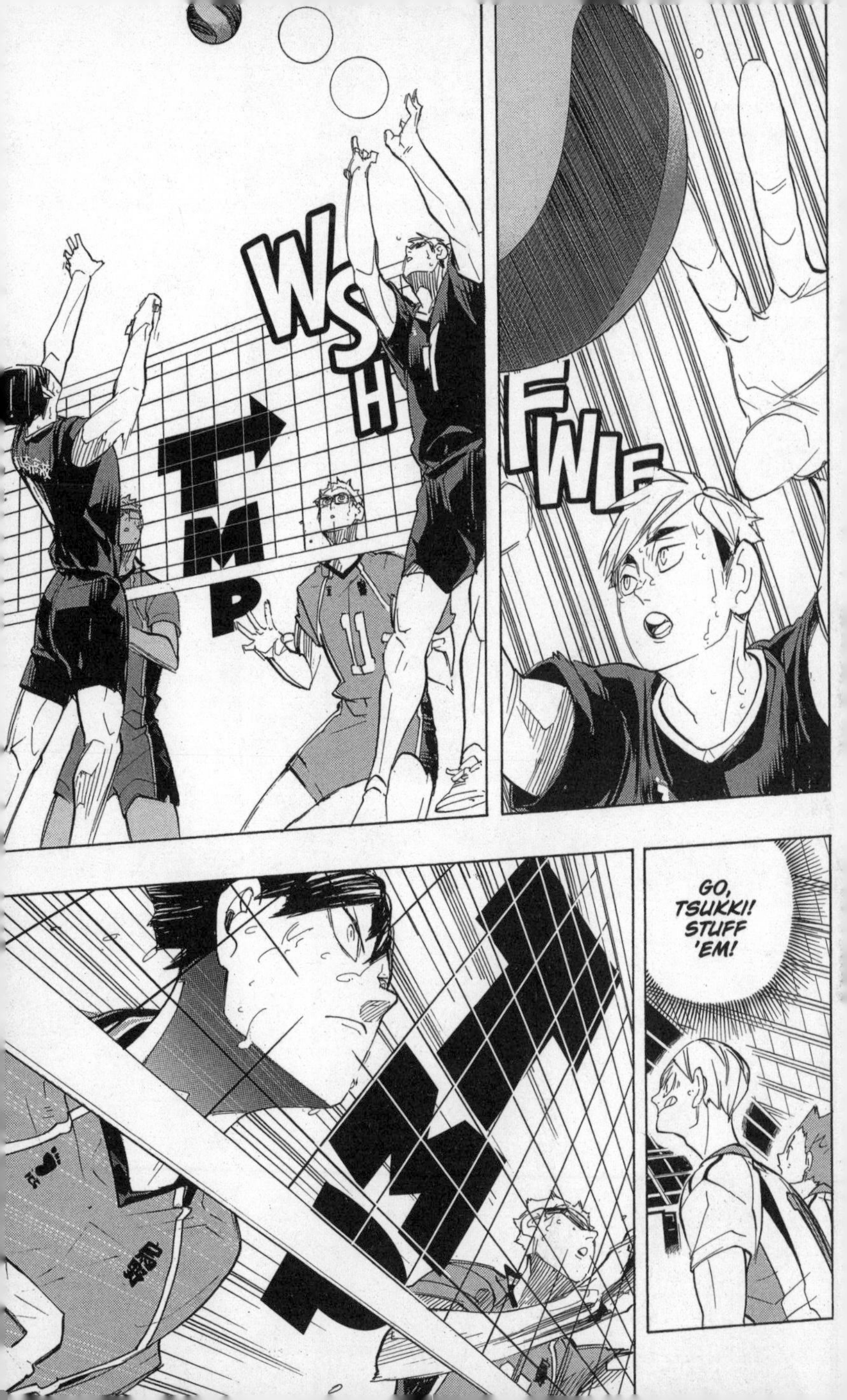
FWIF
WSH
TMP
GO, TSUKKI! STUFF 'EM!

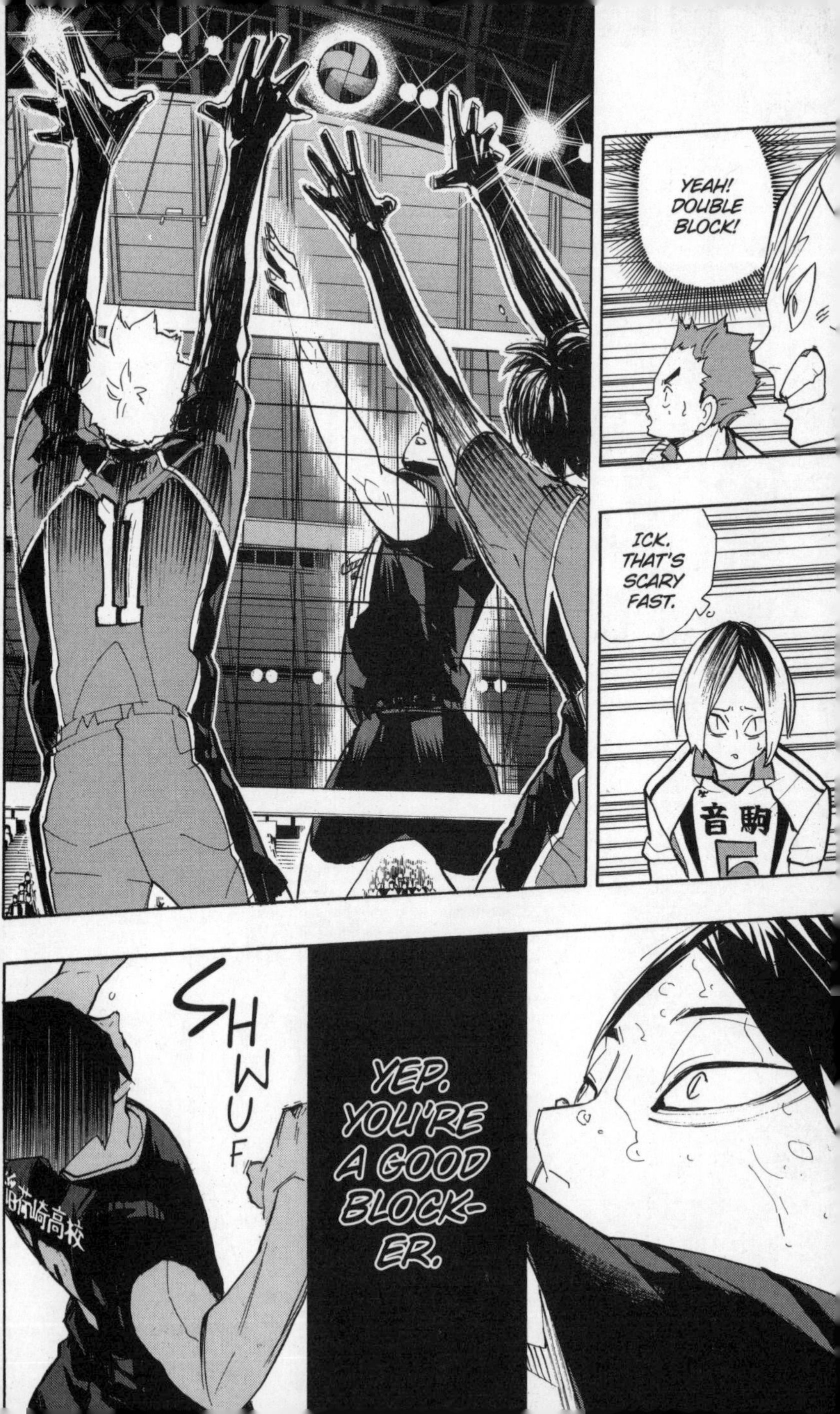
YEAH! DOUBLE BLOCK!
ICK. THAT'S SCARY FAST.
音駒
YEP. YOU'RE A GOOD BLOCK-ER.
SHWUF

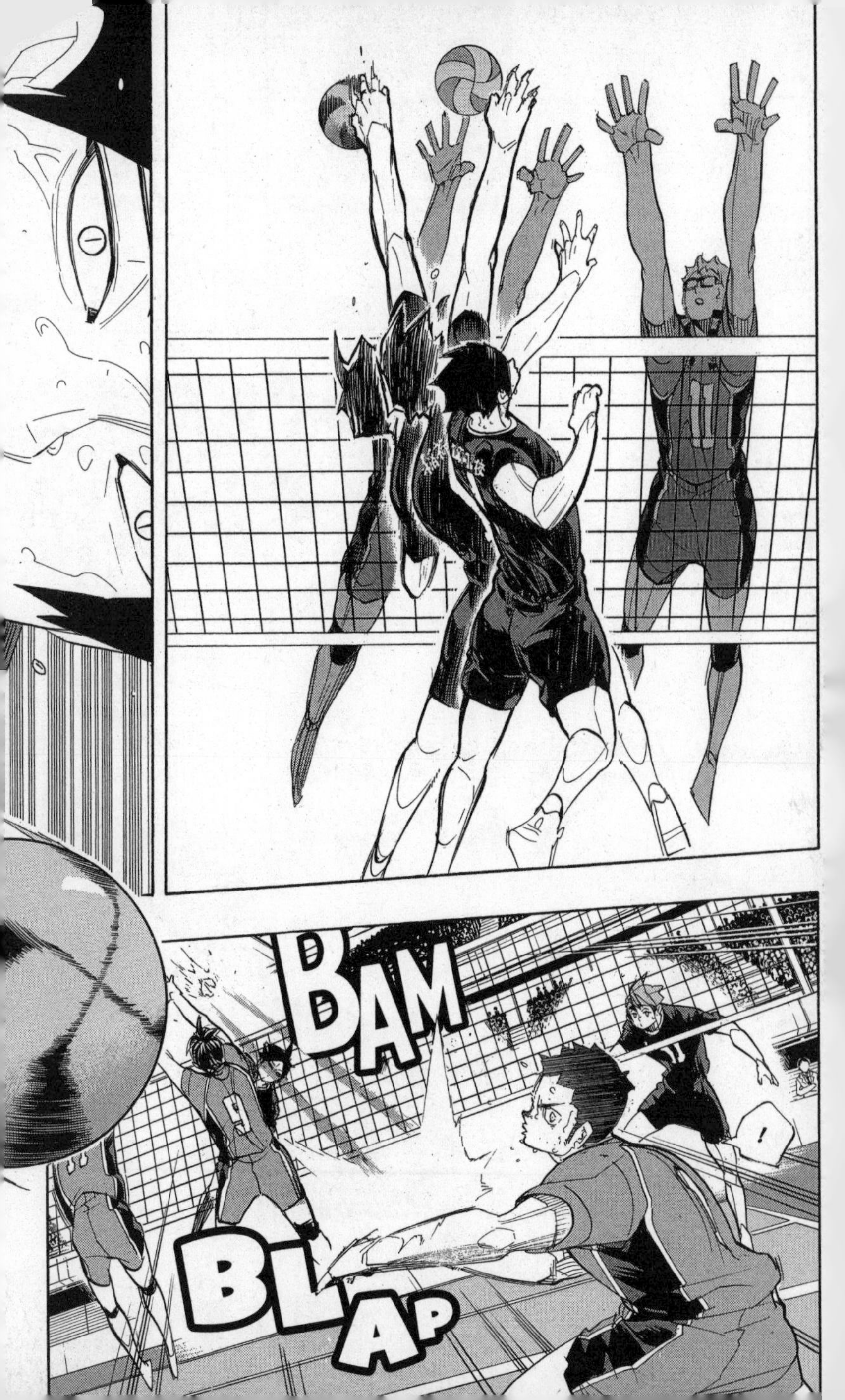

BAM
!
BLAP

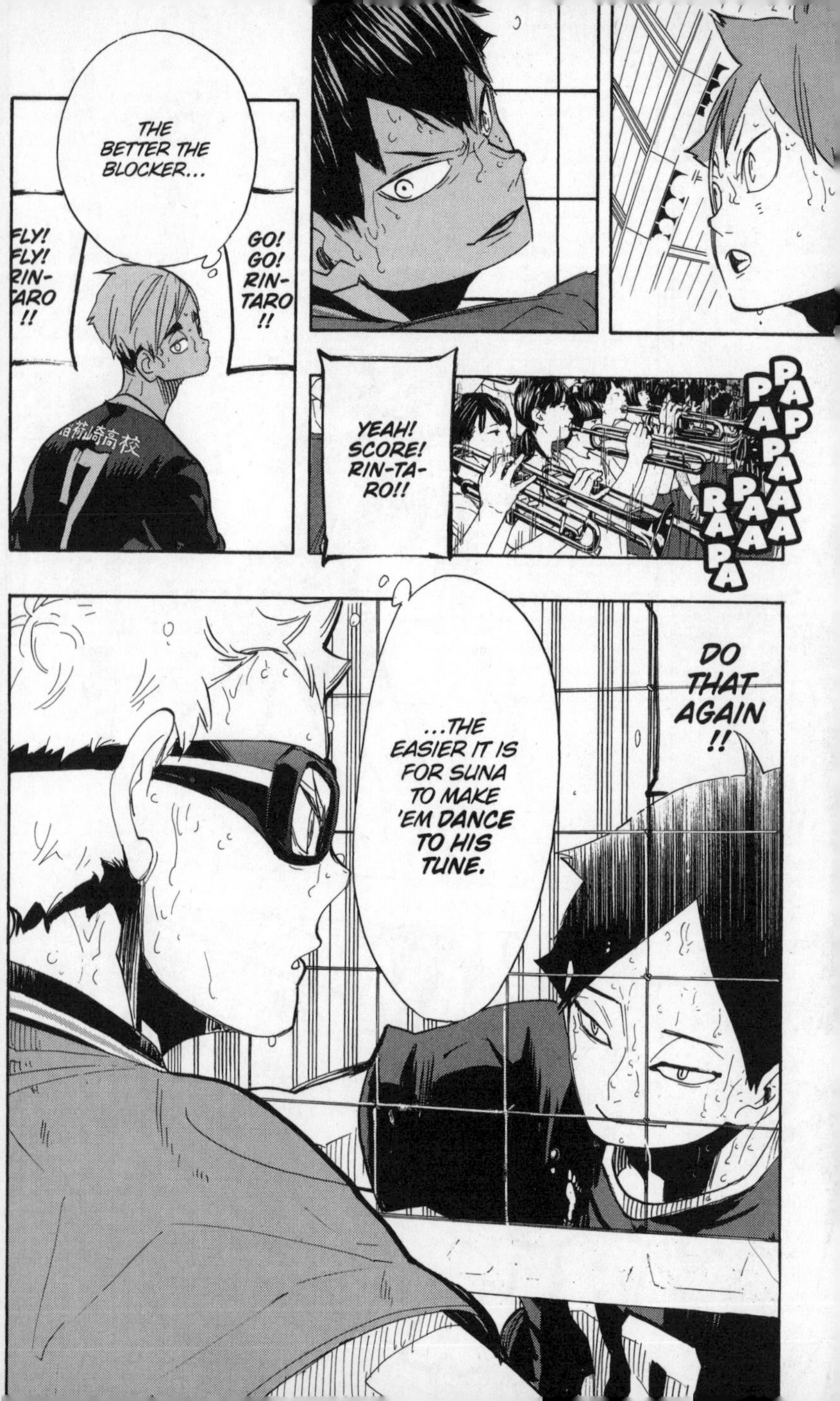
YEAH! SCORE! RIN-TA-RO!!
PAPAPAAA PAAA RAPA
THE BETTER THE BLOCKER...
GO! GO! RIN-TARO!!
FLY! FLY! RIN-TARO!!
DO THAT AGAIN!!
...THE EASIER IT IS FOR SUNA TO MAKE 'EM DANCE TO HIS TUNE.

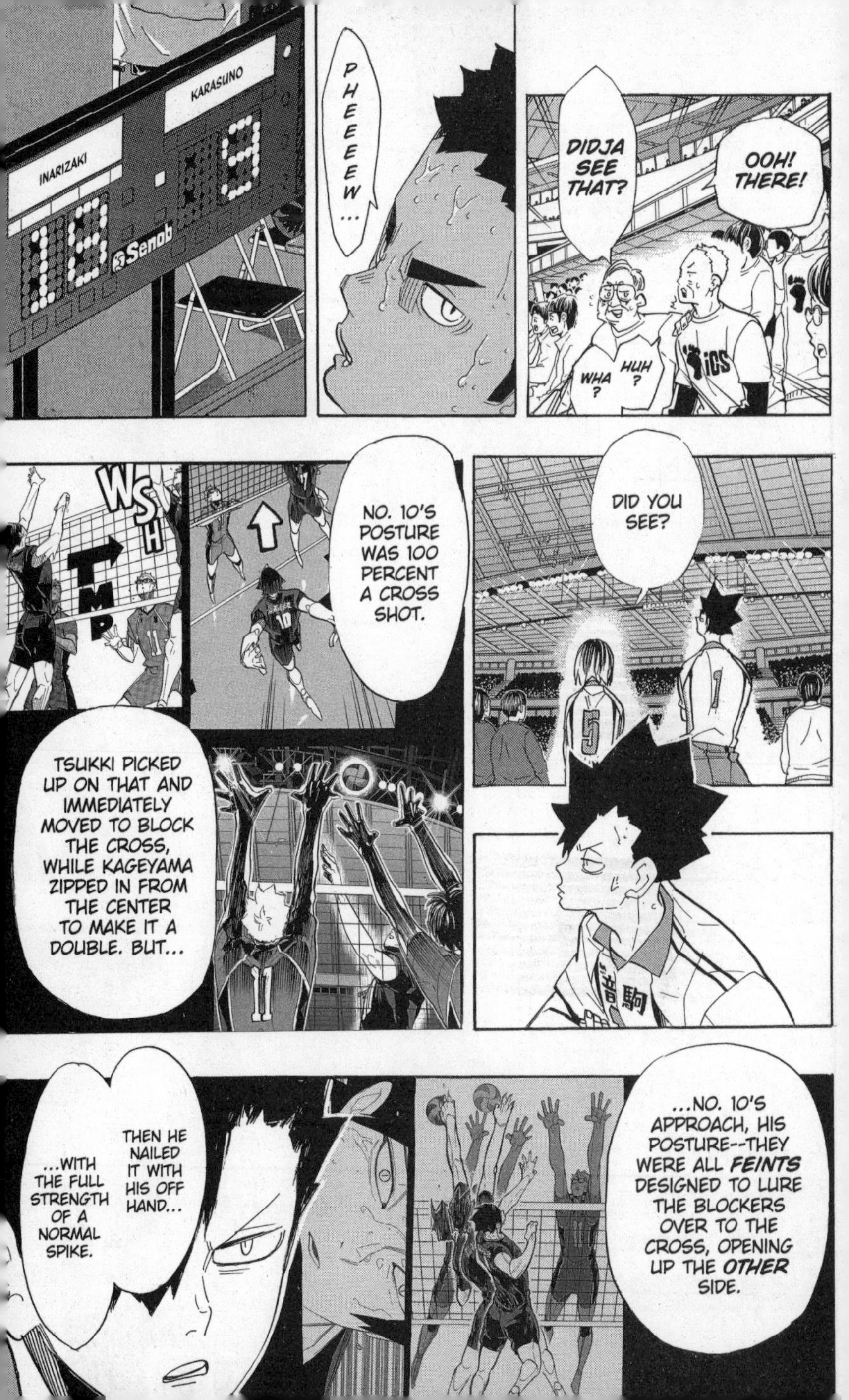
OOH! THERE!
DIDJA SEE THAT?
HUH?
WHA?
PHEEEEW...
KARASUNO
INARIZAKI
Senob
DID YOU SEE?
NO. 10'S POSTURE WAS 100 PERCENT A CROSS SHOT.
WSH
TMP
TSUKKI PICKED UP ON THAT AND IMMEDIATELY MOVED TO BLOCK THE CROSS, WHILE KAGEYAMA ZIPPED IN FROM THE CENTER TO MAKE IT A DOUBLE. BUT...
...NO. 10'S APPROACH, HIS POSTURE--THEY WERE ALL *FEINTS* DESIGNED TO LURE THE BLOCKERS OVER TO THE CROSS, OPENING UP THE *OTHER* SIDE.
THEN HE NAILED IT WITH HIS OFF HAND...
...WITH THE FULL STRENGTH OF A NORMAL SPIKE.

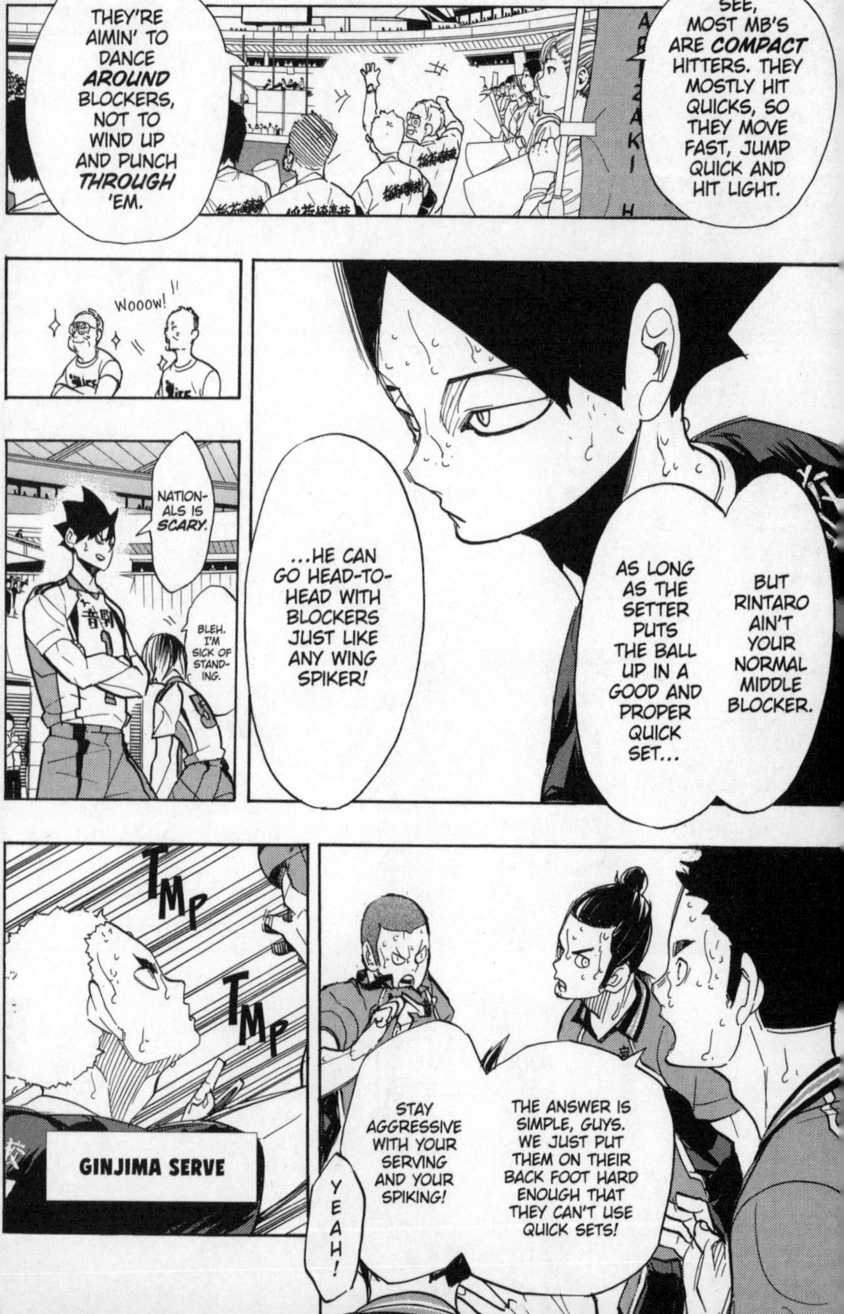
SEE, MOST MB'S ARE COMPACT HITTERS. THEY MOSTLY HIT QUICKS, SO THEY MOVE FAST, JUMP QUICK AND HIT LIGHT.
THEY'RE AIMIN' TO DANCE AROUND BLOCKERS, NOT TO WIND UP AND PUNCH THROUGH 'EM.
BUT RINTARO AIN'T YOUR NORMAL MIDDLE BLOCKER.
AS LONG AS THE SETTER PUTS THE BALL UP IN A GOOD AND PROPER QUICK SET...
...HE CAN GO HEAD-TO-HEAD WITH BLOCKERS JUST LIKE ANY WING SPIKER!
WOOOW!
NATION-ALS IS SCARY.
BLEH. I'M SICK OF STAND-ING.
THE ANSWER IS SIMPLE, GUYS. WE JUST PUT THEM ON THEIR BACK FOOT HARD ENOUGH THAT THEY CAN'T USE QUICK SETS!
STAY AGGRESSIVE WITH YOUR SERVING AND YOUR SPIKING!
YEAH!
TMP
TMP
GINJIMA SERVE

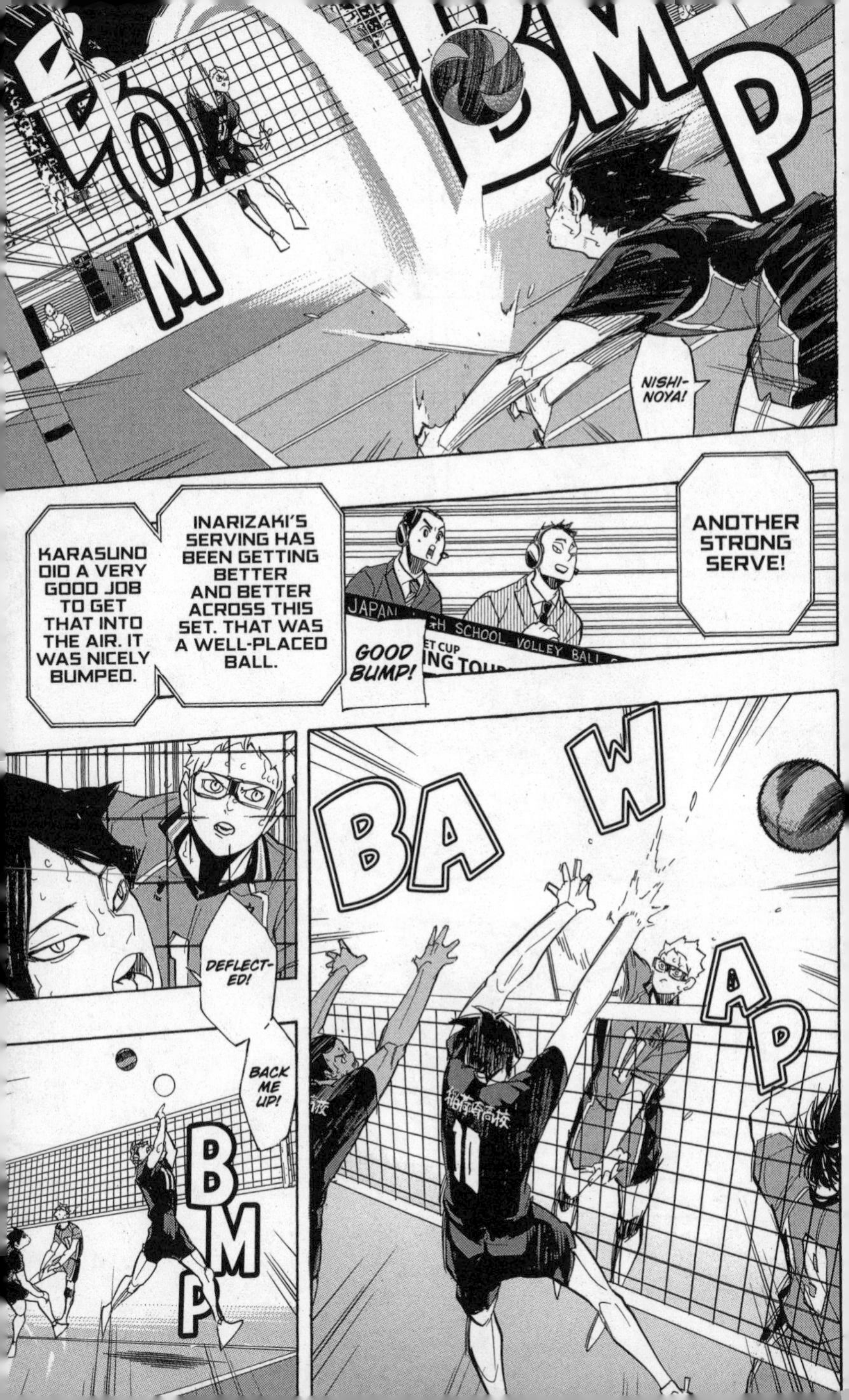
NISHI-NOYA!
ANOTHER STRONG SERVE!
GOOD BUMP!
INARIZAKI'S SERVING HAS BEEN GETTING BETTER AND BETTER ACROSS THIS SET. THAT WAS A WELL-PLACED BALL.
KARASUNO DID A VERY GOOD JOB TO GET THAT INTO THE AIR. IT WAS NICELY BUMPED.
BAWAP
DEFLECT-ED!
BACK ME UP!
BMP

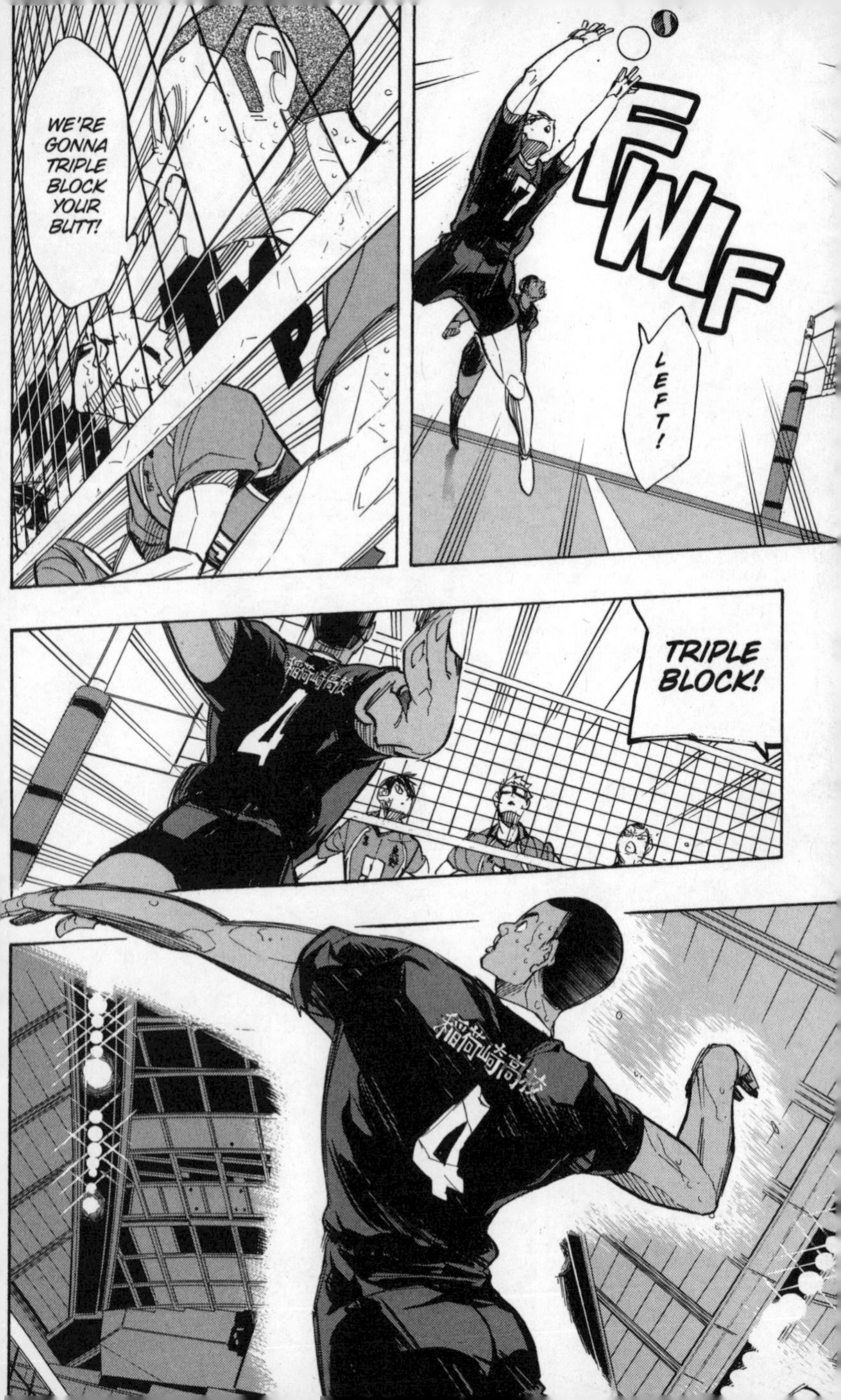
FWIF
LEFT!
WE'RE GONNA TRIPLE BLOCK YOUR BUTT!
TRIPLE BLOCK!

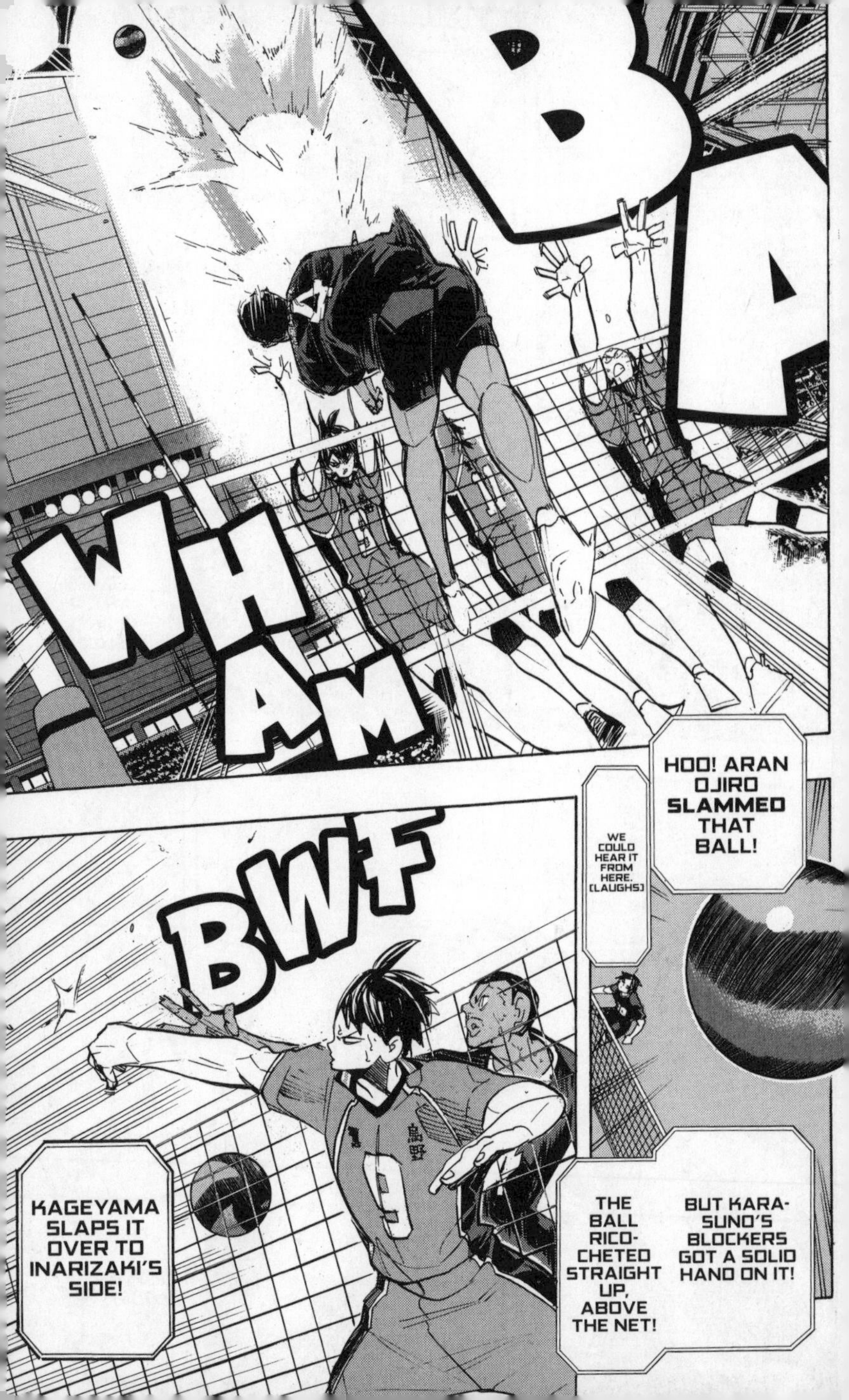
BAP
WHAM
HOO! ARAN OJIRO SLAMMED THAT BALL!
WE COULD HEAR IT FROM HERE. [LAUGHS]
BUT KARA-SUNO'S BLOCKERS GOT A SOLID HAND ON IT!
THE BALL RICO-CHETED STRAIGHT UP, ABOVE THE NET!
BWF
KAGEYAMA SLAPS IT OVER TO INARIZAKI'S SIDE!

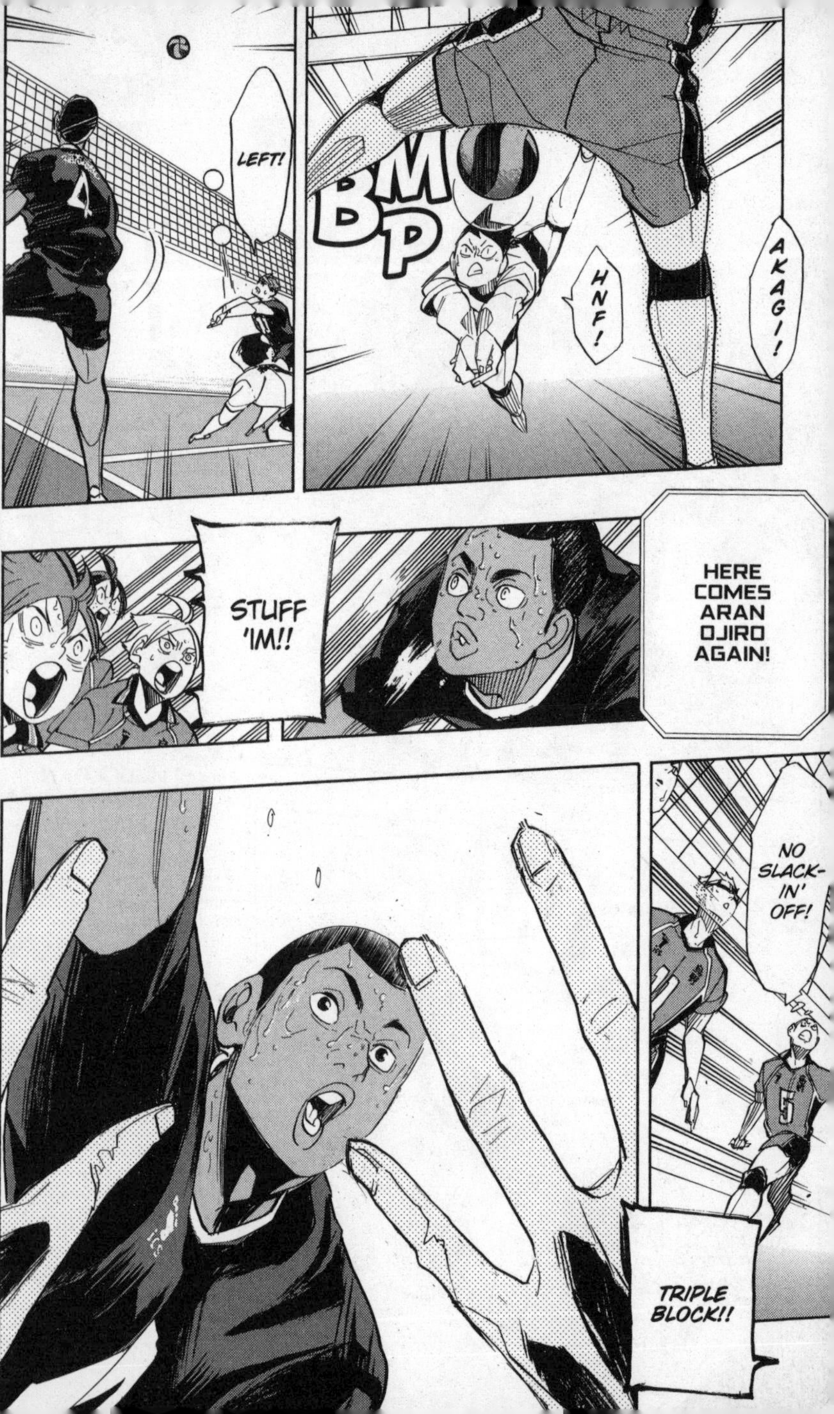
AKAGI!
HNF!
BMP
LEFT!
HERE COMES ARAN OJIRO AGAIN!
STUFF 'IM!!
NO SLACK-IN' OFF!
TRIPLE BLOCK!!

GAH!

OJIRO PUNCHES THE BALL THROUGH A TRIPLE BLOCK WITH INCREDIBLE FORCE!

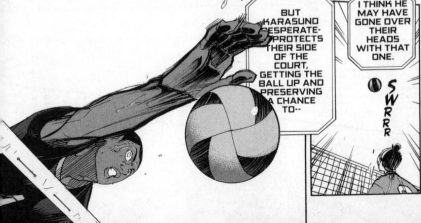

BUT KARASUNO DESPERATE-PROTECTS THEIR SIDE OF THE COURT, GETTING THE BALL UP AND PRESERVING A CHANCE TO--

I THINK HE MAY HAVE GONE OVER THEIR HEADS WITH THAT ONE.

SWRRR

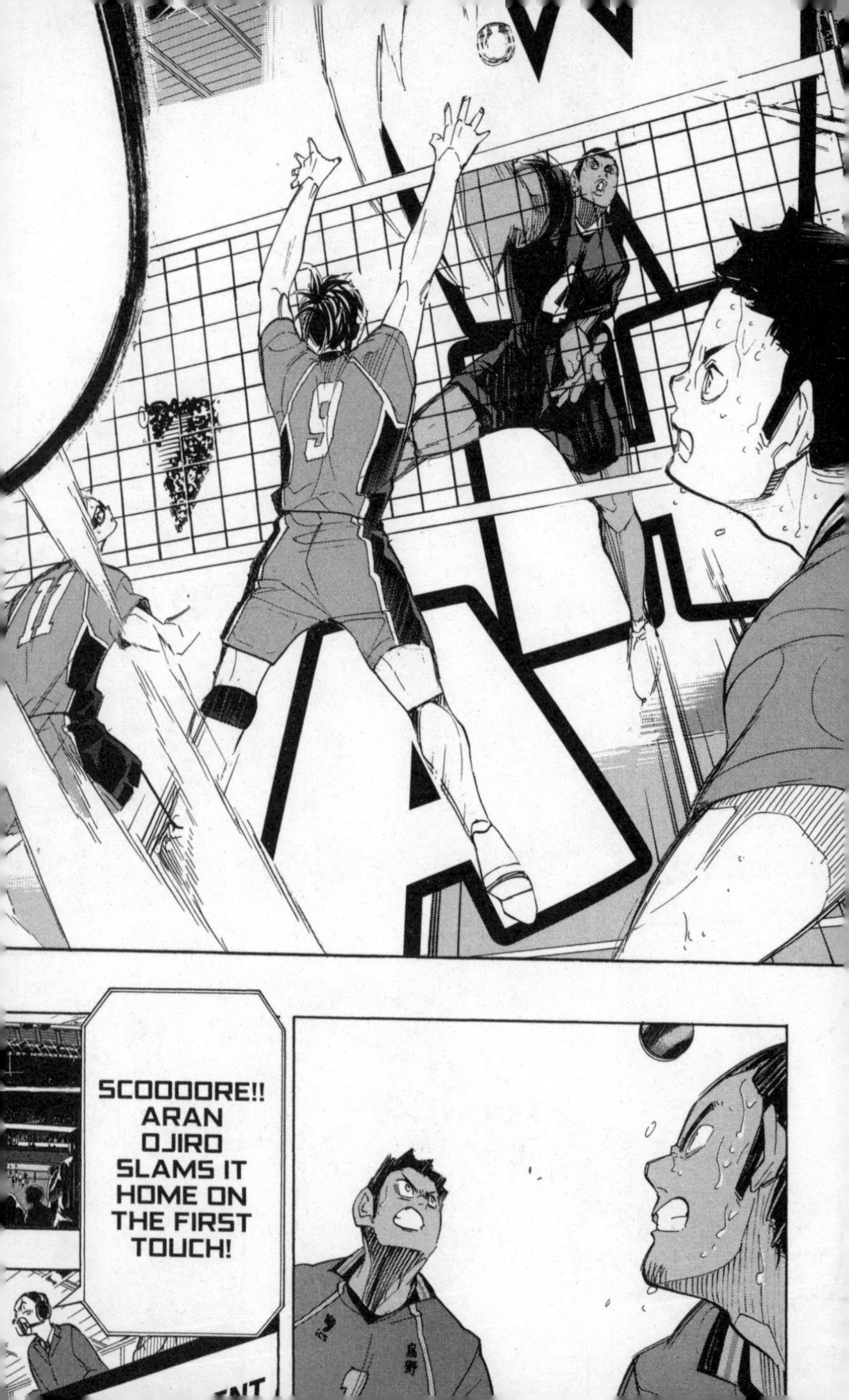
SCOOOORE!! ARAN OJIRO SLAMS IT HOME ON THE FIRST TOUCH!

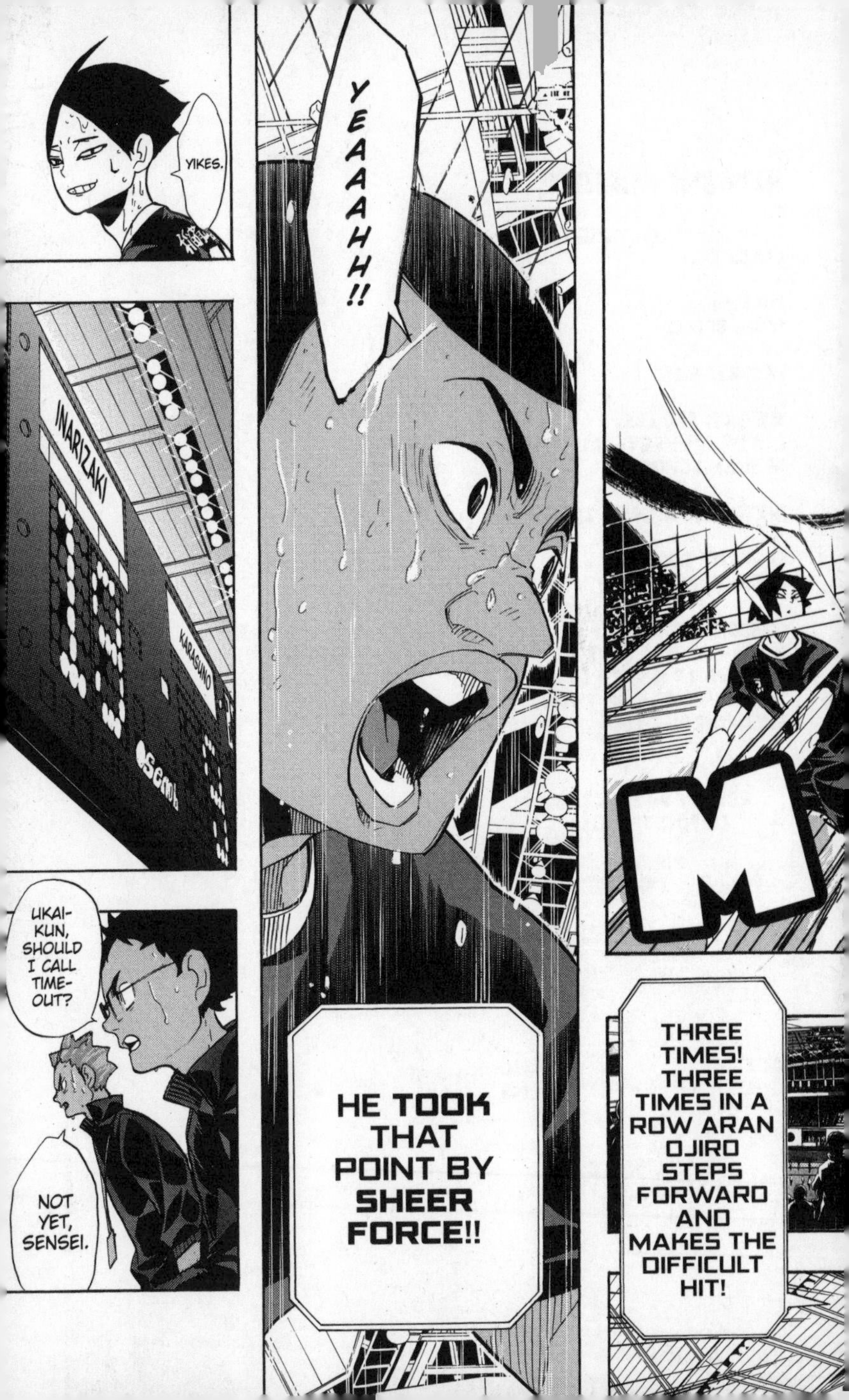
M
THREE TIMES! THREE TIMES IN A ROW ARAN OJIRO STEPS FORWARD AND MAKES THE DIFFICULT HIT!
YEAAAAHH!!
HE TOOK THAT POINT BY SHEER FORCE!!
YIKES.
INARIZAKI
KARASUNO
UKAI-KUN, SHOULD I CALL TIME-OUT?
NOT YET, SENSEI.

HITOSHI GINJIMA

INARIZAKI HIGH SCHOOL
CLASS 2-2

POSITION:
WING SPIKER

HEIGHT: 5′11″

WEIGHT: 160 LBS.
(AS OF JANUARY, 2ND YEAR OF HIGH SCHOOL)

BIRTHDAY: AUGUST 21

FAVORITE FOOD:
BACON-WRAPPED POTATOES

CURRENT WORRY:
OJIRO-SAN HAS STARTED LOOKING TO HIM TO CALL THE TWINS OUT ON THEIR SHENANIGANS TOO.

ABILITY PARAMETERS
(5-POINT SCALE)

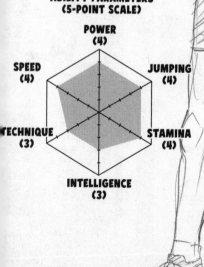

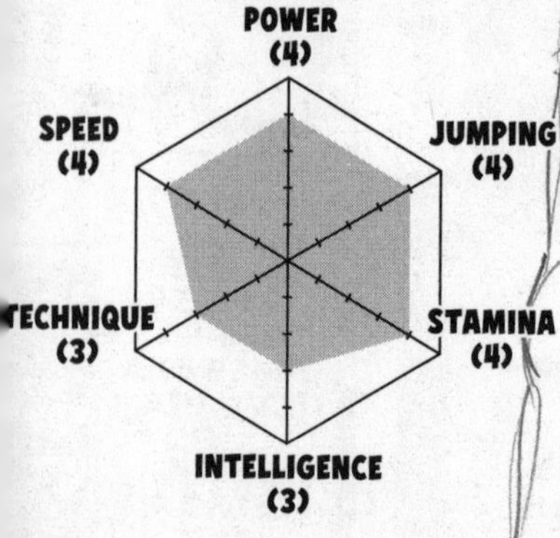
POWER (4)
JUMPING (4)
STAMINA (4)
INTELLIGENCE (3)
TECHNIQUE (3)
SPEED (4)

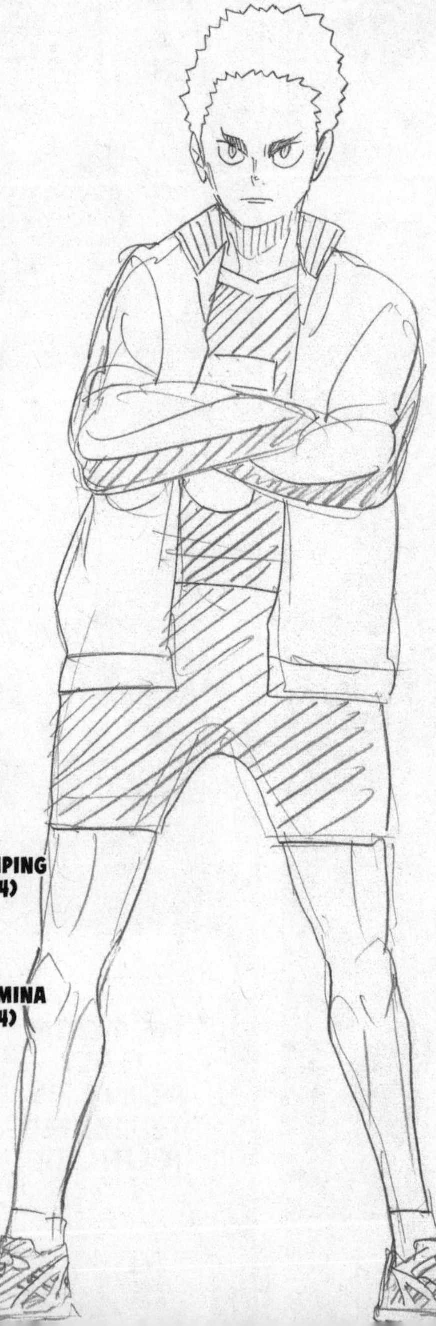

CHAPTER 272: The Greatest Contender

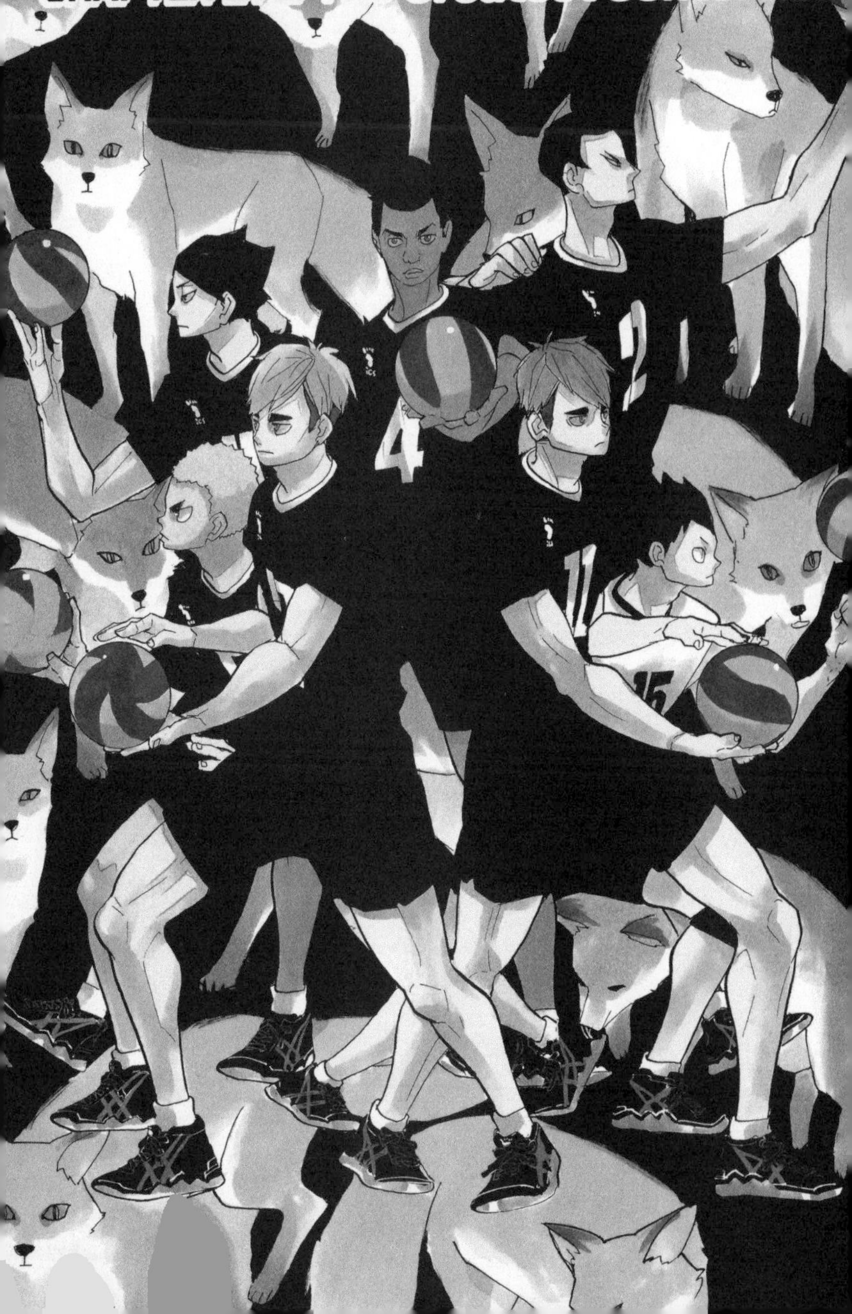

HAIKYU!!

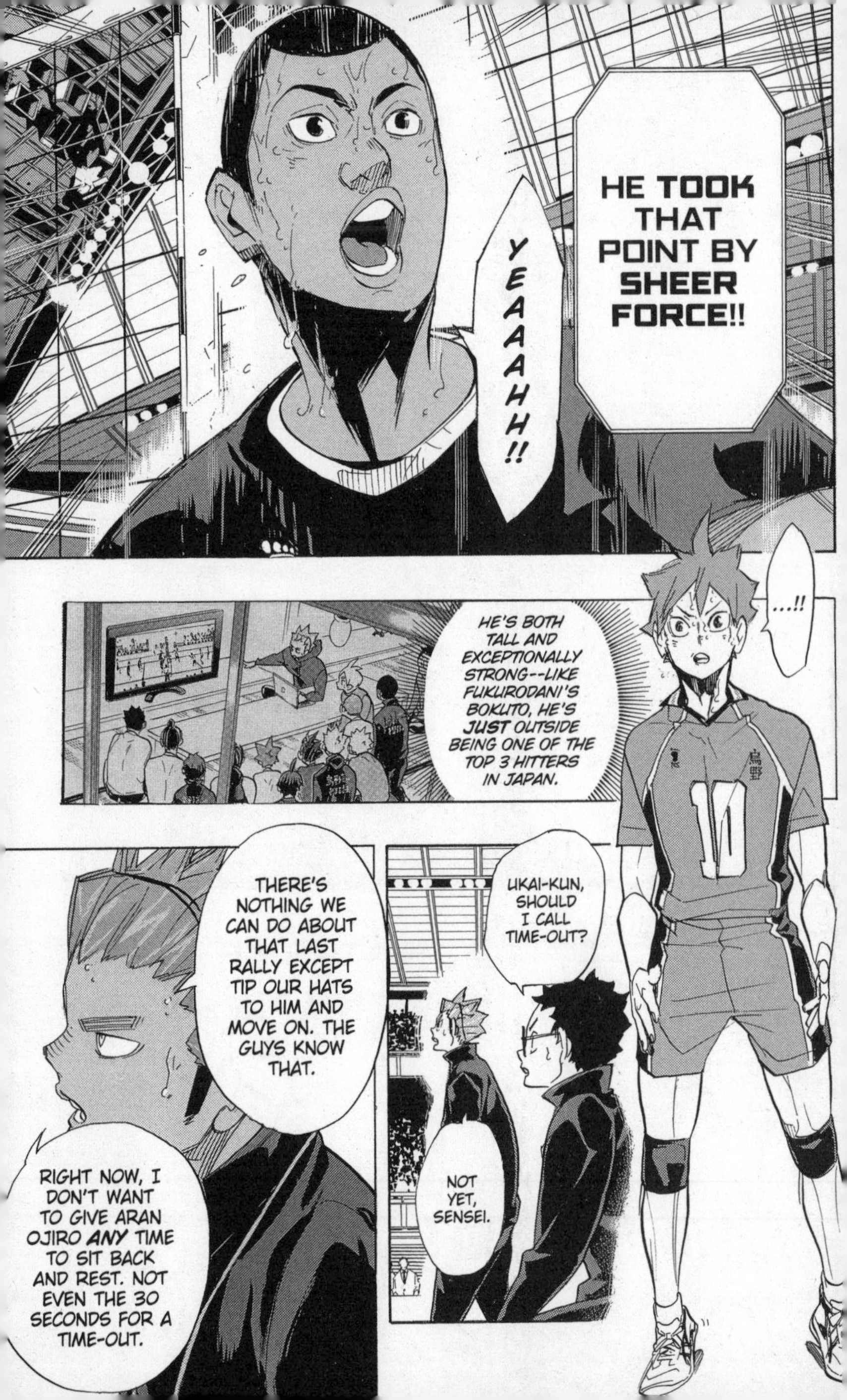
HE TOOK THAT POINT BY SHEER FORCE!!
YEAAAAHH!!
...!!
HE'S BOTH TALL AND EXCEPTIONALLY STRONG--LIKE FUKURODANI'S BOKUTO, HE'S JUST OUTSIDE BEING ONE OF THE TOP 3 HITTERS IN JAPAN.
UKAI-KUN, SHOULD I CALL TIME-OUT?
NOT YET, SENSEI.
THERE'S NOTHING WE CAN DO ABOUT THAT LAST RALLY EXCEPT TIP OUR HATS TO HIM AND MOVE ON. THE GUYS KNOW THAT.
RIGHT NOW, I DON'T WANT TO GIVE ARAN OJIRO ANY TIME TO SIT BACK AND REST. NOT EVEN THE 30 SECONDS FOR A TIME-OUT.

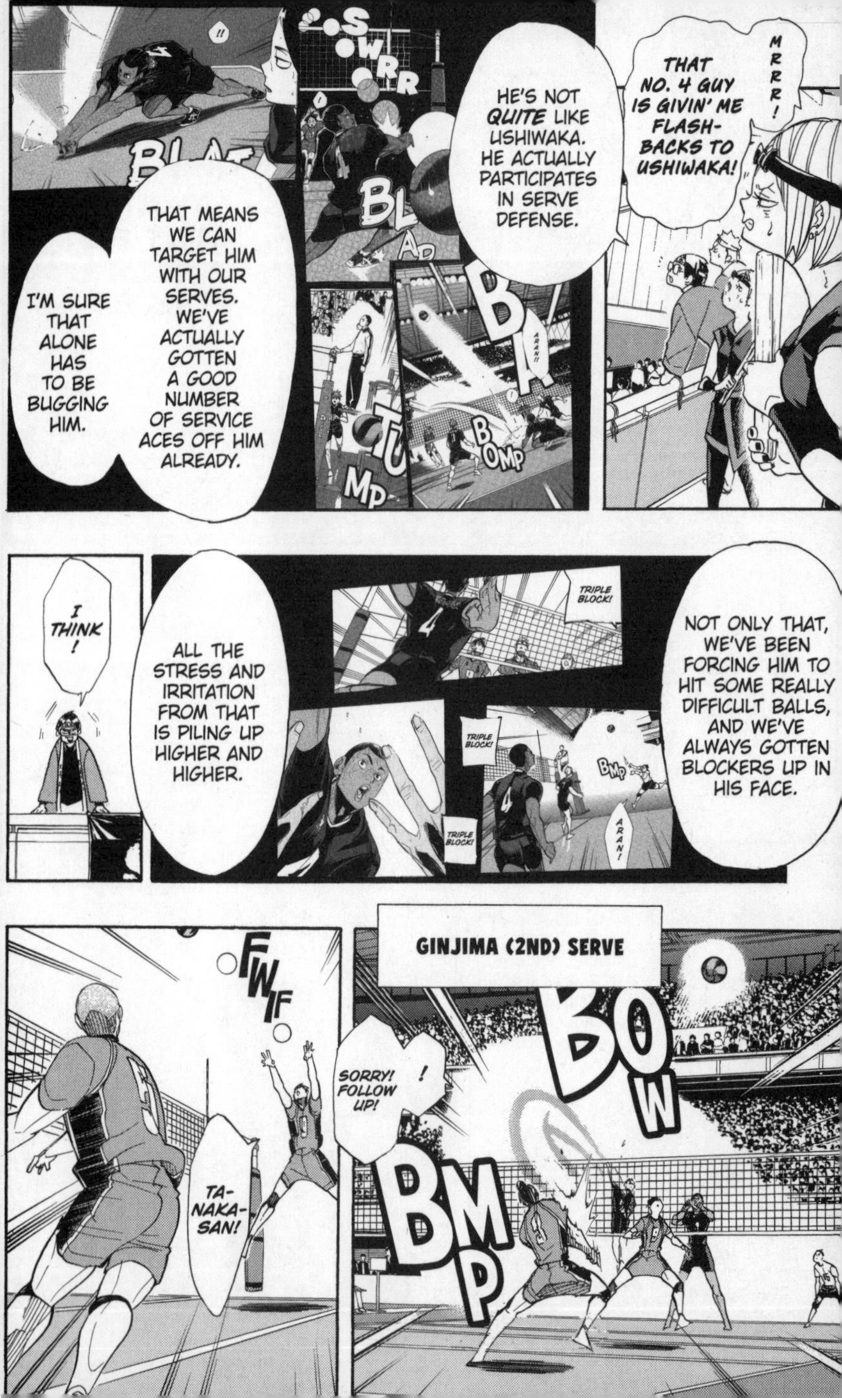
MRRR!
THAT NO. 4 GUY IS GIVIN' ME FLASH-BACKS TO USHIWAKA!
HE'S NOT QUITE LIKE USHIWAKA. HE ACTUALLY PARTICIPATES IN SERVE DEFENSE.
SWRR
!
BLAD
BA
ARAN!!
!
BOMP
TUMP
!!
THAT MEANS WE CAN TARGET HIM WITH OUR SERVES. WE'VE ACTUALLY GOTTEN A GOOD NUMBER OF SERVICE ACES OFF HIM ALREADY.
I'M SURE THAT ALONE HAS TO BE BUGGING HIM.
NOT ONLY THAT, WE'VE BEEN FORCING HIM TO HIT SOME REALLY DIFFICULT BALLS, AND WE'VE ALWAYS GOTTEN BLOCKERS UP IN HIS FACE.
TRIPLE BLOCK!
TRIPLE BLOCK!
BMP
ARAN!
TRIPLE BLOCK!
ALL THE STRESS AND IRRITATION FROM THAT IS PILING UP HIGHER AND HIGHER.
I THINK!
GINJIMA (2ND) SERVE
BOW
!
SORRY! FOLLOW UP!
BMP
FWIF
TA-NAKA-SAN!

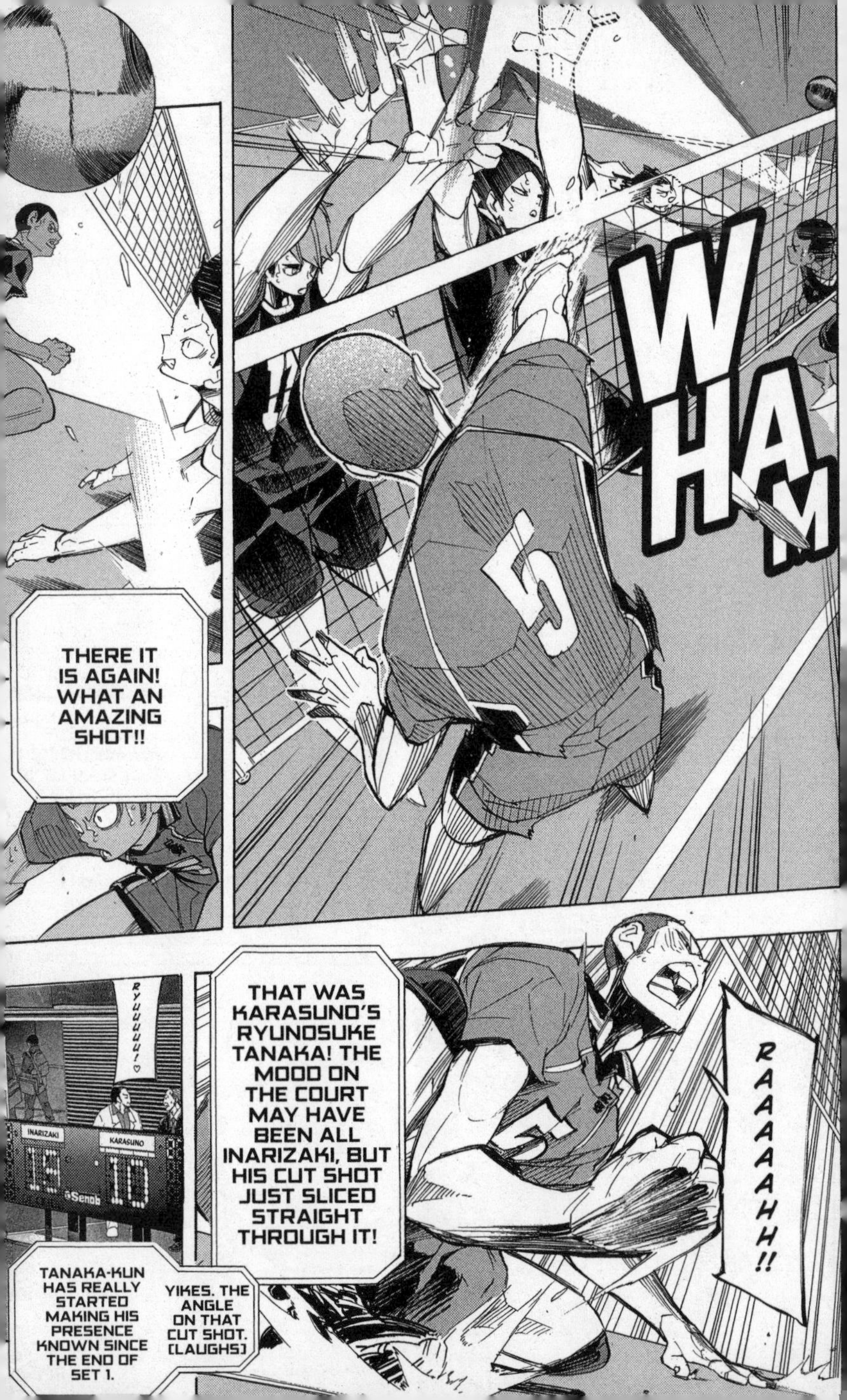
WHAM
THERE IT IS AGAIN! WHAT AN AMAZING SHOT!!
RAAAAAAHH!!
THAT WAS KARASUNO'S RYUNOSUKE TANAKA! THE MOOD ON THE COURT MAY HAVE BEEN ALL INARIZAKI, BUT HIS CUT SHOT JUST SLICED STRAIGHT THROUGH IT!
RYUUUUU!♡
INARIZAKI
KARASUNO
19
10
YIKES. THE ANGLE ON THAT CUT SHOT. [LAUGHS]
TANAKA-KUN HAS REALLY STARTED MAKING HIS PRESENCE KNOWN SINCE THE END OF SET 1.

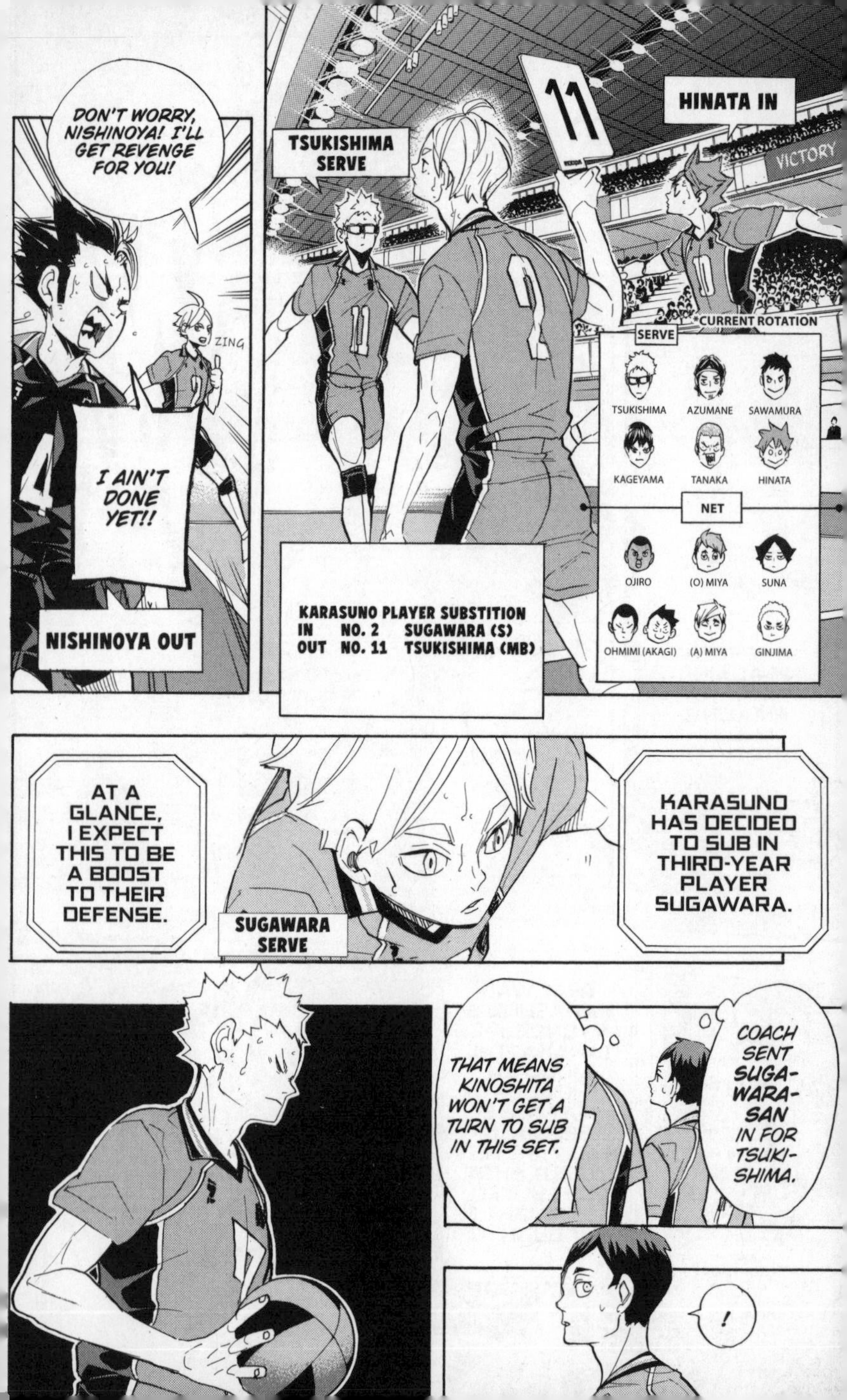

HINATA IN
TSUKISHIMA SERVE
*CURRENT ROTATION
SERVE
TSUKISHIMA
AZUMANE
SAWAMURA
KAGEYAMA
TANAKA
HINATA
NET
OJIRO
(O) MIYA
SUNA
OHMIMI (AKAGI)
(A) MIYA
GINJIMA
KARASUNO PLAYER SUBSTITION
IN NO. 2 SUGAWARA (S)
OUT NO. 11 TSUKISHIMA (MB)
DON'T WORRY, NISHINOYA! I'LL GET REVENGE FOR YOU!
ZING
I AIN'T DONE YET!!
NISHINOYA OUT
KARASUNO HAS DECIDED TO SUB IN THIRD-YEAR PLAYER SUGAWARA.
AT A GLANCE, I EXPECT THIS TO BE A BOOST TO THEIR DEFENSE.
SUGAWARA SERVE
COACH SENT SUGA-WARA-SAN IN FOR TSUKI-SHIMA.
THAT MEANS KINOSHITA WON'T GET A TURN TO SUB IN THIS SET.
!

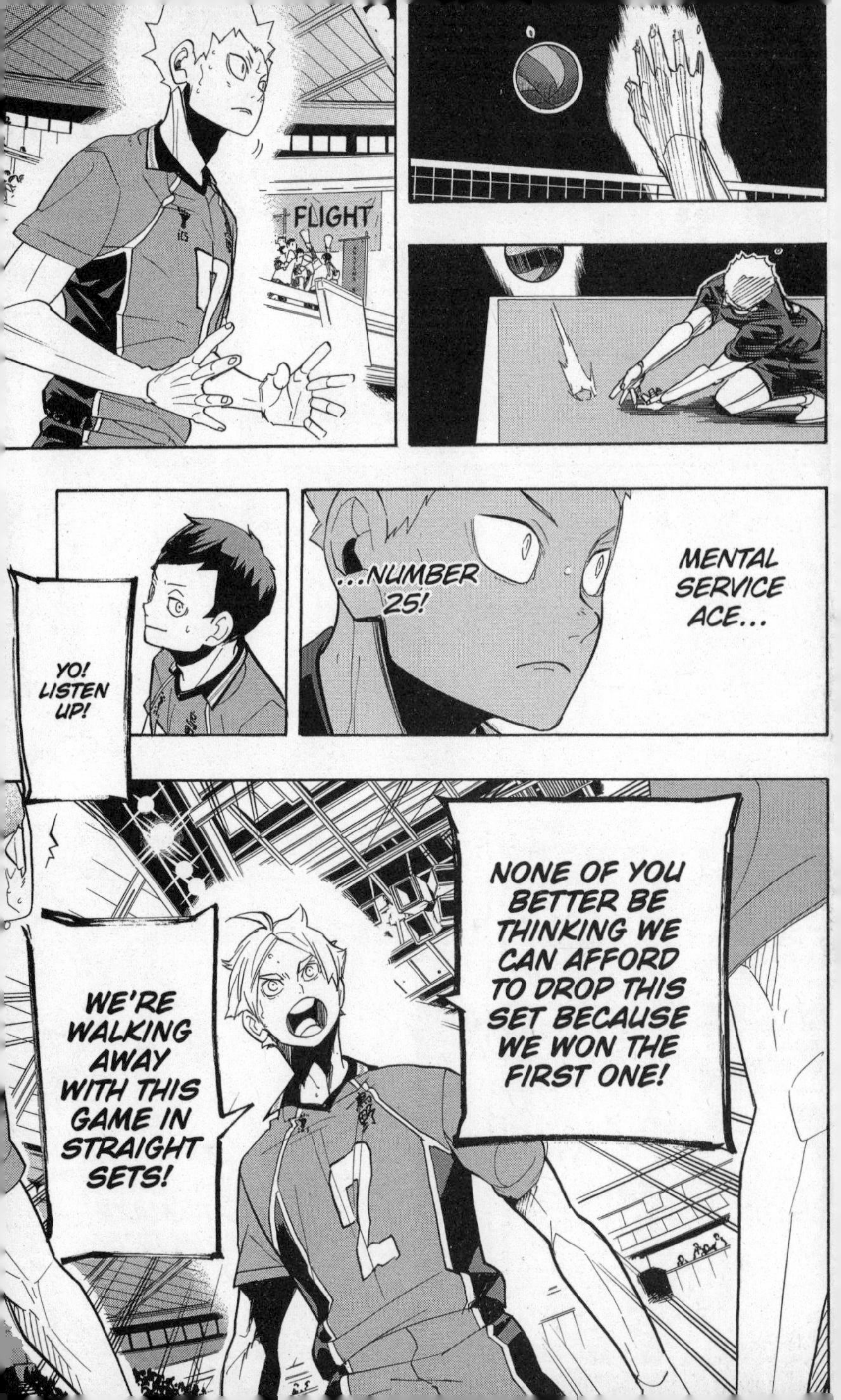
FLIGHT
MENTAL SERVICE ACE...
...NUMBER 25!
YO! LISTEN UP!
NONE OF YOU BETTER BE THINKING WE CAN AFFORD TO DROP THIS SET BECAUSE WE WON THE FIRST ONE!
WE'RE WALKING AWAY WITH THIS GAME IN STRAIGHT SETS!

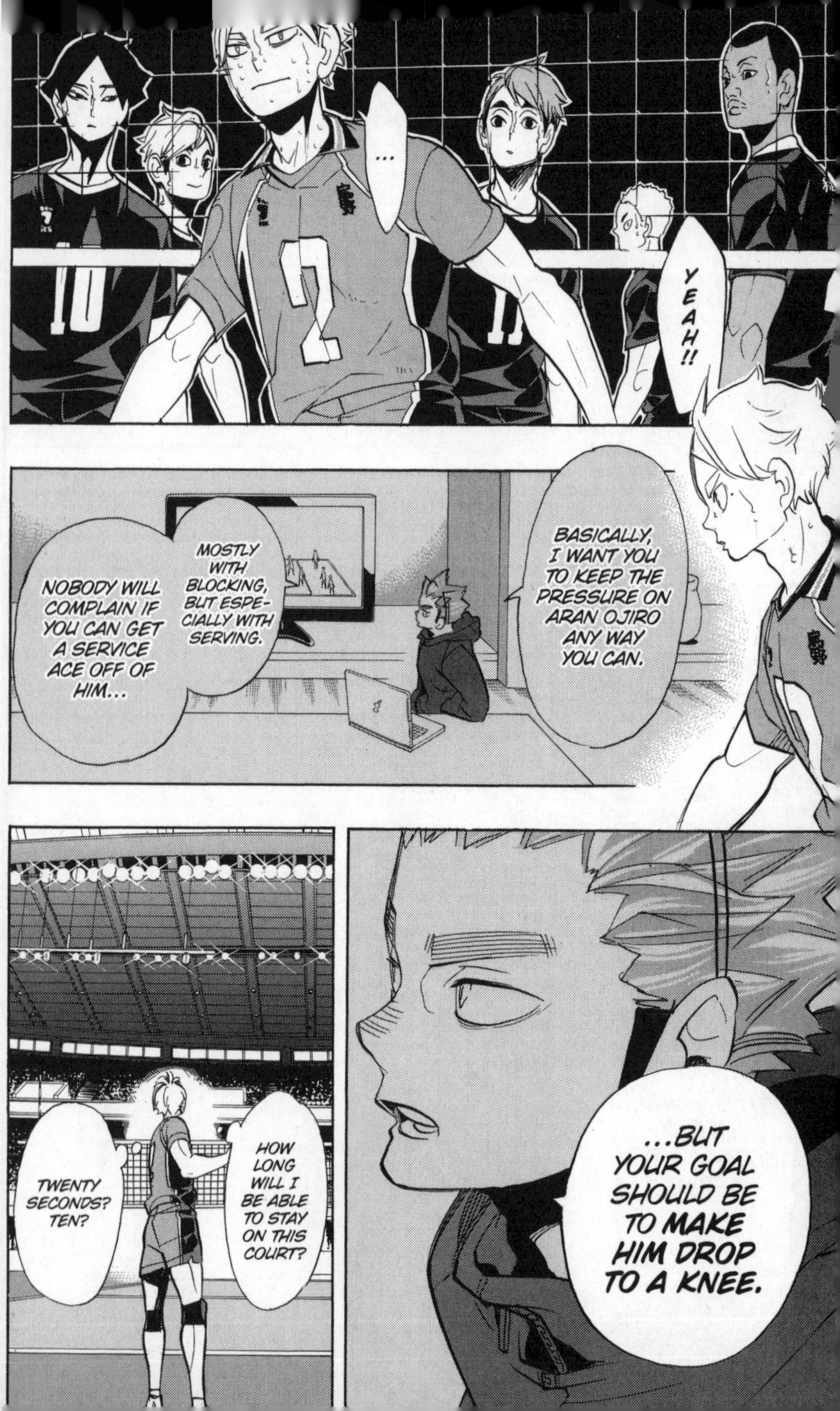
...
YEAH!!
BASICALLY, I WANT YOU TO KEEP THE PRESSURE ON ARAN OJIRO ANY WAY YOU CAN.
MOSTLY WITH BLOCKING, BUT ESPE-CIALLY WITH SERVING.
NOBODY WILL COMPLAIN IF YOU CAN GET A SERVICE ACE OFF OF HIM...
...BUT YOUR GOAL SHOULD BE TO MAKE HIM DROP TO A KNEE.
HOW LONG WILL I BE ABLE TO STAY ON THIS COURT?
TWENTY SECONDS? TEN?

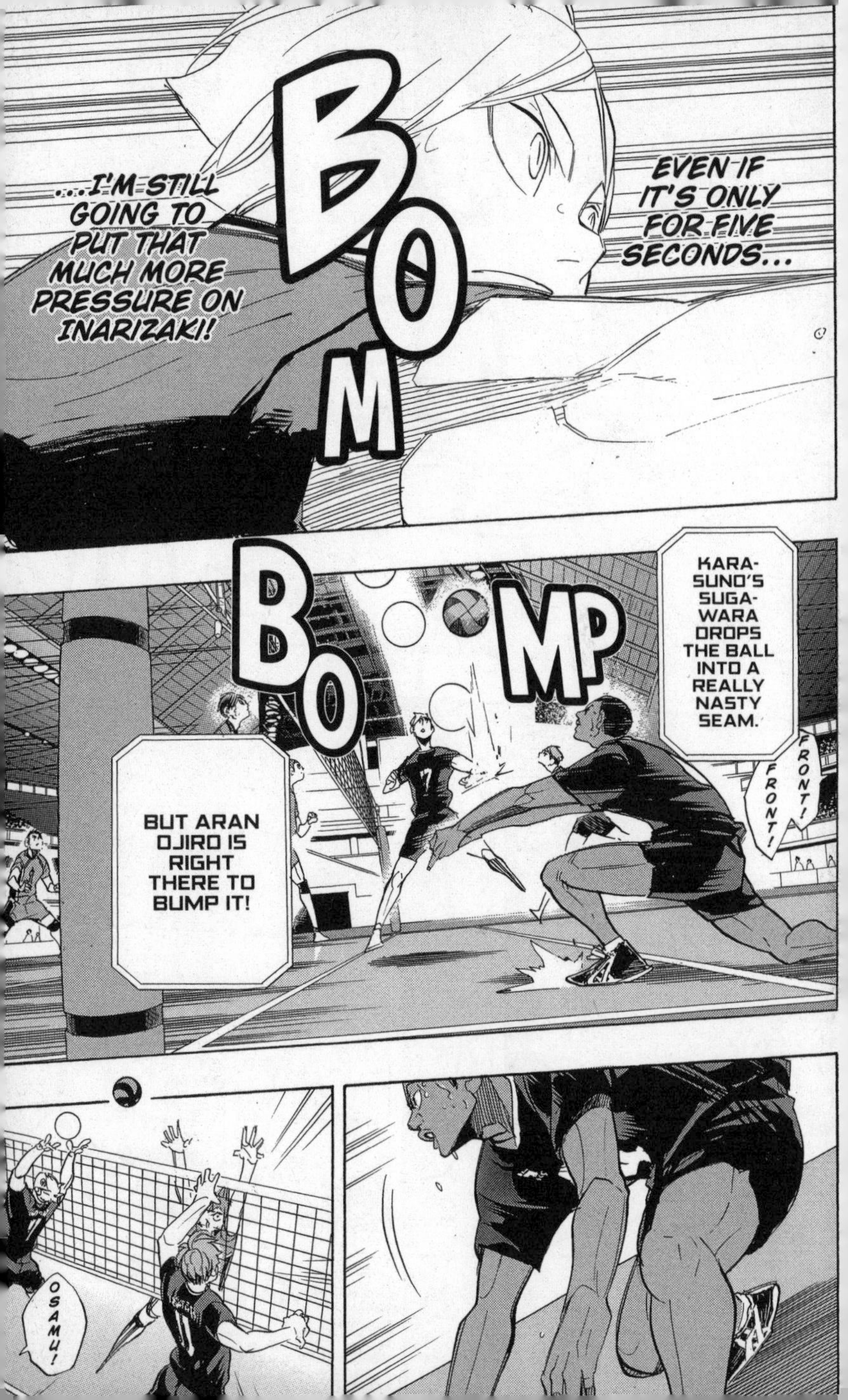

EVEN IF IT'S ONLY FOR FIVE SECONDS...
...I'M STILL GOING TO PUT THAT MUCH MORE PRESSURE ON INARIZAKI!
BOOM
BOOMP
KARA-SUNO'S SUGA-WARA DROPS THE BALL INTO A REALLY NASTY SEAM.
FRONT!
FRONT!
BUT ARAN OJIRO IS RIGHT THERE TO BUMP IT!
OSAMU!

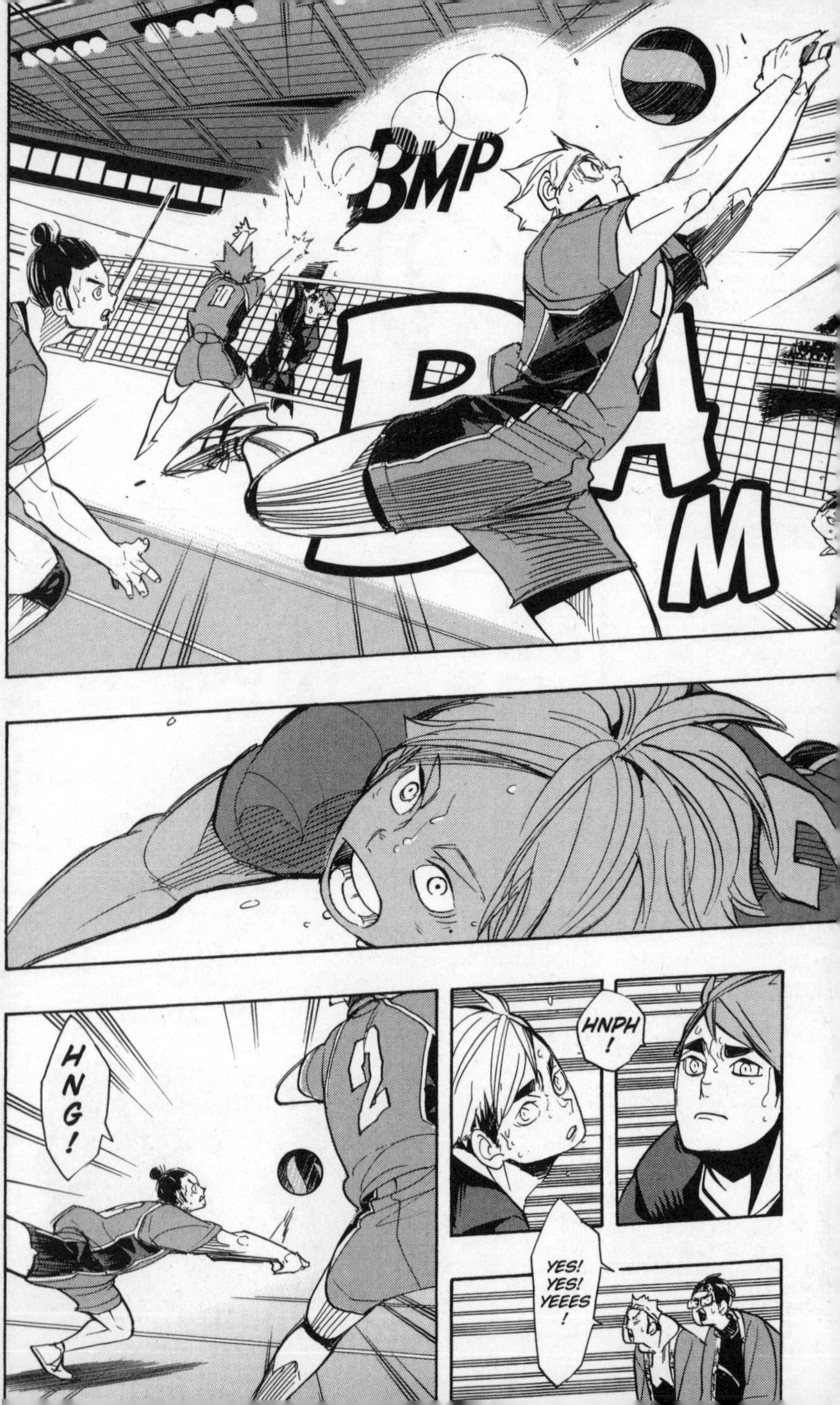
BMP
BAM
HNPH!
YES! YES! YEEES!
HNG!

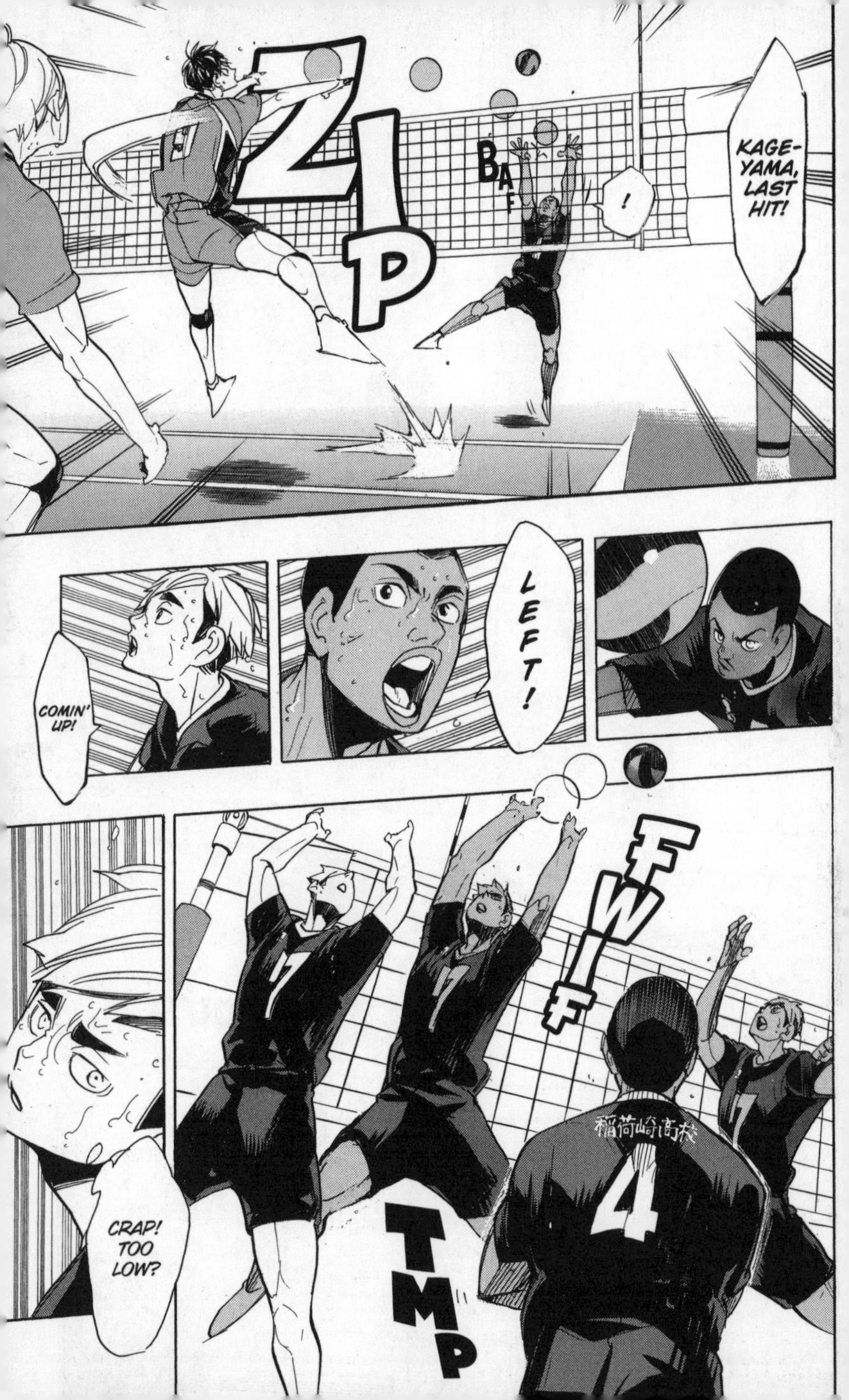
KAGE-YAMA, LAST HIT!
!
BAF
ZIP
LEFT!
COMIN' UP!
FWF
稲荷崎高校
4
TMP
CRAP! TOO LOW?

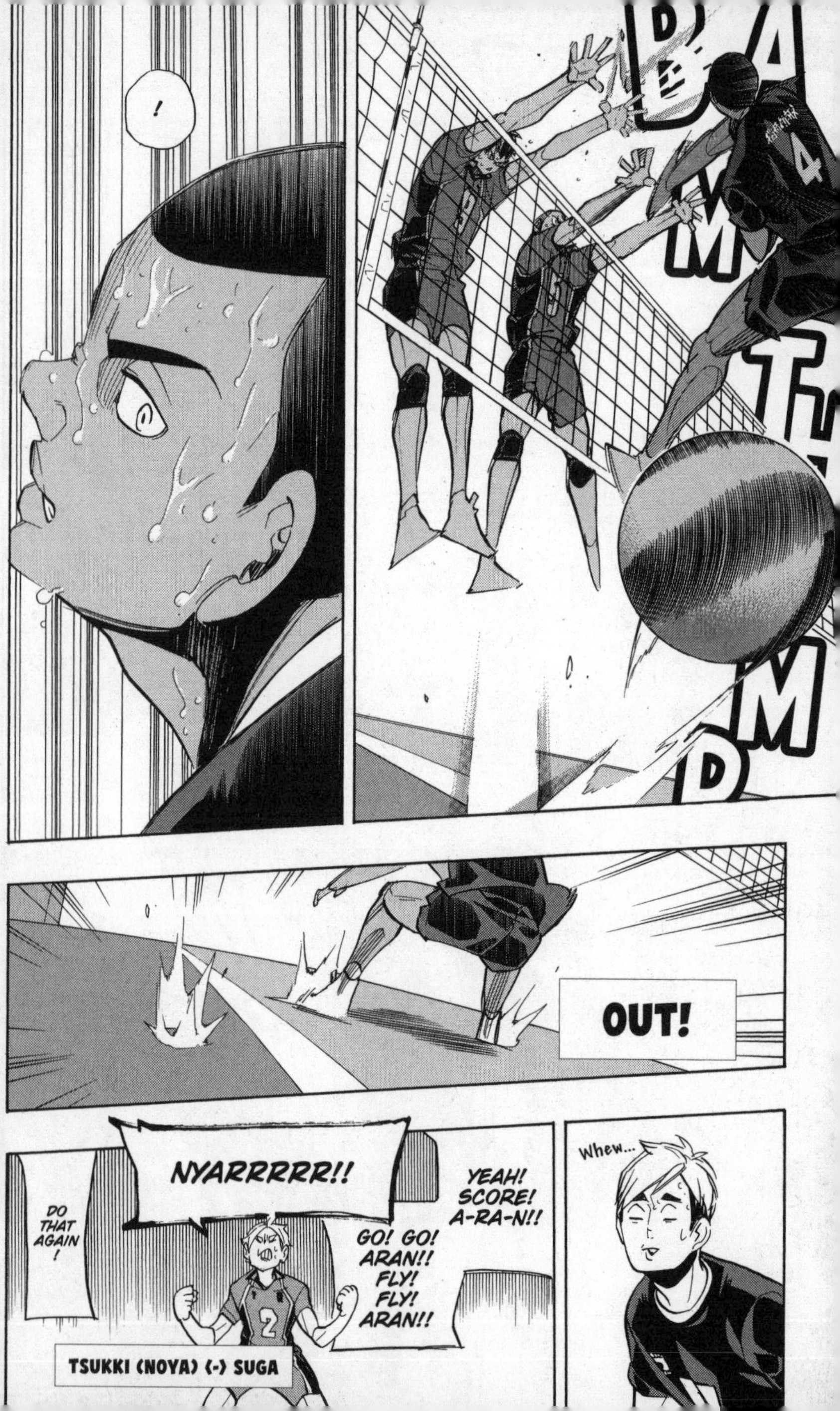
!
OUT!
Whew...
YEAH! SCORE! A-RA-N!!
GO! GO! ARAN!! FLY! FLY! ARAN!!
NYARRRRR!!
DO THAT AGAIN!
TSUKKI (NOYA) (-) SUGA

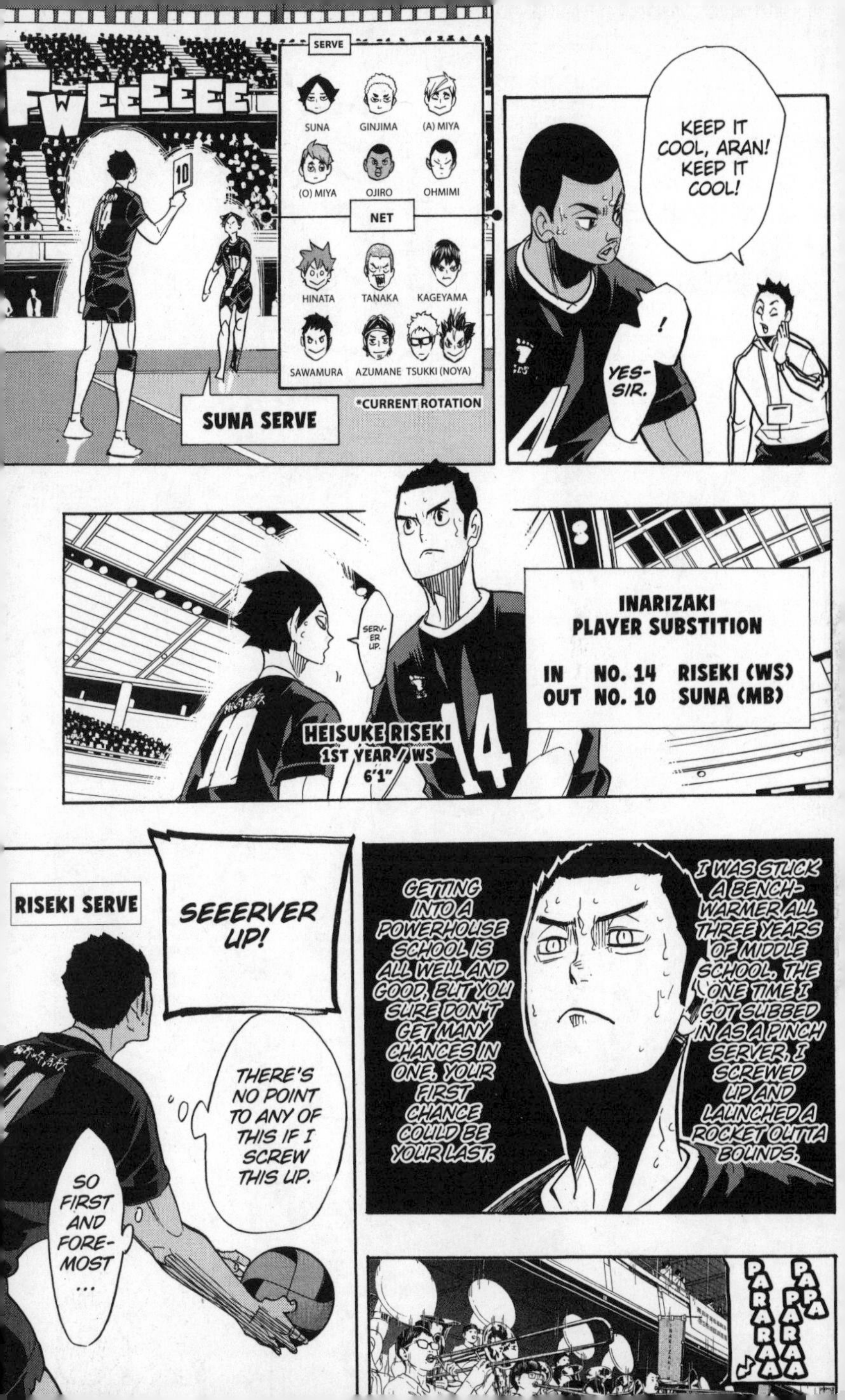
KEEP IT COOL, ARAN! KEEP IT COOL!
!
YES-SIR.
FWEEEEE
SERVE
SUNA
GINJIMA
(A) MIYA
(O) MIYA
OJIRO
OHMIMI
NET
HINATA
TANAKA
KAGEYAMA
SAWAMURA
AZUMANE
TSUKKI (NOYA)
*CURRENT ROTATION
SUNA SERVE
INARIZAKI PLAYER SUBSTITION
IN NO. 14 RISEKI (WS)
OUT NO. 10 SUNA (MB)
SERV-ER UP.
HEISUKE RISEKI
1ST YEAR / WS
6'1"
I WAS STUCK A BENCH-WARMER ALL THREE YEARS OF MIDDLE SCHOOL. THE ONE TIME I GOT SUBBED IN AS A PINCH SERVER, I SCREWED UP AND LAUNCHED A ROCKET OUTTA BOUNDS.
GETTING INTO A POWERHOUSE SCHOOL IS ALL WELL AND GOOD, BUT YOU SURE DON'T GET MANY CHANCES IN ONE. YOUR FIRST CHANCE COULD BE YOUR LAST.
PAPAPARARAA
PARARARAA♪
RISEKI SERVE
SEEERVER UP!
THERE'S NO POINT TO ANY OF THIS IF I SCREW THIS UP.
SO FIRST AND FORE-MOST...

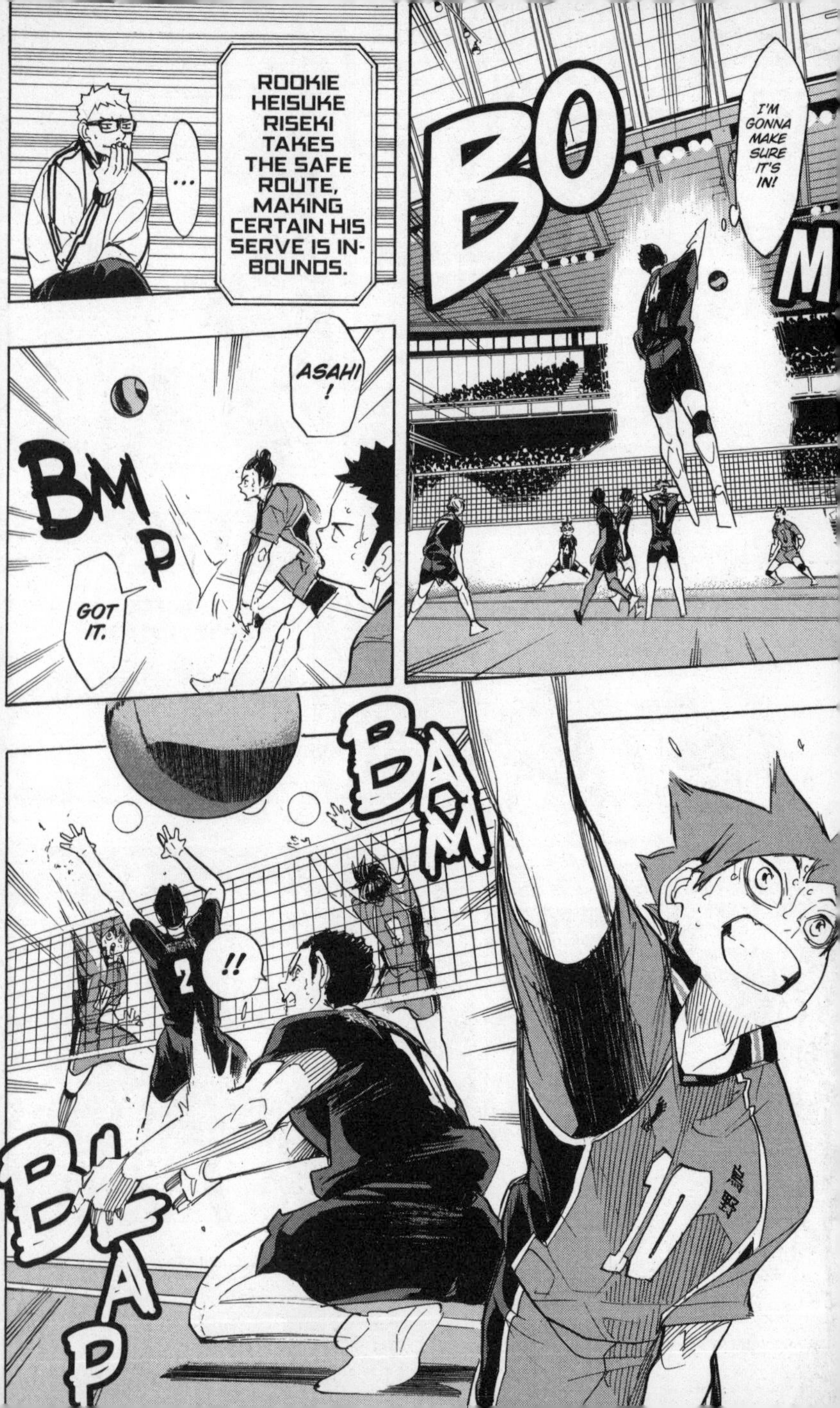
BOM
I'M GONNA MAKE SURE IT'S IN!
ROOKIE HEISUKE RISEKI TAKES THE SAFE ROUTE, MAKING CERTAIN HIS SERVE IS IN-BOUNDS.
...
ASAHI!
BMP
GOT IT.
BAM
!!
BLAP

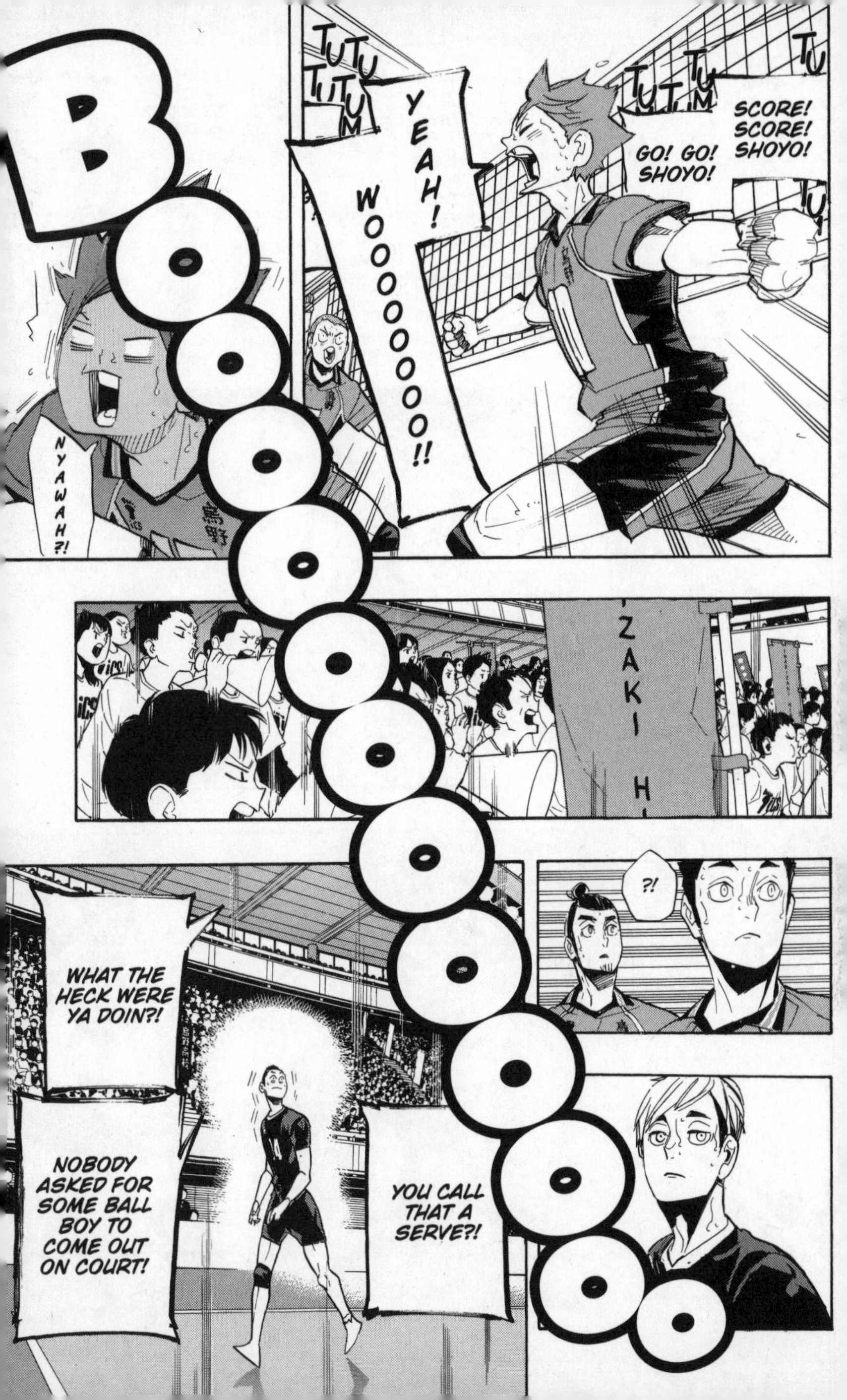
TU TU TUTUM
TU
SCORE! SCORE! SHOYO!
GO! GO! SHOYO!
TU TU TUTUM
YEAH! WOOOOOOOOO!!
NYAWAH?!
BOOOOOOOOOOOOOO
ZAKI H
?!
YOU CALL THAT A SERVE?!
WHAT THE HECK WERE YA DOIN?!
NOBODY ASKED FOR SOME BALL BOY TO COME OUT ON COURT!

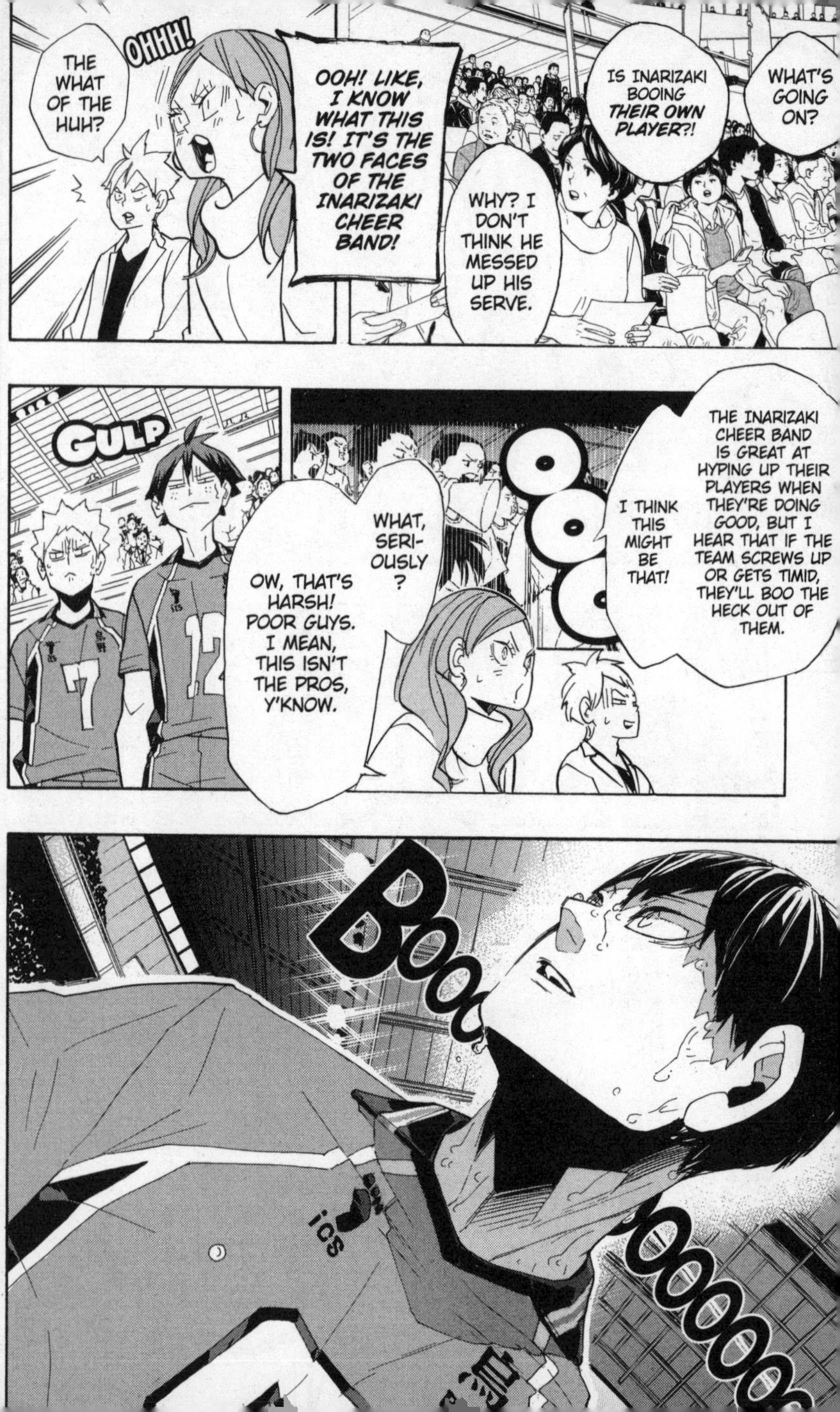
WHAT'S GOING ON?
IS INARIZAKI BOOING THEIR OWN PLAYER?!
WHY? I DON'T THINK HE MESSED UP HIS SERVE.
OOH! LIKE, I KNOW WHAT THIS IS! IT'S THE TWO FACES OF THE INARIZAKI CHEER BAND!
OHHH!
THE WHAT OF THE HUH?
THE INARIZAKI CHEER BAND IS GREAT AT HYPING UP THEIR PLAYERS WHEN THEY'RE DOING GOOD, BUT I HEAR THAT IF THE TEAM SCREWS UP OR GETS TIMID, THEY'LL BOO THE HECK OUT OF THEM.
I THINK THIS MIGHT BE THAT!
WHAT, SERI-OUSLY?
OW, THAT'S HARSH! POOR GUYS. I MEAN, THIS ISN'T THE PROS, Y'KNOW.
GULP
BOOOOOOOOO

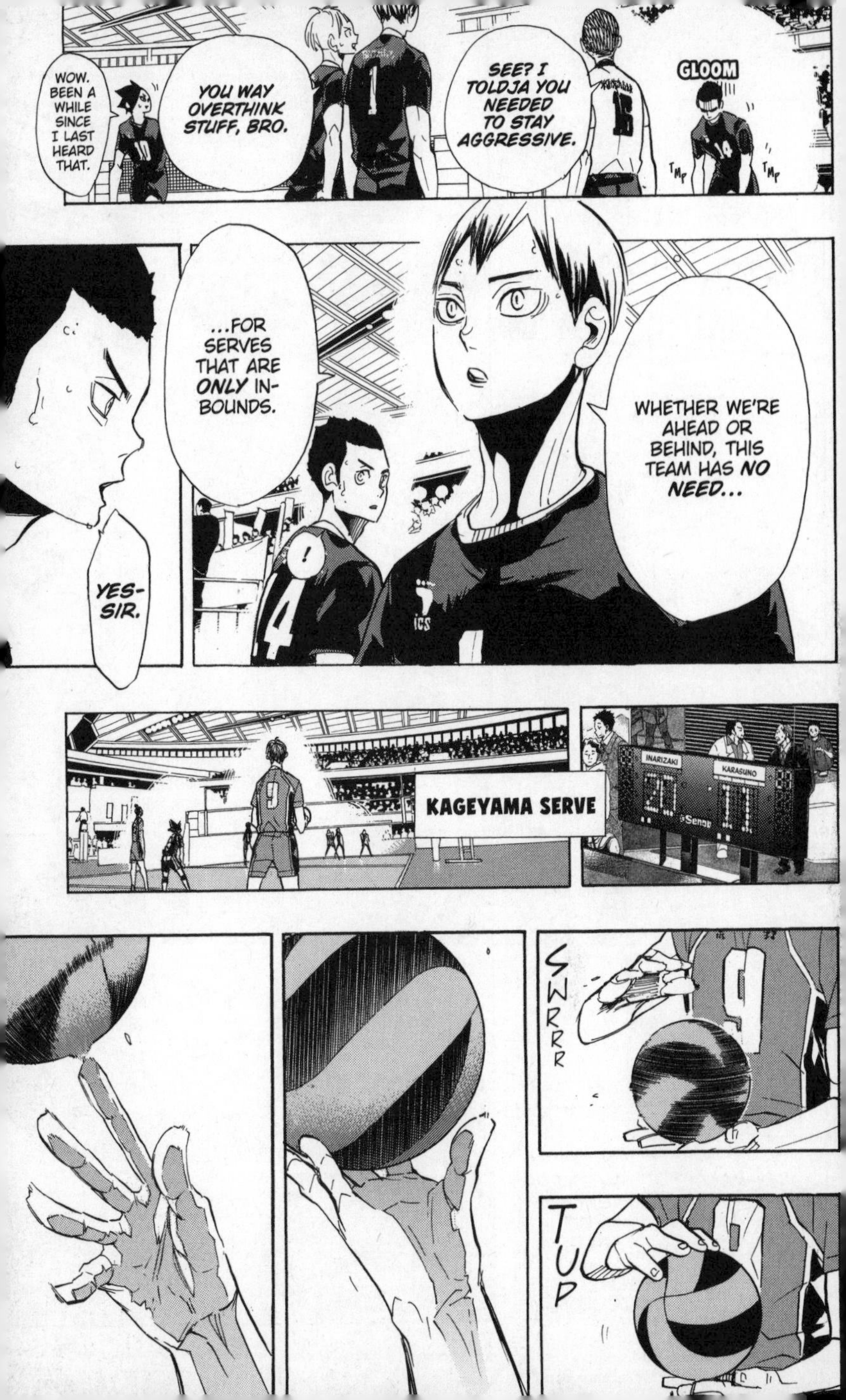
GLOOM
TMP TMP
SEE? I TOLDJA YOU NEEDED TO STAY AGGRESSIVE.
YOU WAY OVERTHINK STUFF, BRO.
WOW. BEEN A WHILE SINCE I LAST HEARD THAT.
WHETHER WE'RE AHEAD OR BEHIND, THIS TEAM HAS NO NEED...
...FOR SERVES THAT ARE ONLY IN-BOUNDS.
!
YES-SIR.
INARIZAKI
KARASUNO
KAGEYAMA SERVE
SWRRR
TUP

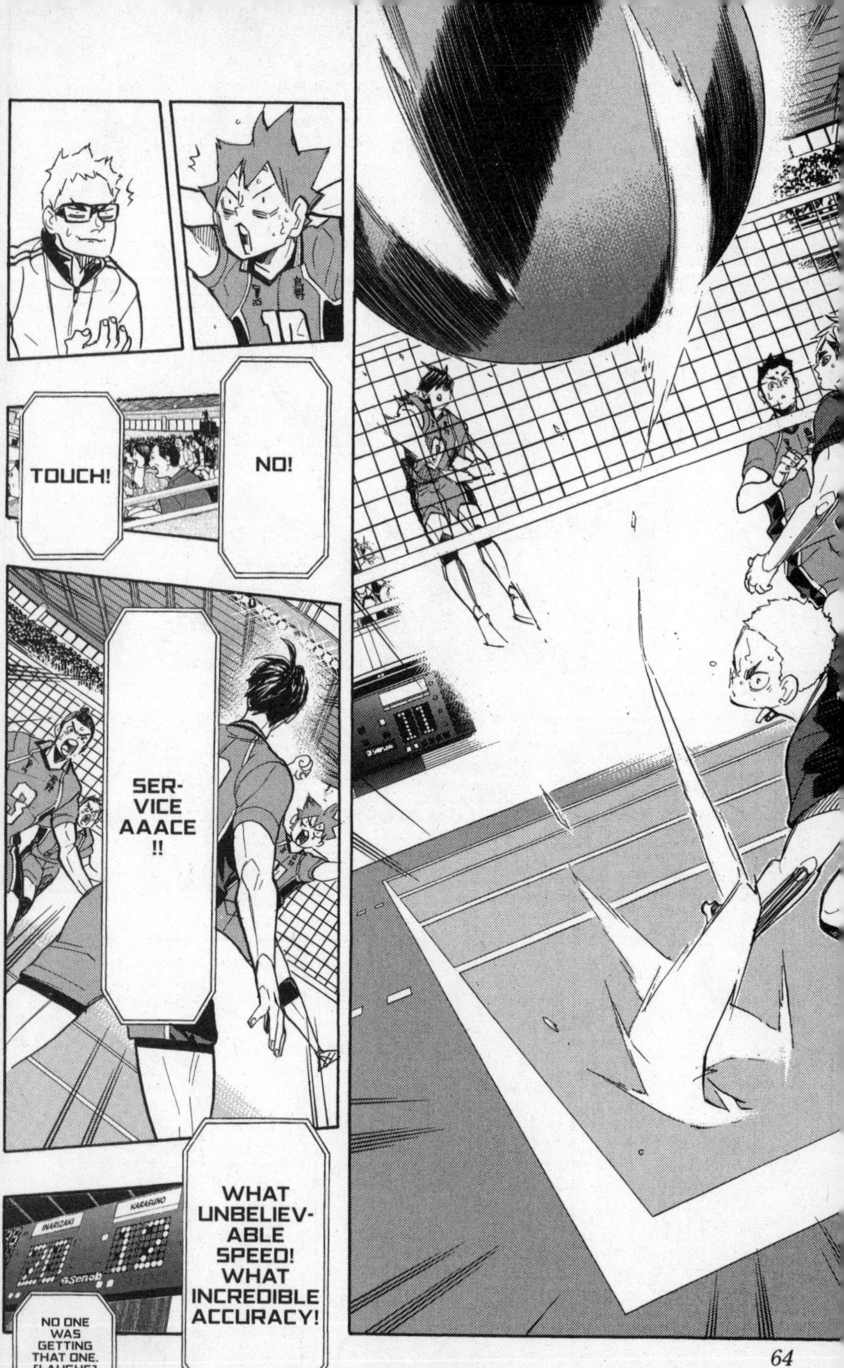
NO!
TOUCH!
SERVICE AAACE!!
WHAT UNBELIEVABLE SPEED! WHAT INCREDIBLE ACCURACY!
KARASUNO
INARIZAKI
NO ONE WAS GETTING THAT ONE. [LAUGHS]

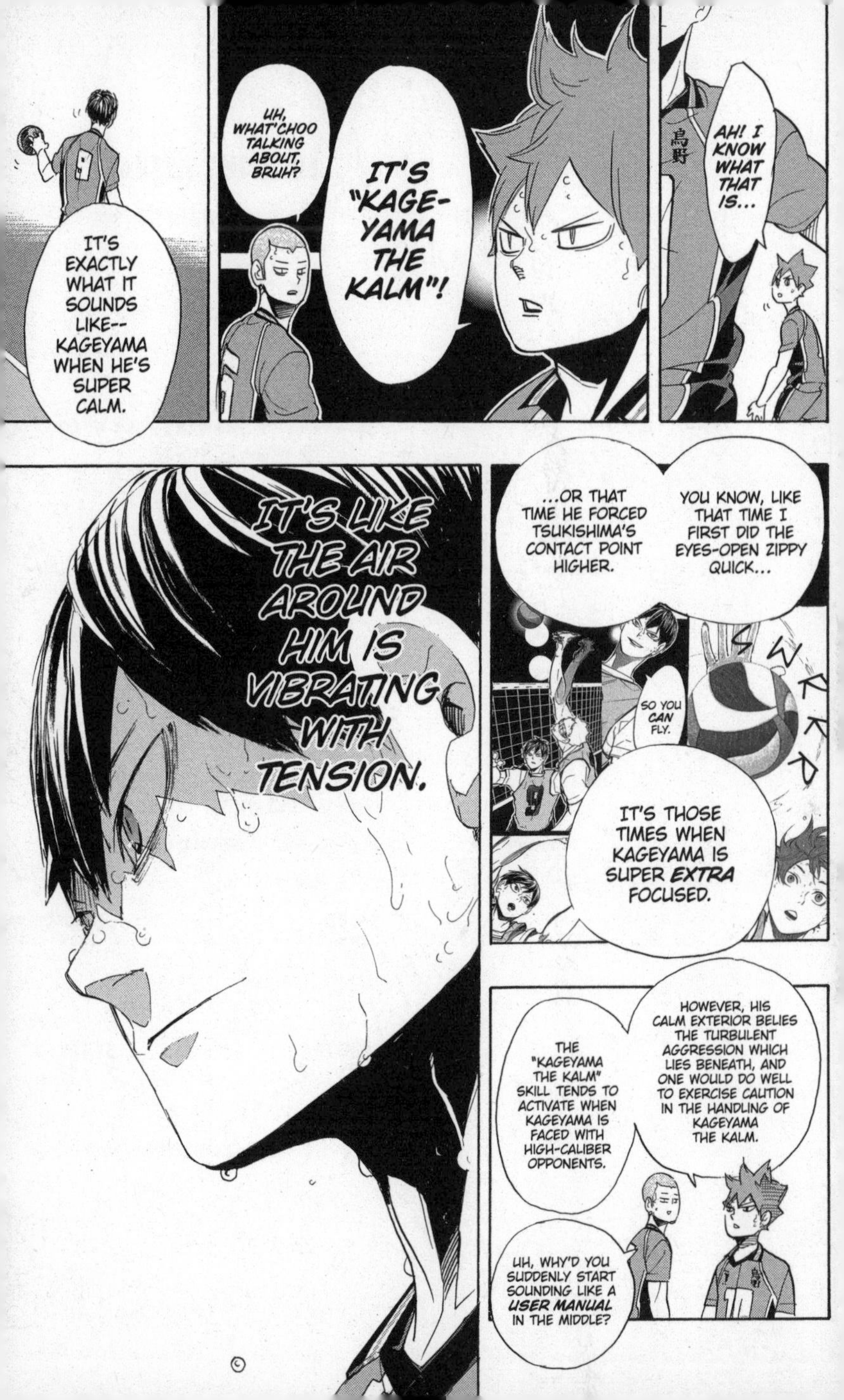
AH! I KNOW WHAT THAT IS...
IT'S "KAGE-YAMA THE KALM"!
UH, WHAT'CHOO TALKING ABOUT, BRUH?
IT'S EXACTLY WHAT IT SOUNDS LIKE-- KAGEYAMA WHEN HE'S SUPER CALM.
YOU KNOW, LIKE THAT TIME I FIRST DID THE EYES-OPEN ZIPPY QUICK...
...OR THAT TIME HE FORCED TSUKISHIMA'S CONTACT POINT HIGHER.
SWRRR
SO YOU *CAN* FLY.
IT'S THOSE TIMES WHEN KAGEYAMA IS SUPER ***EXTRA*** FOCUSED.
HOWEVER, HIS CALM EXTERIOR BELIES THE TURBULENT AGGRESSION WHICH LIES BENEATH, AND ONE WOULD DO WELL TO EXERCISE CAUTION IN THE HANDLING OF KAGEYAMA THE KALM.
THE "KAGEYAMA THE KALM" SKILL TENDS TO ACTIVATE WHEN KAGEYAMA IS FACED WITH HIGH-CALIBER OPPONENTS.
UH, WHY'D YOU SUDDENLY START SOUNDING LIKE A ***USER MANUAL*** IN THE MIDDLE?
IT'S LIKE THE AIR AROUND HIM IS VIBRATING WITH TENSION.

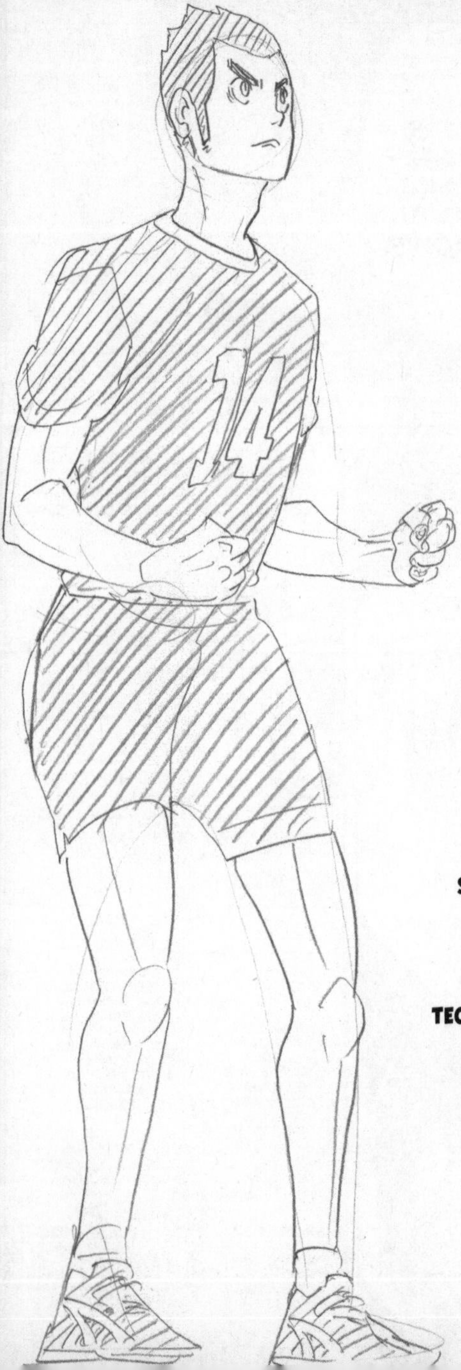

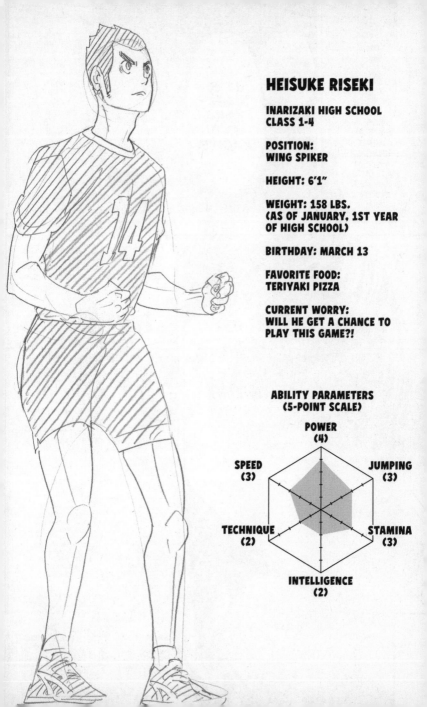

HEISUKE RISEKI

INARIZAKI HIGH SCHOOL
CLASS 1-4

POSITION:
WING SPIKER

HEIGHT: 6'1"

WEIGHT: 158 LBS.
(AS OF JANUARY, 1ST YEAR OF HIGH SCHOOL)

BIRTHDAY: MARCH 13

FAVORITE FOOD:
TERIYAKI PIZZA

CURRENT WORRY:
WILL HE GET A CHANCE TO PLAY THIS GAME?!

ABILITY PARAMETERS
(5-POINT SCALE)

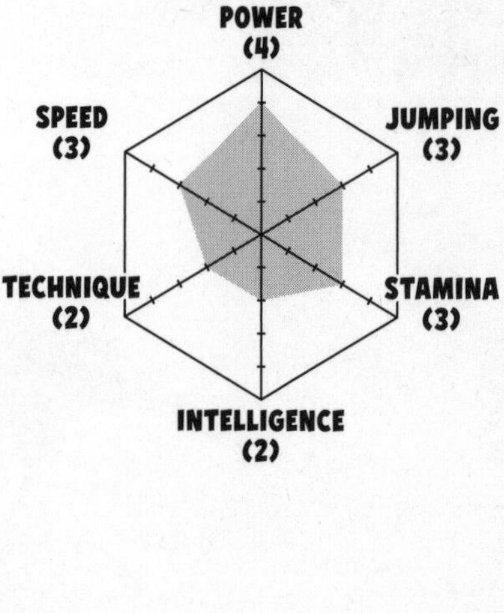

POWER (4)
JUMPING (3)
STAMINA (3)
INTELLIGENCE (2)
TECHNIQUE (2)
SPEED (3)

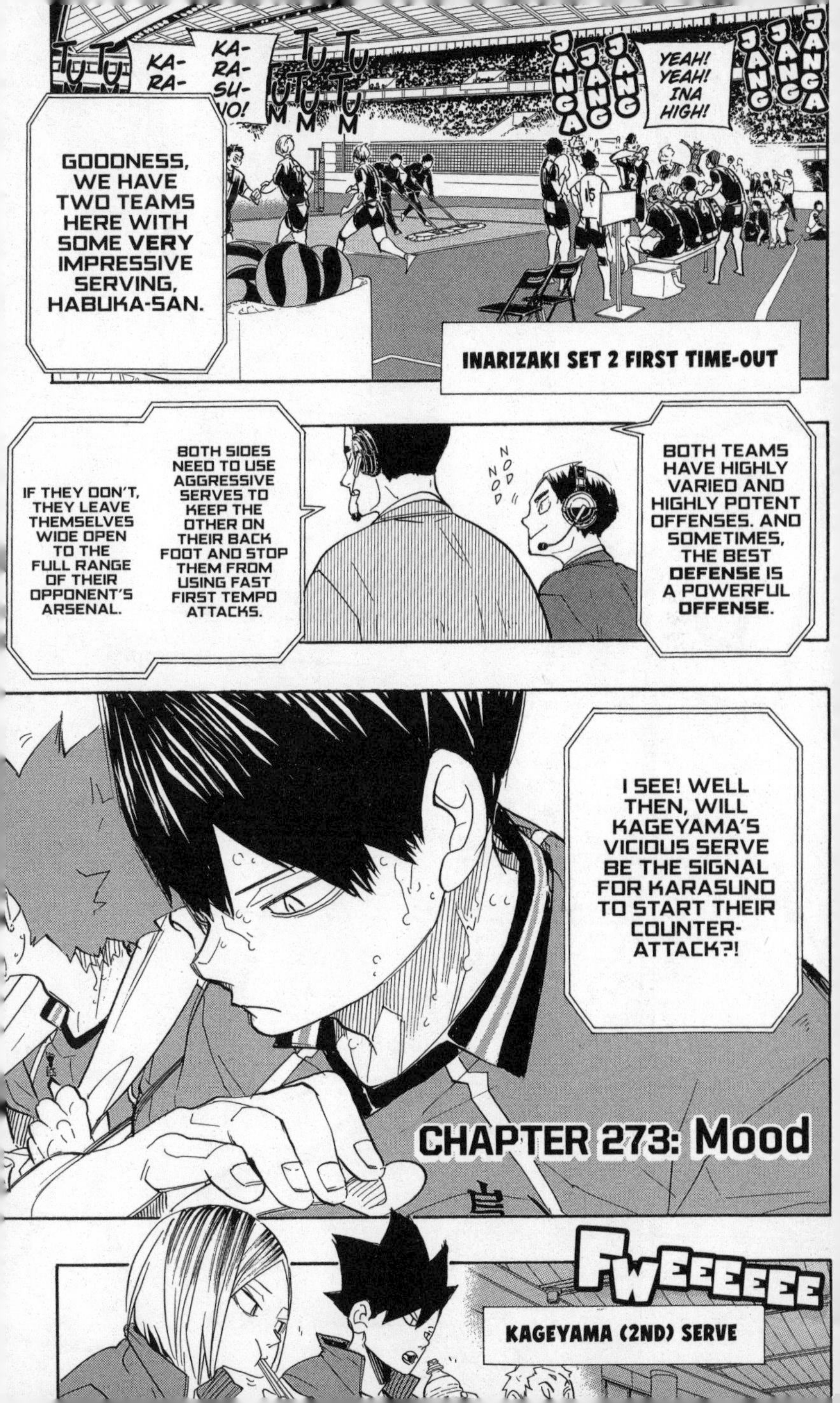
JANGA JANGA JANGA
YEAH! YEAH! INA HIGH!
JANG JANG JANGA
TU TU TUM TUM
KA-RA-SU-NO!
KA-RA-
TU TU TUM TUM
GOODNESS, WE HAVE TWO TEAMS HERE WITH SOME VERY IMPRESSIVE SERVING, HABUKA-SAN.
INARIZAKI SET 2 FIRST TIME-OUT
BOTH TEAMS HAVE HIGHLY VARIED AND HIGHLY POTENT OFFENSES. AND SOMETIMES, THE BEST DEFENSE IS A POWERFUL OFFENSE.
NOD NOD
BOTH SIDES NEED TO USE AGGRESSIVE SERVES TO KEEP THE OTHER ON THEIR BACK FOOT AND STOP THEM FROM USING FAST FIRST TEMPO ATTACKS.
IF THEY DON'T, THEY LEAVE THEMSELVES WIDE OPEN TO THE FULL RANGE OF THEIR OPPONENT'S ARSENAL.
I SEE! WELL THEN, WILL KAGEYAMA'S VICIOUS SERVE BE THE SIGNAL FOR KARASUNO TO START THEIR COUNTER-ATTACK?!
CHAPTER 273: Mood
FWEEEEEE
KAGEYAMA (2ND) SERVE

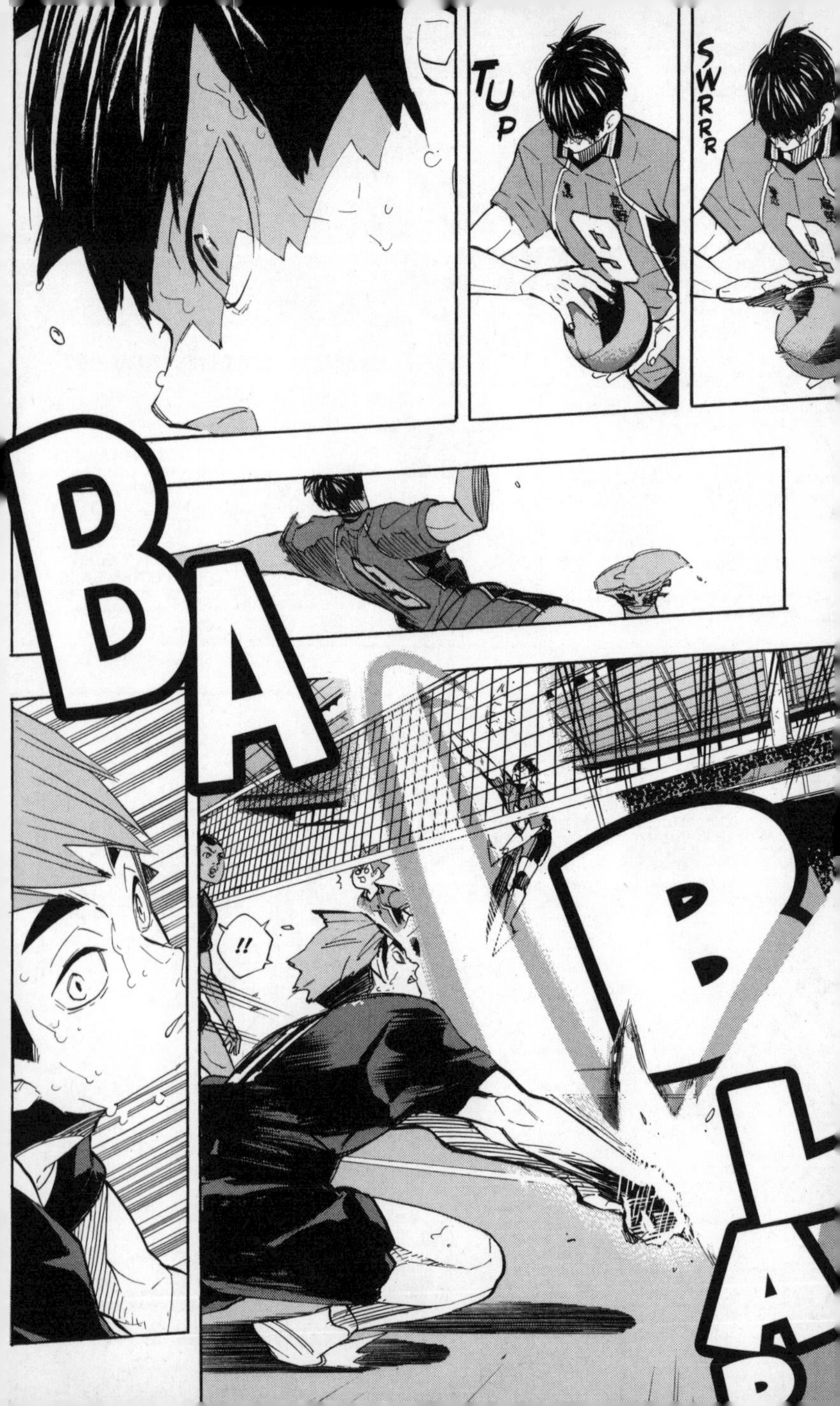
SWRRR
TUP
BA
!!
BLA

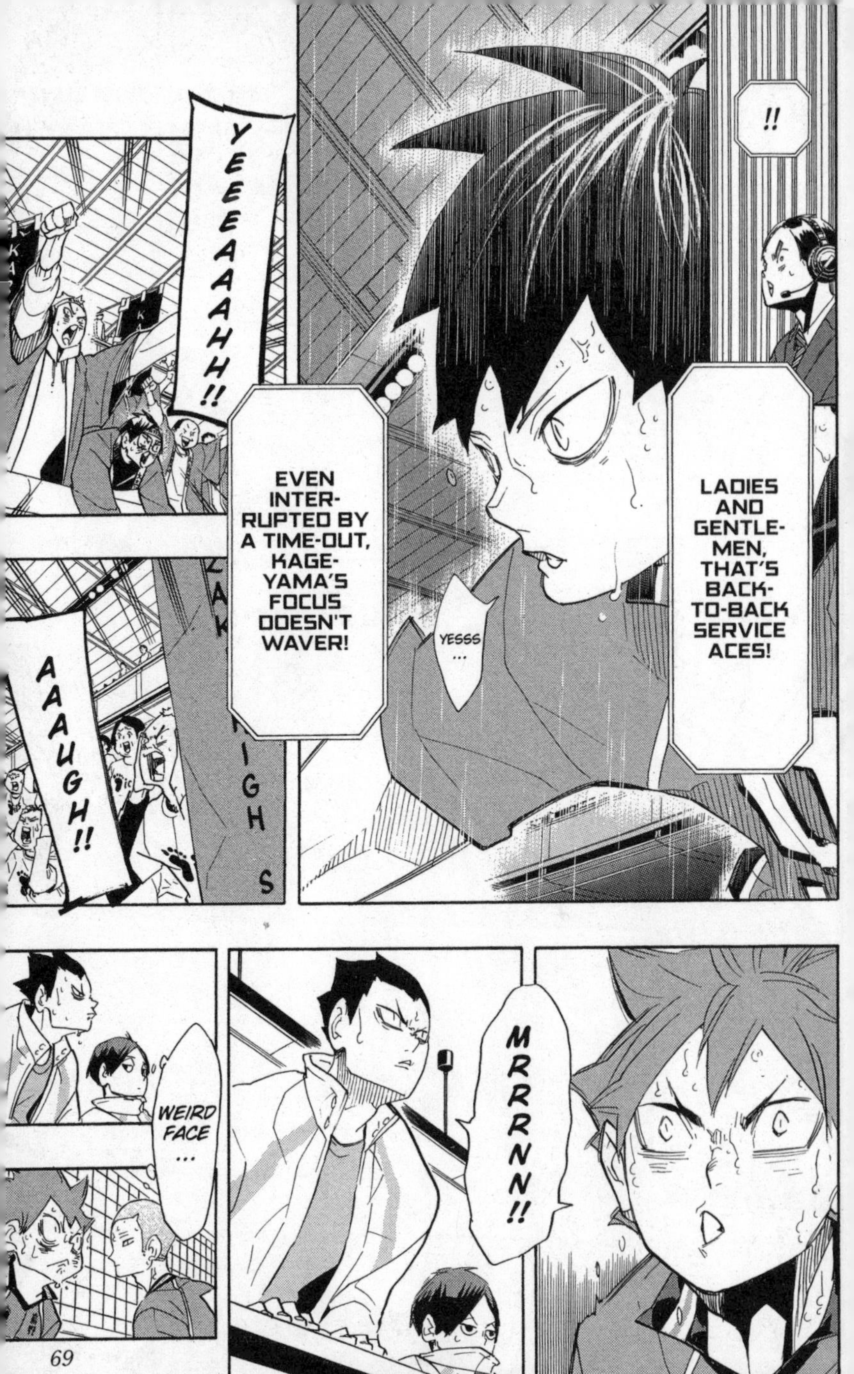
!!
LADIES AND GENTLEMEN, THAT'S BACK-TO-BACK SERVICE ACES!
YESSS...
EVEN INTERRUPTED BY A TIME-OUT, KAGEYAMA'S FOCUS DOESN'T WAVER!
YEEEAAAAHH!!
AAAAUGH!!
MRRRNN!!
WEIRD FACE...

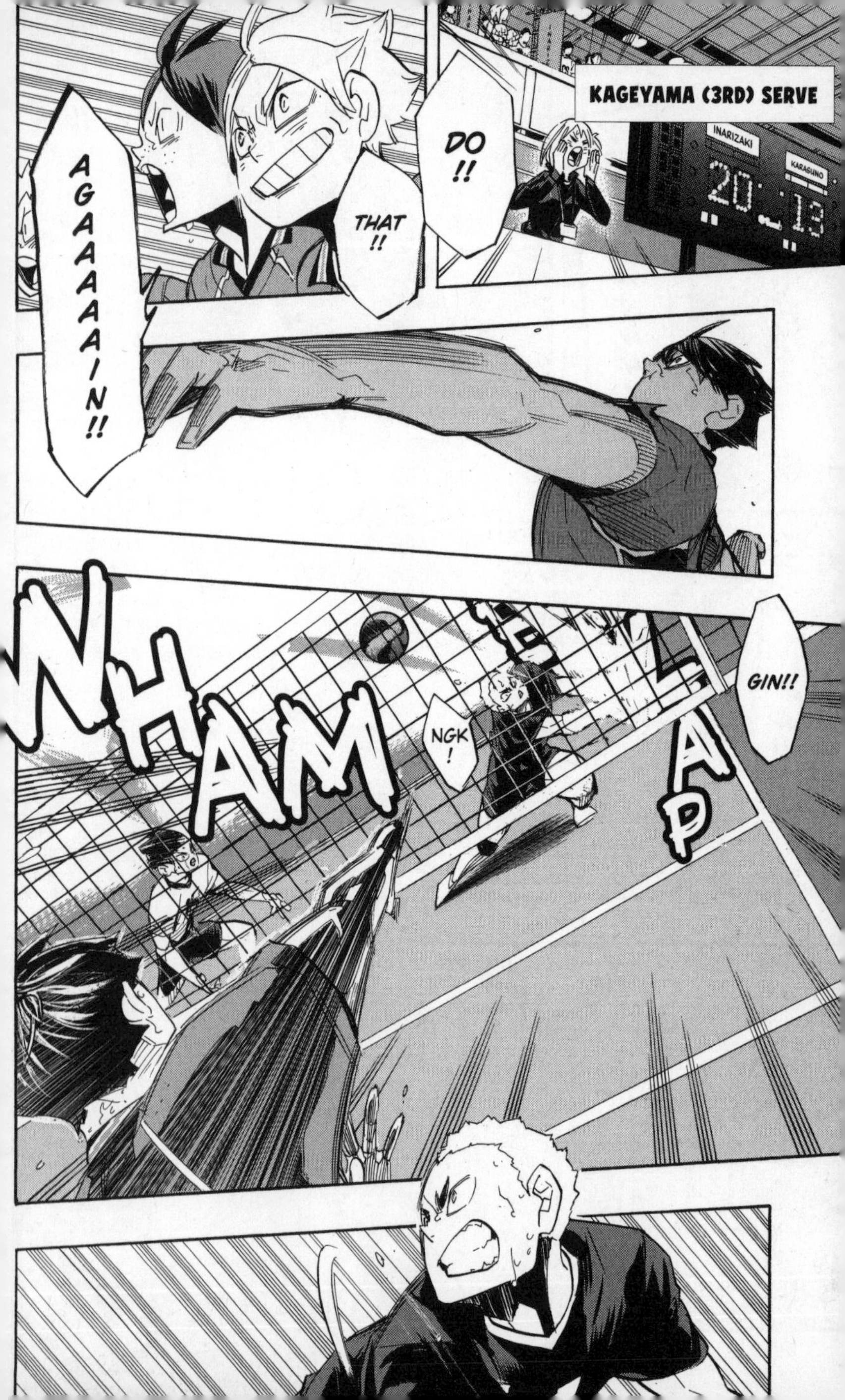
KAGEYAMA (3RD) SERVE
INARIZAKI
KARASUNO
20
13
DO!!
THAT!!
AGAAAAAAIN!!
GIN!!
NGK!
WHAM

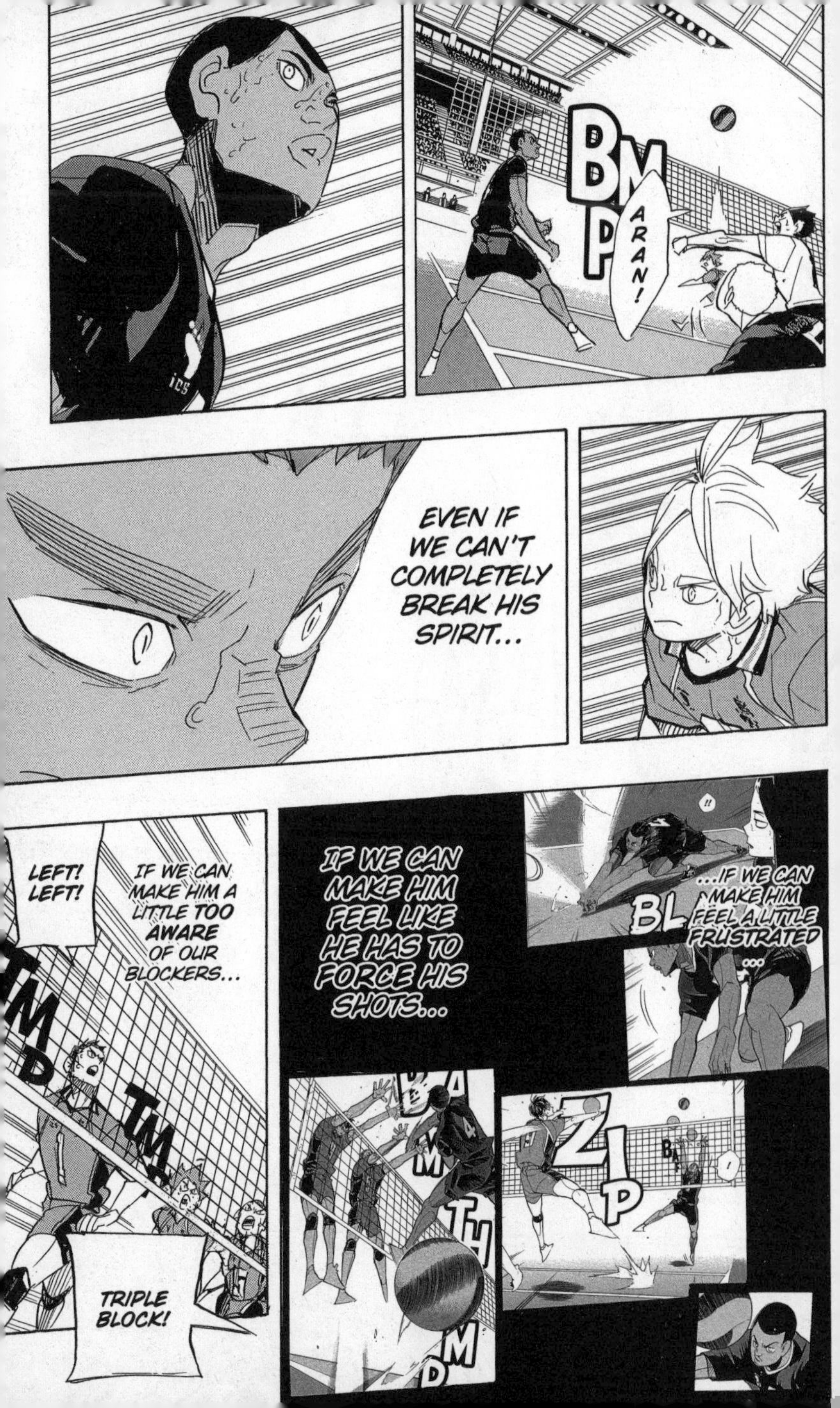
BMP
ARAN!
EVEN IF WE CAN'T COMPLETELY BREAK HIS SPIRIT...
!!
BL
...IF WE CAN MAKE HIM FEEL A LITTLE FRUSTRATED...
IF WE CAN MAKE HIM FEEL LIKE HE HAS TO FORCE HIS SHOTS...
ZIP
BAM
!
BAM
THMD
LEFT! LEFT!
IF WE CAN MAKE HIM A LITTLE TOO AWARE OF OUR BLOCKERS...
TMD
TMP
TRIPLE BLOCK!

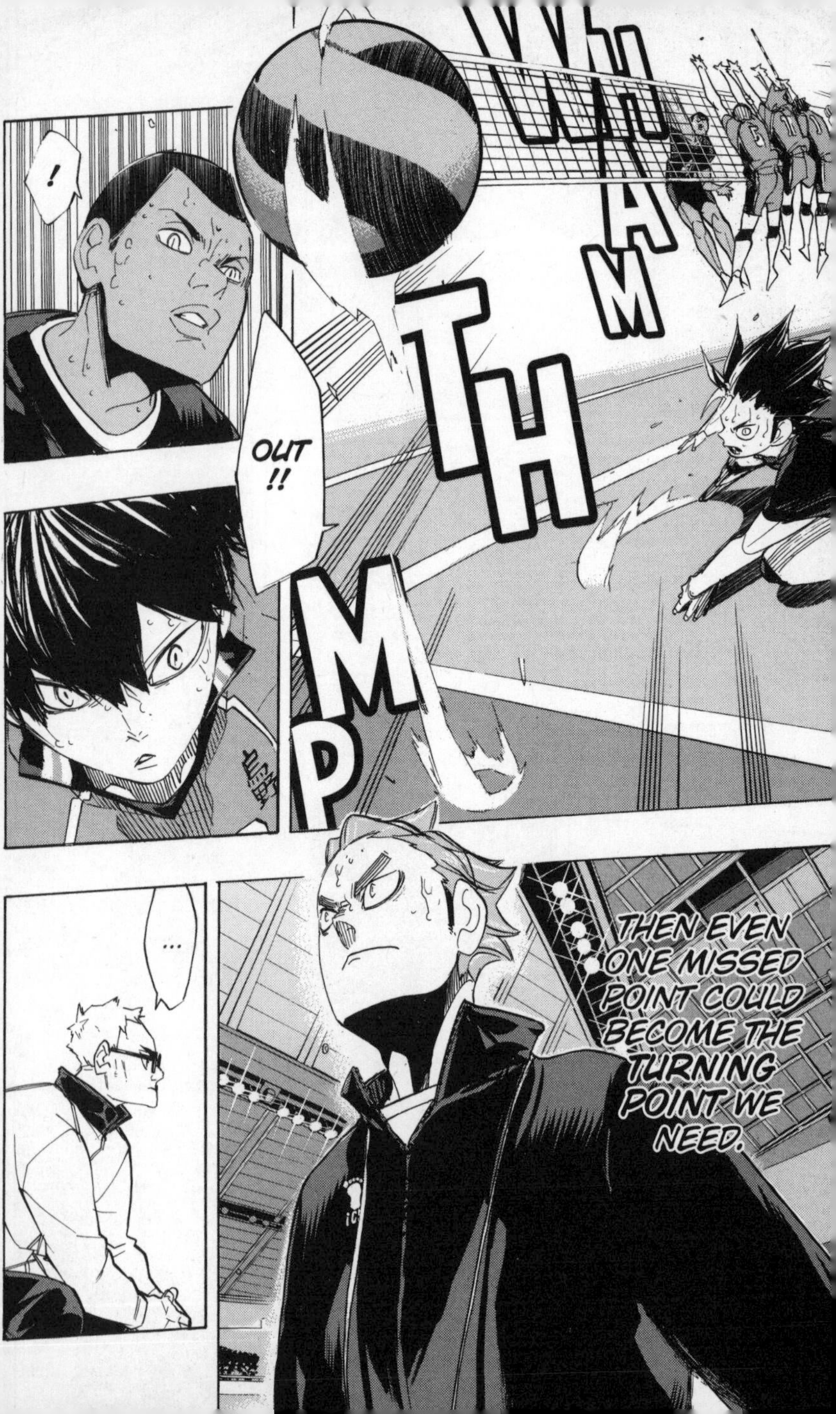
WHAM
!
OUT !!
THUMP
THEN EVEN ONE MISSED POINT COULD BECOME THE TURNING POINT WE NEED.
...

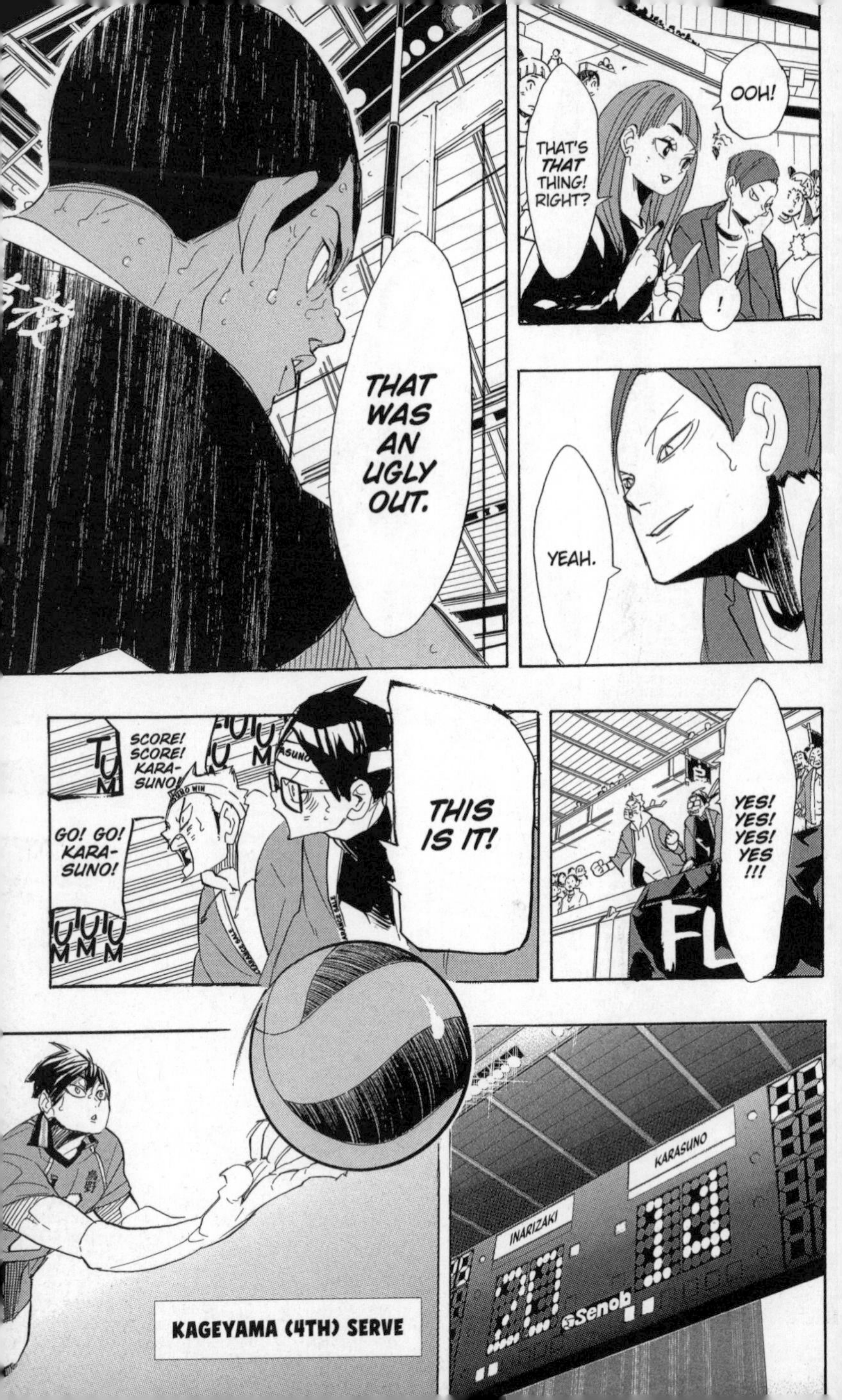
OOH!
THAT'S *THAT* THING! RIGHT?
!
YEAH.
THAT WAS AN UGLY OUT.
YES! YES! YES! YES!!!
FL
THIS IS IT!
TUM
UUUM
SCORE! SCORE! KARA-SUNO!
GO! GO! KARA-SUNO!
UUUUMMM
KARASUNO
INARIZAKI
Senob
KAGEYAMA (4TH) SERVE

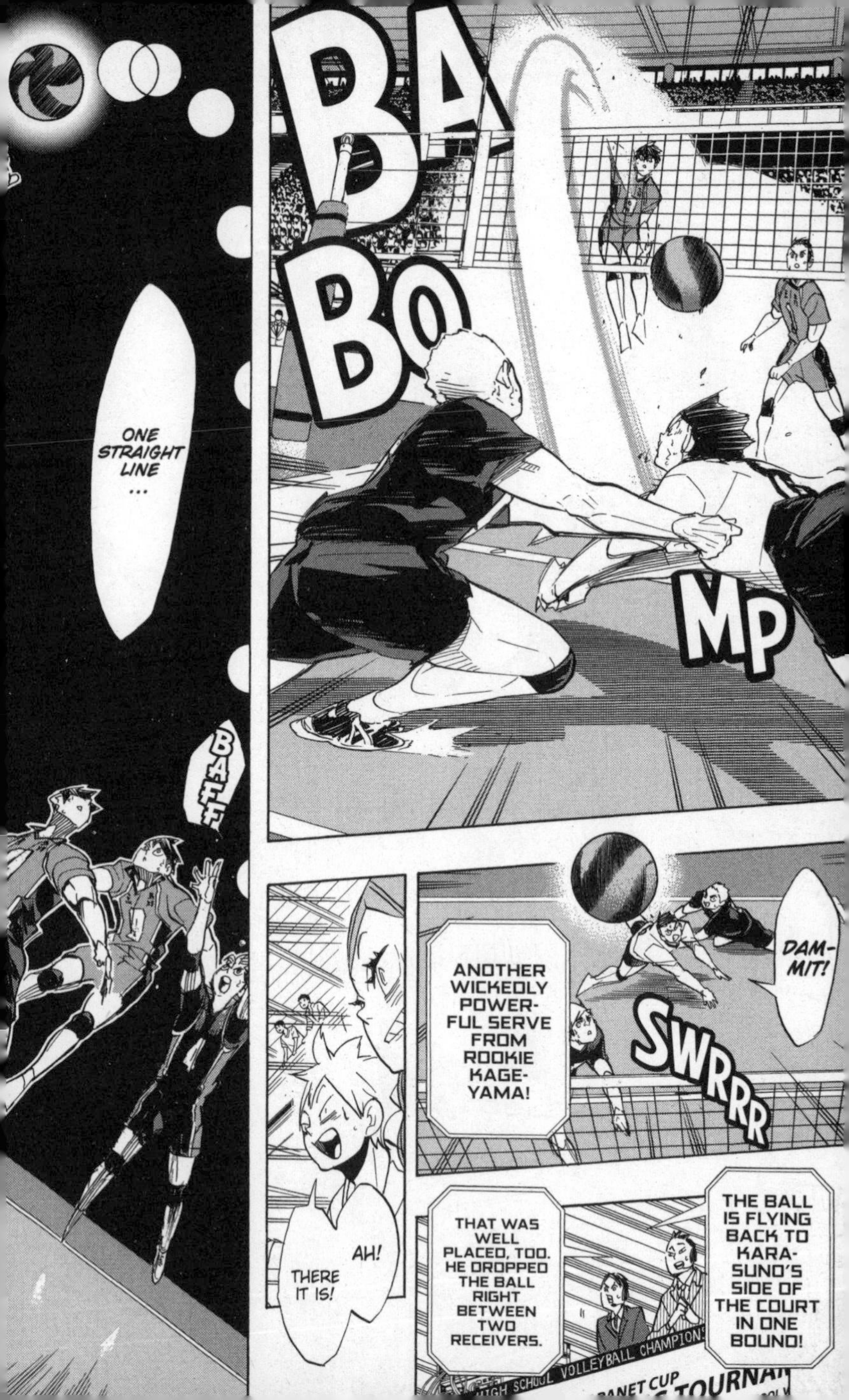
BA
BO
MP
DAM-MIT!
ANOTHER WICKEDLY POWERFUL SERVE FROM ROOKIE KAGEYAMA!
SWRRR
THE BALL IS FLYING BACK TO KARASUNO'S SIDE OF THE COURT IN ONE BOUND!
THAT WAS WELL PLACED, TOO. HE DROPPED THE BALL RIGHT BETWEEN TWO RECEIVERS.
AH!
THERE IT IS!
ONE STRAIGHT LINE ...
BAFF

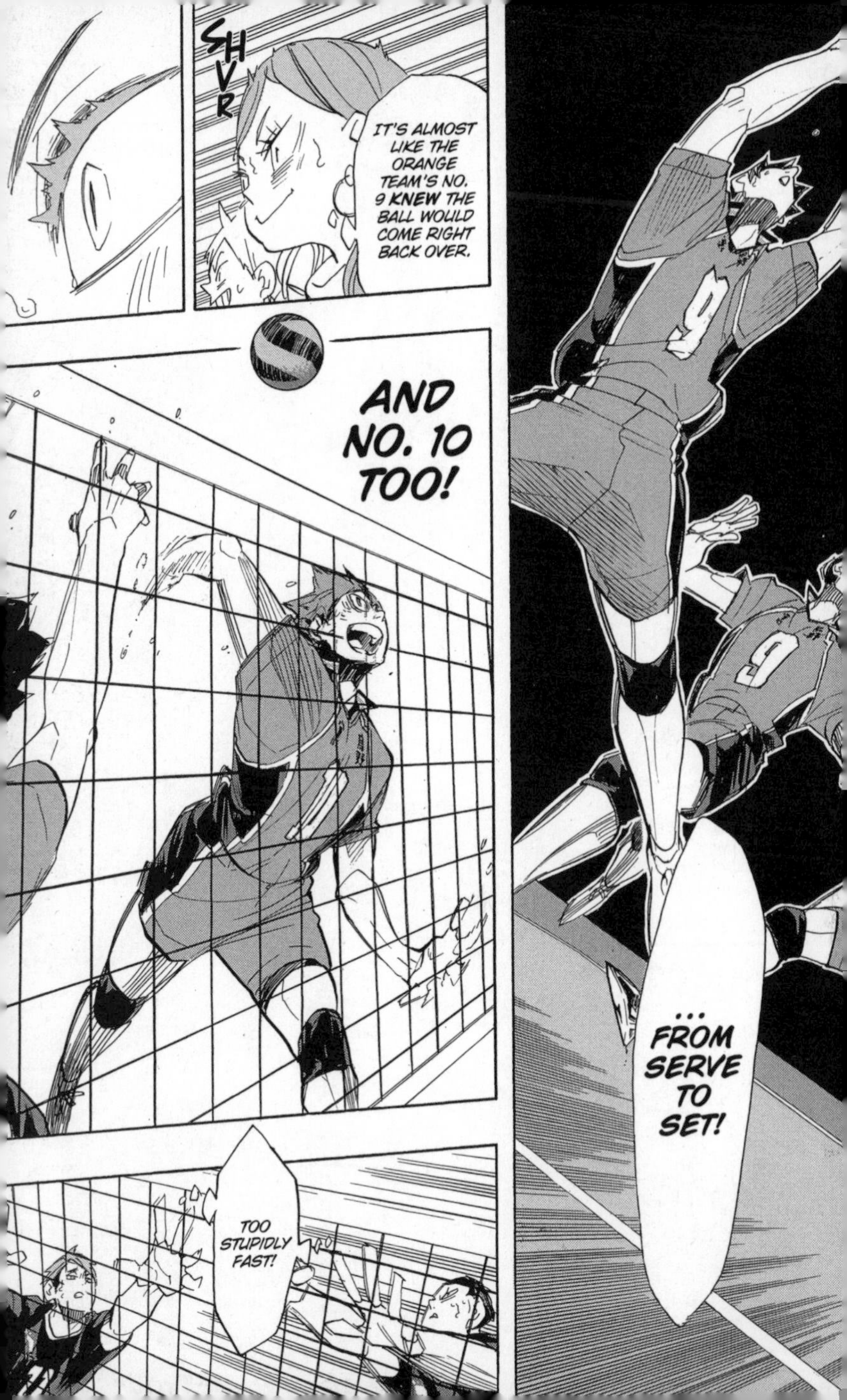
...FROM SERVE TO SET!
SHVR
IT'S ALMOST LIKE THE ORANGE TEAM'S NO. 9 KNEW THE BALL WOULD COME RIGHT BACK OVER.
AND NO. 10 TOO!
TOO STUPIDLY FAST!

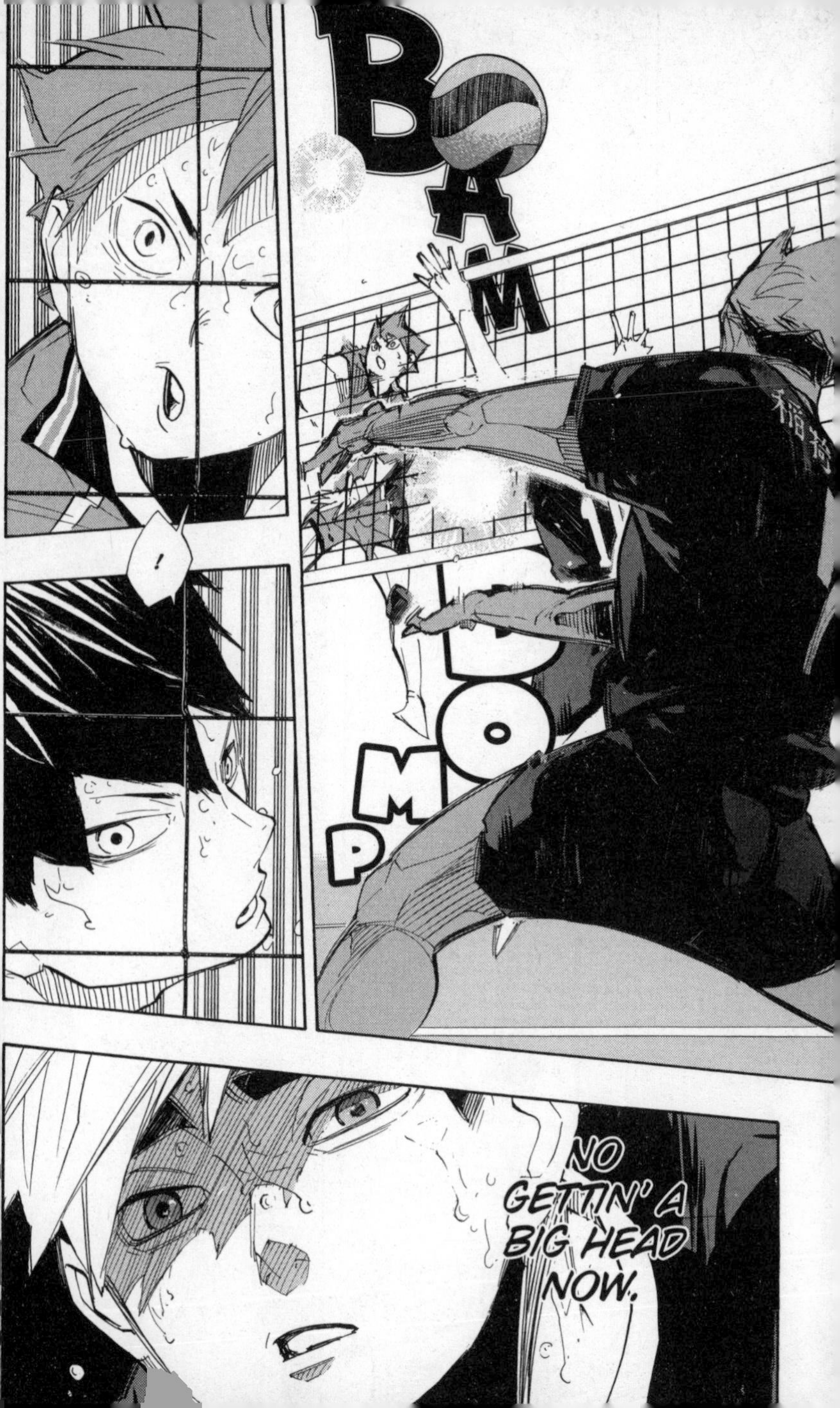

BAM
!
NO GETTIN' A BIG HEAD NOW.

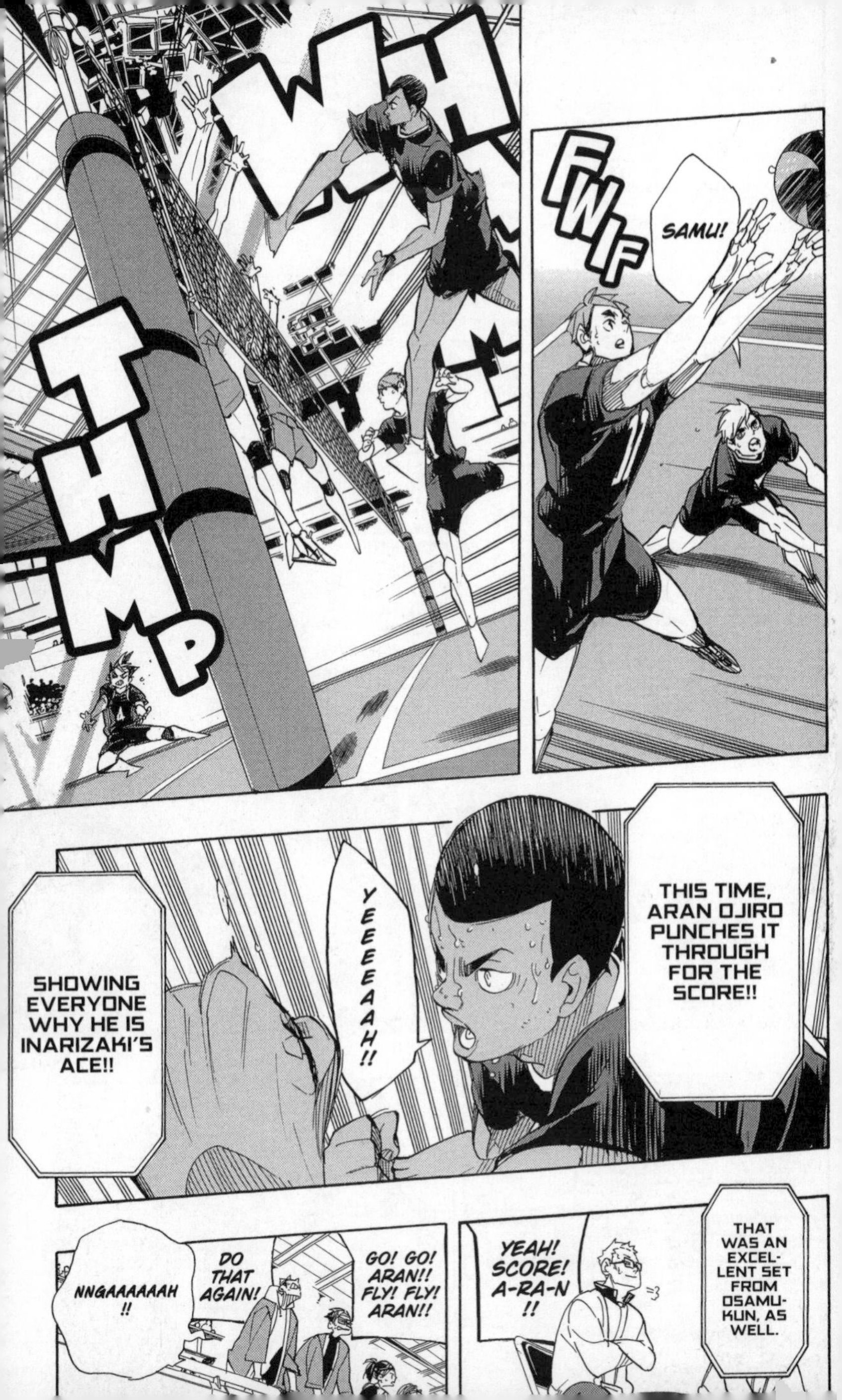
FWIP
SAMU!
THUMP
THIS TIME, ARAN OJIRO PUNCHES IT THROUGH FOR THE SCORE!!
YEEEEEAAAH!!
SHOWING EVERYONE WHY HE IS INARIZAKI'S ACE!!
THAT WAS AN EXCEL-LENT SET FROM OSAMU-KUN, AS WELL.
YEAH! SCORE! A-RA-N!!
GO! GO! ARAN!! FLY! FLY! ARAN!!
DO THAT AGAIN!
NNGAAAAAAAH!!

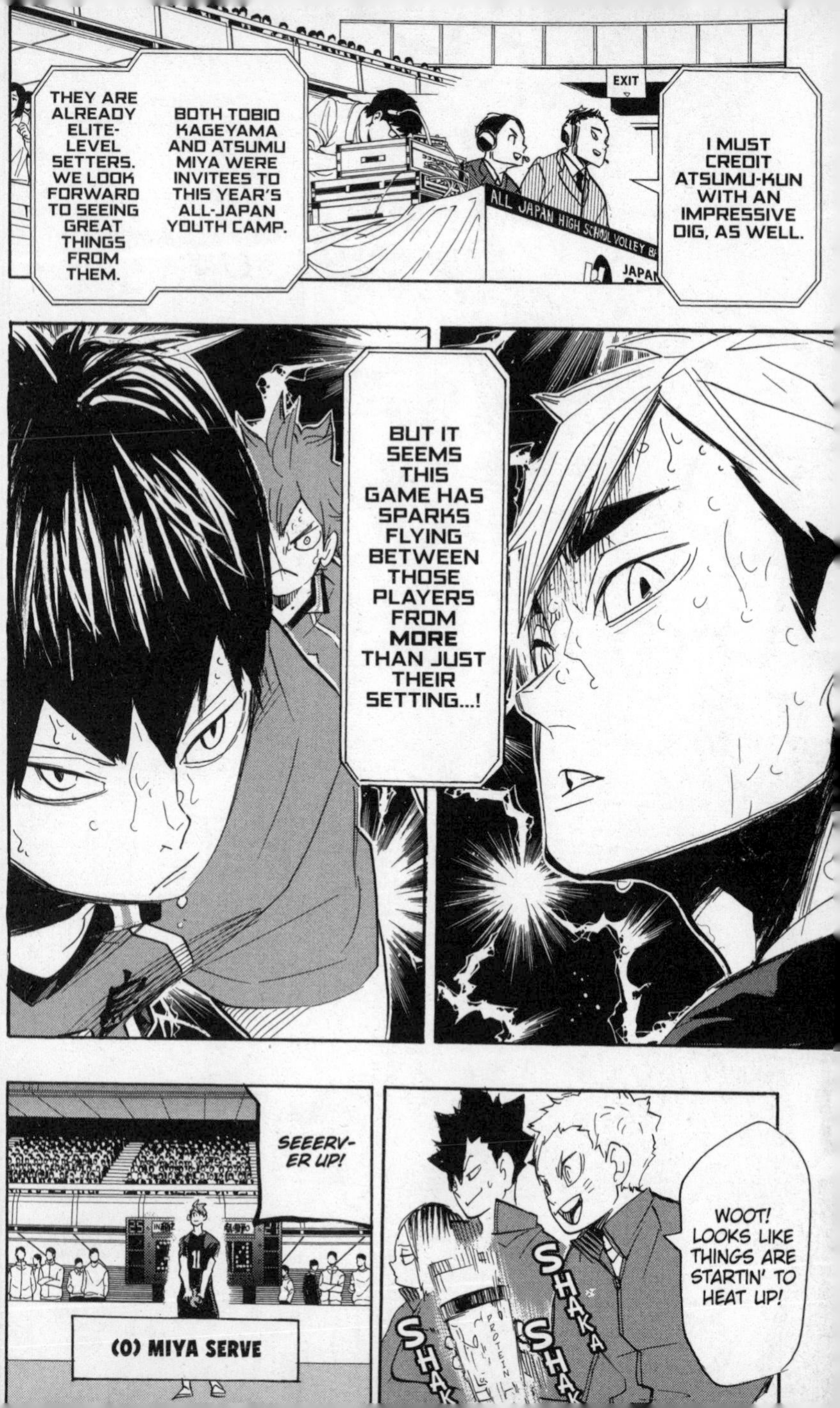
I MUST CREDIT ATSUMU-KUN WITH AN IMPRESSIVE DIG, AS WELL.
BOTH TOBIO KAGEYAMA AND ATSUMU MIYA WERE INVITEES TO THIS YEAR'S ALL-JAPAN YOUTH CAMP.
THEY ARE ALREADY ELITE-LEVEL SETTERS. WE LOOK FORWARD TO SEEING GREAT THINGS FROM THEM.
EXIT
ALL JAPAN HIGH SCHOOL VOLLEY B
BUT IT SEEMS THIS GAME HAS SPARKS FLYING BETWEEN THOSE PLAYERS FROM **MORE** THAN JUST THEIR SETTING...!
WOOT! LOOKS LIKE THINGS ARE STARTIN' TO HEAT UP!
SHAKA
SHAKA
PROTEIN
SEEERV-ER UP!
(0) MIYA SERVE

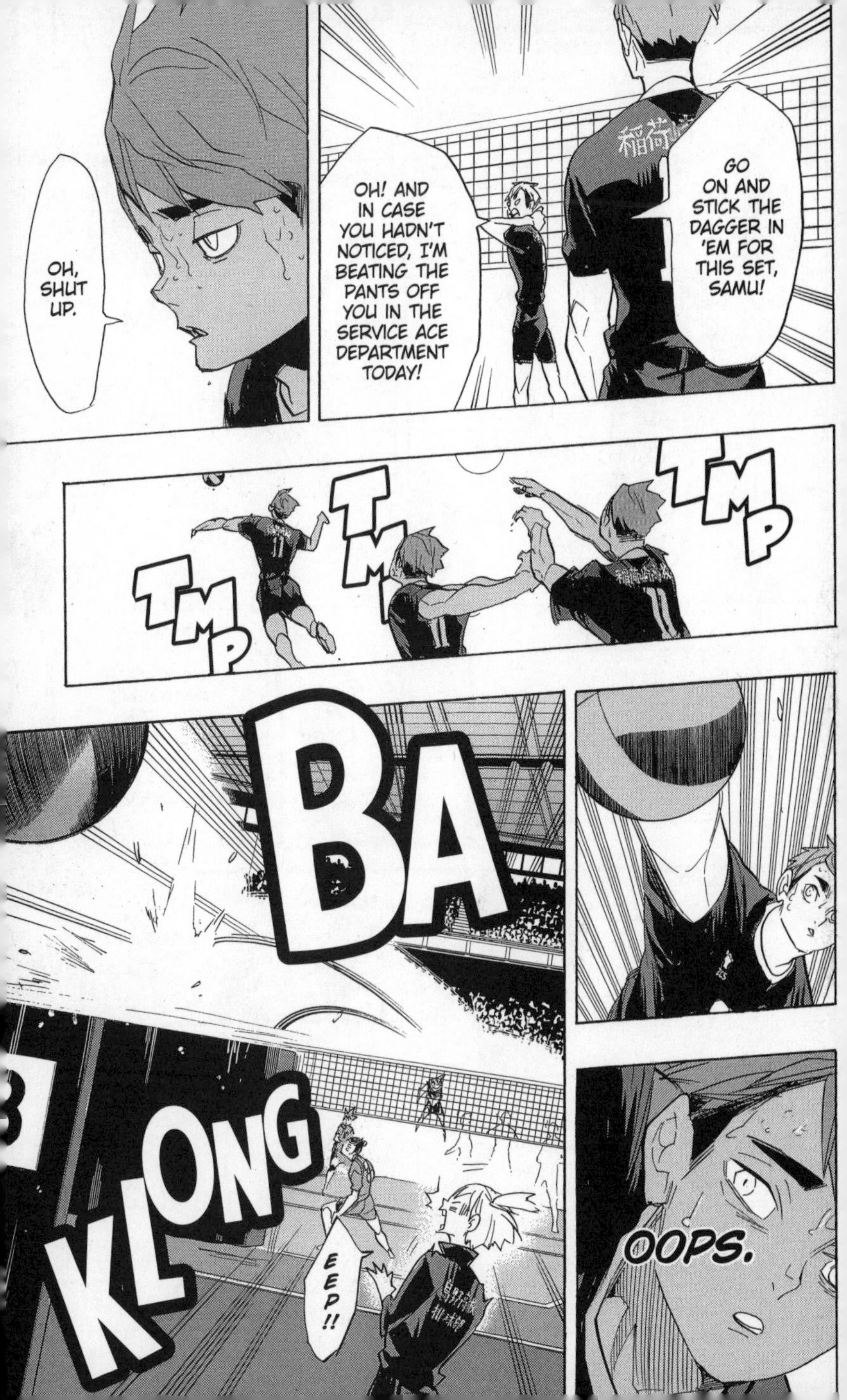
GO ON AND STICK THE DAGGER IN 'EM FOR THIS SET, SAMU!
OH! AND IN CASE YOU HADN'T NOTICED, I'M BEATING THE PANTS OFF YOU IN THE SERVICE ACE DEPARTMENT TODAY!
OH, SHUT UP.
TMP
TMP
TMP
OOPS.
BA
KLONG
EEP!!

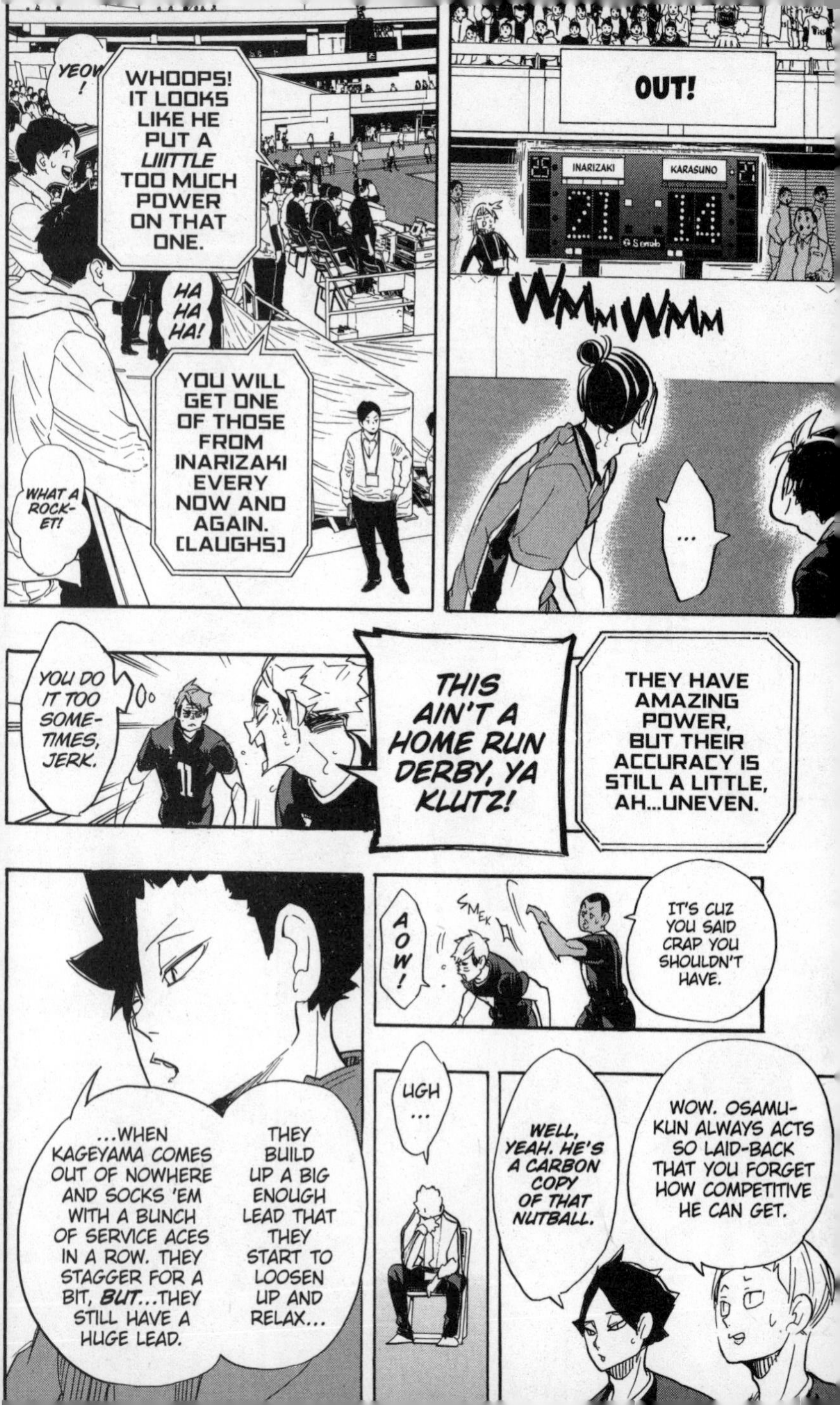
OUT!
INARIZAKI
KARASUNO
WMM WMM
...
WHOOPS! IT LOOKS LIKE HE PUT A *LIIITTLE* TOO MUCH POWER ON THAT ONE.
YEOW!
HA HA HA!
YOU WILL GET ONE OF THOSE FROM INARIZAKI EVERY NOW AND AGAIN. [LAUGHS]
WHAT A ROCKET!
THEY HAVE AMAZING POWER, BUT THEIR ACCURACY IS STILL A LITTLE, AH...UNEVEN.
THIS AIN'T A HOME RUN DERBY, YA KLUTZ!
YOU DO IT TOO SOMETIMES, JERK.
IT'S CUZ YOU SAID CRAP YOU SHOULDN'T HAVE.
SMEK
AOW!
WOW. OSAMU-KUN ALWAYS ACTS SO LAID-BACK THAT YOU FORGET HOW COMPETITIVE HE CAN GET.
WELL, YEAH. HE'S A CARBON COPY OF THAT NUTBALL.
UGH...
THEY BUILD UP A BIG ENOUGH LEAD THAT THEY START TO LOOSEN UP AND RELAX...
...WHEN KAGEYAMA COMES OUT OF NOWHERE AND SOCKS 'EM WITH A BUNCH OF SERVICE ACES IN A ROW. THEY STAGGER FOR A BIT, *BUT*...THEY STILL HAVE A HUGE LEAD.

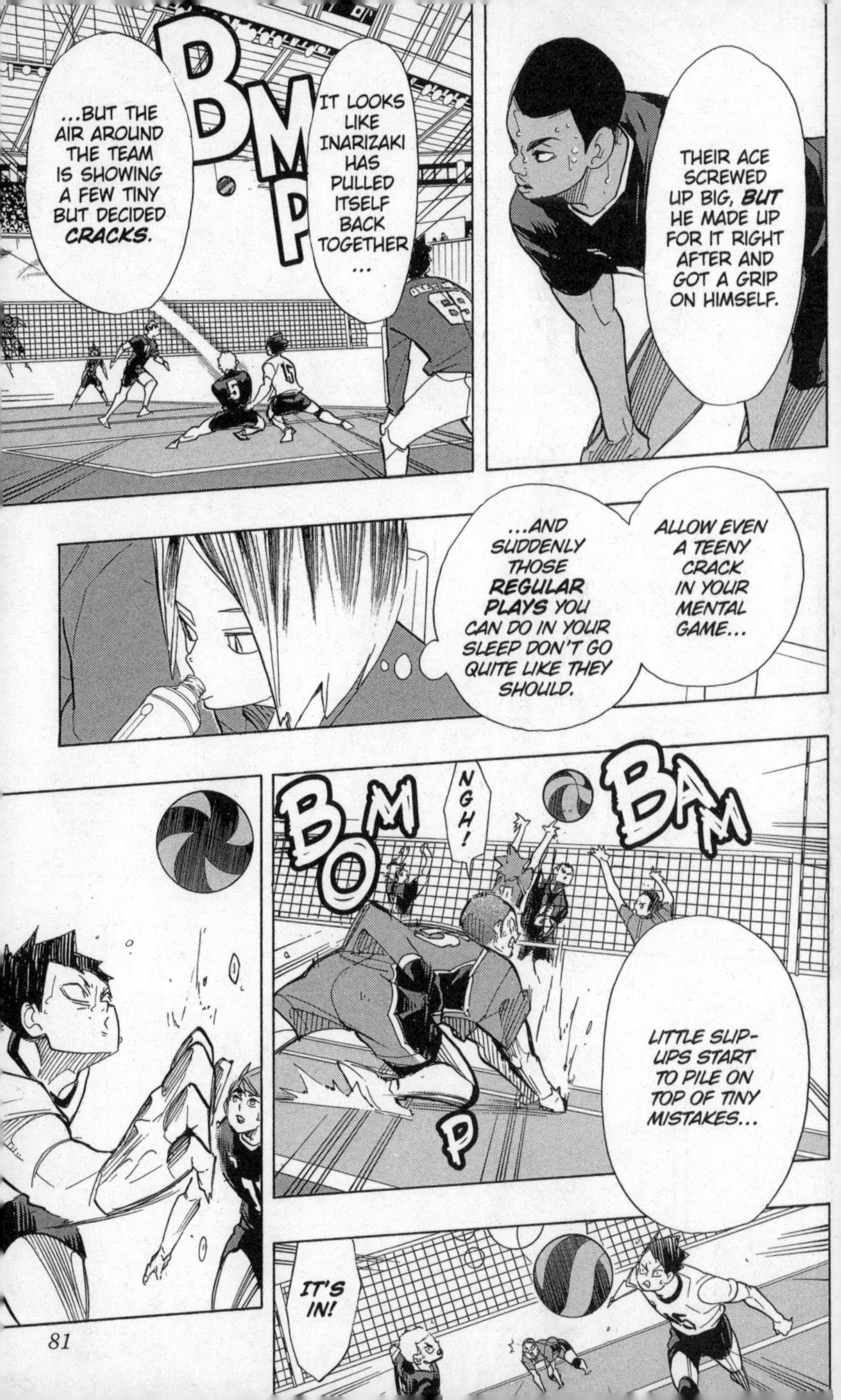
THEIR ACE SCREWED UP BIG, BUT HE MADE UP FOR IT RIGHT AFTER AND GOT A GRIP ON HIMSELF.
IT LOOKS LIKE INARIZAKI HAS PULLED ITSELF BACK TOGETHER...
BMP
...BUT THE AIR AROUND THE TEAM IS SHOWING A FEW TINY BUT DECIDED CRACKS.
ALLOW EVEN A TEENY CRACK IN YOUR MENTAL GAME...
...AND SUDDENLY THOSE REGULAR PLAYS YOU CAN DO IN YOUR SLEEP DON'T GO QUITE LIKE THEY SHOULD.
BAM
NGH!
BOMP
LITTLE SLIP-UPS START TO PILE ON TOP OF TINY MISTAKES...
IT'S IN!

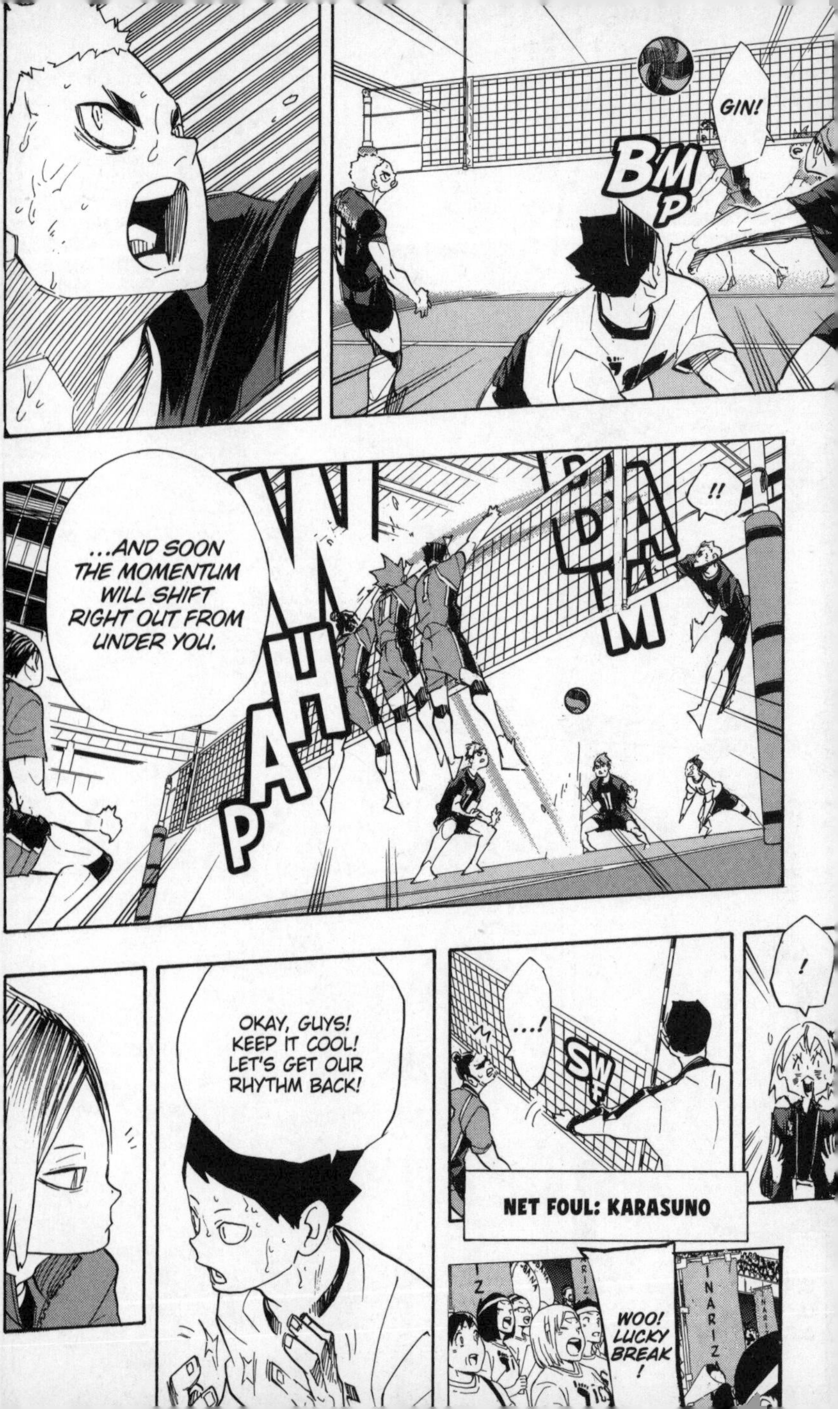
GIN!
BMP
!!
...AND SOON THE MOMENTUM WILL SHIFT RIGHT OUT FROM UNDER YOU.
!
...!
SWF
NET FOUL: KARASUNO
WOO! LUCKY BREAK!
OKAY, GUYS! KEEP IT COOL! LET'S GET OUR RHYTHM BACK!

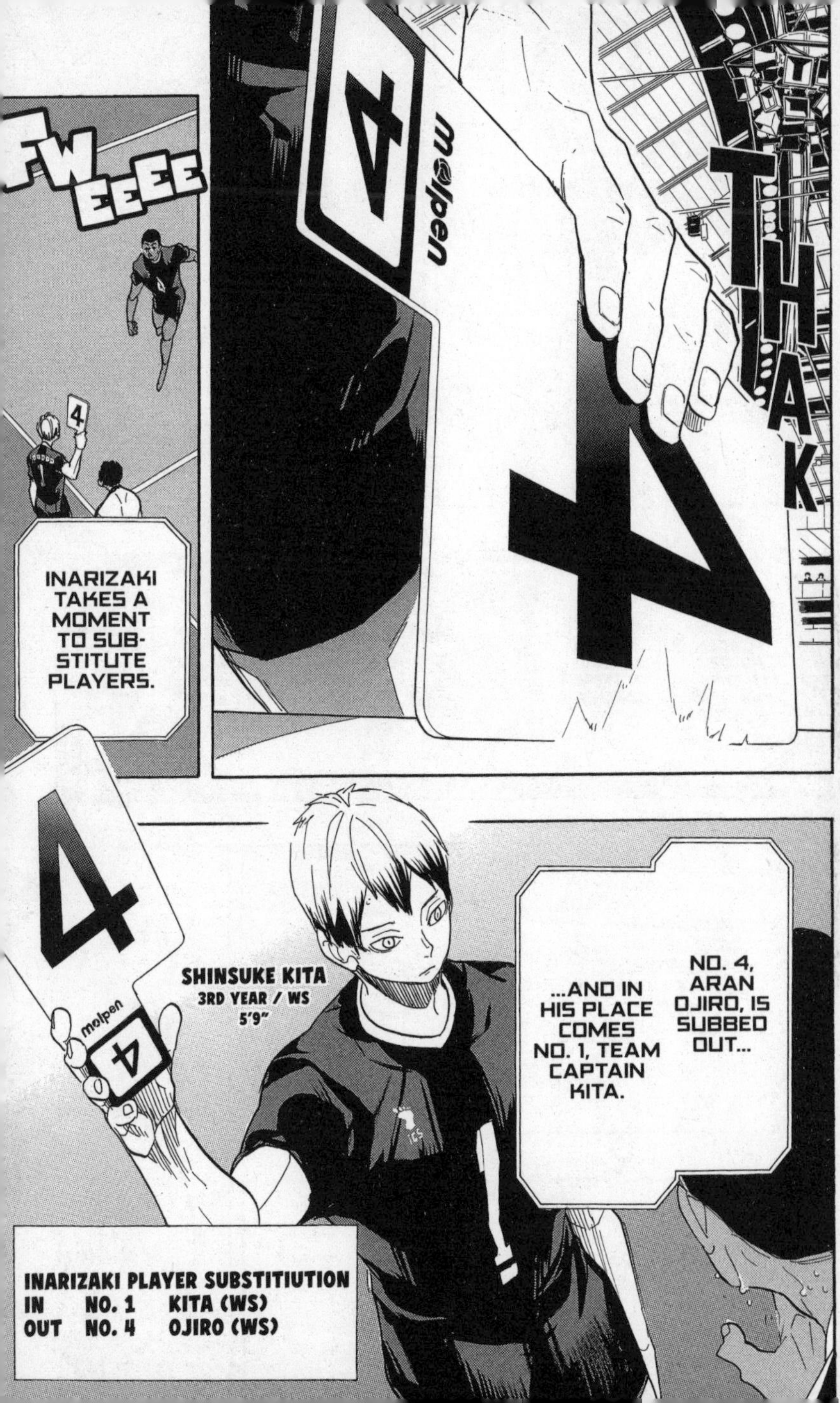

THWAK
FWEEEE
INARIZAKI TAKES A MOMENT TO SUB-STITUTE PLAYERS.
NO. 4, ARAN OJIRO, IS SUBBED OUT...
...AND IN HIS PLACE COMES NO. 1, TEAM CAPTAIN KITA.
SHINSUKE KITA
3RD YEAR / WS
5'9"
INARIZAKI PLAYER SUBSTITIUTION
IN NO. 1 KITA (WS)
OUT NO. 4 OJIRO (WS)

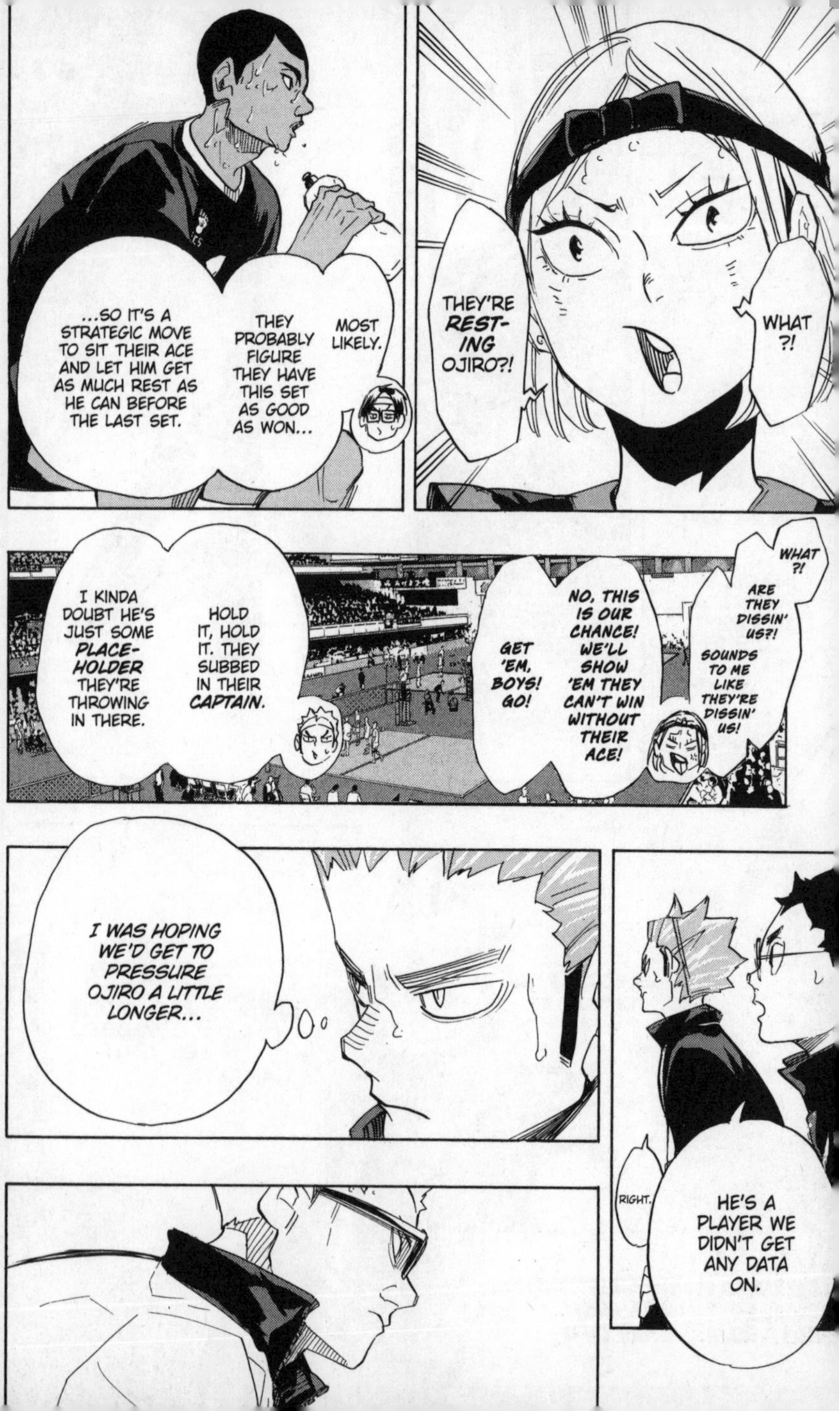
WHAT?!
THEY'RE RESTING OJIRO?!
MOST LIKELY.
THEY PROBABLY FIGURE THEY HAVE THIS SET AS GOOD AS WON...
...SO IT'S A STRATEGIC MOVE TO SIT THEIR ACE AND LET HIM GET AS MUCH REST AS HE CAN BEFORE THE LAST SET.
WHAT?! ARE THEY DISSIN' US?!
SOUNDS TO ME LIKE THEY'RE DISSIN' US!
NO, THIS IS OUR CHANCE! WE'LL SHOW 'EM THEY CAN'T WIN WITHOUT THEIR ACE!
GET 'EM, BOYS! GO!
HOLD IT, HOLD IT. THEY SUBBED IN THEIR CAPTAIN.
I KINDA DOUBT HE'S JUST SOME PLACEHOLDER THEY'RE THROWING IN THERE.
HE'S A PLAYER WE DIDN'T GET ANY DATA ON.
RIGHT.
I WAS HOPING WE'D GET TO PRESSURE OJIRO A LITTLE LONGER...

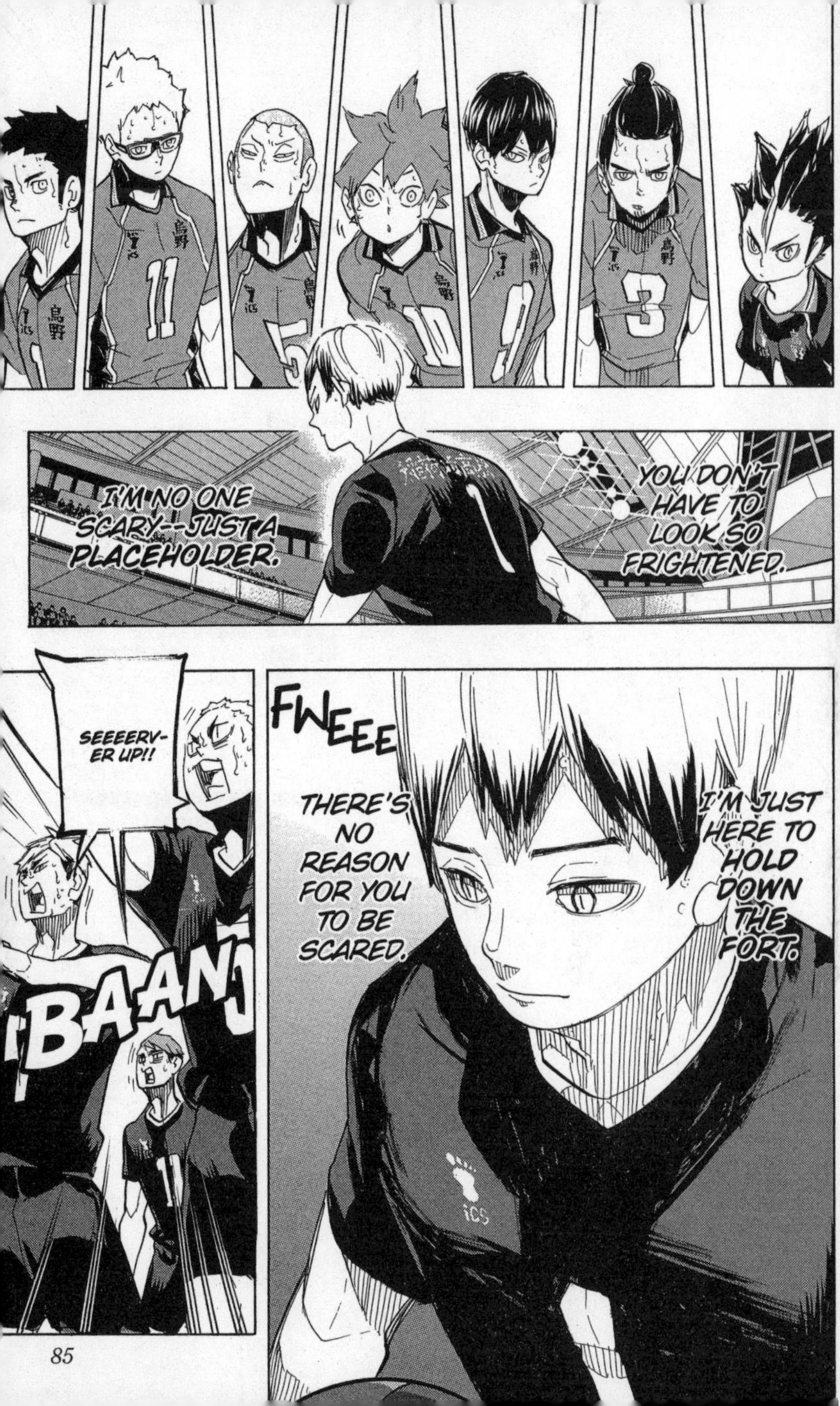
YOU DON'T HAVE TO LOOK SO FRIGHTENED.
I'M NO ONE SCARY--JUST A PLACEHOLDER.
FWEEE
I'M JUST HERE TO HOLD DOWN THE FORT.
THERE'S NO REASON FOR YOU TO BE SCARED.
SEEEERV-ER UP!!
BAAN

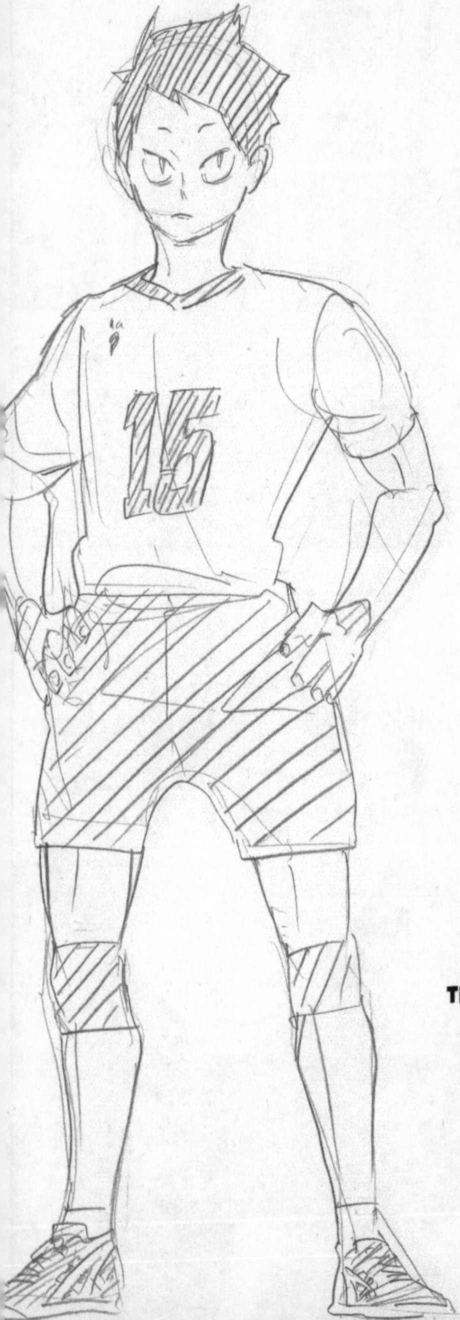
15

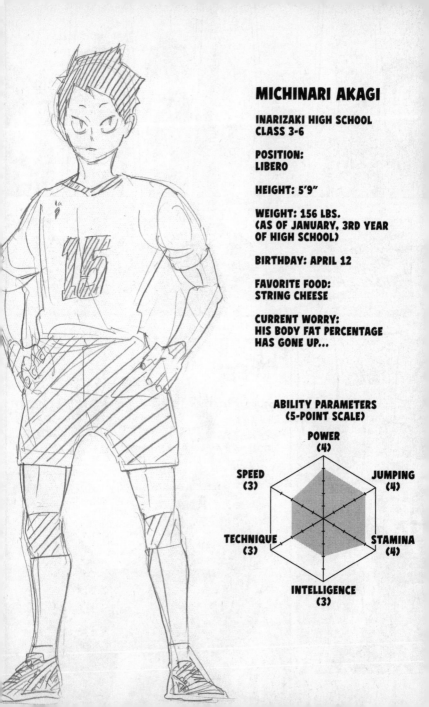

MICHINARI AKAGI

INARIZAKI HIGH SCHOOL
CLASS 3-6

POSITION:
LIBERO

HEIGHT: 5'9"

WEIGHT: 156 LBS.
(AS OF JANUARY, 3RD YEAR OF HIGH SCHOOL)

BIRTHDAY: APRIL 12

FAVORITE FOOD:
STRING CHEESE

CURRENT WORRY:
HIS BODY FAT PERCENTAGE HAS GONE UP...

ABILITY PARAMETERS
(5-POINT SCALE)

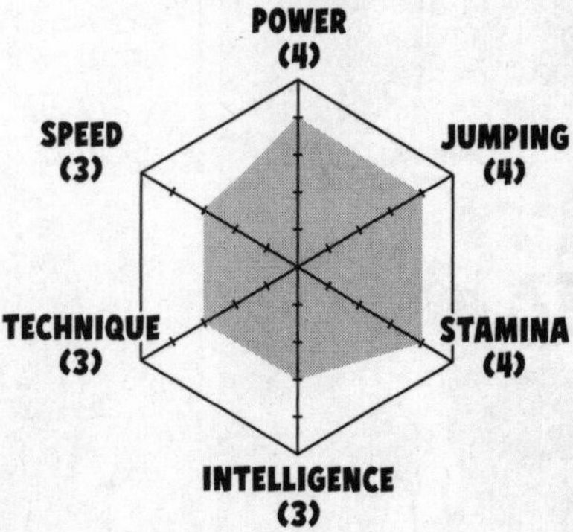
POWER
(4)
JUMPING
(4)
STAMINA
(4)
INTELLIGENCE
(3)
TECHNIQUE
(3)
SPEED
(3)

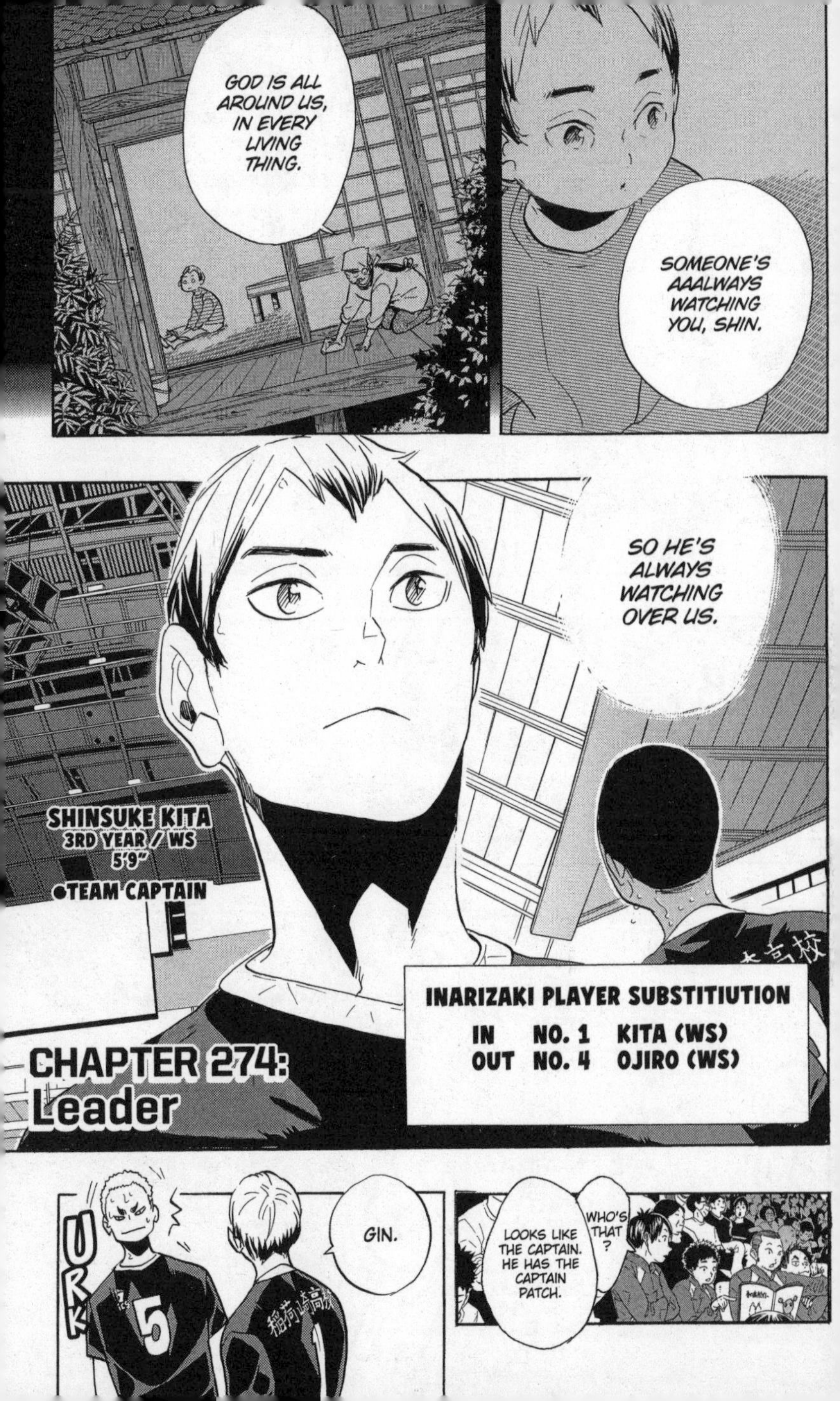
SOMEONE'S AAALWAYS WATCHING YOU, SHIN.
GOD IS ALL AROUND US, IN EVERY LIVING THING.
SO HE'S ALWAYS WATCHING OVER US.
INARIZAKI PLAYER SUBSTITIUTION
IN NO. 1 KITA (WS)
OUT NO. 4 OJIRO (WS)
SHINSUKE KITA
3RD YEAR / WS
5'9"
•TEAM CAPTAIN
CHAPTER 274:
Leader
WHO'S THAT?
LOOKS LIKE THE CAPTAIN. HE HAS THE CAPTAIN PATCH.
GIN.
URK

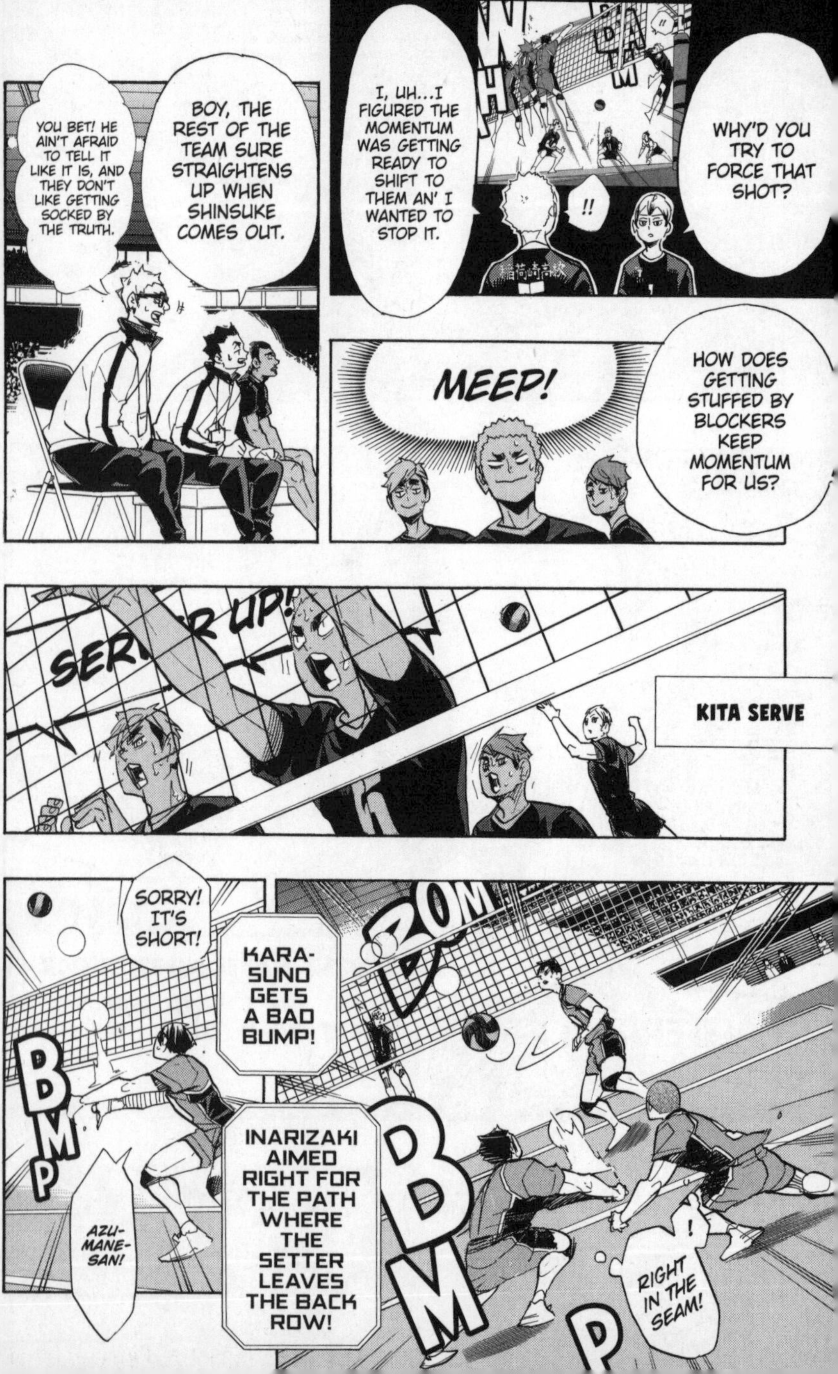

WHY'D YOU TRY TO FORCE THAT SHOT?
!!
!!
I, UH...I FIGURED THE MOMENTUM WAS GETTING READY TO SHIFT TO THEM AN' I WANTED TO STOP IT.
BOY, THE REST OF THE TEAM SURE STRAIGHTENS UP WHEN SHINSUKE COMES OUT.
YOU BET! HE AIN'T AFRAID TO TELL IT LIKE IT IS, AND THEY DON'T LIKE GETTING SOCKED BY THE TRUTH.
HOW DOES GETTING STUFFED BY BLOCKERS KEEP MOMENTUM FOR US?
MEEP!
KITA SERVE
!
RIGHT IN THE SEAM!
INARIZAKI AIMED RIGHT FOR THE PATH WHERE THE SETTER LEAVES THE BACK ROW!
KARA-SUNO GETS A BAD BUMP!
SORRY! IT'S SHORT!
AZU-MANE-SAN!

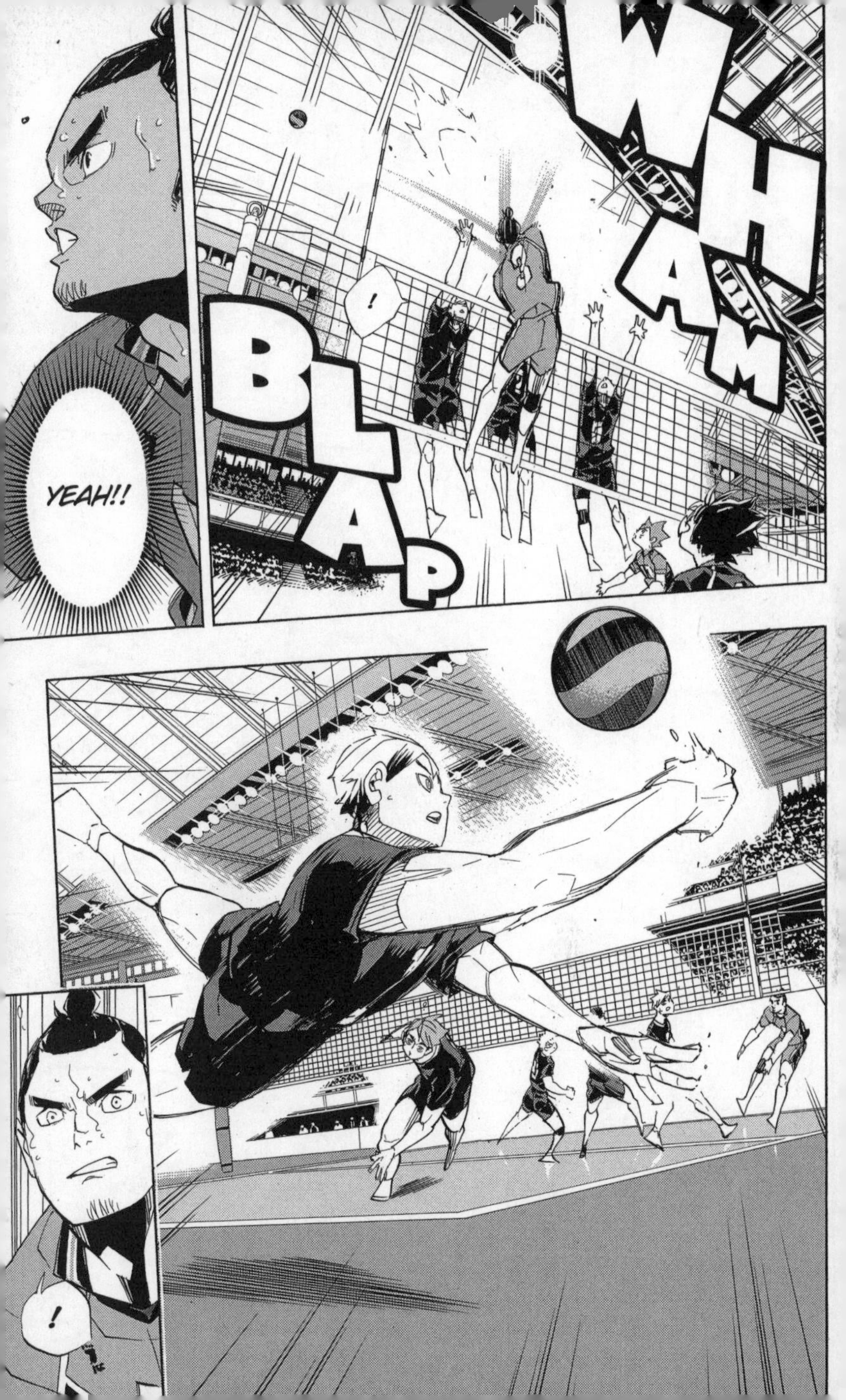
WHAM
!
BLAP
YEAH!!
!

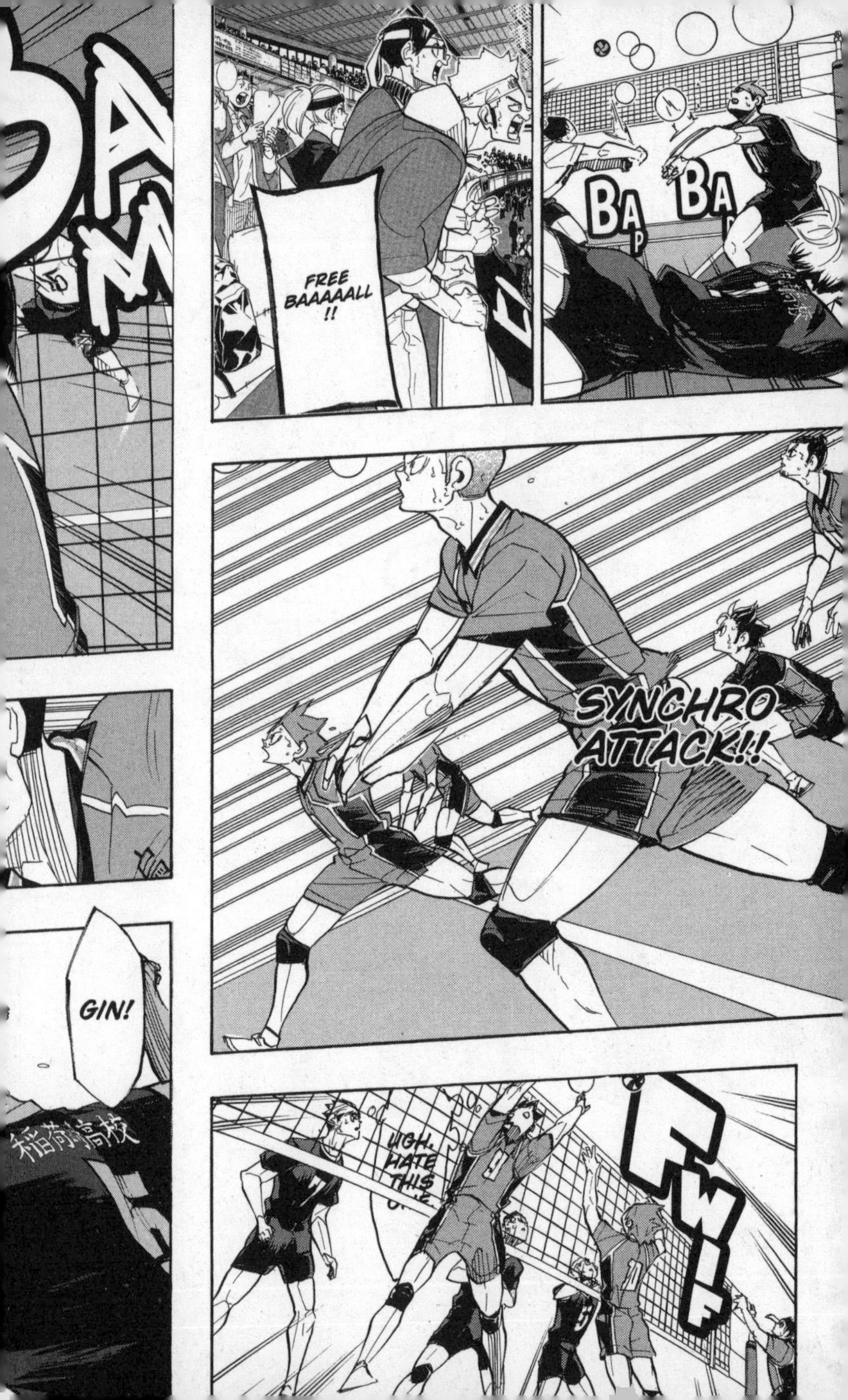

BAP BAP
FREE BAAAAALL !!
SYNCHRO ATTACK!!
FWIF
UGH. HATE THIS
GIN!
稲荷崎高校

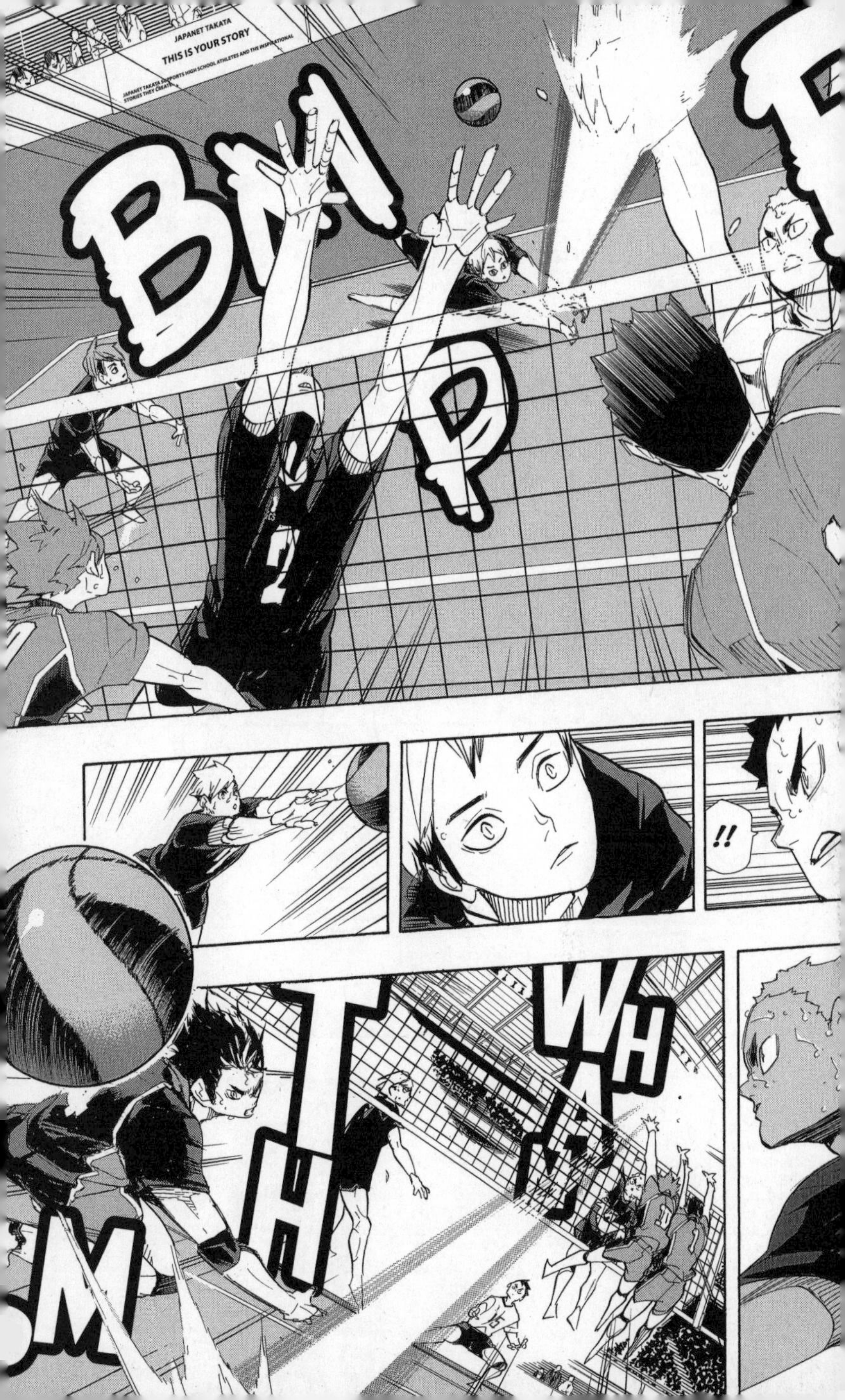
JAPANET TAKATA
THIS IS YOUR STORY
JAPANET TAKATA SUPPORTS HIGH SCHOOL ATHLETES AND THE INSPIRATIONAL STORIES THEY CREATE
!!

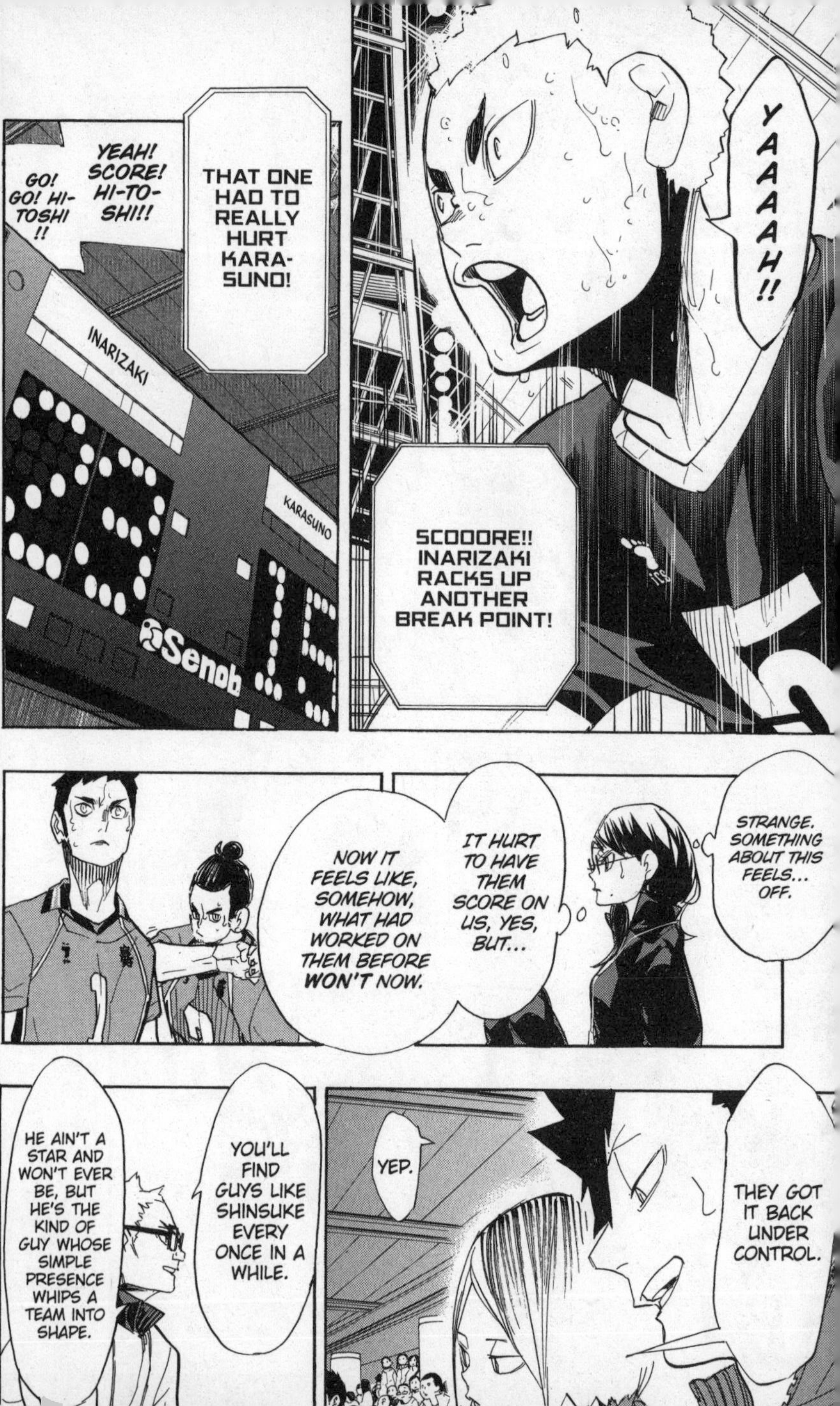
YAAAAAH!!
SCOOORE!! INARIZAKI RACKS UP ANOTHER BREAK POINT!
THAT ONE HAD TO REALLY HURT KARASUNO!
YEAH! SCORE! HI-TO-SHI!!
GO! GO! HI-TOSHI!!
INARIZAKI
KARASUNO
STRANGE. SOMETHING ABOUT THIS FEELS... OFF.
IT HURT TO HAVE THEM SCORE ON US, YES, BUT...
NOW IT FEELS LIKE, SOMEHOW, WHAT HAD WORKED ON THEM BEFORE WON'T NOW.
THEY GOT IT BACK UNDER CONTROL.
YEP.
YOU'LL FIND GUYS LIKE SHINSUKE EVERY ONCE IN A WHILE.
HE AIN'T A STAR AND WON'T EVER BE, BUT HE'S THE KIND OF GUY WHOSE SIMPLE PRESENCE WHIPS A TEAM INTO SHAPE.

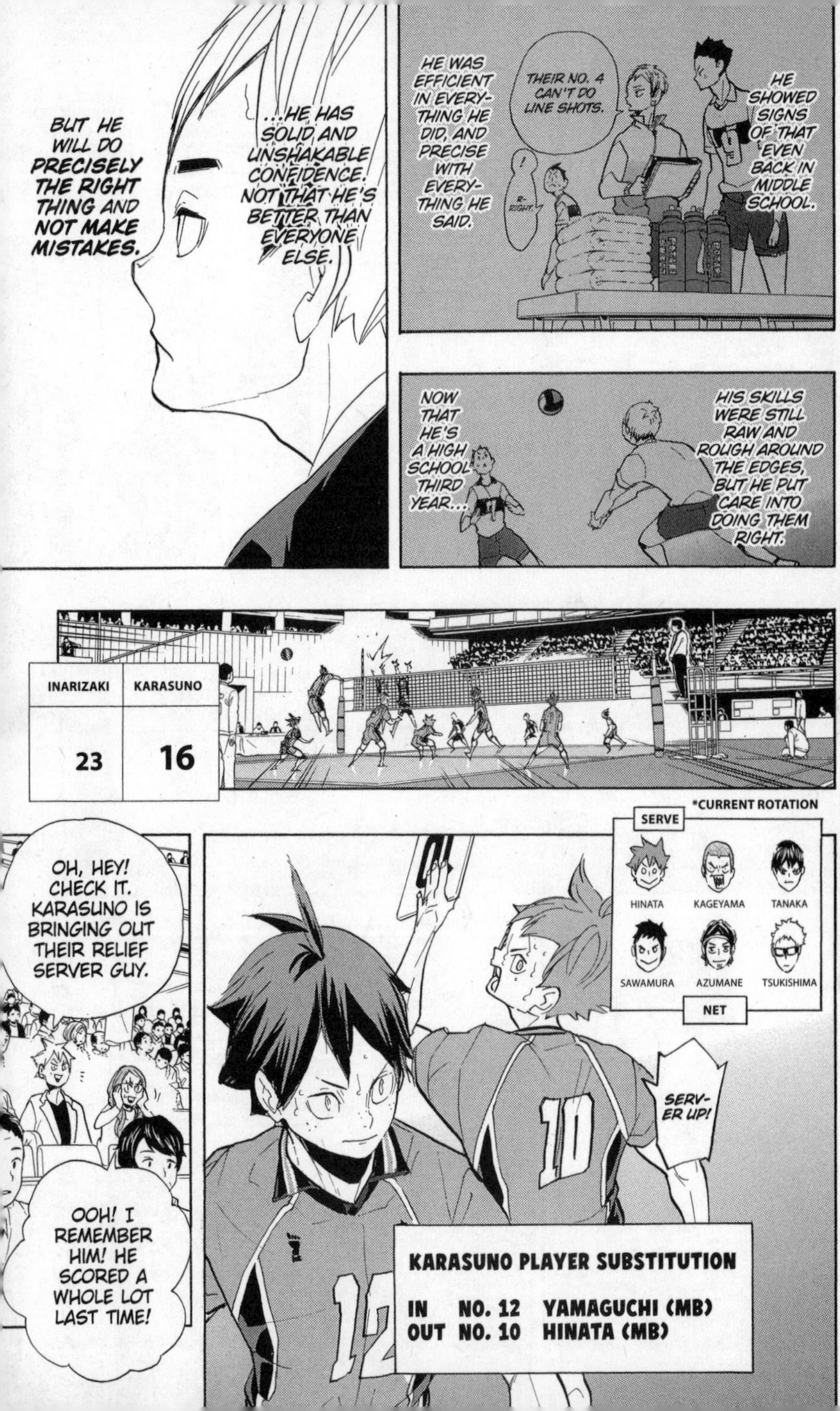
HE SHOWED SIGNS OF THAT EVEN BACK IN MIDDLE SCHOOL.
THEIR NO. 4 CAN'T DO LINE SHOTS.
!
R-RIGHT.
HE WAS EFFICIENT IN EVERYTHING HE DID, AND PRECISE WITH EVERYTHING HE SAID.
HIS SKILLS WERE STILL RAW AND ROUGH AROUND THE EDGES, BUT HE PUT CARE INTO DOING THEM RIGHT.
NOW THAT HE'S A HIGH SCHOOL THIRD YEAR...
...HE HAS SOLID AND UNSHAKABLE CONFIDENCE. NOT THAT HE'S BETTER THAN EVERYONE ELSE.
BUT HE WILL DO PRECISELY THE RIGHT THING AND NOT MAKE MISTAKES.
INARIZAKI
KARASUNO
23
16
*CURRENT ROTATION
SERVE
HINATA
KAGEYAMA
TANAKA
SAWAMURA
AZUMANE
TSUKISHIMA
NET
SERVER UP!
KARASUNO PLAYER SUBSTITUTION
IN NO. 12 YAMAGUCHI (MB)
OUT NO. 10 HINATA (MB)
OH, HEY! CHECK IT. KARASUNO IS BRINGING OUT THEIR RELIEF SERVER GUY.
OOH! I REMEMBER HIM! HE SCORED A WHOLE LOT LAST TIME!

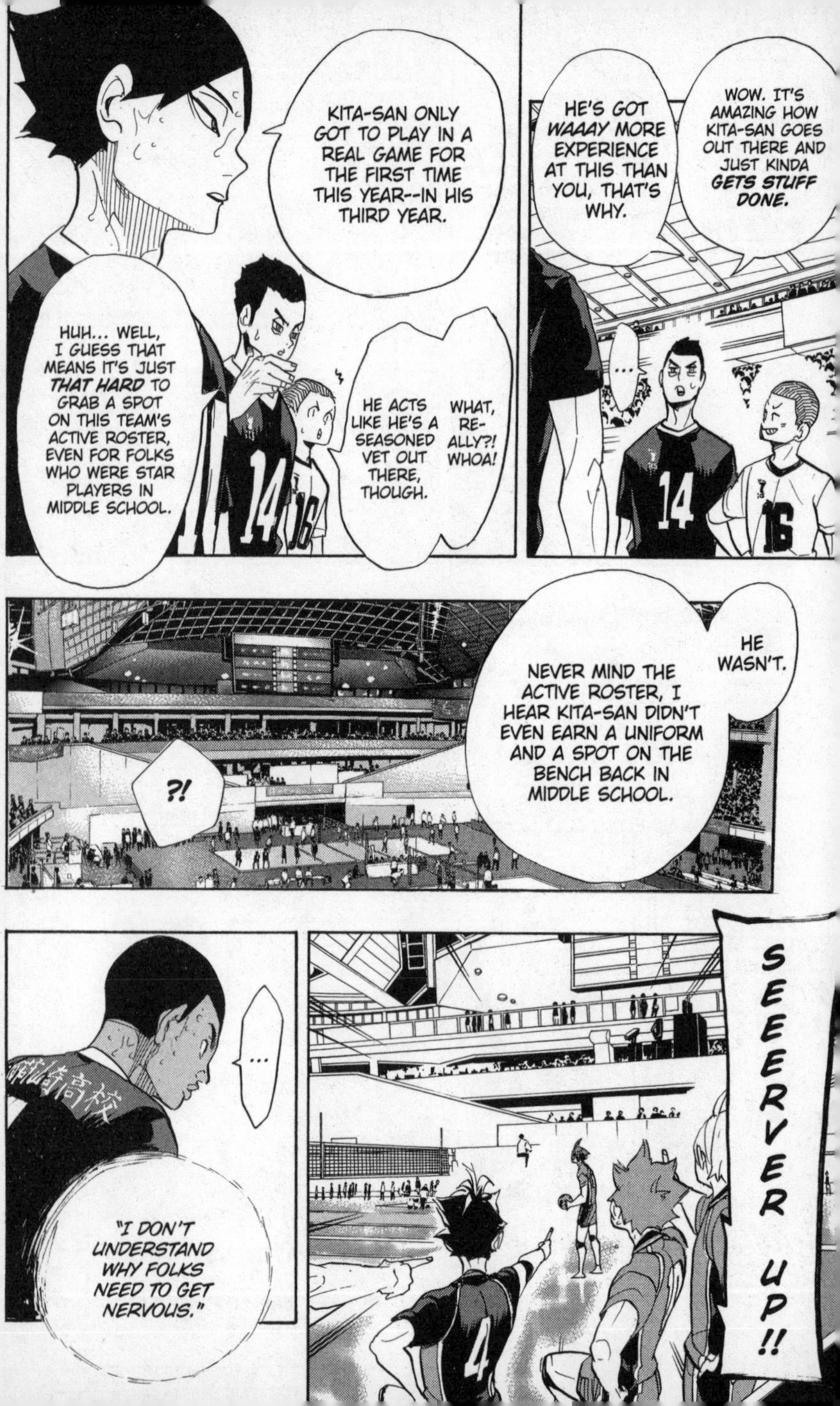
WOW. IT'S AMAZING HOW KITA-SAN GOES OUT THERE AND JUST KINDA GETS STUFF DONE.
HE'S GOT WAAAY MORE EXPERIENCE AT THIS THAN YOU, THAT'S WHY.
...
KITA-SAN ONLY GOT TO PLAY IN A REAL GAME FOR THE FIRST TIME THIS YEAR--IN HIS THIRD YEAR.
WHAT, RE-ALLY?! WHOA!
HE ACTS LIKE HE'S A SEASONED VET OUT THERE, THOUGH.
HUH... WELL, I GUESS THAT MEANS IT'S JUST THAT HARD TO GRAB A SPOT ON THIS TEAM'S ACTIVE ROSTER, EVEN FOR FOLKS WHO WERE STAR PLAYERS IN MIDDLE SCHOOL.
HE WASN'T.
NEVER MIND THE ACTIVE ROSTER, I HEAR KITA-SAN DIDN'T EVEN EARN A UNIFORM AND A SPOT ON THE BENCH BACK IN MIDDLE SCHOOL.
?!
SEEERVER UP!!
...
"I DON'T UNDERSTAND WHY FOLKS NEED TO GET NERVOUS."

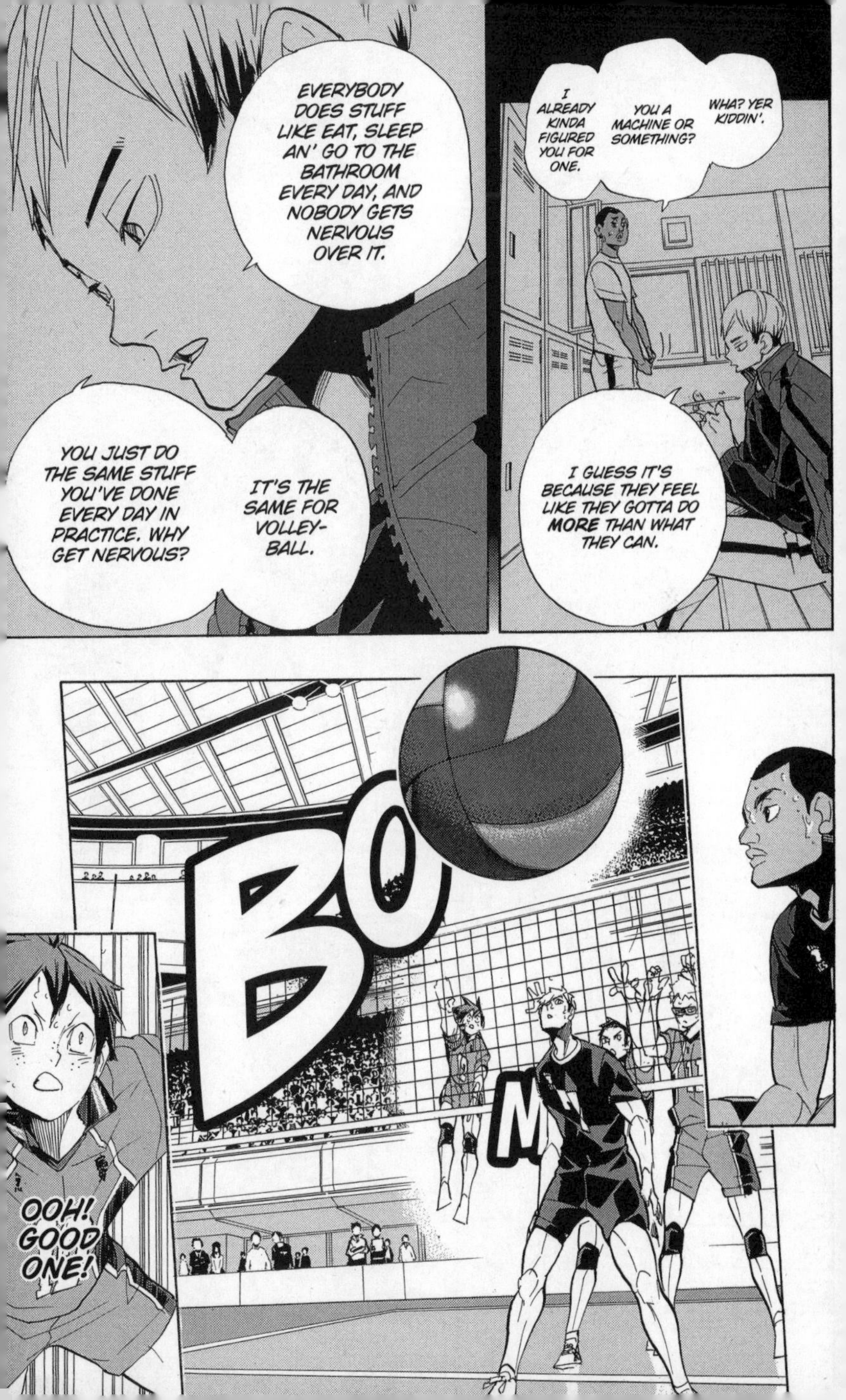
WHA? YER KIDDIN'.
YOU A MACHINE OR SOMETHING?
I ALREADY KINDA FIGURED YOU FOR ONE.
I GUESS IT'S BECAUSE THEY FEEL LIKE THEY GOTTA DO **MORE** THAN WHAT THEY CAN.
EVERYBODY DOES STUFF LIKE EAT, SLEEP AN' GO TO THE BATHROOM EVERY DAY, AND NOBODY GETS NERVOUS OVER IT.
IT'S THE SAME FOR VOLLEY-BALL.
YOU JUST DO THE SAME STUFF YOU'VE DONE EVERY DAY IN PRACTICE. WHY GET NERVOUS?
BO
M
OOH! GOOD ONE!

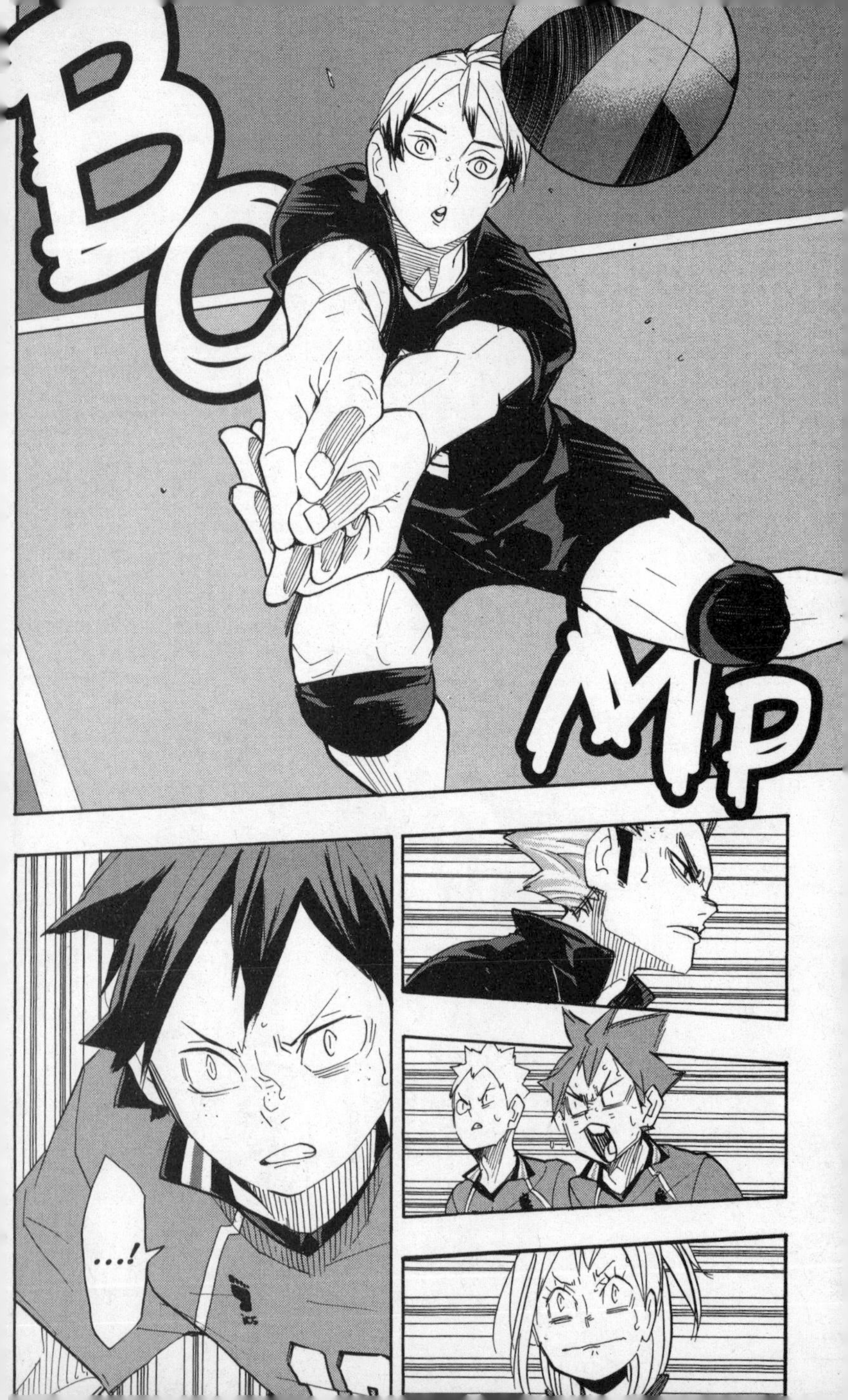
BOMP
...!

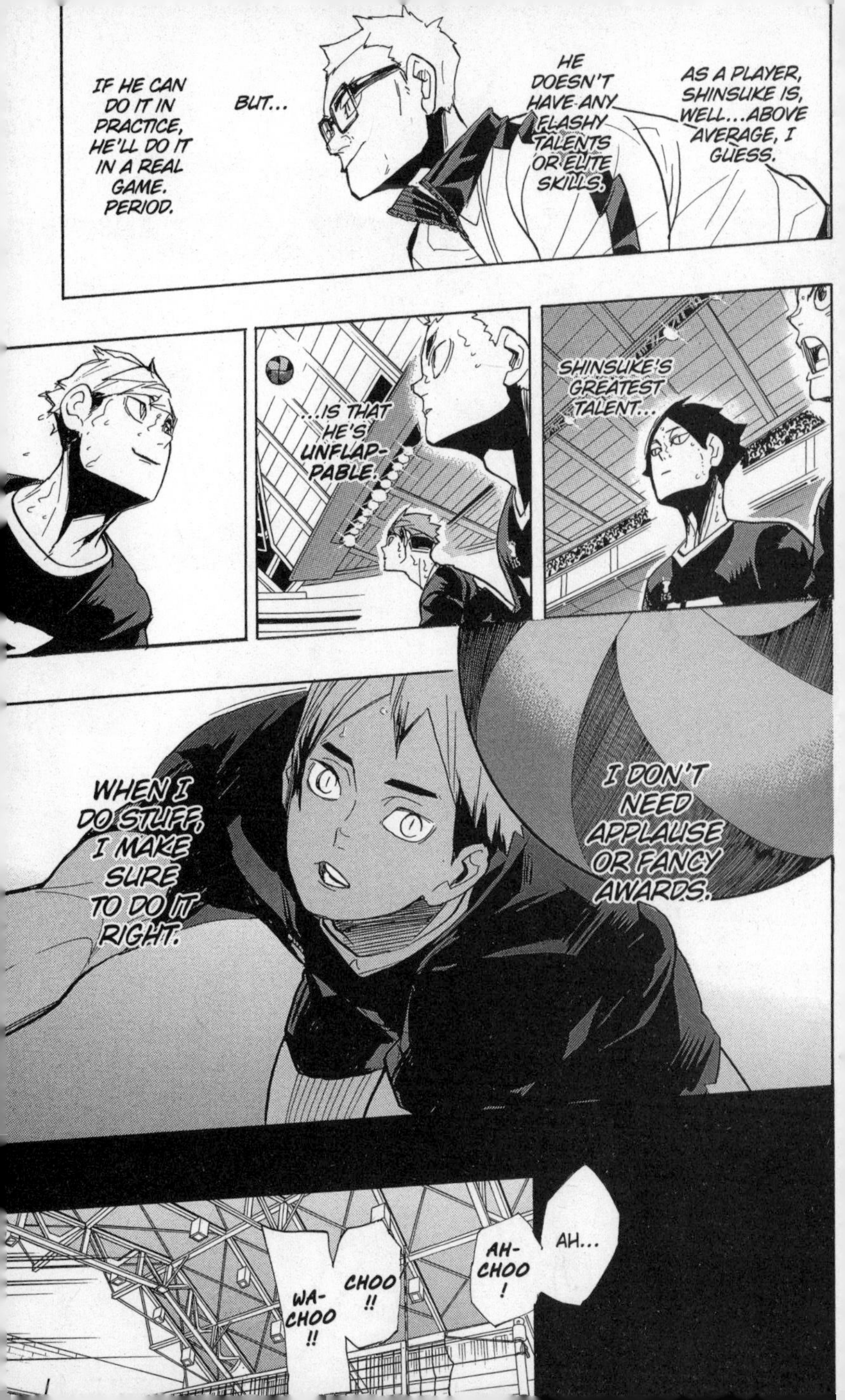
AS A PLAYER, SHINSUKE IS, WELL...ABOVE AVERAGE, I GUESS.
HE DOESN'T HAVE ANY FLASHY TALENTS OR ELITE SKILLS.
BUT...
IF HE CAN DO IT IN PRACTICE, HE'LL DO IT IN A REAL GAME. PERIOD.
SHINSUKE'S GREATEST TALENT...
...IS THAT HE'S UNFLAP-PABLE.
I DON'T NEED APPLAUSE OR FANCY AWARDS.
WHEN I DO STUFF, I MAKE SURE TO DO IT RIGHT.
AH...
AH-CHOO!
CHOO!!
WA-CHOO!!

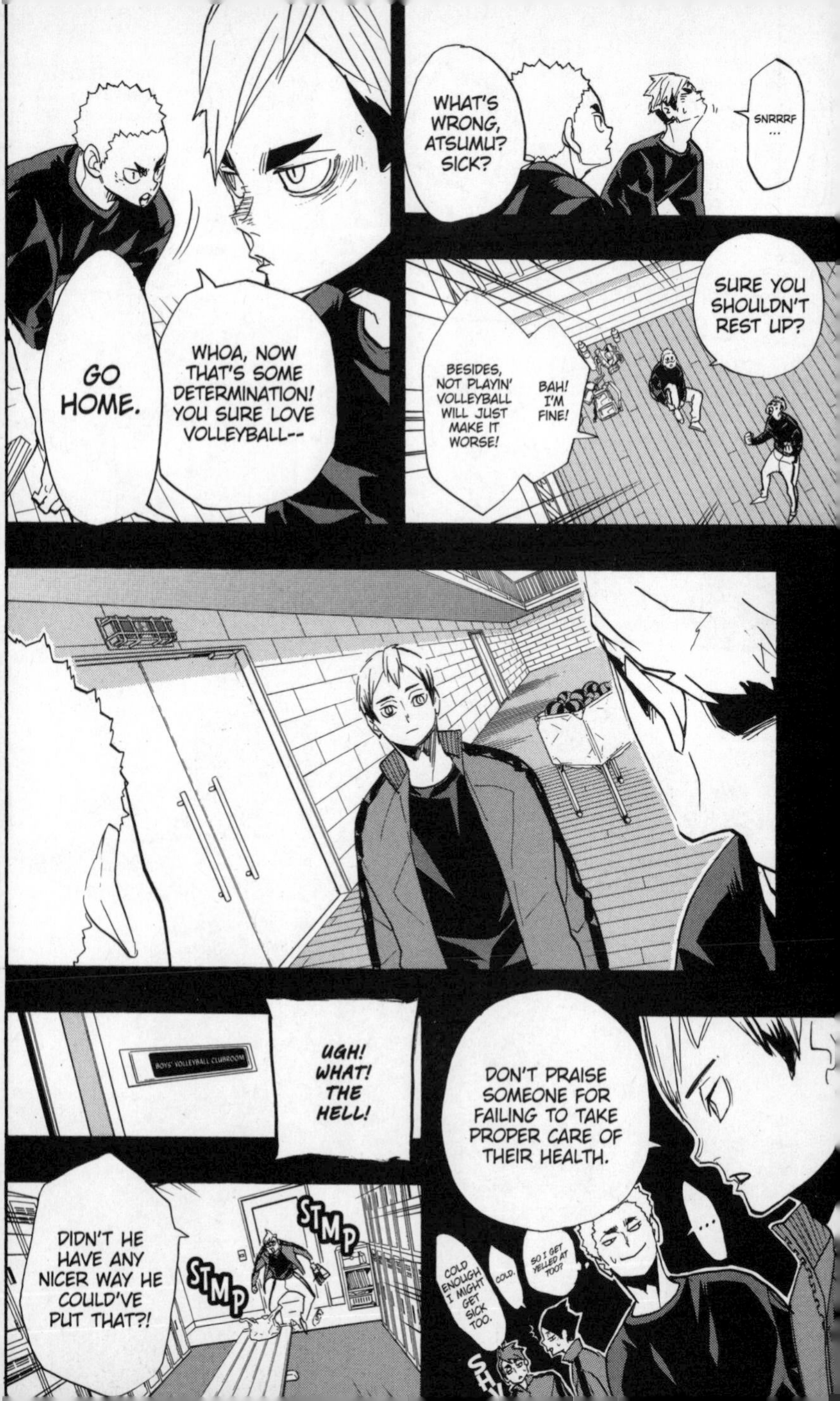
SNRRRF ...
WHAT'S WRONG, ATSUMU? SICK?
SURE YOU SHOULDN'T REST UP?
BAH! I'M FINE!
BESIDES, NOT PLAYIN' VOLLEYBALL WILL JUST MAKE IT WORSE!
WHOA, NOW THAT'S SOME DETERMINATION! YOU SURE LOVE VOLLEYBALL--
GO HOME.
DON'T PRAISE SOMEONE FOR FAILING TO TAKE PROPER CARE OF THEIR HEALTH.
...
SO I GET YELLED AT TOO?
COLD.
COLD ENOUGH I MIGHT GET SICK TOO.
BOYS' VOLLEYBALL CLUBROOM
UGH! WHAT! THE HELL!
STMP
STMP
DIDN'T HE HAVE ANY NICER WAY HE COULD'VE PUT THAT?!

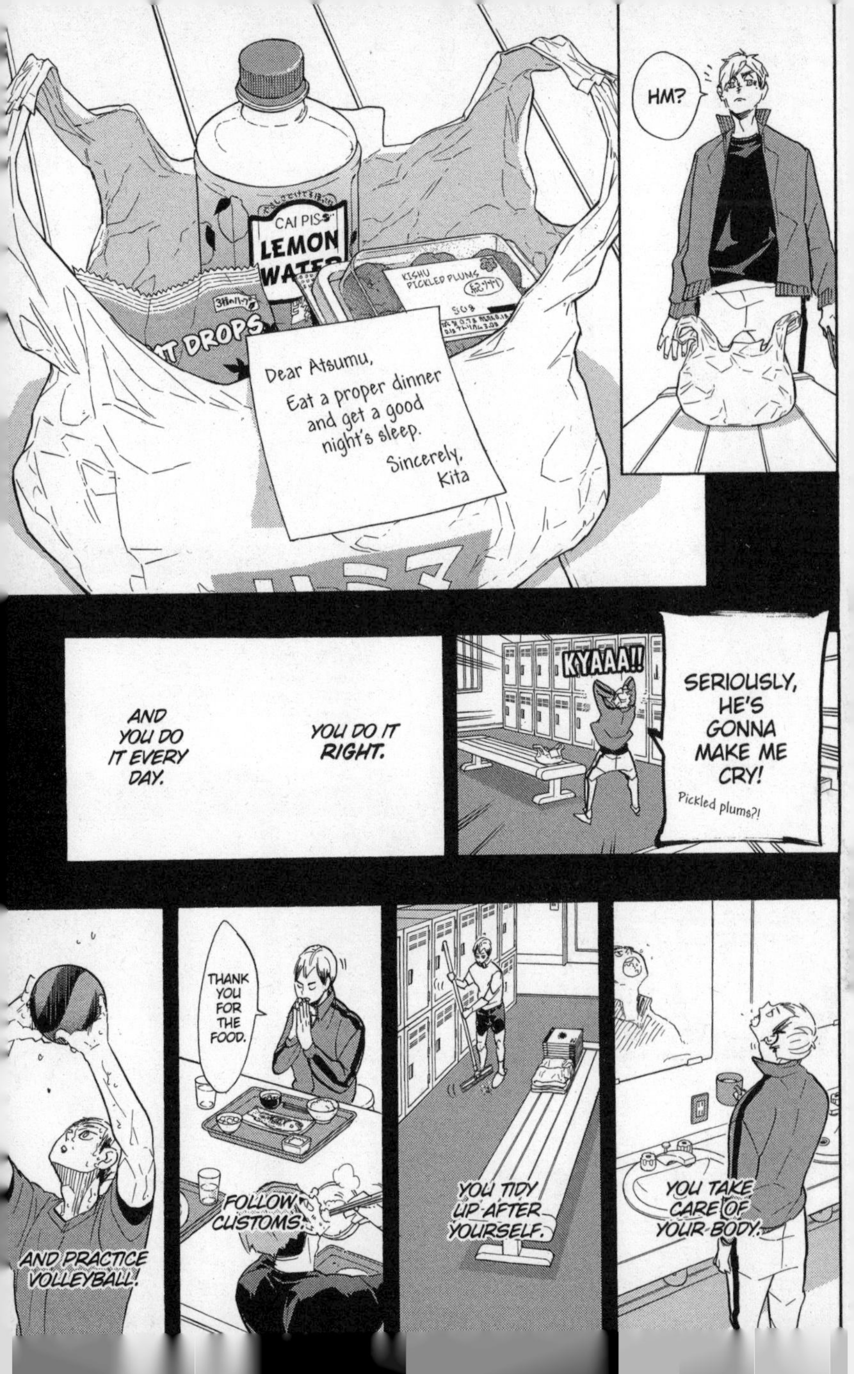
HM?
CAI PIS
LEMON
KISHU PICKLED PLUMS
Dear Atsumu,
Eat a proper dinner and get a good night's sleep.
Sincerely, Kita
KYAAA!!
SERIOUSLY, HE'S GONNA MAKE ME CRY!
Pickled plums?!
YOU DO IT RIGHT.
AND YOU DO IT EVERY DAY.
YOU TAKE CARE OF YOUR BODY.
YOU TIDY UP AFTER YOURSELF.
THANK YOU FOR THE FOOD.
FOLLOW CUSTOMS.
AND PRACTICE VOLLEYBALL!

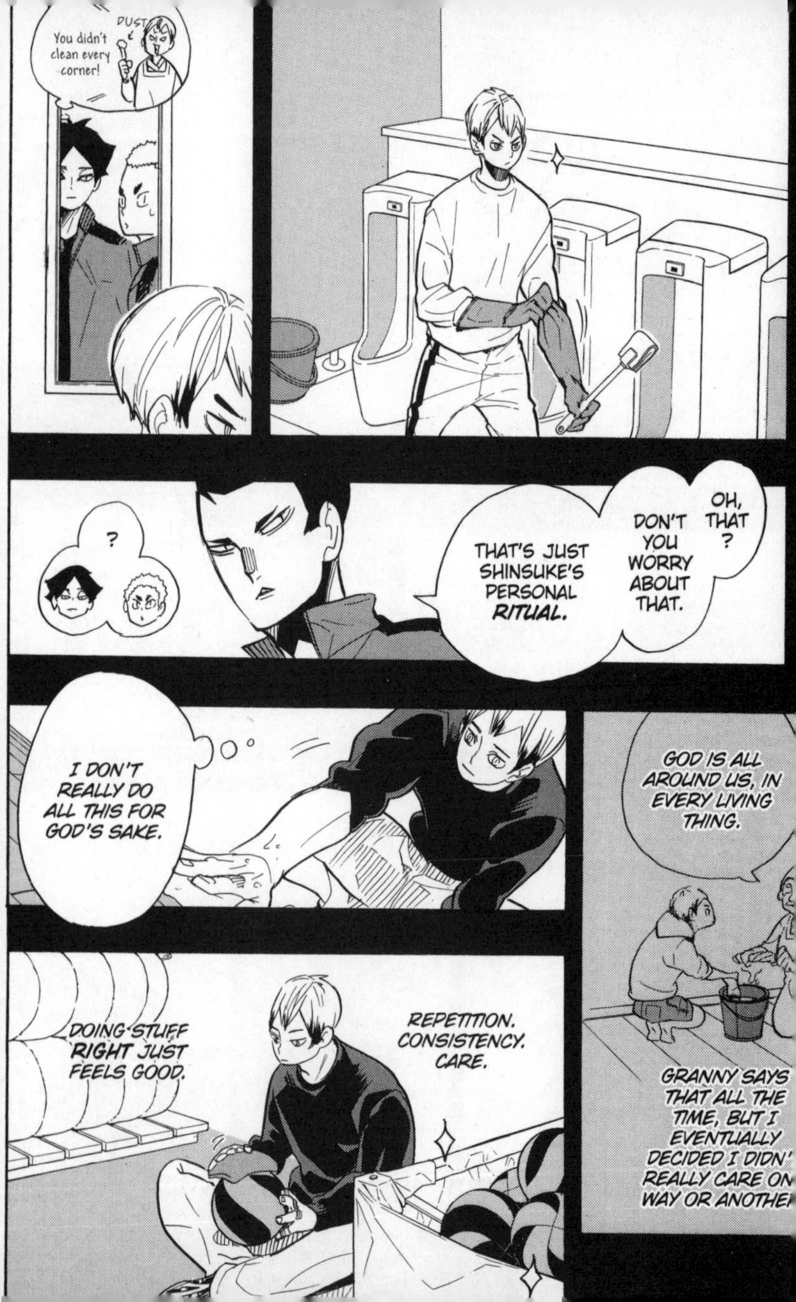
DUST
You didn't clean every corner!
OH, THAT?
DON'T YOU WORRY ABOUT THAT.
THAT'S JUST SHINSUKE'S PERSONAL RITUAL.
?
GOD IS ALL AROUND US, IN EVERY LIVING THING.
GRANNY SAYS THAT ALL THE TIME, BUT I EVENTUALLY DECIDED I DIDN' REALLY CARE ON WAY OR ANOTHE
I DON'T REALLY DO ALL THIS FOR GOD'S SAKE.
REPETITION. CONSISTENCY. CARE.
DOING STUFF RIGHT JUST FEELS GOOD.

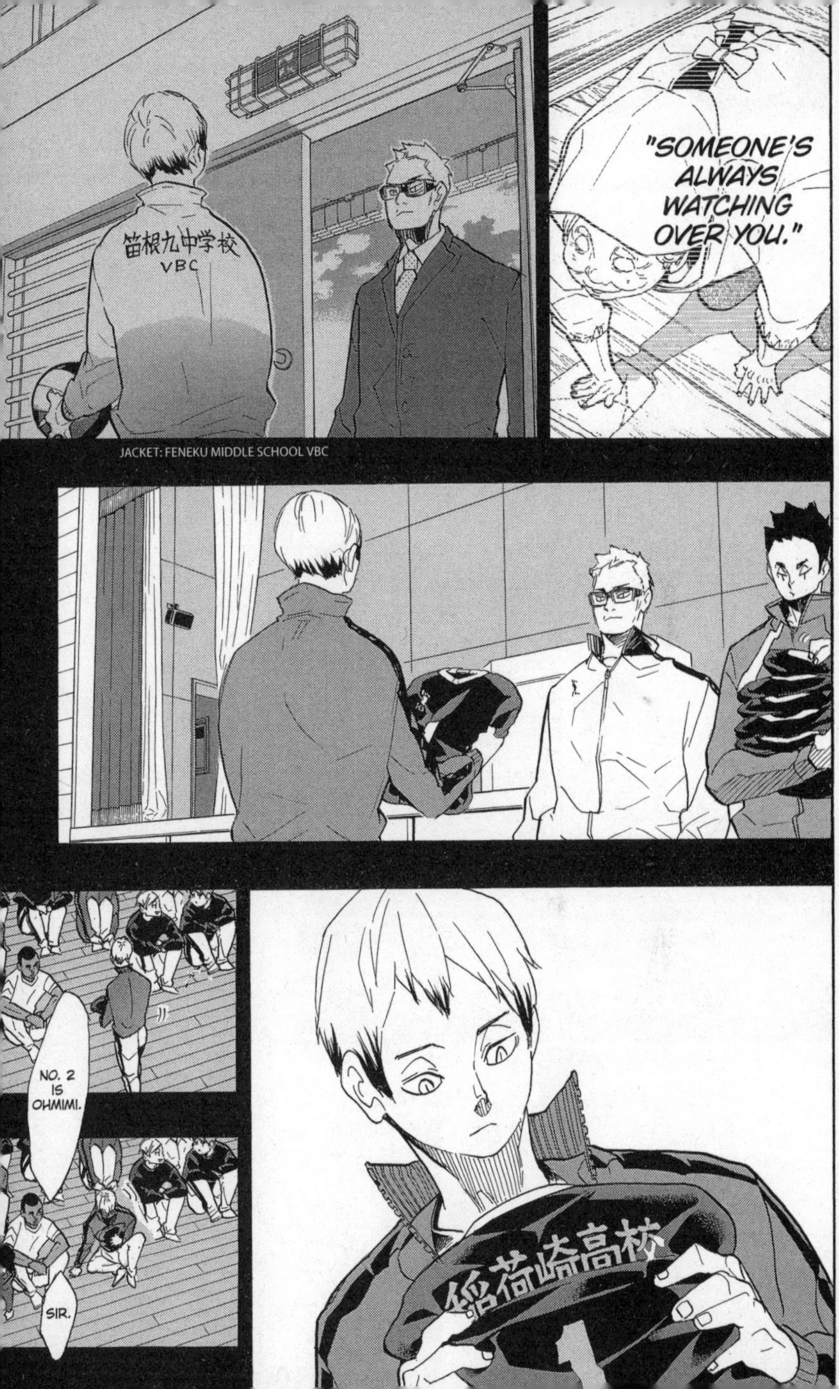
"SOMEONE'S ALWAYS WATCHING OVER YOU."
JACKET: FENEKU MIDDLE SCHOOL VBC
NO. 2 IS OHMIMI.
SIR.

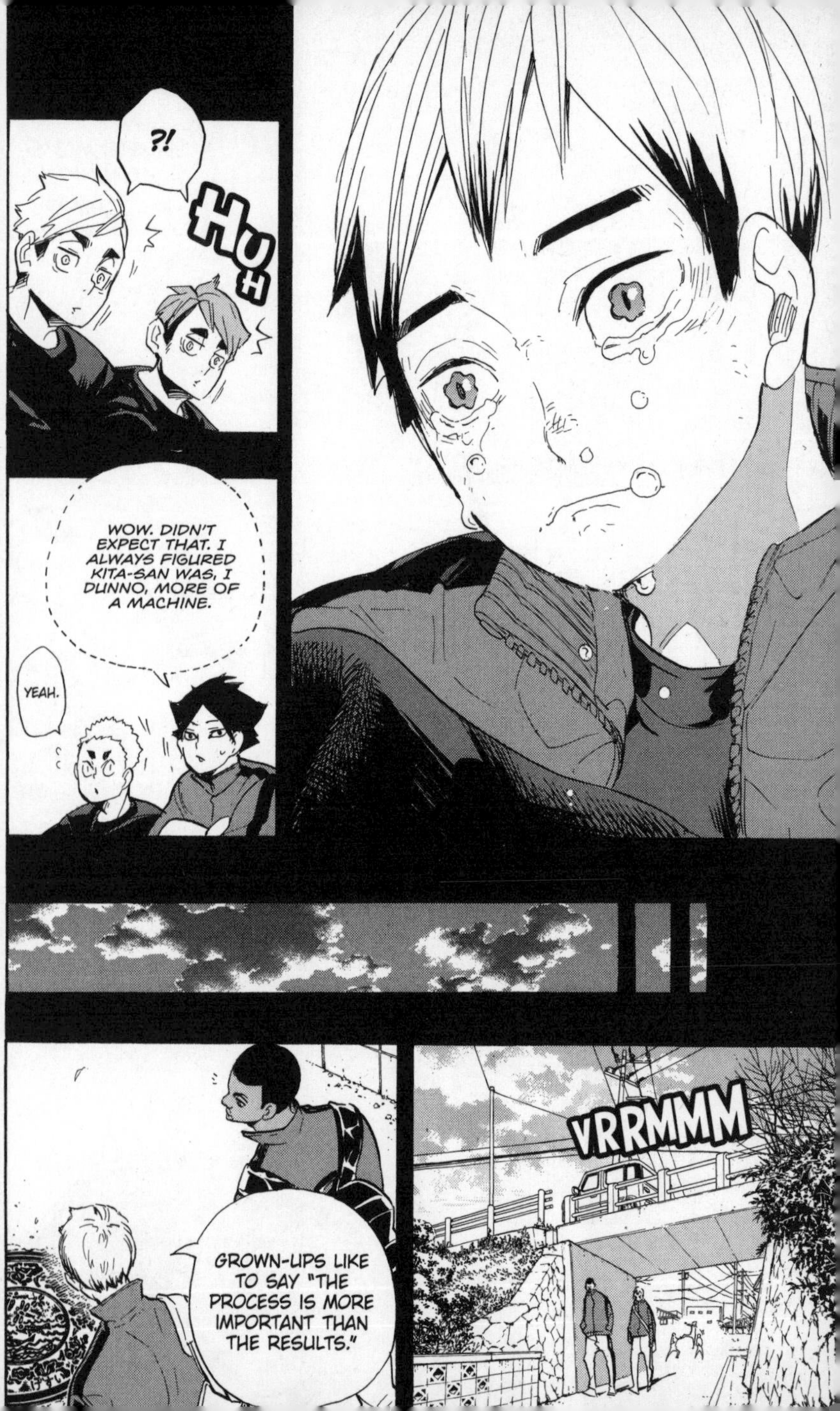
?!
HUH
WOW. DIDN'T EXPECT THAT. I ALWAYS FIGURED KITA-SAN WAS, I DUNNO, MORE OF A MACHINE.
YEAH.
VRRMMM
GROWN-UPS LIKE TO SAY "THE PROCESS IS MORE IMPORTANT THAN THE RESULTS."

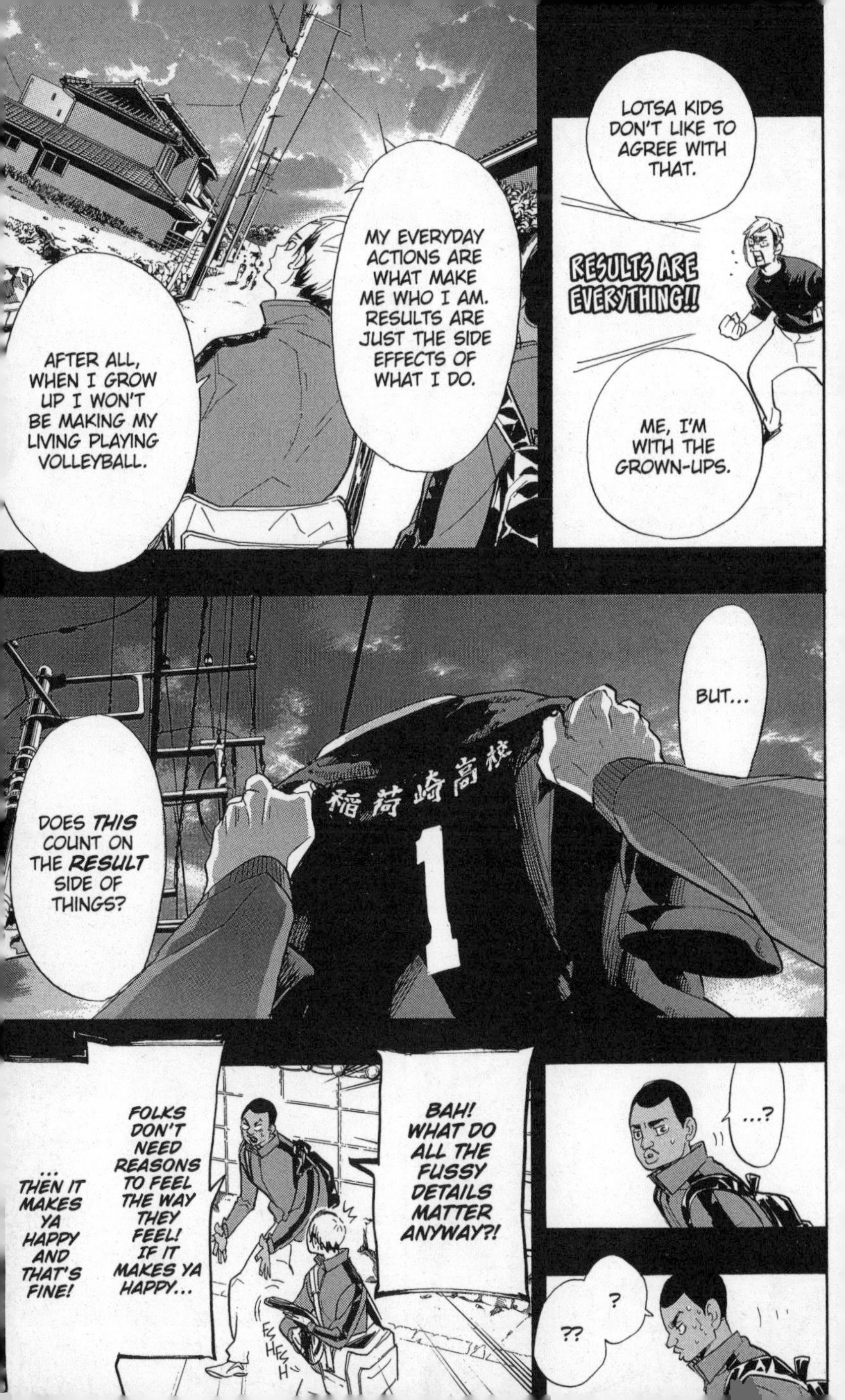
LOTSA KIDS DON'T LIKE TO AGREE WITH THAT.
RESULTS ARE EVERYTHING!!
ME, I'M WITH THE GROWN-UPS.
MY EVERYDAY ACTIONS ARE WHAT MAKE ME WHO I AM. RESULTS ARE JUST THE SIDE EFFECTS OF WHAT I DO.
AFTER ALL, WHEN I GROW UP I WON'T BE MAKING MY LIVING PLAYING VOLLEYBALL.
BUT...
稲荷崎高校
1
DOES THIS COUNT ON THE RESULT SIDE OF THINGS?
...?
?
??
BAH! WHAT DO ALL THE FUSSY DETAILS MATTER ANYWAY?!
FOLKS DON'T NEED REASONS TO FEEL THE WAY THEY FEEL! IF IT MAKES YA HAPPY...
...THEN IT MAKES YA HAPPY AND THAT'S FINE!

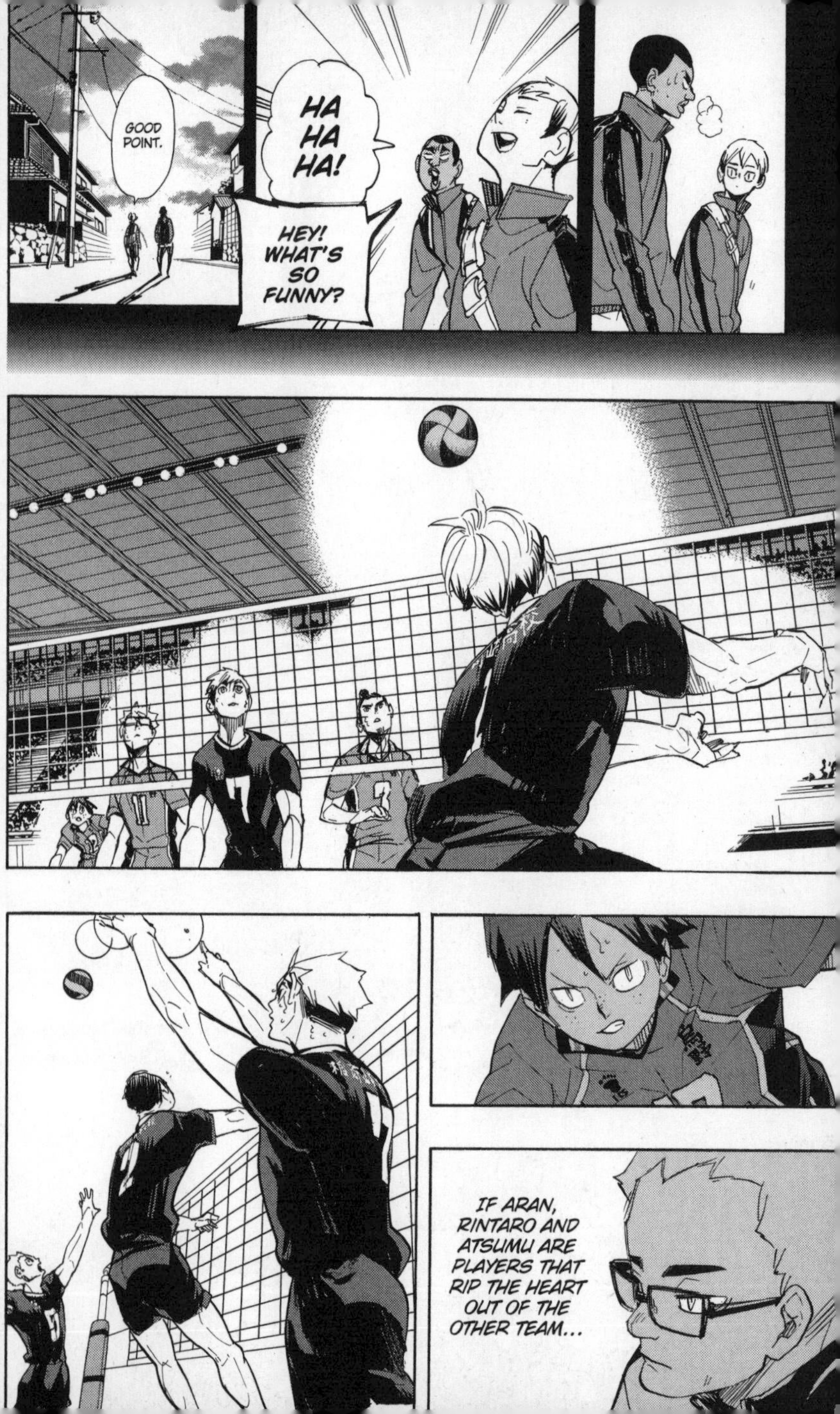
HA HA HA!
HEY! WHAT'S SO FUNNY?
GOOD POINT.
IF ARAN, RINTARO AND ATSUMU ARE PLAYERS THAT RIP THE HEART OUT OF THE OTHER TEAM...

THEN SHINSUKE'S JOB IS TO KEEP 'EM FROM TAKING IT BACK.

*SHIRT: GOOD LUCK

ZAKI

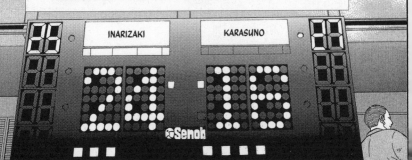

INARIZAKI HIGH SCHOOL, SET 2 SET POINT

INARIZAKI　　KARASUNO

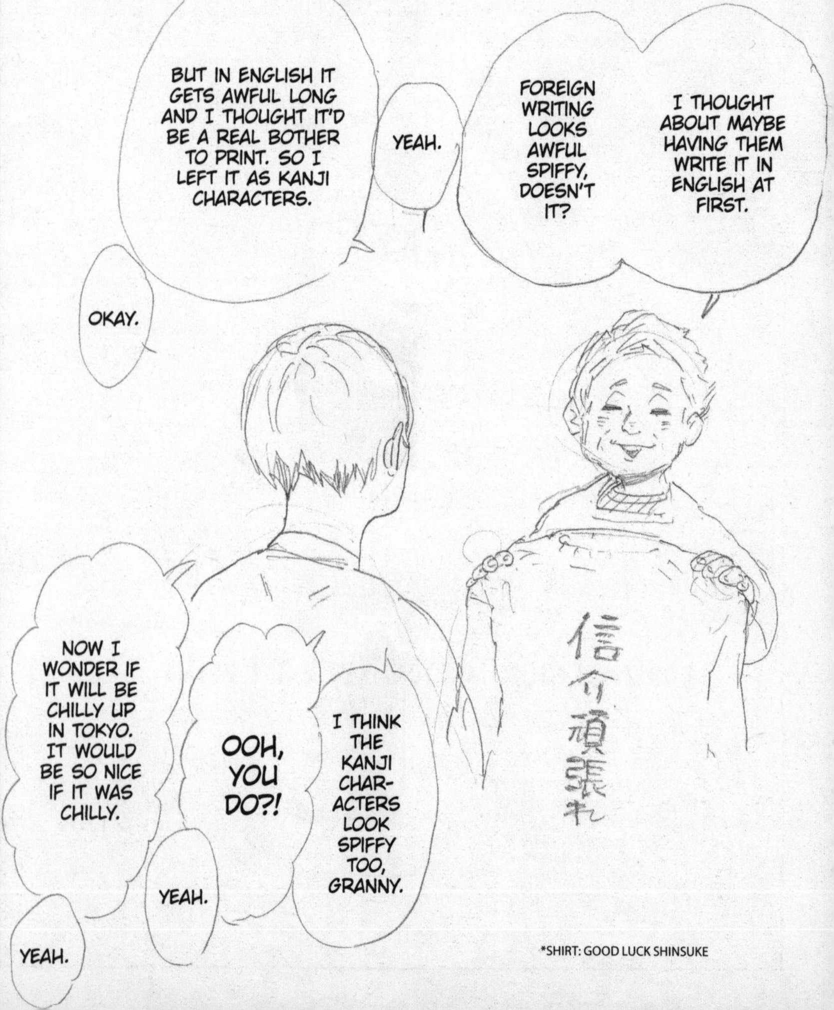
I THOUGHT ABOUT MAYBE HAVING THEM WRITE IT IN ENGLISH AT FIRST.
FOREIGN WRITING LOOKS AWFUL SPIFFY, DOESN'T IT?
YEAH.
BUT IN ENGLISH IT GETS AWFUL LONG AND I THOUGHT IT'D BE A REAL BOTHER TO PRINT. SO I LEFT IT AS KANJI CHARACTERS.
OKAY.
信介頑張れ
I THINK THE KANJI CHAR-ACTERS LOOK SPIFFY TOO, GRANNY.
OOH, YOU DO?!
NOW I WONDER IF IT WILL BE CHILLY UP IN TOKYO. IT WOULD BE SO NICE IF IT WAS CHILLY.
YEAH.
YEAH.

*SHIRT: GOOD LUCK SHINSUKE

CHAPTER 275:
Continuity and Accumulation

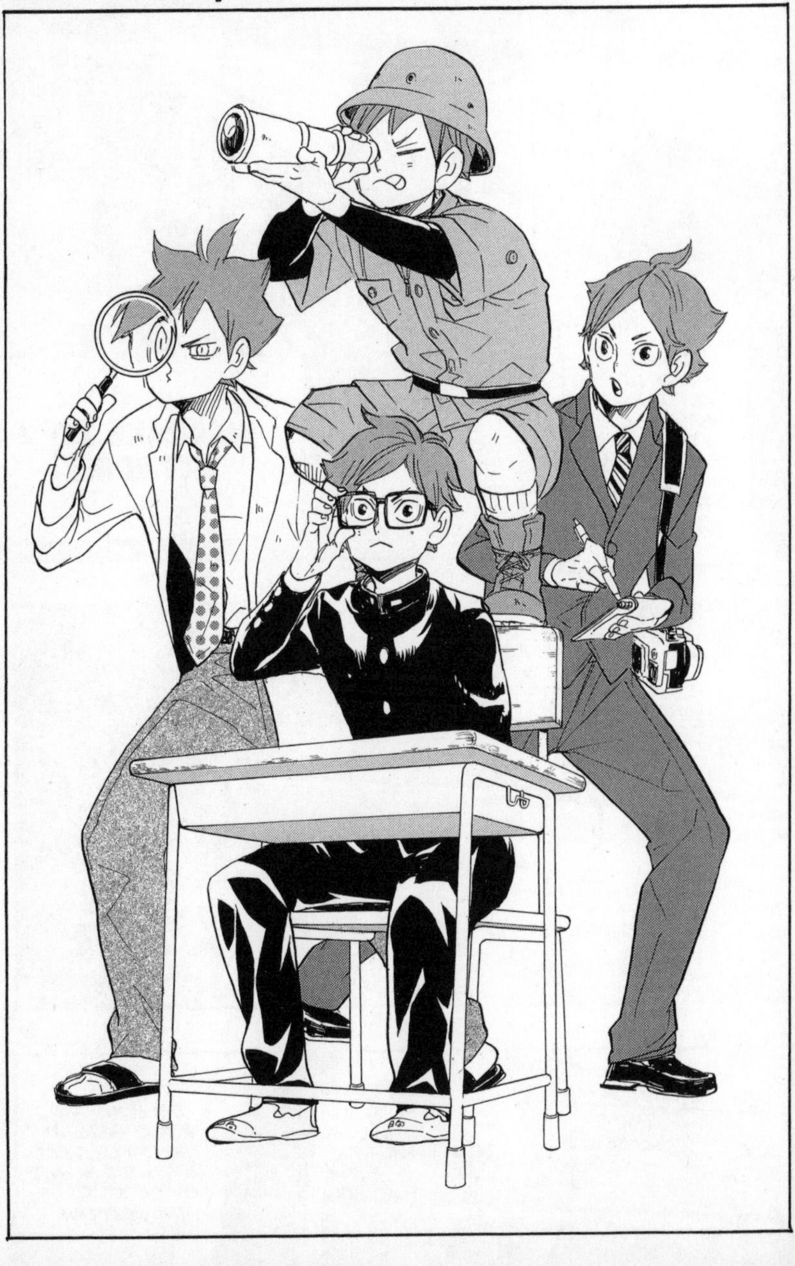

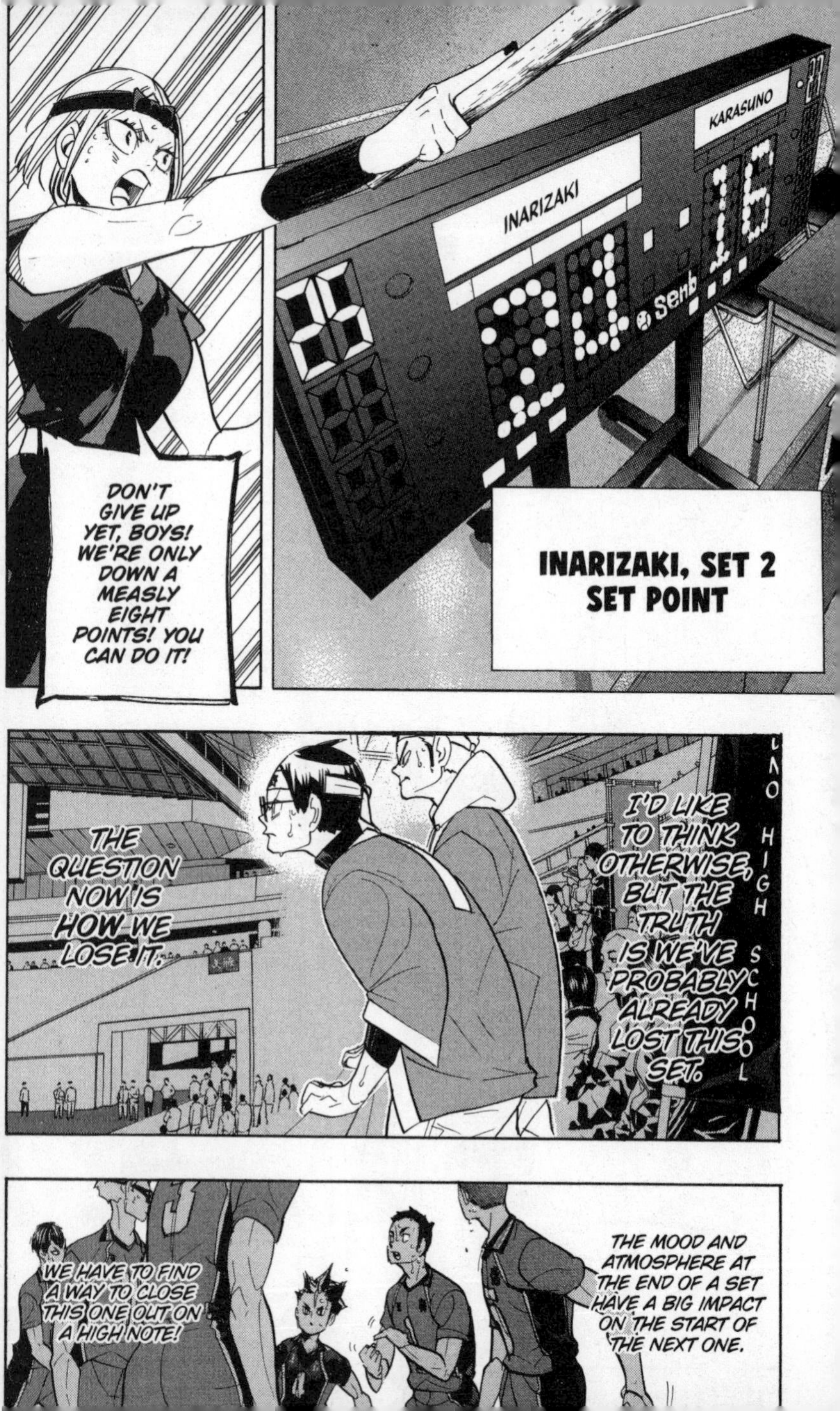
KARASUNO
INARIZAKI
INARIZAKI, SET 2 SET POINT
DON'T GIVE UP YET, BOYS! WE'RE ONLY DOWN A MEASLY EIGHT POINTS! YOU CAN DO IT!
I'D LIKE TO THINK OTHERWISE, BUT THE TRUTH IS WE'VE PROBABLY ALREADY LOST THIS SET.
THE QUESTION NOW IS HOW WE LOSE IT.
THE MOOD AND ATMOSPHERE AT THE END OF A SET HAVE A BIG IMPACT ON THE START OF THE NEXT ONE.
WE HAVE TO FIND A WAY TO CLOSE THIS ONE OUT ON A HIGH NOTE!

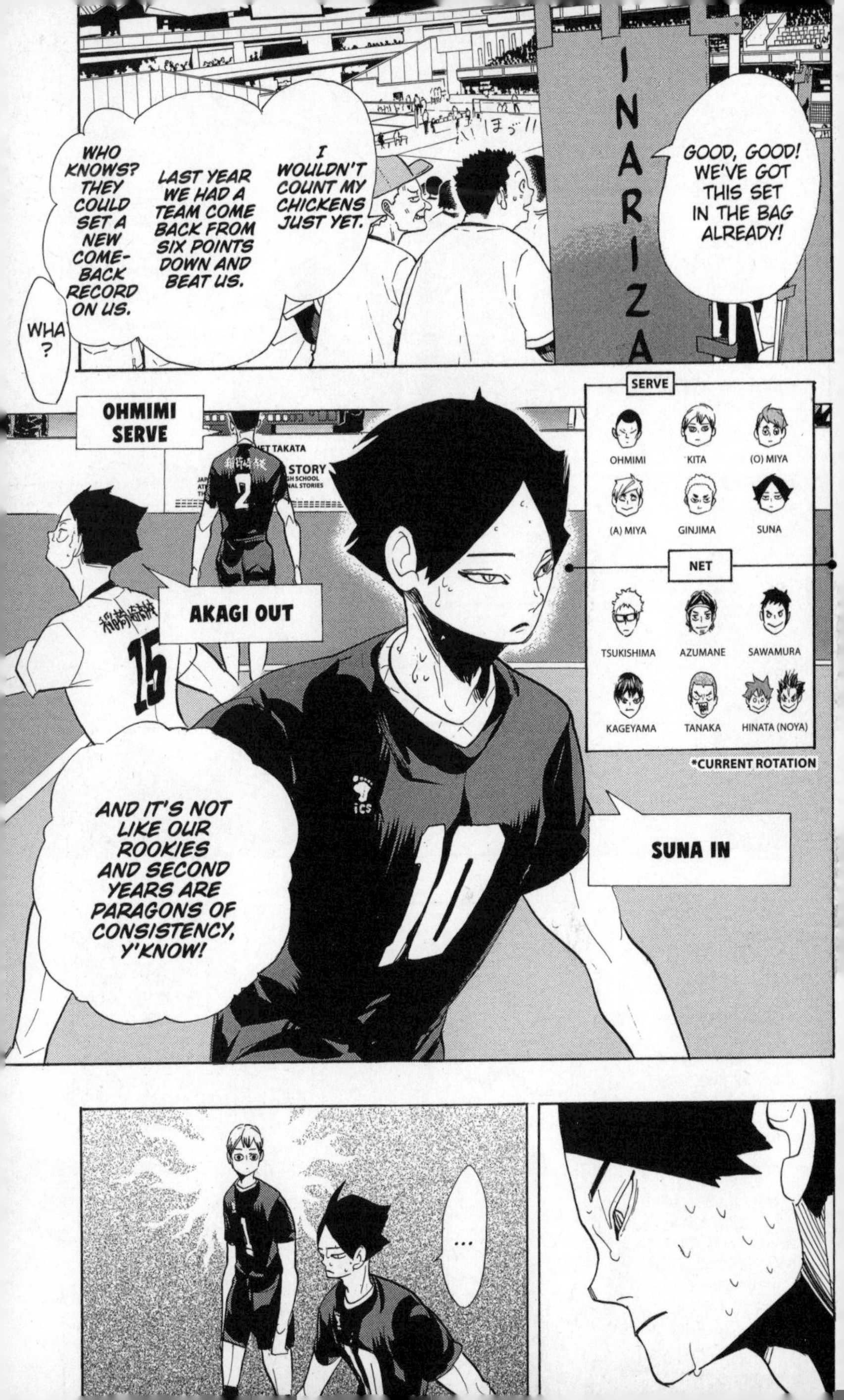
INARIZA
GOOD, GOOD! WE'VE GOT THIS SET IN THE BAG ALREADY!
I WOULDN'T COUNT MY CHICKENS JUST YET.
LAST YEAR WE HAD A TEAM COME BACK FROM SIX POINTS DOWN AND BEAT US.
WHO KNOWS? THEY COULD SET A NEW COME-BACK RECORD ON US.
WHA?
SERVE
OHMIMI
KITA
(O) MIYA
(A) MIYA
GINJIMA
SUNA
NET
TSUKISHIMA
AZUMANE
SAWAMURA
KAGEYAMA
TANAKA
HINATA (NOYA)
*CURRENT ROTATION
SUNA IN
OHMIMI SERVE
AKAGI OUT
AND IT'S NOT LIKE OUR ROOKIES AND SECOND YEARS ARE PARAGONS OF CONSISTENCY, Y'KNOW!
...

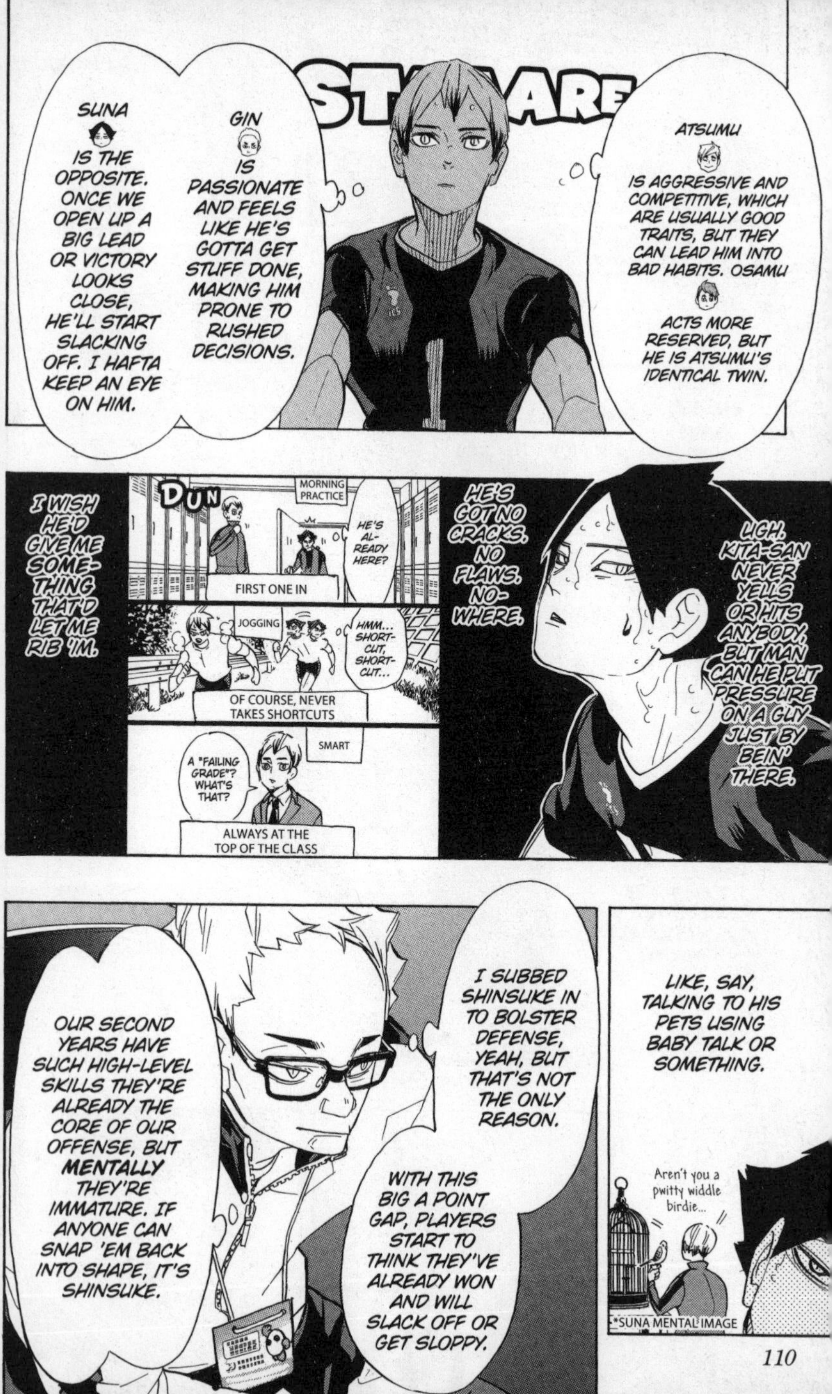

ATSUMU IS AGGRESSIVE AND COMPETITIVE, WHICH ARE USUALLY GOOD TRAITS, BUT THEY CAN LEAD HIM INTO BAD HABITS. OSAMU ACTS MORE RESERVED, BUT HE IS ATSUMU'S IDENTICAL TWIN.
GIN IS PASSIONATE AND FEELS LIKE HE'S GOTTA GET STUFF DONE, MAKING HIM PRONE TO RUSHED DECISIONS.
SUNA IS THE OPPOSITE. ONCE WE OPEN UP A BIG LEAD OR VICTORY LOOKS CLOSE, HE'LL START SLACKING OFF. I HAFTA KEEP AN EYE ON HIM.
UGH. KITA-SAN NEVER YELLS OR HITS ANYBODY, BUT MAN CAN HE PUT PRESSURE ON A GUY JUST BY BEIN' THERE.
HE'S GOT NO CRACKS. NO FLAWS. NOWHERE.
MORNING PRACTICE
DUN
HE'S ALREADY HERE?
FIRST ONE IN
HMM... SHORTCUT, SHORTCUT...
JOGGING
OF COURSE, NEVER TAKES SHORTCUTS
SMART
A "FAILING GRADE"? WHAT'S THAT?
ALWAYS AT THE TOP OF THE CLASS
I WISH HE'D GIVE ME SOMETHING THAT'D LET ME RIB 'IM.
LIKE, SAY, TALKING TO HIS PETS USING BABY TALK OR SOMETHING.
Aren't you a pwitty widdle birdie...
*SUNA MENTAL IMAGE
I SUBBED SHINSUKE IN TO BOLSTER DEFENSE, YEAH, BUT THAT'S NOT THE ONLY REASON.
WITH THIS BIG A POINT GAP, PLAYERS START TO THINK THEY'VE ALREADY WON AND WILL SLACK OFF OR GET SLOPPY.
OUR SECOND YEARS HAVE SUCH HIGH-LEVEL SKILLS THEY'RE ALREADY THE CORE OF OUR OFFENSE, BUT MENTALLY THEY'RE IMMATURE. IF ANYONE CAN SNAP 'EM BACK INTO SHAPE, IT'S SHINSUKE.

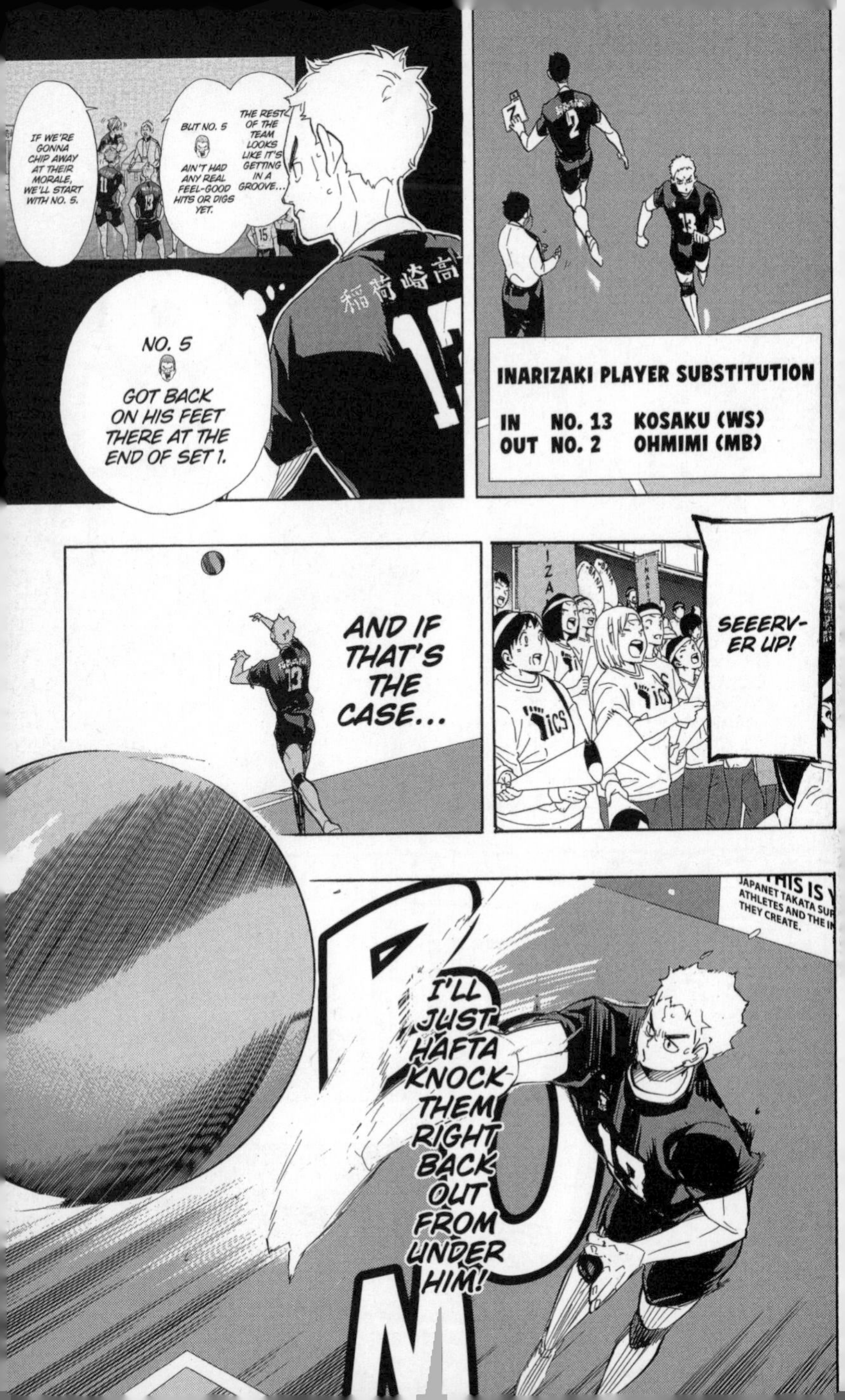
INARIZAKI PLAYER SUBSTITUTION
IN NO. 13 KOSAKU (WS)
OUT NO. 2 OHMIMI (MB)
THE REST OF THE TEAM LOOKS LIKE IT'S GETTING IN A GROOVE...
BUT NO. 5 AIN'T HAD ANY REAL FEEL-GOOD HITS OR DIGS YET.
IF WE'RE GONNA CHIP AWAY AT THEIR MORALE, WE'LL START WITH NO. 5.
NO. 5 GOT BACK ON HIS FEET THERE AT THE END OF SET 1.
SEEERV-ER UP!
AND IF THAT'S THE CASE...
I'LL JUST HAFTA KNOCK THEM RIGHT BACK OUT FROM UNDER HIM!

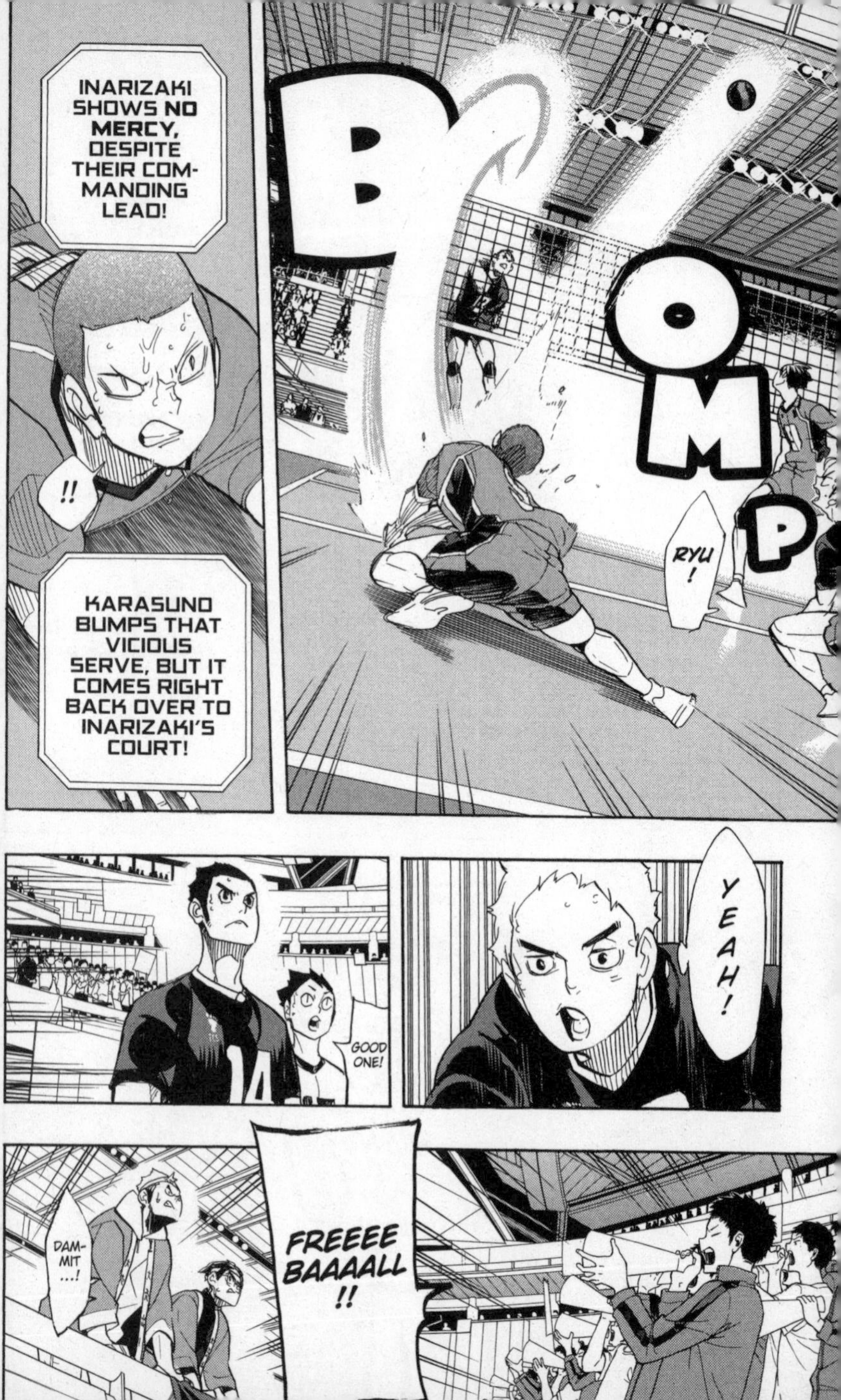
BOMP
RYU!
INARIZAKI SHOWS NO MERCY, DESPITE THEIR COMMANDING LEAD!
!!
KARASUNO BUMPS THAT VICIOUS SERVE, BUT IT COMES RIGHT BACK OVER TO INARIZAKI'S COURT!
YEAH!
GOOD ONE!
FREEEE BAAAALL!!
DAMMIT...!

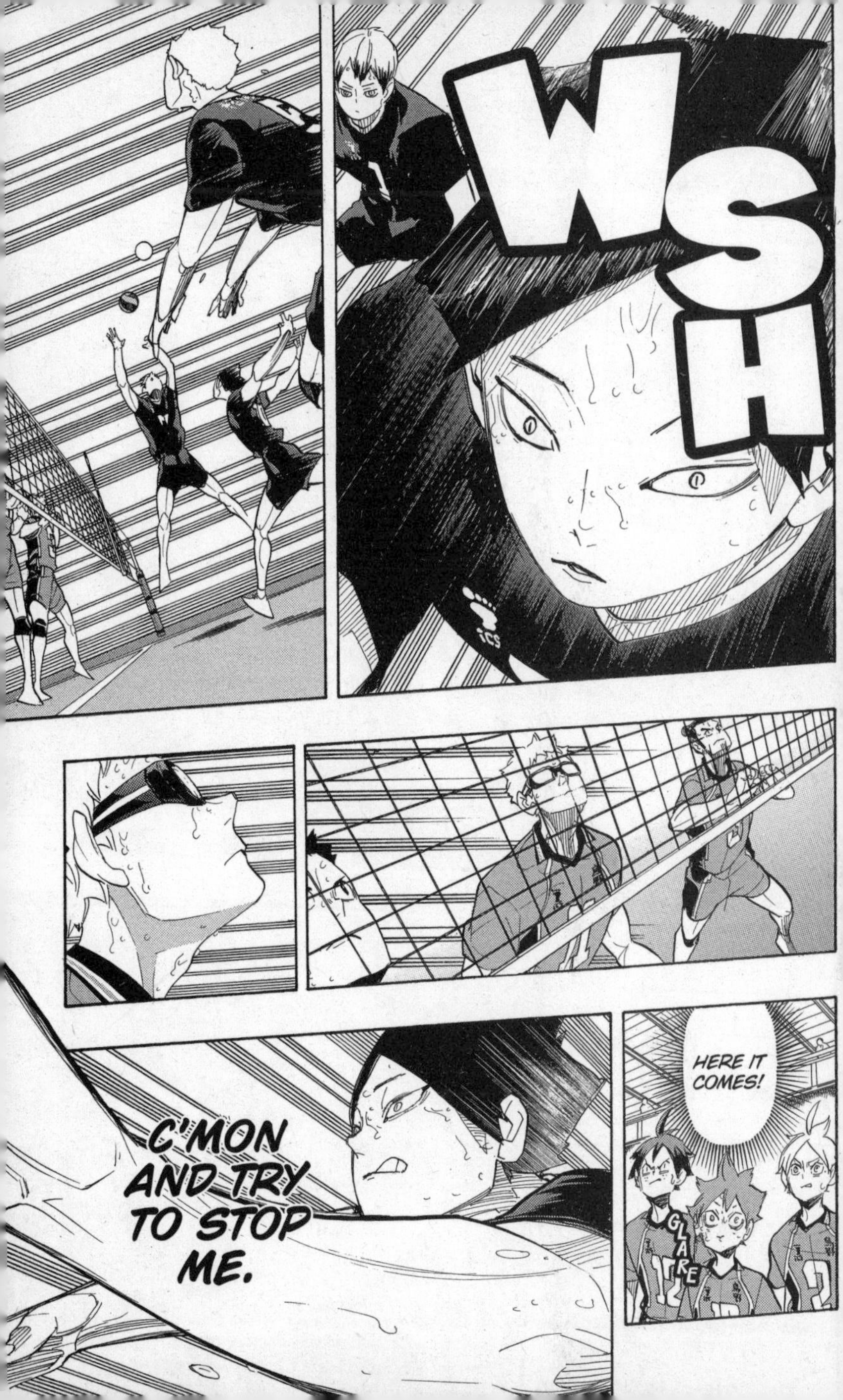
WSH
HERE IT COMES!
GLARE
C'MON AND TRY TO STOP ME.

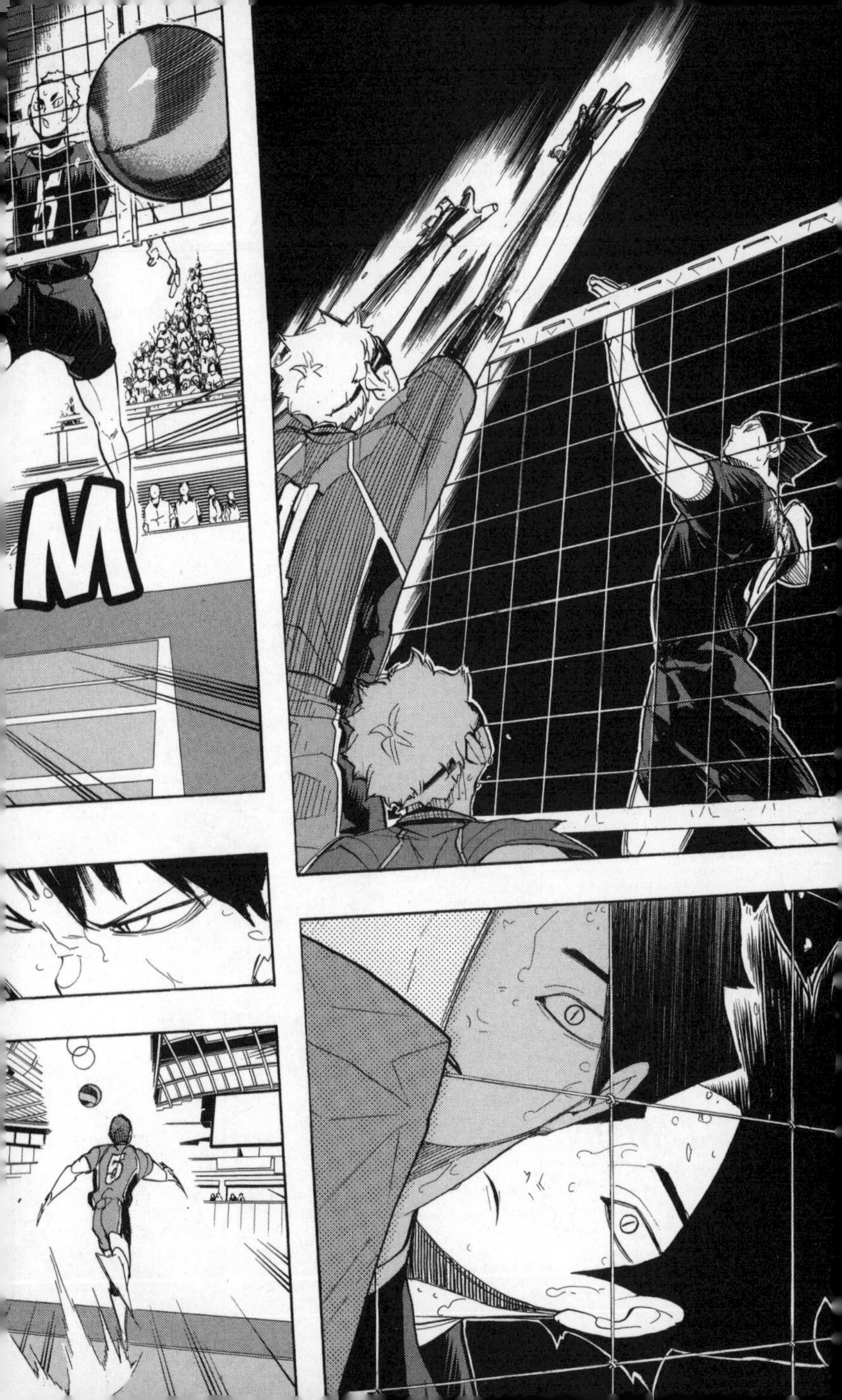
M

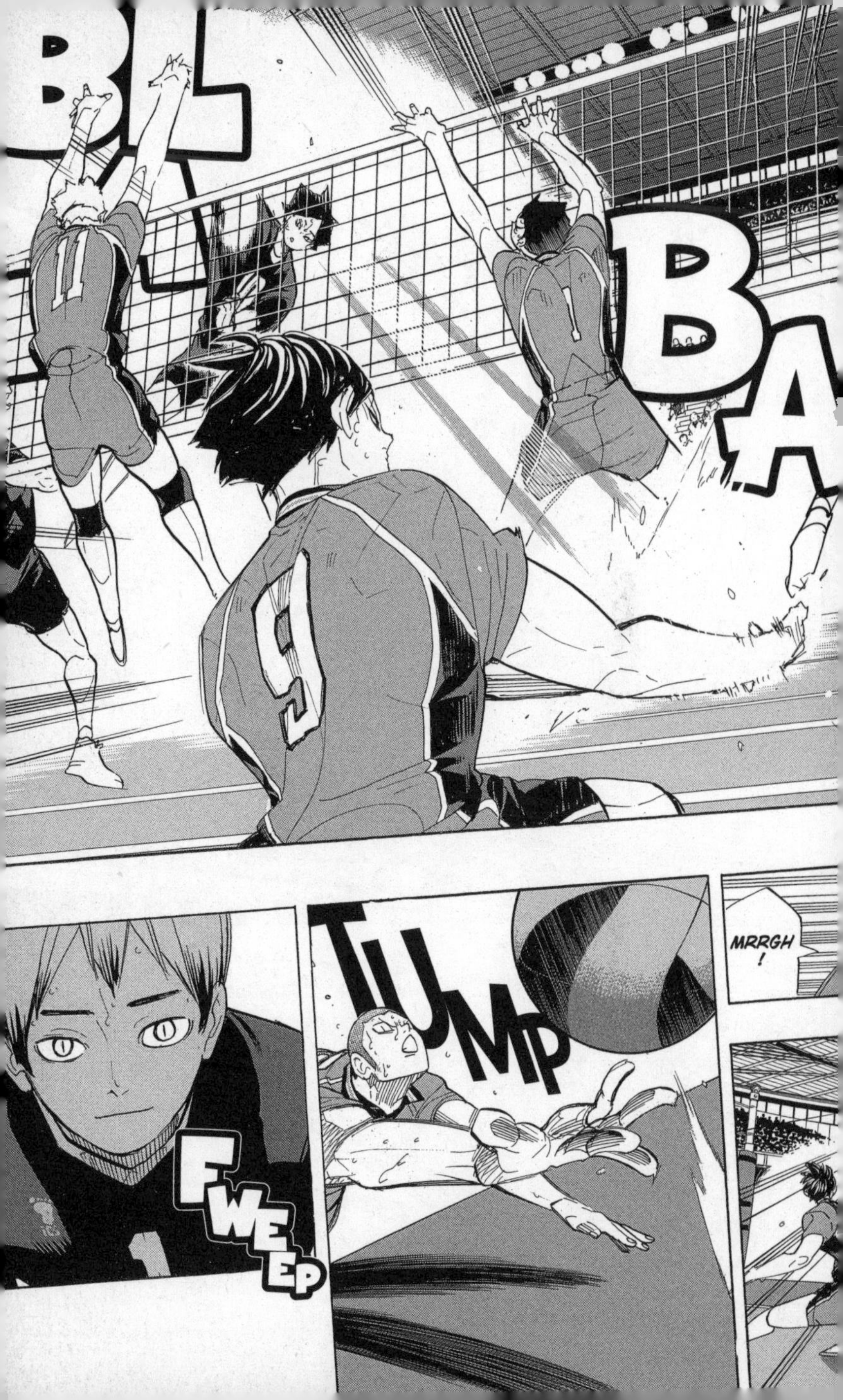
BL
BA
MRRGH !
TUMP
FWEEP

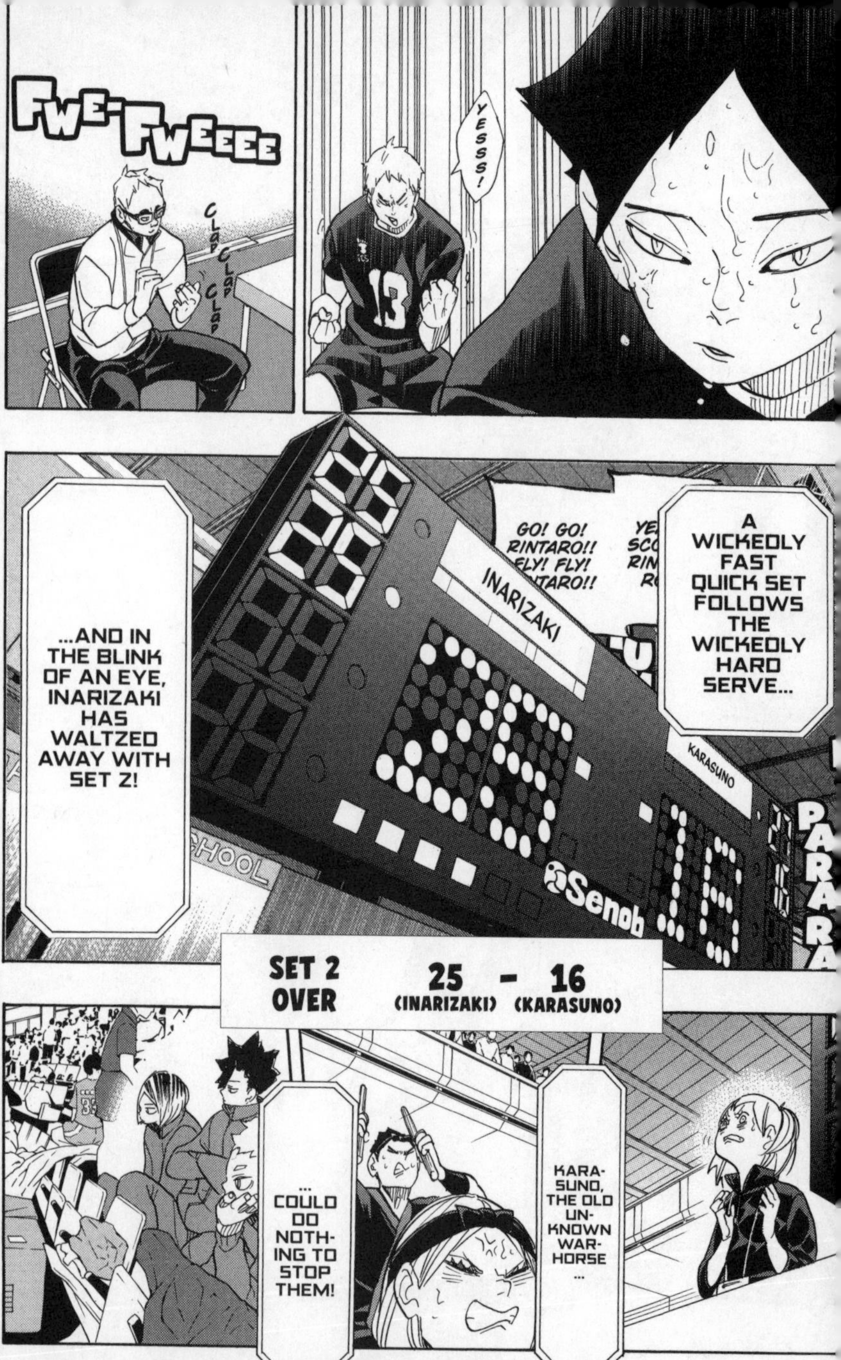
YESSS!
FWE-FWEEEE
CLAP
CLAP
CLAP
A WICKEDLY FAST QUICK SET FOLLOWS THE WICKEDLY HARD SERVE...
GO! GO! RINTARO!! FLY! FLY!
INARIZAKI
KARASUNO
Senob
PARARA
...AND IN THE BLINK OF AN EYE, INARIZAKI HAS WALTZED AWAY WITH SET 2!
SET 2 OVER 25 - 16 (INARIZAKI) (KARASUNO)
KARASUNO, THE OLD UNKNOWN WARHORSE ...
...COULD DO NOTHING TO STOP THEM!

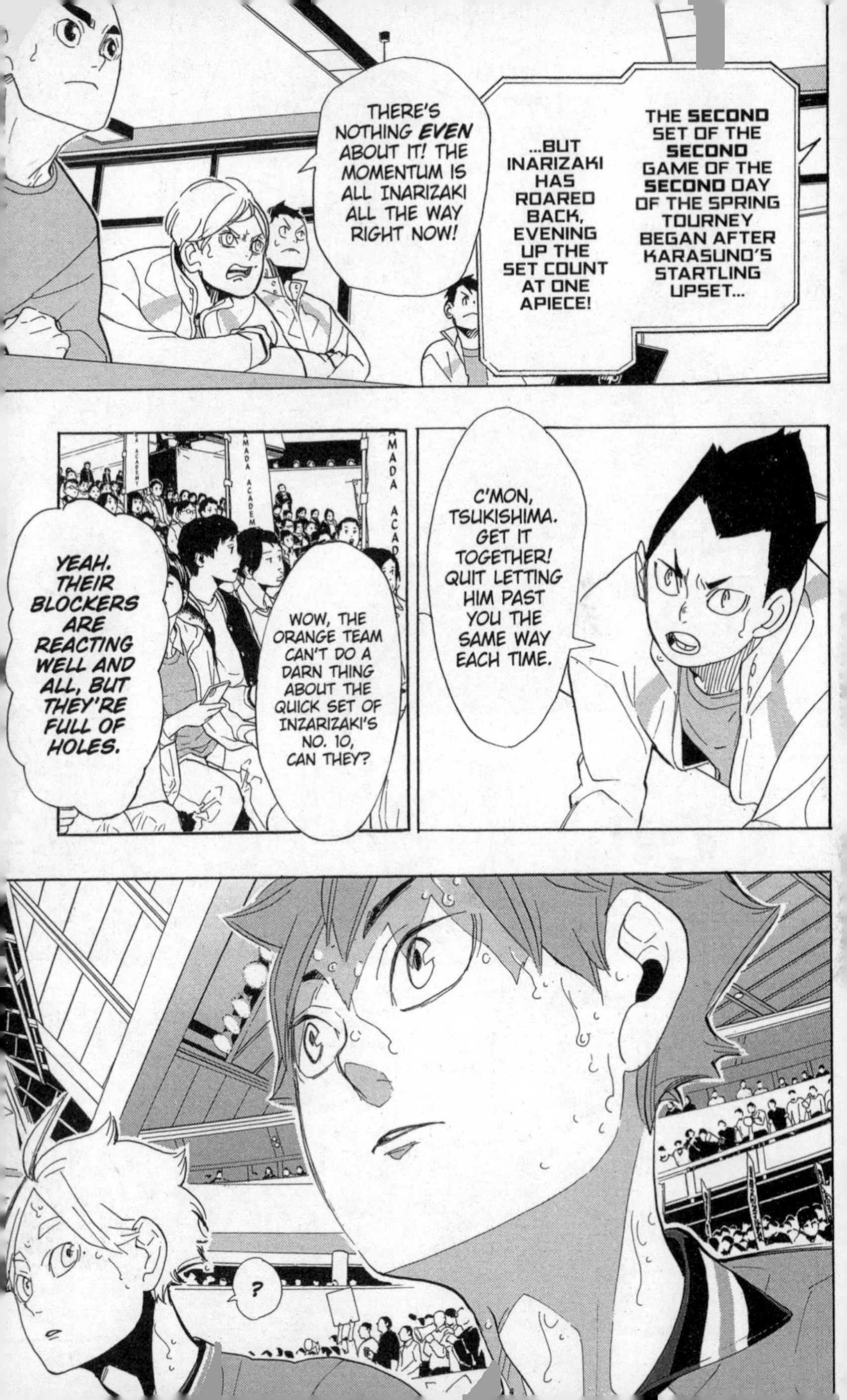
THE **SECOND** SET OF THE **SECOND** GAME OF THE **SECOND** DAY OF THE SPRING TOURNEY BEGAN AFTER KARASUNO'S STARTLING UPSET...
...BUT INARIZAKI HAS ROARED BACK, EVENING UP THE SET COUNT AT ONE APIECE!
THERE'S NOTHING ***EVEN*** ABOUT IT! THE MOMENTUM IS ALL INARIZAKI ALL THE WAY RIGHT NOW!
C'MON, TSUKISHIMA. GET IT TOGETHER! QUIT LETTING HIM PAST YOU THE SAME WAY EACH TIME.
WOW, THE ORANGE TEAM CAN'T DO A DARN THING ABOUT THE QUICK SET OF INZARIZAKI'S NO. 10, CAN THEY?
YEAH. THEIR BLOCKERS ARE REACTING WELL AND ALL, BUT THEY'RE FULL OF HOLES.
?

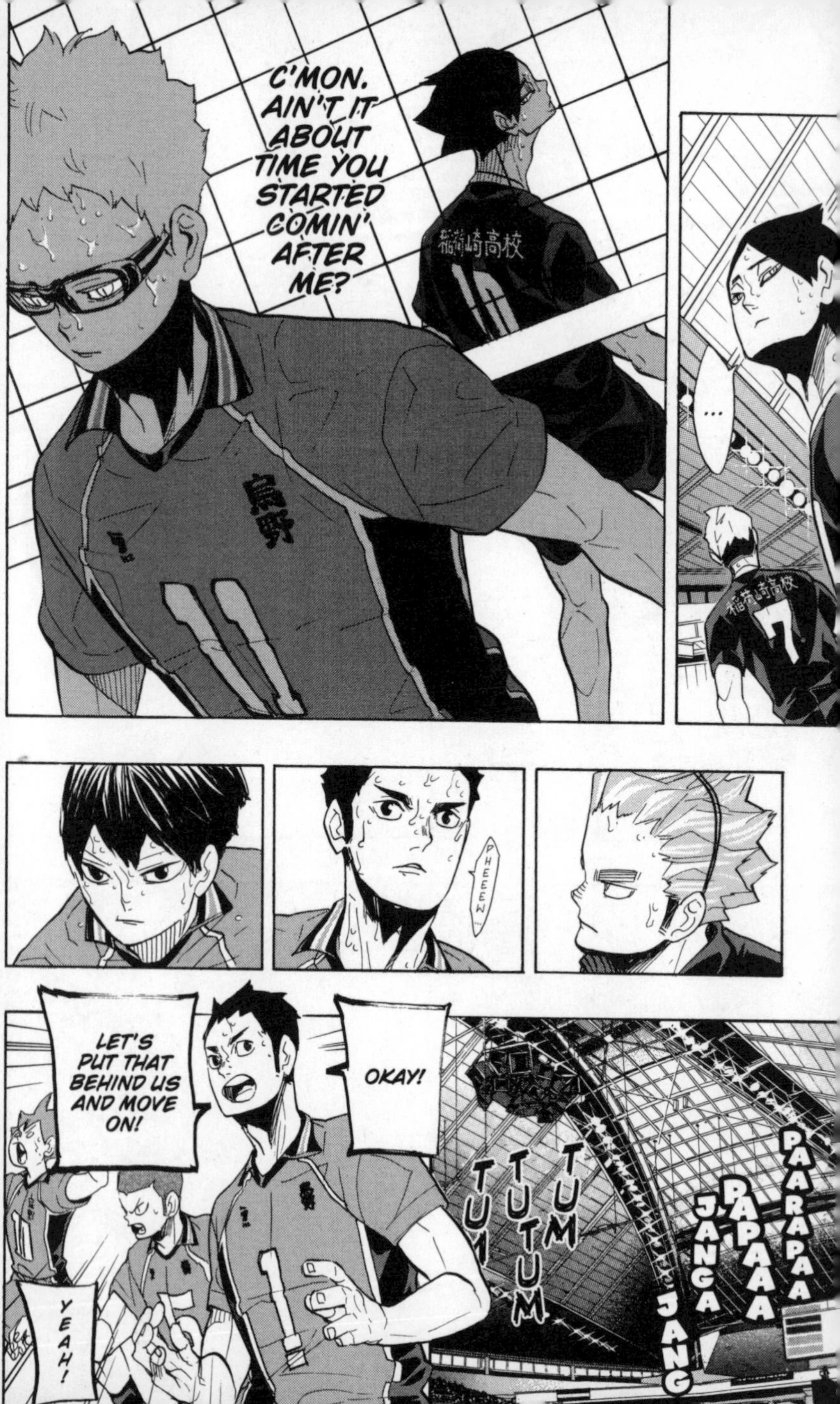
...
C'MON. AIN'T IT ABOUT TIME YOU STARTED COMIN' AFTER ME?
PHEEEEW...
PAARAPAA
PAPAAA
JANGA
JANG
TUM
TUTUM
TUM
LET'S PUT THAT BEHIND US AND MOVE ON!
OKAY!
YEAH!

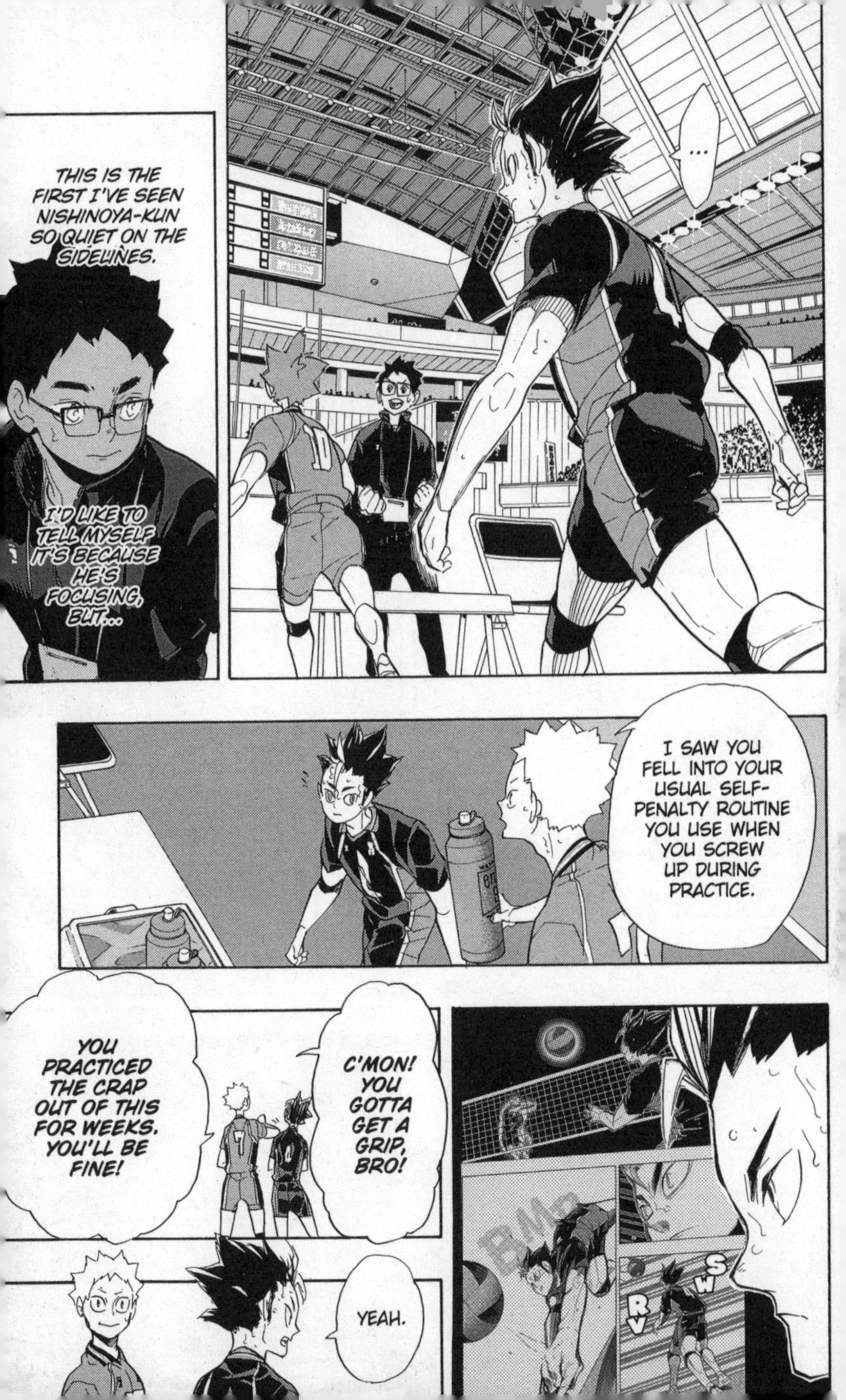
...
THIS IS THE FIRST I'VE SEEN NISHINOYA-KUN SO QUIET ON THE SIDELINES.
I'D LIKE TO TELL MYSELF IT'S BECAUSE HE'S FOCUSING, BUT...
I SAW YOU FELL INTO YOUR USUAL SELF-PENALTY ROUTINE YOU USE WHEN YOU SCREW UP DURING PRACTICE.
C'MON! YOU GOTTA GET A GRIP, BRO!
YOU PRACTICED THE CRAP OUT OF THIS FOR WEEKS. YOU'LL BE FINE!
YEAH.

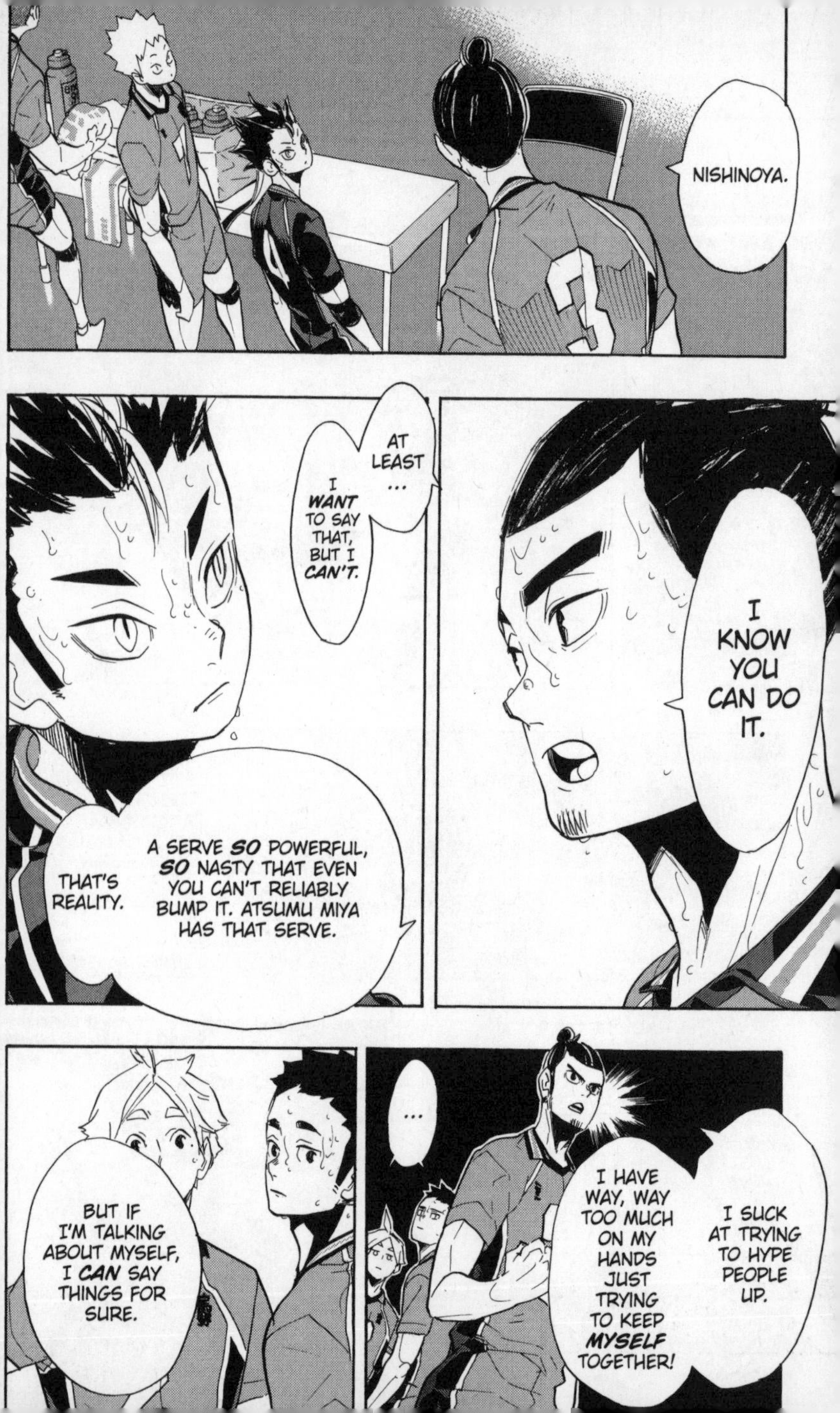
NISHINOYA.
I KNOW YOU CAN DO IT.
AT LEAST...
I *WANT* TO SAY THAT, BUT I *CAN'T*.
A SERVE *SO* POWERFUL, *SO* NASTY THAT EVEN YOU CAN'T RELIABLY BUMP IT. ATSUMU MIYA HAS THAT SERVE.
THAT'S REALITY.
I SUCK AT TRYING TO HYPE PEOPLE UP.
I HAVE WAY, WAY TOO MUCH ON MY HANDS JUST TRYING TO KEEP *MYSELF* TOGETHER!
...
BUT IF I'M TALKING ABOUT MYSELF, I *CAN* SAY THINGS FOR SURE.

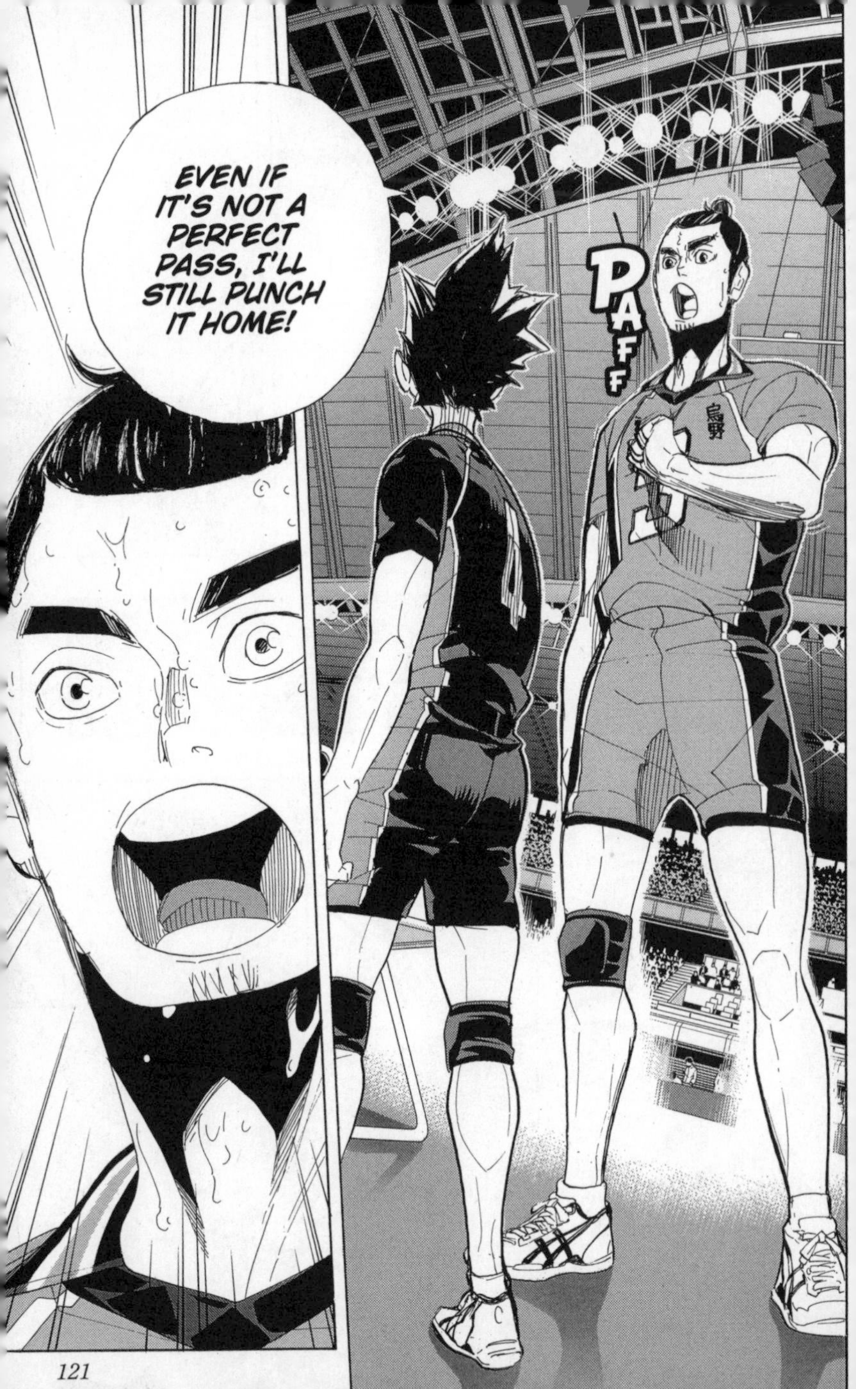
PAFF
EVEN IF IT'S NOT A PERFECT PASS, I'LL STILL PUNCH IT HOME!

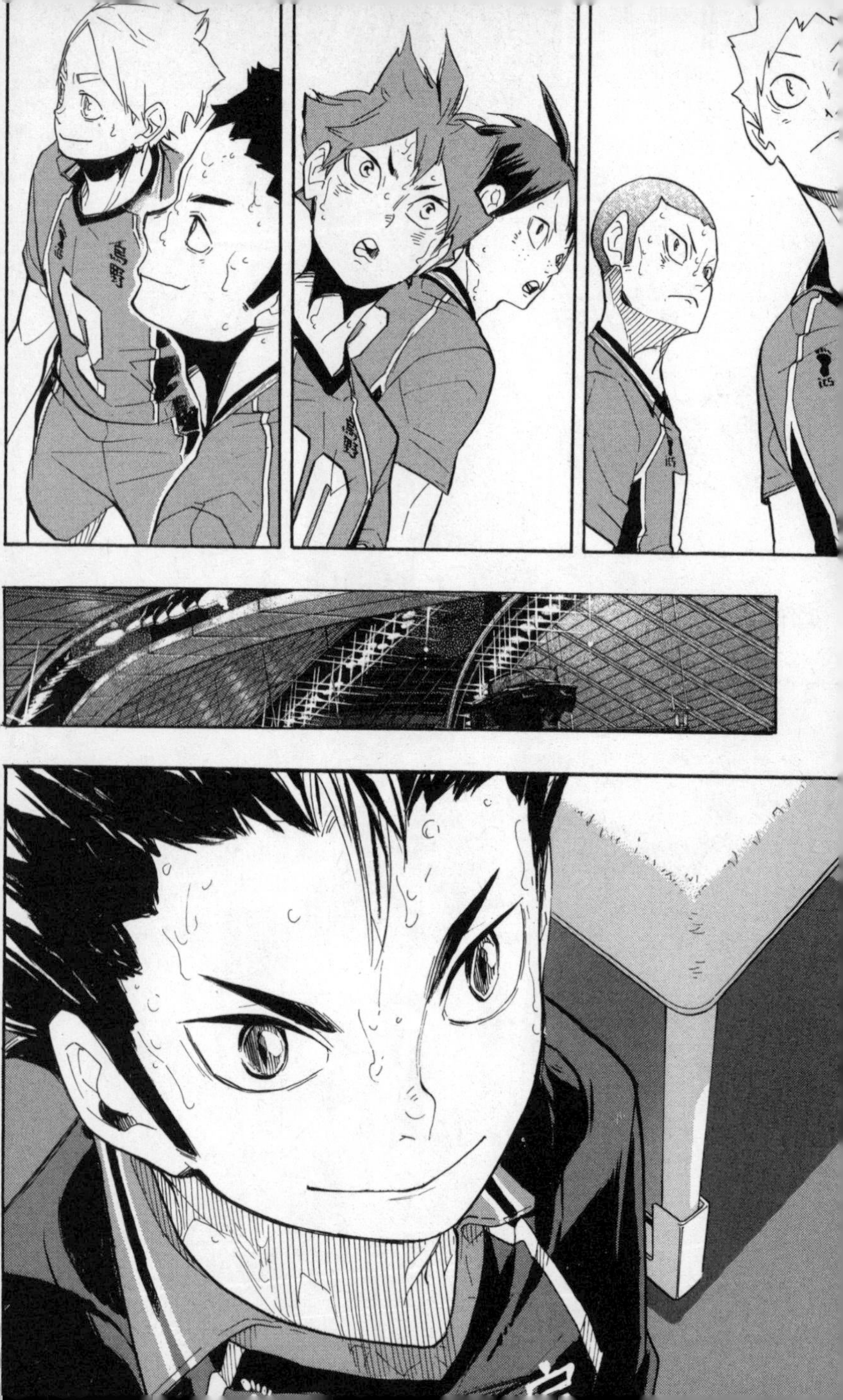

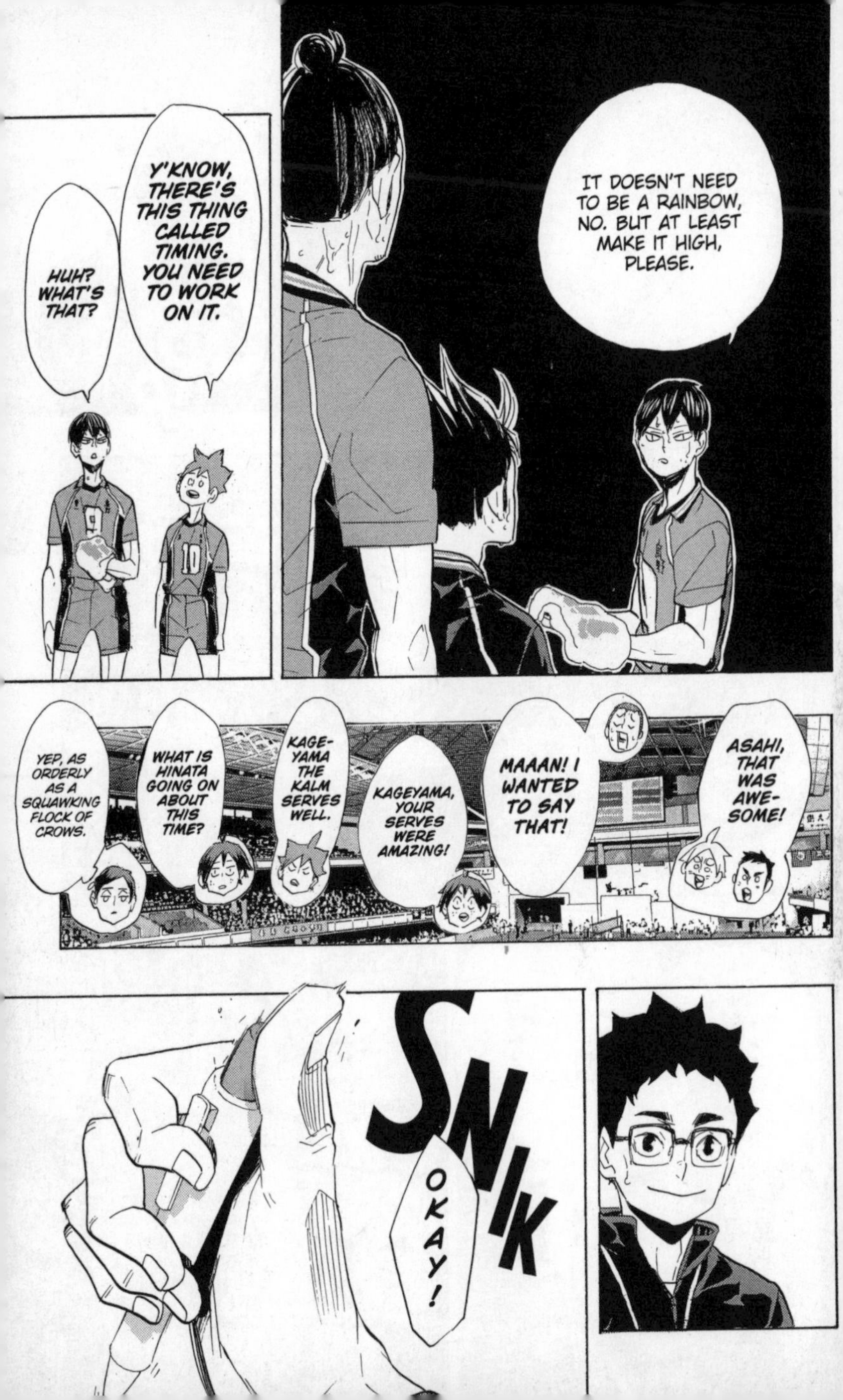
IT DOESN'T NEED TO BE A RAINBOW, NO. BUT AT LEAST MAKE IT HIGH, PLEASE.
Y'KNOW, THERE'S THIS THING CALLED TIMING. YOU NEED TO WORK ON IT.
HUH? WHAT'S THAT?
ASAHI, THAT WAS AWESOME!
MAAAN! I WANTED TO SAY THAT!
KAGEYAMA, YOUR SERVES WERE AMAZING!
KAGE-YAMA THE KALM SERVES WELL.
WHAT IS HINATA GOING ON ABOUT THIS TIME?
YEP, AS ORDERLY AS A SQUAWKING FLOCK OF CROWS.
SNIK
OKAY!

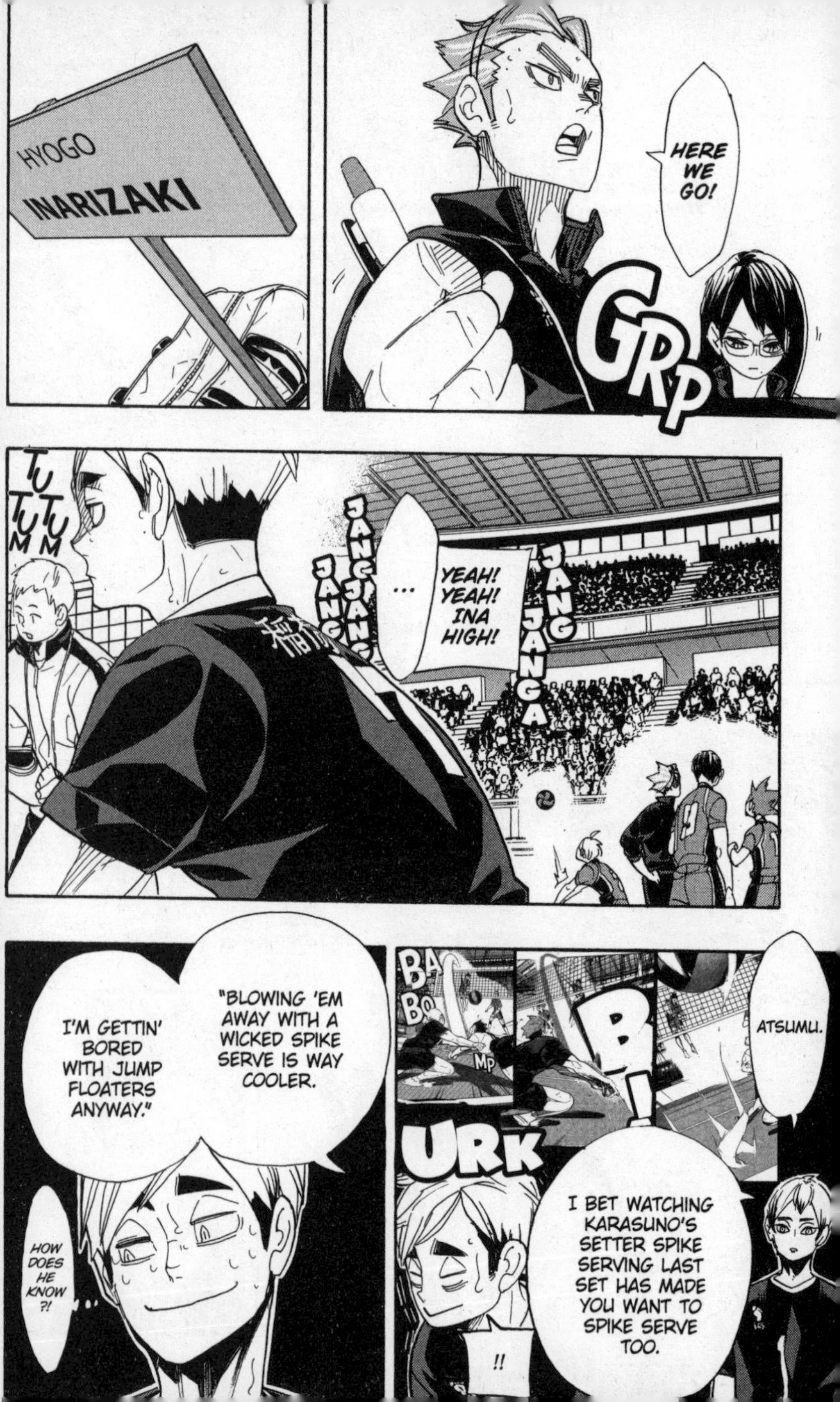
HERE WE GO!
GRP
HYOGO
INARIZAKI
JANG JANGA
YEAH! YEAH! INA HIGH!
...
JANG JANG JANG
TUTUM TUTUM
ATSUMU.
B!
BABOMP
URK
I BET WATCHING KARASUNO'S SETTER SPIKE SERVING LAST SET HAS MADE YOU WANT TO SPIKE SERVE TOO.
!!
"BLOWING 'EM AWAY WITH A WICKED SPIKE SERVE IS WAY COOLER.
I'M GETTIN' BORED WITH JUMP FLOATERS ANYWAY."
HOW DOES HE KNOW ?!
...

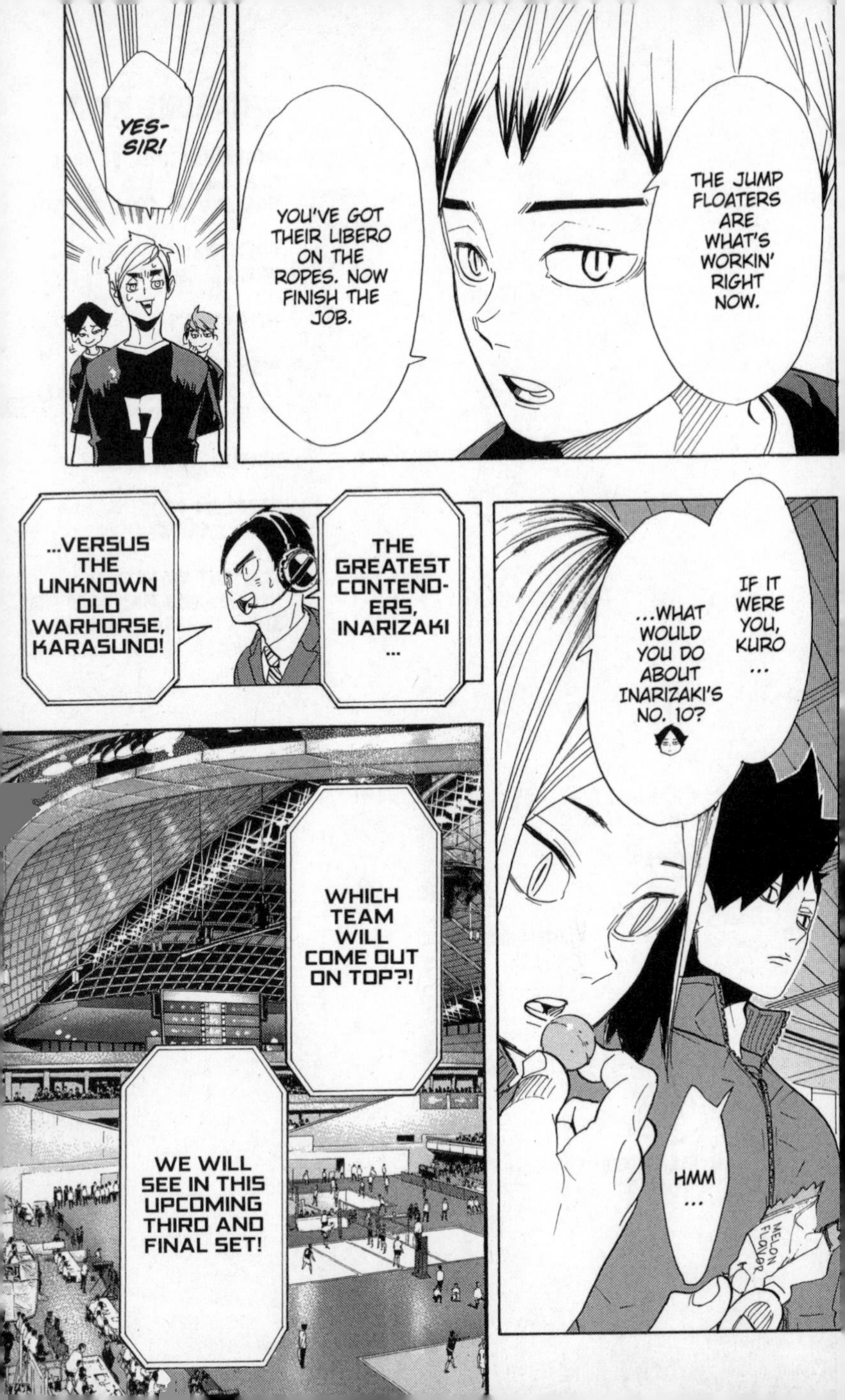
THE JUMP FLOATERS ARE WHAT'S WORKIN' RIGHT NOW.
YOU'VE GOT THEIR LIBERO ON THE ROPES. NOW FINISH THE JOB.
YES-SIR!
IF IT WERE YOU, KURO...
...WHAT WOULD YOU DO ABOUT INARIZAKI'S NO. 10?
HMM...
MELON FLAVOR
THE GREATEST CONTENDERS, INARIZAKI...
...VERSUS THE UNKNOWN OLD WARHORSE, KARASUNO!
WHICH TEAM WILL COME OUT ON TOP?!
WE WILL SEE IN THIS UPCOMING THIRD AND FINAL SET!

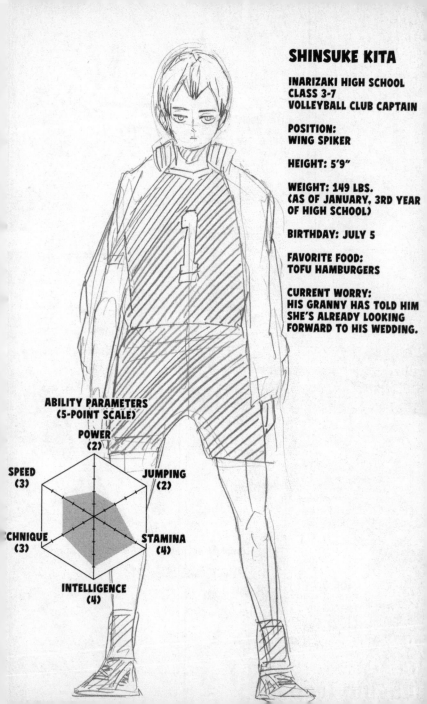

SHINSUKE KITA

**INARIZAKI HIGH SCHOOL
CLASS 3-7
VOLLEYBALL CLUB CAPTAIN**

**POSITION:
WING SPIKER**

HEIGHT: 5'9"

**WEIGHT: 149 LBS.
(AS OF JANUARY, 3RD YEAR
OF HIGH SCHOOL)**

BIRTHDAY: JULY 5

**FAVORITE FOOD:
TOFU HAMBURGERS**

**CURRENT WORRY:
HIS GRANNY HAS TOLD HIM
SHE'S ALREADY LOOKING
FORWARD TO HIS WEDDING.**

**ABILITY PARAMETERS
(5-POINT SCALE)**

POWER
(2)

SPEED
(3)

JUMPING
(2)

CHNIQUE
(3)

STAMINA
(4)

INTELLIGENCE
(4)

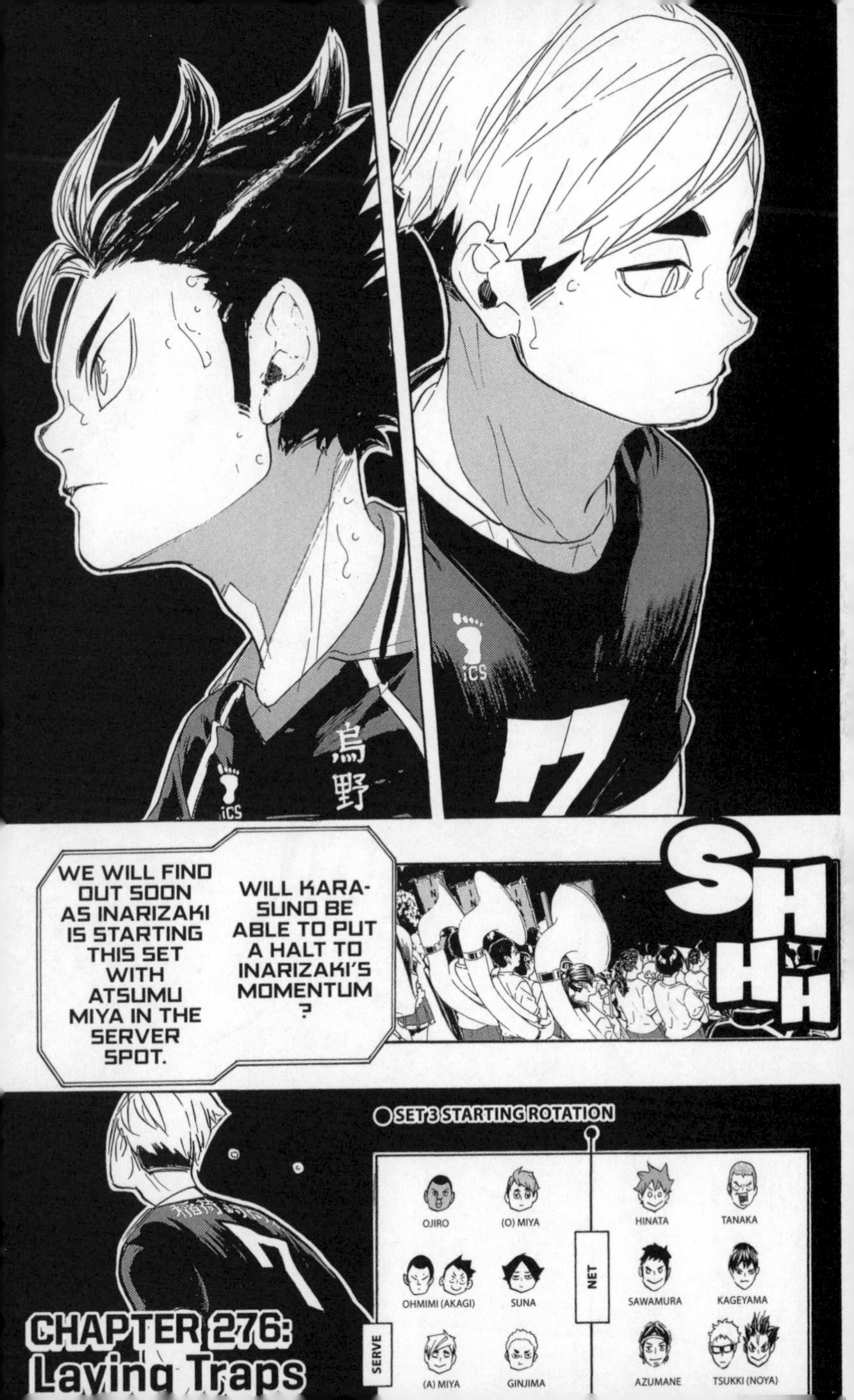
SHHHH
WILL KARA-SUNO BE ABLE TO PUT A HALT TO INARIZAKI'S MOMENTUM ?
WE WILL FIND OUT SOON AS INARIZAKI IS STARTING THIS SET WITH ATSUMU MIYA IN THE SERVER SPOT.
SET 3 STARTING ROTATION
NET
SERVE
OJIRO
(O) MIYA
HINATA
TANAKA
OHMIMI (AKAGI)
SUNA
SAWAMURA
KAGEYAMA
(A) MIYA
GINJIMA
AZUMANE
TSUKKI (NOYA)
CHAPTER 276:
Laying Traps

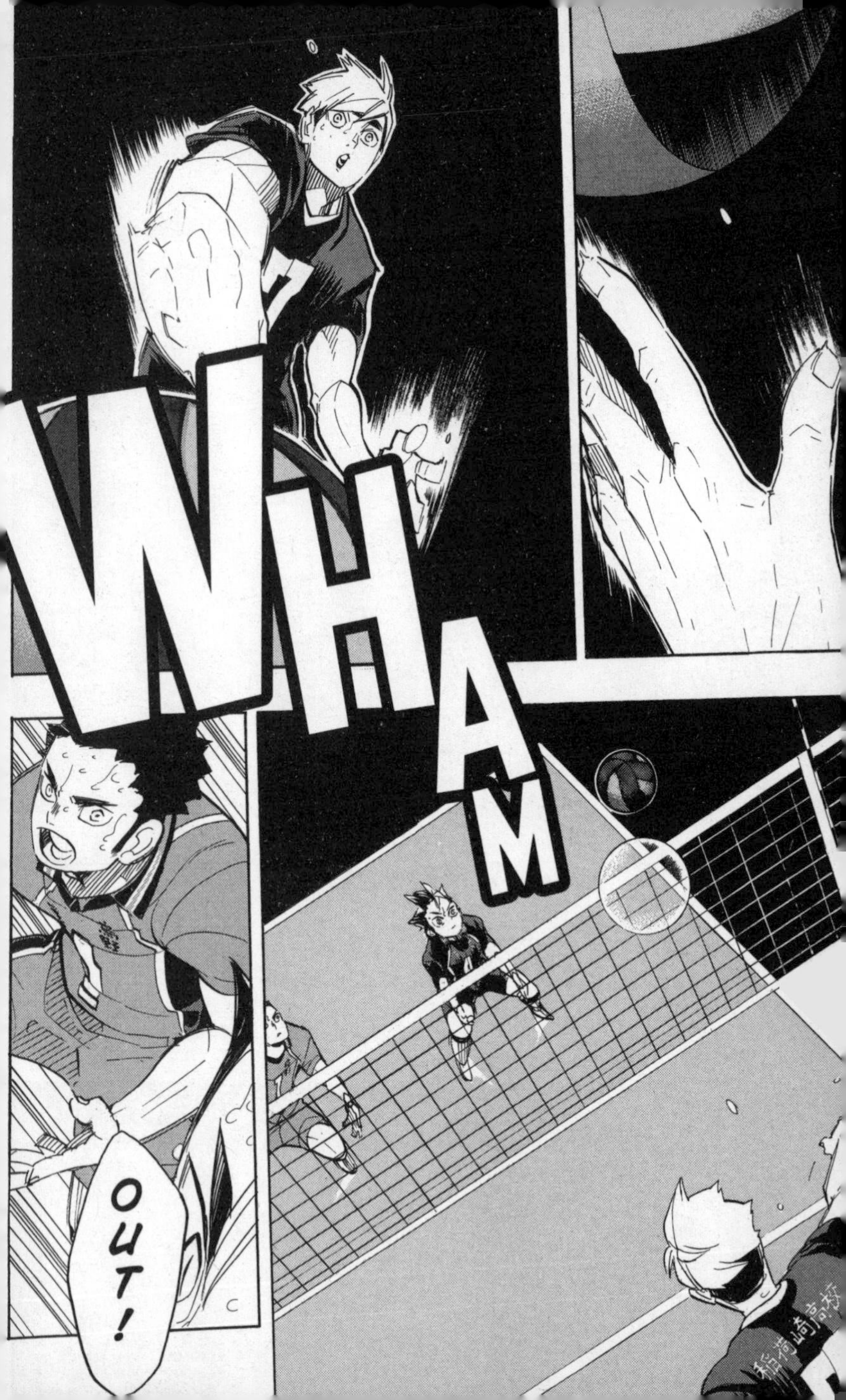
WHAM
OUT!

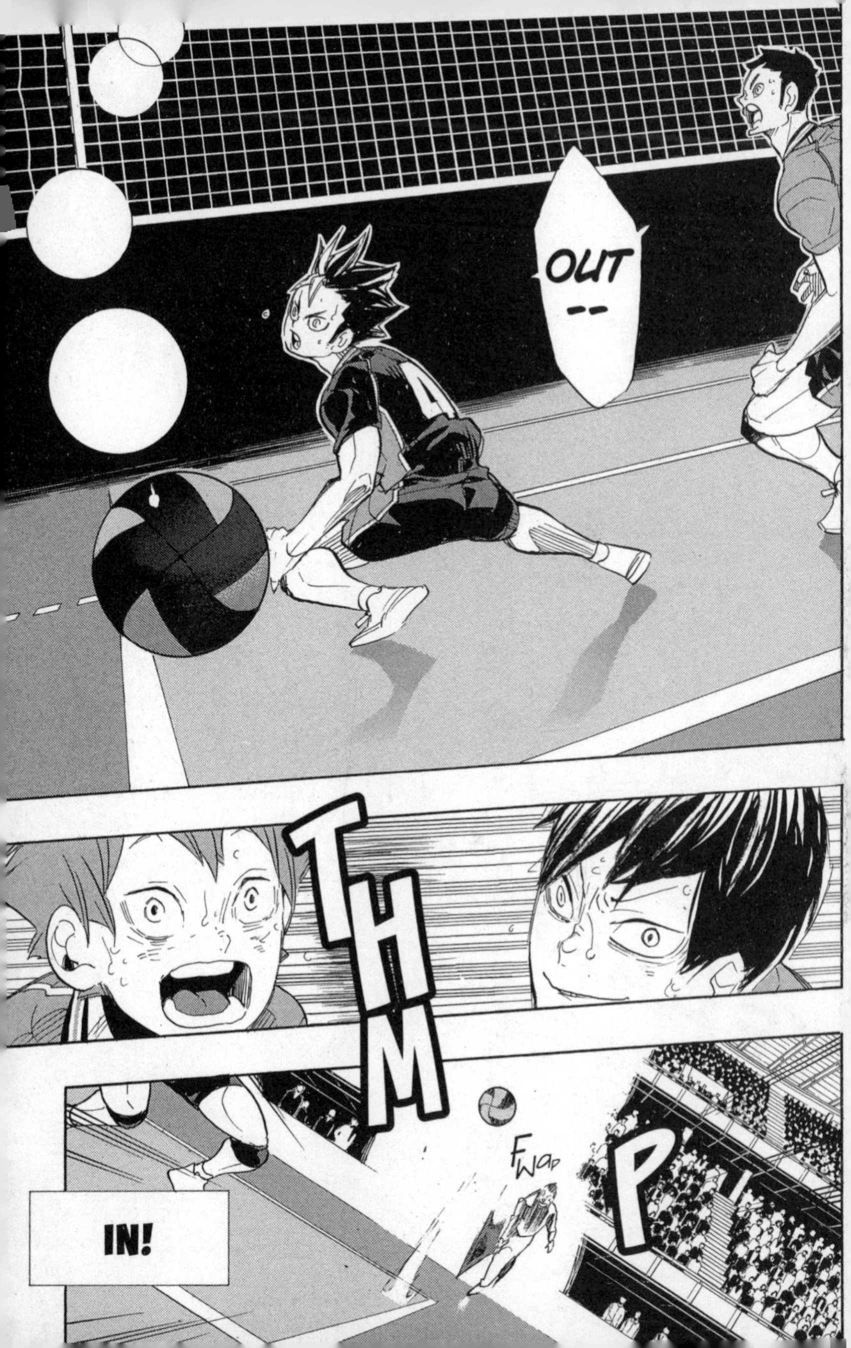
OUT --
THMP
FWAP
IN!

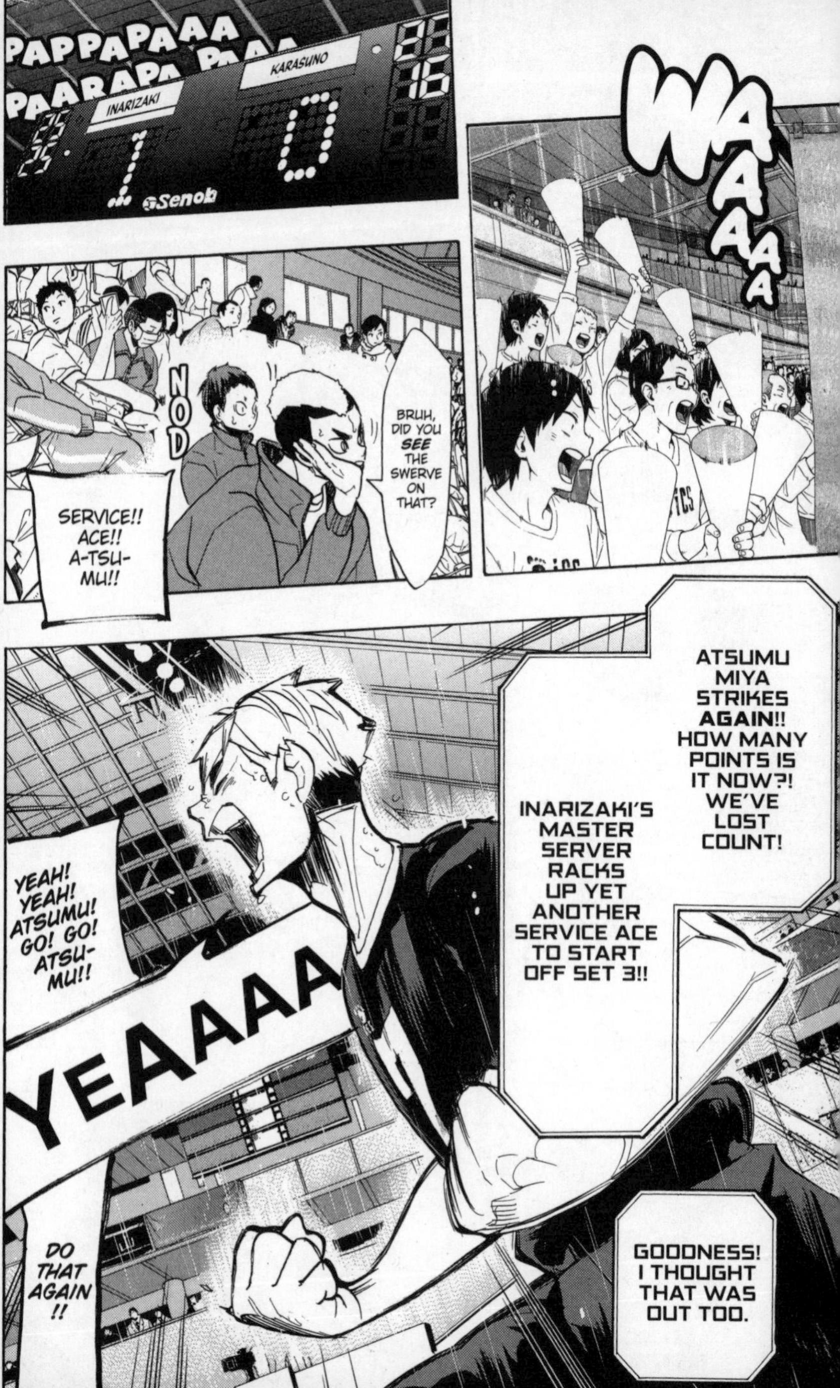
WAAAAAA
PAPPAPAAA
PAARAPA PAAA
KARASUNO
INARIZAKI
1
0
16
Senoh
BRUH, DID YOU SEE THE SWERVE ON THAT?
NOD
SERVICE!! ACE!! A-TSU-MU!!
ATSUMU MIYA STRIKES AGAIN!! HOW MANY POINTS IS IT NOW?! WE'VE LOST COUNT!
INARIZAKI'S MASTER SERVER RACKS UP YET ANOTHER SERVICE ACE TO START OFF SET 3!!
YEAH! YEAH! ATSUMU! GO! GO! ATSU-MU!!
YEAAAA
GOODNESS! I THOUGHT THAT WAS OUT TOO.
DO THAT AGAIN!!

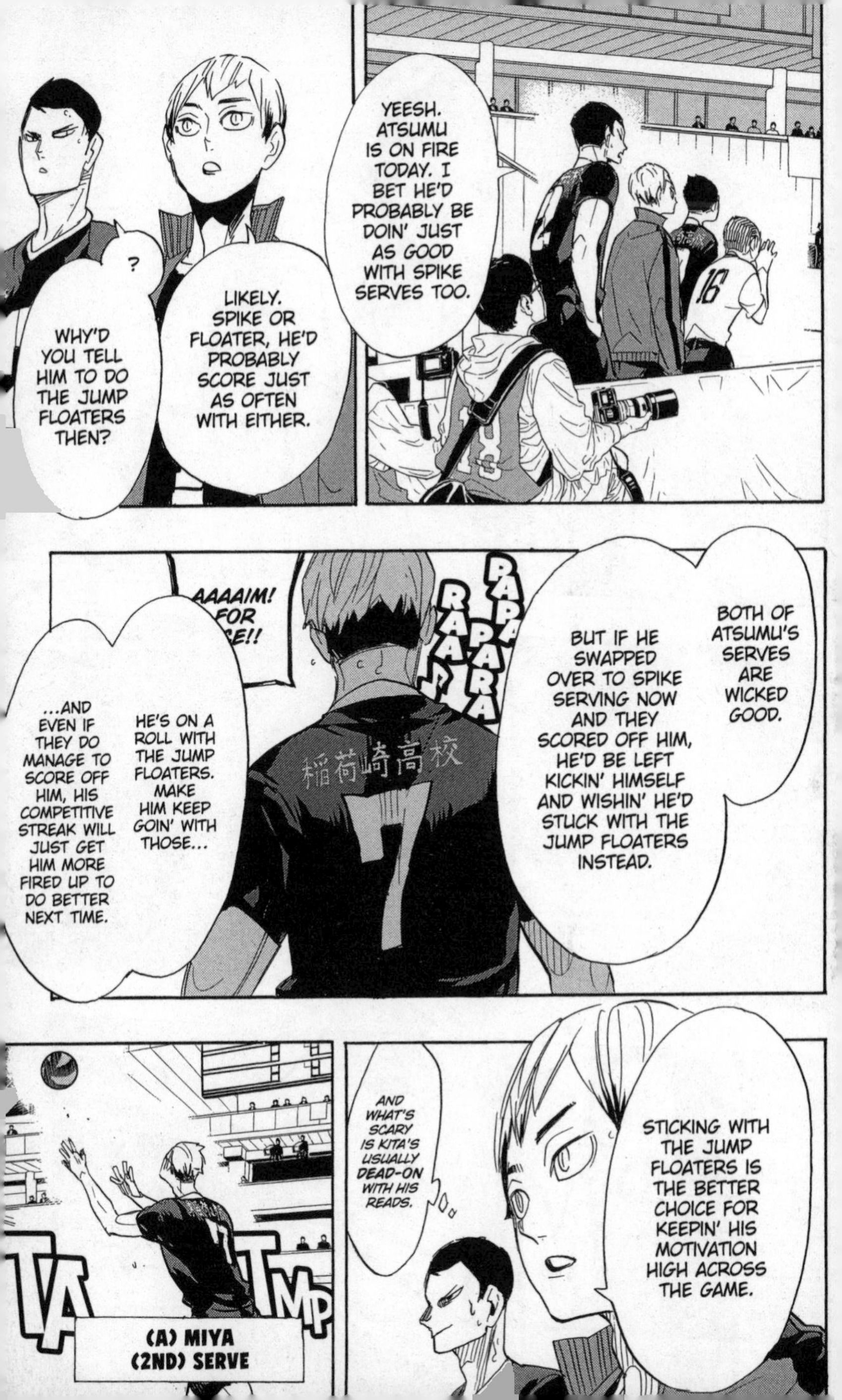
YEESH. ATSUMU IS ON FIRE TODAY. I BET HE'D PROBABLY BE DOIN' JUST AS GOOD WITH SPIKE SERVES TOO.
LIKELY. SPIKE OR FLOATER, HE'D PROBABLY SCORE JUST AS OFTEN WITH EITHER.
?
WHY'D YOU TELL HIM TO DO THE JUMP FLOATERS THEN?
BOTH OF ATSUMU'S SERVES ARE WICKED GOOD.
BUT IF HE SWAPPED OVER TO SPIKE SERVING NOW AND THEY SCORED OFF HIM, HE'D BE LEFT KICKIN' HIMSELF AND WISHIN' HE'D STUCK WITH THE JUMP FLOATERS INSTEAD.
PAPA
PARA
AAAAIM! FOR
HE'S ON A ROLL WITH THE JUMP FLOATERS. MAKE HIM KEEP GOIN' WITH THOSE...
...AND EVEN IF THEY DO MANAGE TO SCORE OFF HIM, HIS COMPETITIVE STREAK WILL JUST GET HIM MORE FIRED UP TO DO BETTER NEXT TIME.
STICKING WITH THE JUMP FLOATERS IS THE BETTER CHOICE FOR KEEPIN' HIS MOTIVATION HIGH ACROSS THE GAME.
AND WHAT'S SCARY IS KITA'S USUALLY DEAD-ON WITH HIS READS.
TA
TMP
(A) MIYA (2ND) SERVE

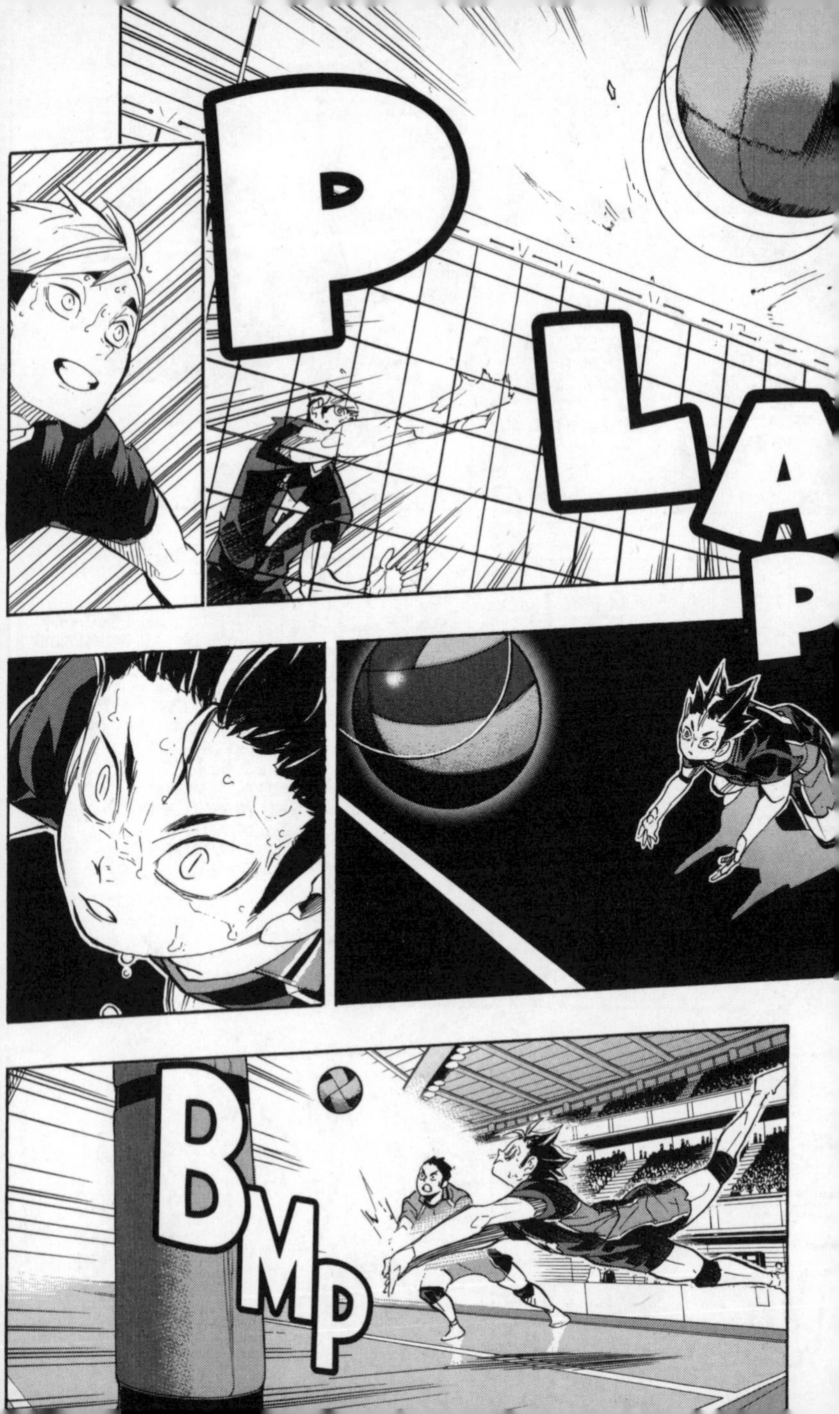
PLAP
BMP

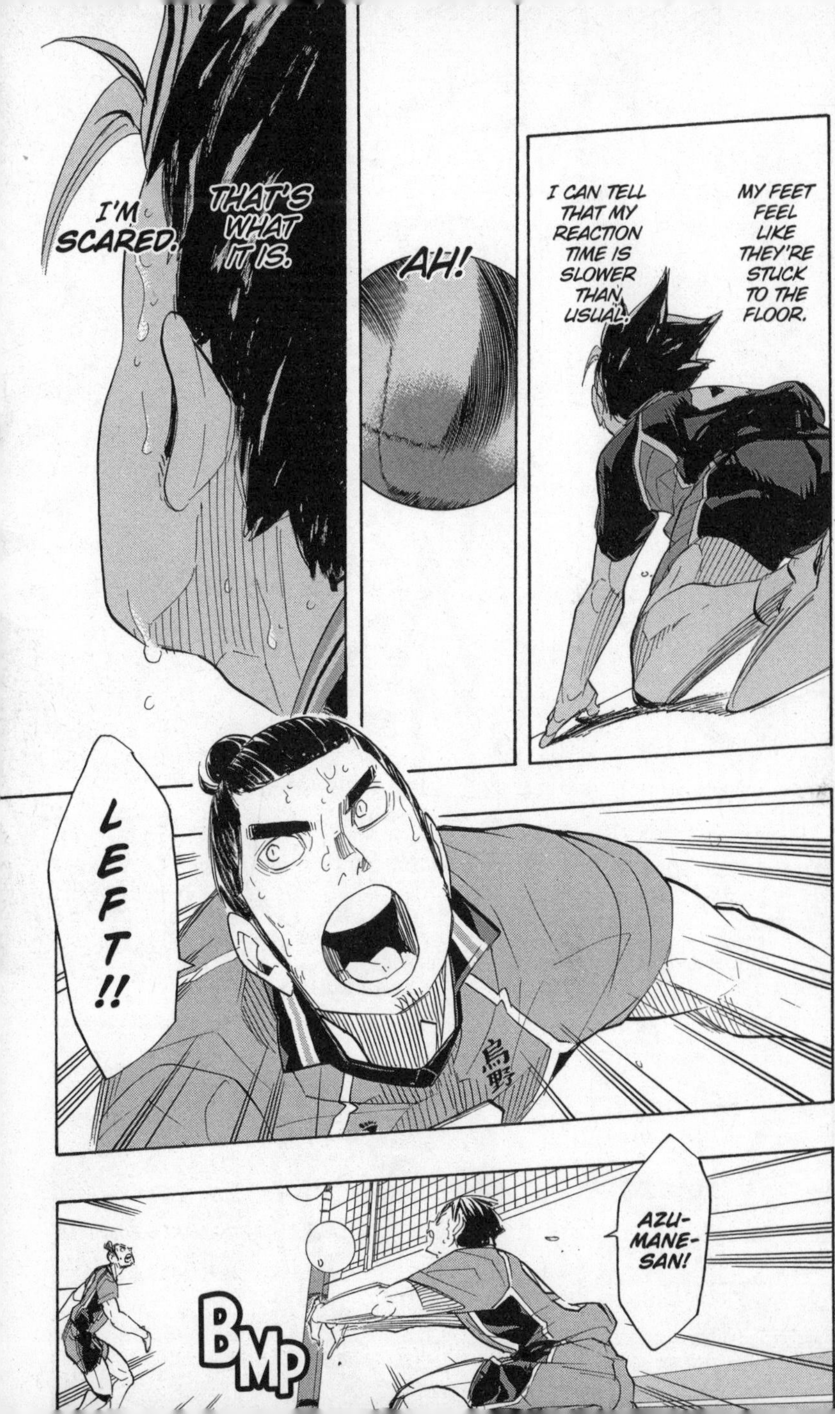
MY FEET FEEL LIKE THEY'RE STUCK TO THE FLOOR.
I CAN TELL THAT MY REACTION TIME IS SLOWER THAN USUAL.
AH!
THAT'S WHAT IT IS.
I'M SCARED.
LEFT!!
AZU-MANE-SAN!
BMP

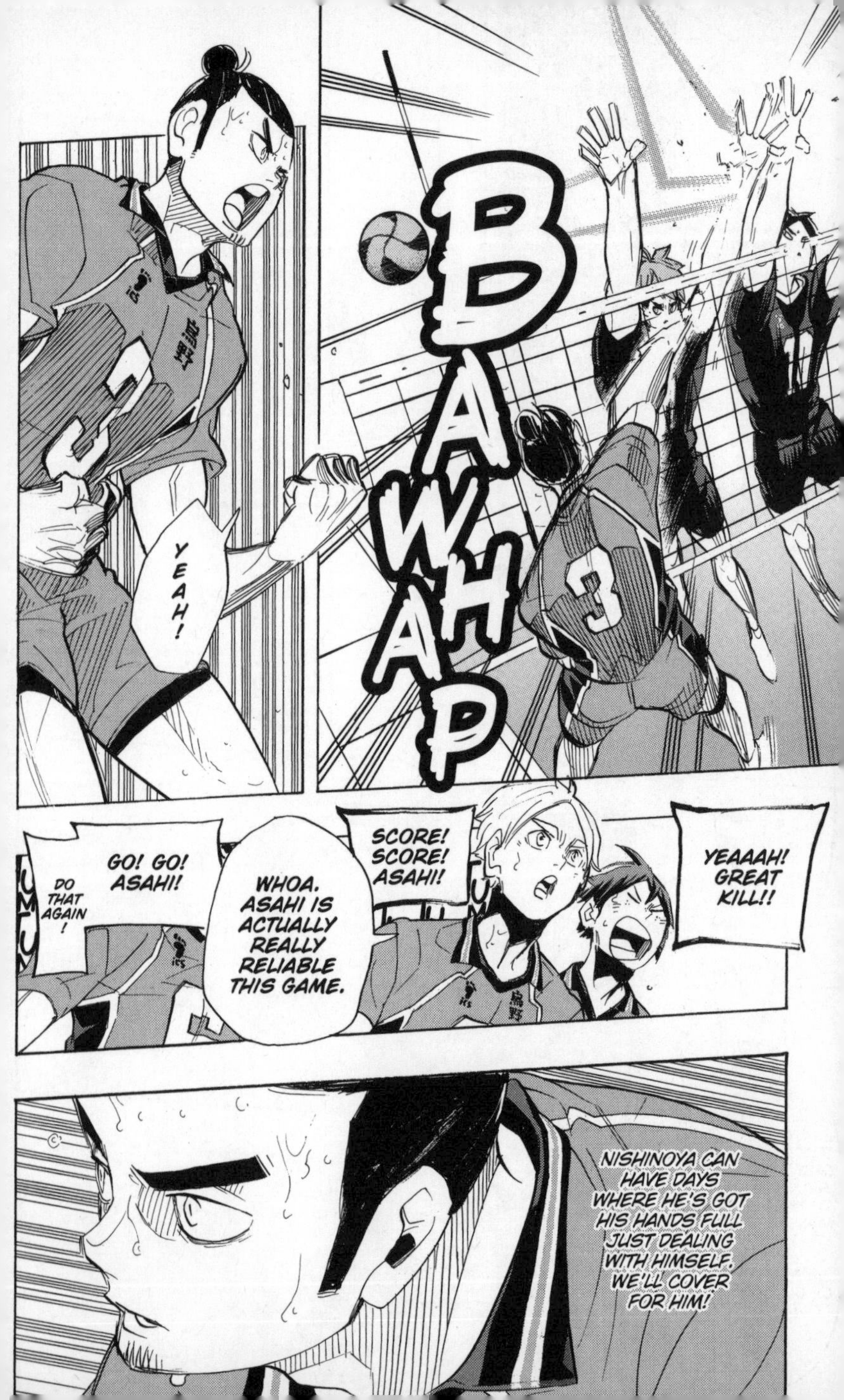
BAWHAP
YEAH!
YEAAAH! GREAT KILL!!
SCORE! SCORE! ASAHI!
WHOA. ASAHI IS ACTUALLY REALLY RELIABLE THIS GAME.
GO! GO! ASAHI!
DO THAT AGAIN!
NISHINOYA CAN HAVE DAYS WHERE HE'S GOT HIS HANDS FULL JUST DEALING WITH HIMSELF. WE'LL COVER FOR HIM!

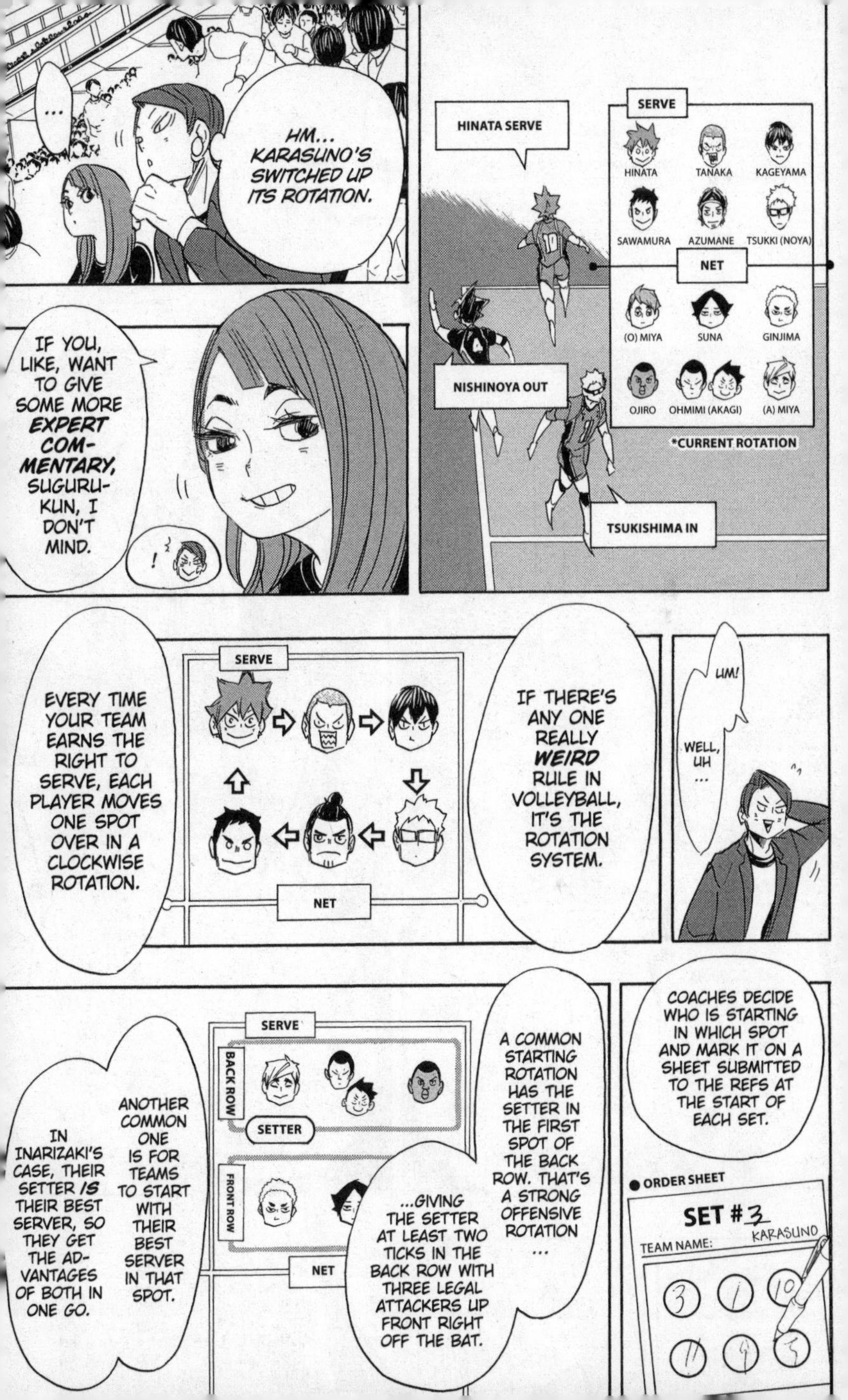
HINATA SERVE
SERVE
HINATA
TANAKA
KAGEYAMA
SAWAMURA
AZUMANE
TSUKKI (NOYA)
NET
(O) MIYA
SUNA
GINJIMA
OJIRO
OHMIMI (AKAGI)
(A) MIYA
*CURRENT ROTATION
NISHINOYA OUT
TSUKISHIMA IN
HM... KARASUNO'S SWITCHED UP ITS ROTATION.
...
IF YOU, LIKE, WANT TO GIVE SOME MORE *EXPERT COMMENTARY,* SUGURU-KUN, I DON'T MIND.
!
UM!
WELL, UH...
IF THERE'S ANY ONE REALLY *WEIRD* RULE IN VOLLEYBALL, IT'S THE ROTATION SYSTEM.
SERVE
EVERY TIME YOUR TEAM EARNS THE RIGHT TO SERVE, EACH PLAYER MOVES ONE SPOT OVER IN A CLOCKWISE ROTATION.
NET
COACHES DECIDE WHO IS STARTING IN WHICH SPOT AND MARK IT ON A SHEET SUBMITTED TO THE REFS AT THE START OF EACH SET.
ORDER SHEET
SET #3
TEAM NAME: KARASUNO
A COMMON STARTING ROTATION HAS THE SETTER IN THE FIRST SPOT OF THE BACK ROW. THAT'S A STRONG OFFENSIVE ROTATION...
...GIVING THE SETTER AT LEAST TWO TICKS IN THE BACK ROW WITH THREE LEGAL ATTACKERS UP FRONT RIGHT OFF THE BAT.
SERVE
BACK ROW
SETTER
FRONT ROW
NET
ANOTHER COMMON ONE IS FOR TEAMS TO START WITH THEIR BEST SERVER IN THAT SPOT.
IN INARIZAKI'S CASE, THEIR SETTER *IS* THEIR BEST SERVER, SO THEY GET THE ADVANTAGES OF BOTH IN ONE GO.

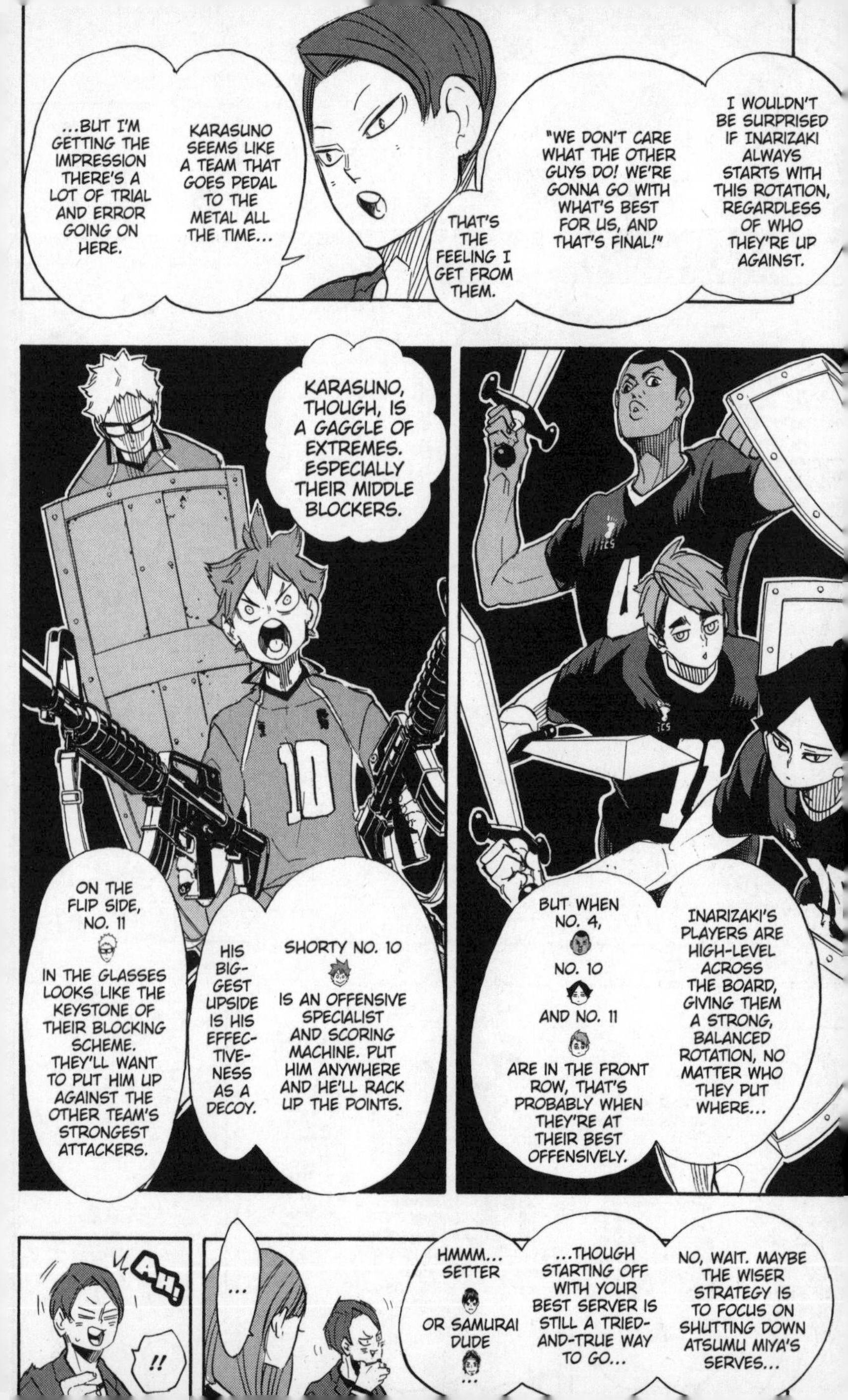
I WOULDN'T BE SURPRISED IF INARIZAKI ALWAYS STARTS WITH THIS ROTATION, REGARDLESS OF WHO THEY'RE UP AGAINST.
"WE DON'T CARE WHAT THE OTHER GUYS DO! WE'RE GONNA GO WITH WHAT'S BEST FOR US, AND THAT'S FINAL!"
THAT'S THE FEELING I GET FROM THEM.
KARASUNO SEEMS LIKE A TEAM THAT GOES PEDAL TO THE METAL ALL THE TIME...
...BUT I'M GETTING THE IMPRESSION THERE'S A LOT OF TRIAL AND ERROR GOING ON HERE.
INARIZAKI'S PLAYERS ARE HIGH-LEVEL ACROSS THE BOARD, GIVING THEM A STRONG, BALANCED ROTATION, NO MATTER WHO THEY PUT WHERE...
BUT WHEN NO. 4, NO. 10 AND NO. 11 ARE IN THE FRONT ROW, THAT'S PROBABLY WHEN THEY'RE AT THEIR BEST OFFENSIVELY.
KARASUNO, THOUGH, IS A GAGGLE OF EXTREMES. ESPECIALLY THEIR MIDDLE BLOCKERS.
SHORTY NO. 10 IS AN OFFENSIVE SPECIALIST AND SCORING MACHINE. PUT HIM ANYWHERE AND HE'LL RACK UP THE POINTS.
HIS BIGGEST UPSIDE IS HIS EFFECTIVENESS AS A DECOY.
ON THE FLIP SIDE, NO. 11 IN THE GLASSES LOOKS LIKE THE KEYSTONE OF THEIR BLOCKING SCHEME. THEY'LL WANT TO PUT HIM UP AGAINST THE OTHER TEAM'S STRONGEST ATTACKERS.
NO, WAIT. MAYBE THE WISER STRATEGY IS TO FOCUS ON SHUTTING DOWN ATSUMU MIYA'S SERVES...
...THOUGH STARTING OFF WITH YOUR BEST SERVER IS STILL A TRIED-AND-TRUE WAY TO GO...
HMMM... SETTER OR SAMURAI DUDE ...
...
AH!
!!

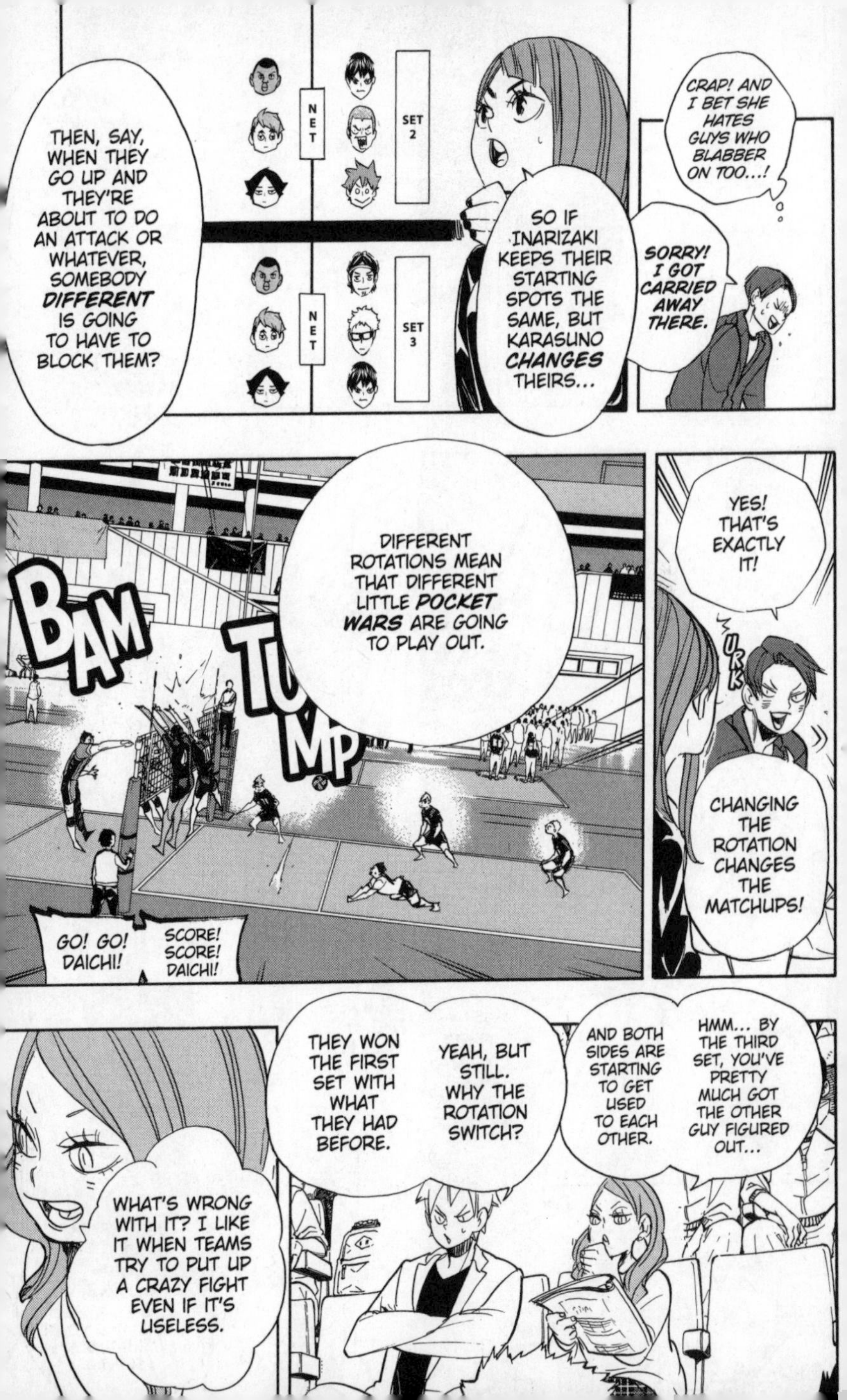
CRAP! AND I BET SHE HATES GUYS WHO BLABBER ON TOO...!
SORRY! I GOT CARRIED AWAY THERE.
SO IF INARIZAKI KEEPS THEIR STARTING SPOTS THE SAME, BUT KARASUNO CHANGES THEIRS...
SET 2
NET
SET 3
NET
THEN, SAY, WHEN THEY GO UP AND THEY'RE ABOUT TO DO AN ATTACK OR WHATEVER, SOMEBODY DIFFERENT IS GOING TO HAVE TO BLOCK THEM?
YES! THAT'S EXACTLY IT!
URK
CHANGING THE ROTATION CHANGES THE MATCHUPS!
DIFFERENT ROTATIONS MEAN THAT DIFFERENT LITTLE POCKET WARS ARE GOING TO PLAY OUT.
BAM
TUMP
SCORE! SCORE! DAICHI!
GO! GO! DAICHI!
HMM... BY THE THIRD SET, YOU'VE PRETTY MUCH GOT THE OTHER GUY FIGURED OUT...
AND BOTH SIDES ARE STARTING TO GET USED TO EACH OTHER.
YEAH, BUT STILL. WHY THE ROTATION SWITCH?
THEY WON THE FIRST SET WITH WHAT THEY HAD BEFORE.
WHAT'S WRONG WITH IT? I LIKE IT WHEN TEAMS TRY TO PUT UP A CRAZY FIGHT EVEN IF IT'S USELESS.

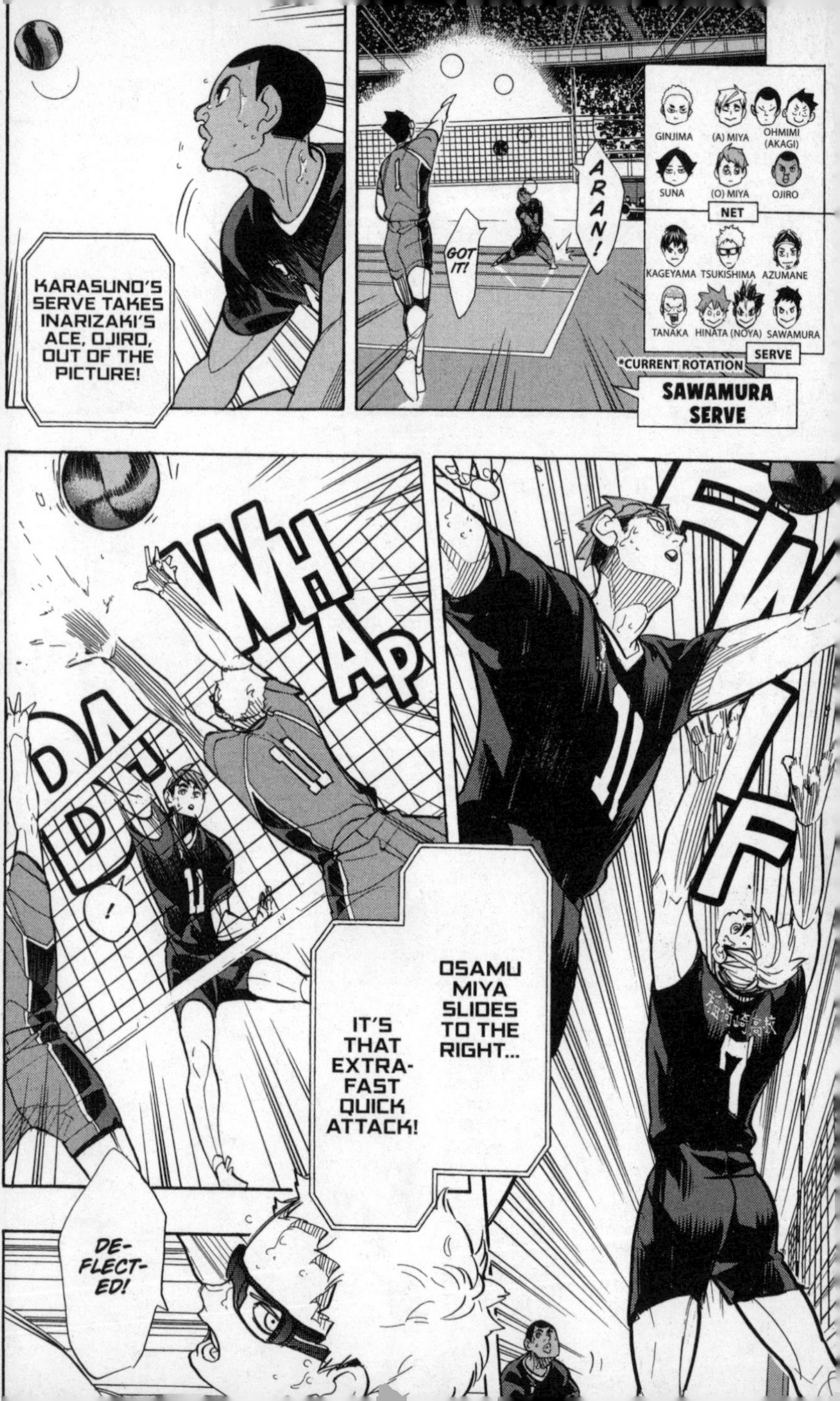
GINJIMA
(A) MIYA
OHMIMI (AKAGI)
SUNA
(O) MIYA
OJIRO
NET
KAGEYAMA
TSUKISHIMA
AZUMANE
TANAKA
HINATA (NOYA)
SAWAMURA
SERVE
*CURRENT ROTATION
ARAN!
GOT IT!
SAWAMURA SERVE
KARASUNO'S SERVE TAKES INARIZAKI'S ACE, OJIRO, OUT OF THE PICTURE!
OSAMU MIYA SLIDES TO THE RIGHT...
IT'S THAT EXTRA-FAST QUICK ATTACK!
WHAP
!
DE-FLECT-ED!

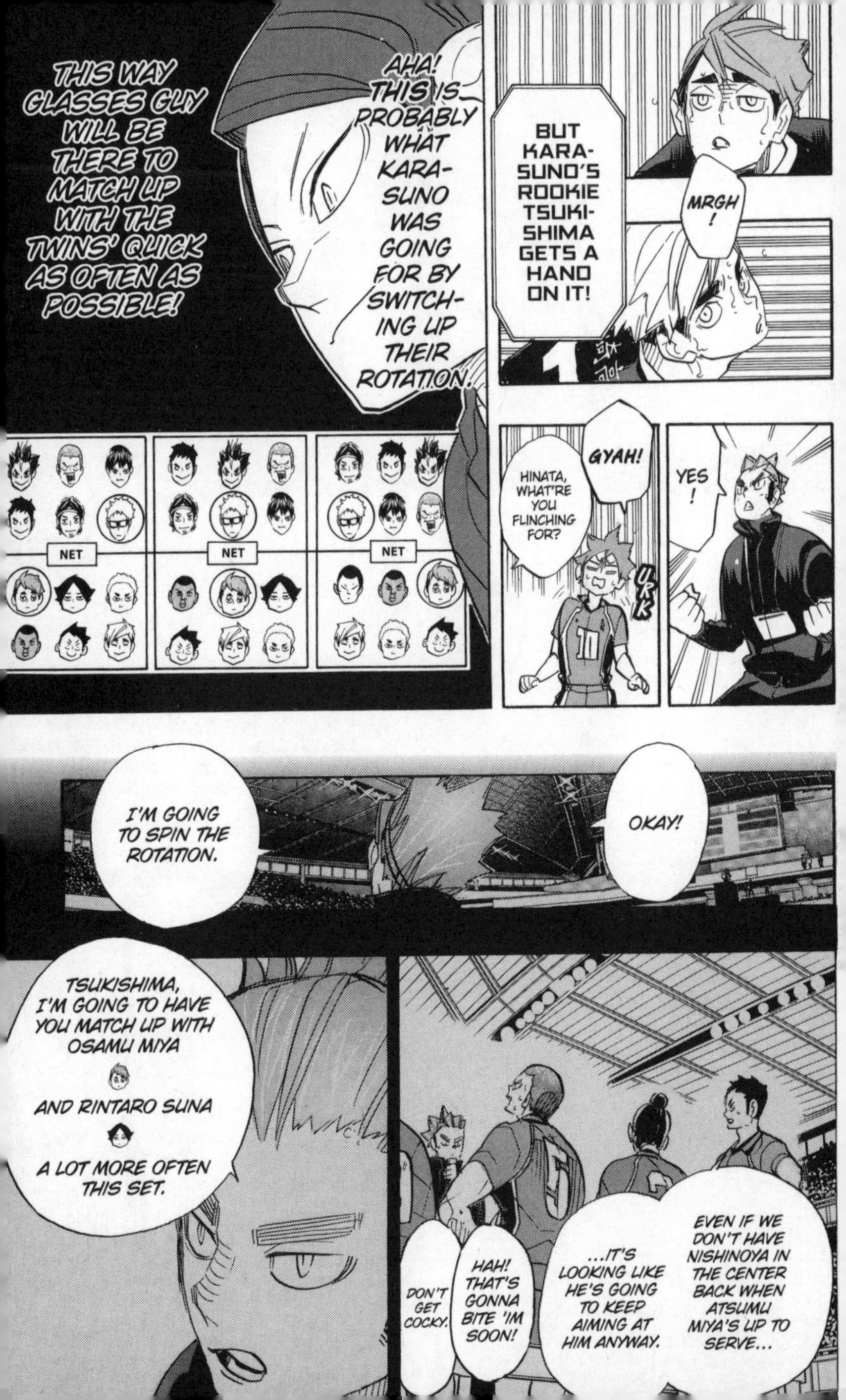
BUT KARASUNO'S ROOKIE TSUKISHIMA GETS A HAND ON IT!
MRGH!
AHA! THIS IS PROBABLY WHAT KARASUNO WAS GOING FOR BY SWITCHING UP THEIR ROTATION.
THIS WAY GLASSES GUY WILL BE THERE TO MATCH UP WITH THE TWINS' QUICK AS OFTEN AS POSSIBLE!
NET
NET
NET
YES!
GYAH!
HINATA, WHAT'RE YOU FLINCHING FOR?
URK
I'M GOING TO SPIN THE ROTATION.
OKAY!
EVEN IF WE DON'T HAVE NISHINOYA IN THE CENTER BACK WHEN ATSUMU MIYA'S UP TO SERVE...
...IT'S LOOKING LIKE HE'S GOING TO KEEP AIMING AT HIM ANYWAY.
HAH! THAT'S GONNA BITE 'IM SOON!
DON'T GET COCKY.
TSUKISHIMA, I'M GOING TO HAVE YOU MATCH UP WITH OSAMU MIYA
AND RINTARO SUNA
A LOT MORE OFTEN THIS SET.

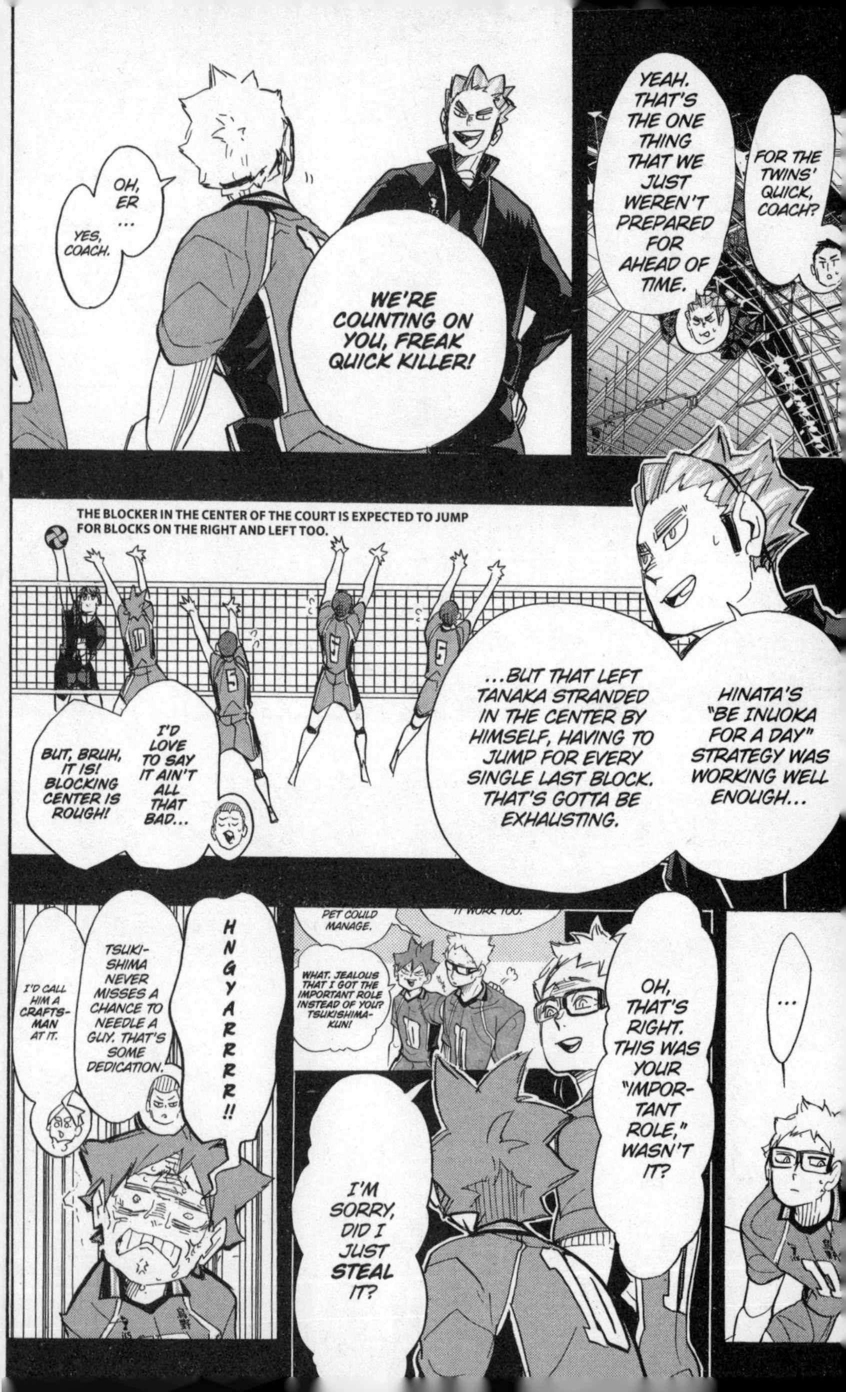
FOR THE TWINS' QUICK, COACH?
YEAH. THAT'S THE ONE THING THAT WE JUST WEREN'T PREPARED FOR AHEAD OF TIME.
WE'RE COUNTING ON YOU, FREAK QUICK KILLER!
OH, ER ...
YES, COACH.
HINATA'S "BE INUOKA FOR A DAY" STRATEGY WAS WORKING WELL ENOUGH...
...BUT THAT LEFT TANAKA STRANDED IN THE CENTER BY HIMSELF, HAVING TO JUMP FOR EVERY SINGLE LAST BLOCK. THAT'S GOTTA BE EXHAUSTING.
THE BLOCKER IN THE CENTER OF THE COURT IS EXPECTED TO JUMP FOR BLOCKS ON THE RIGHT AND LEFT TOO.
I'D LOVE TO SAY IT AIN'T ALL THAT BAD...
BUT, BRUH, IT IS! BLOCKING CENTER IS ROUGH!
...
IT WORK TOO.
PET COULD MANAGE.
WHAT. JEALOUS THAT I GOT THE IMPORTANT ROLE INSTEAD OF YOU? TSUKISHIMA-KUN!
OH, THAT'S RIGHT. THIS WAS YOUR "IMPORTANT ROLE," WASN'T IT?
I'M SORRY, DID I JUST STEAL IT?
HNGYARRRR!!
TSUKISHIMA NEVER MISSES A CHANCE TO NEEDLE A GUY. THAT'S SOME DEDICATION.
I'D CALL HIM A CRAFTSMAN AT IT.

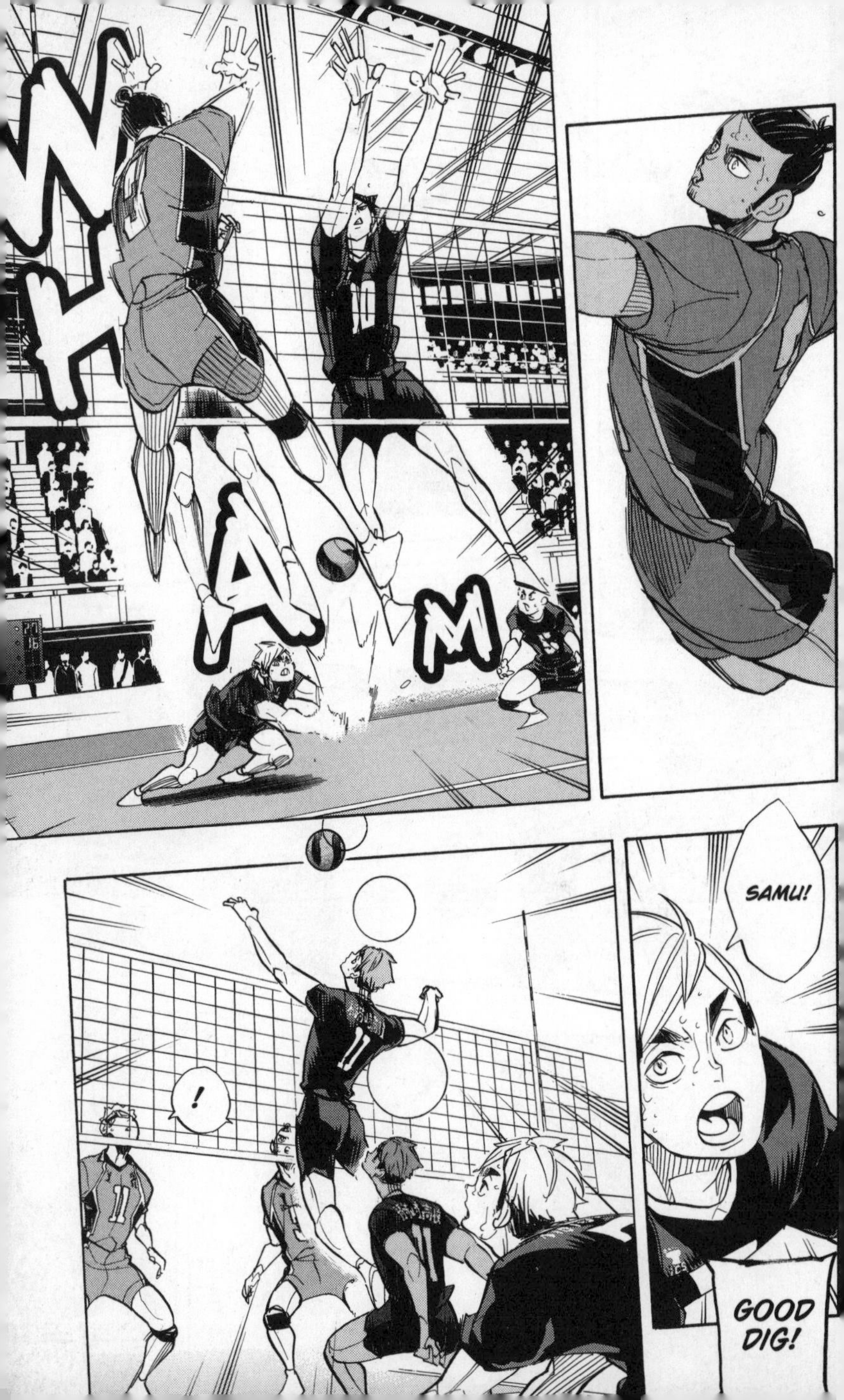
WHAM
SAMU!
GOOD DIG!
!

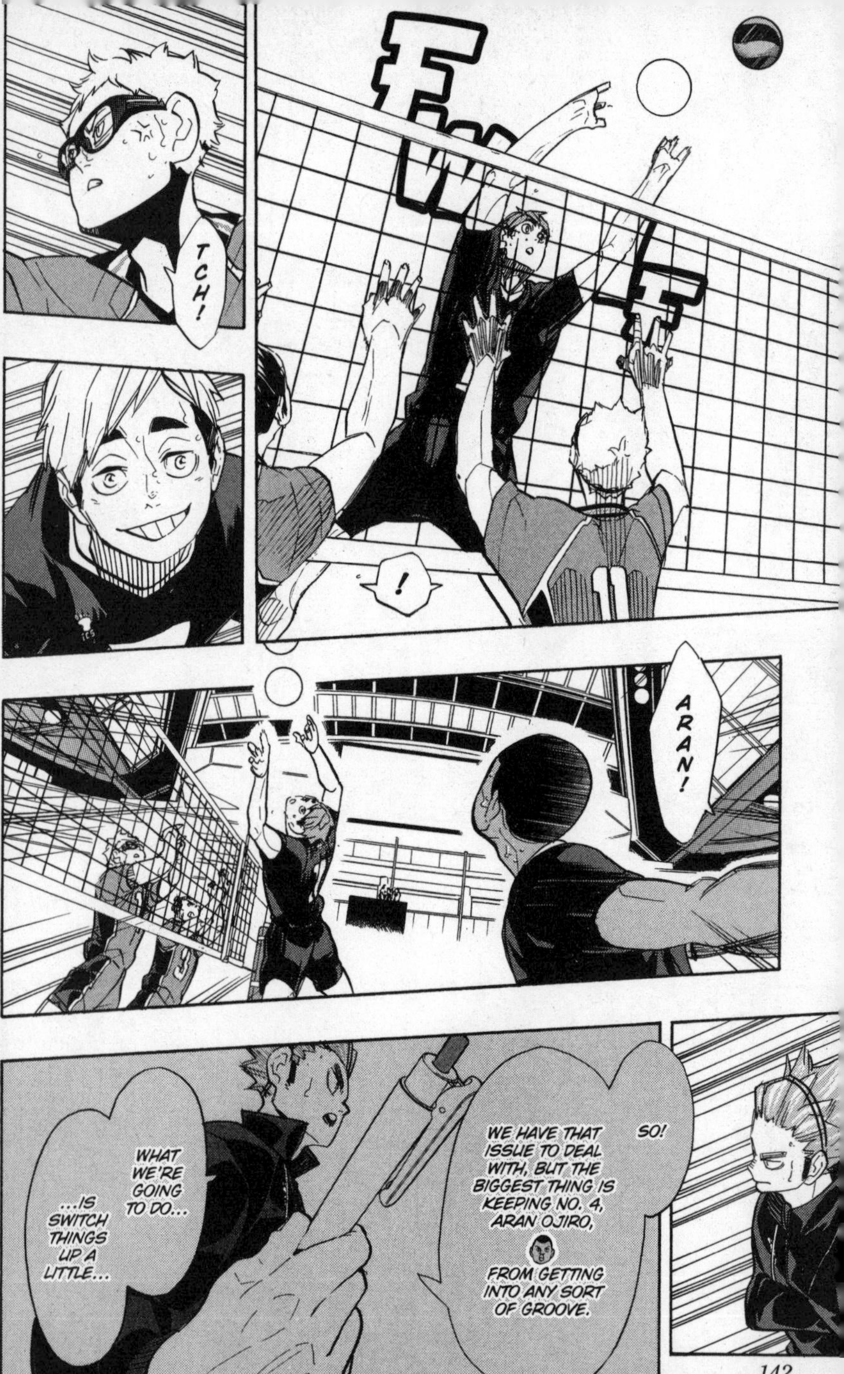
TCH!
!
ARAN!
SO!
WE HAVE THAT ISSUE TO DEAL WITH, BUT THE BIGGEST THING IS KEEPING NO. 4, ARAN OJIRO, FROM GETTING INTO ANY SORT OF GROOVE.
WHAT WE'RE GOING TO DO...
...IS SWITCH THINGS UP A LITTLE...

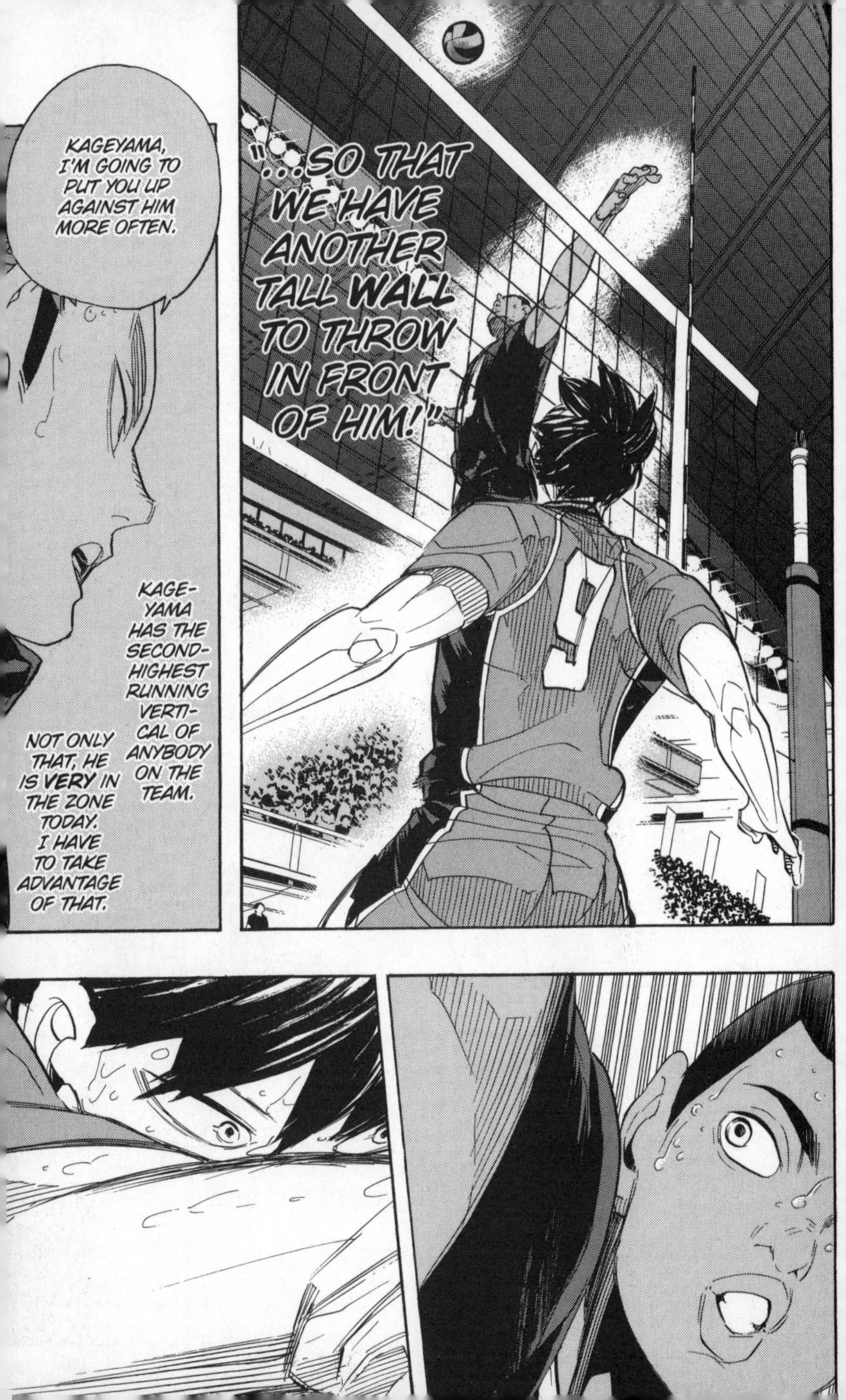
"...SO THAT WE HAVE ANOTHER TALL WALL TO THROW IN FRONT OF HIM!"
KAGEYAMA, I'M GOING TO PUT YOU UP AGAINST HIM MORE OFTEN.
KAGEYAMA HAS THE SECOND-HIGHEST RUNNING VERTICAL OF ANYBODY ON THE TEAM.
NOT ONLY THAT, HE IS VERY IN THE ZONE TODAY. I HAVE TO TAKE ADVANTAGE OF THAT.

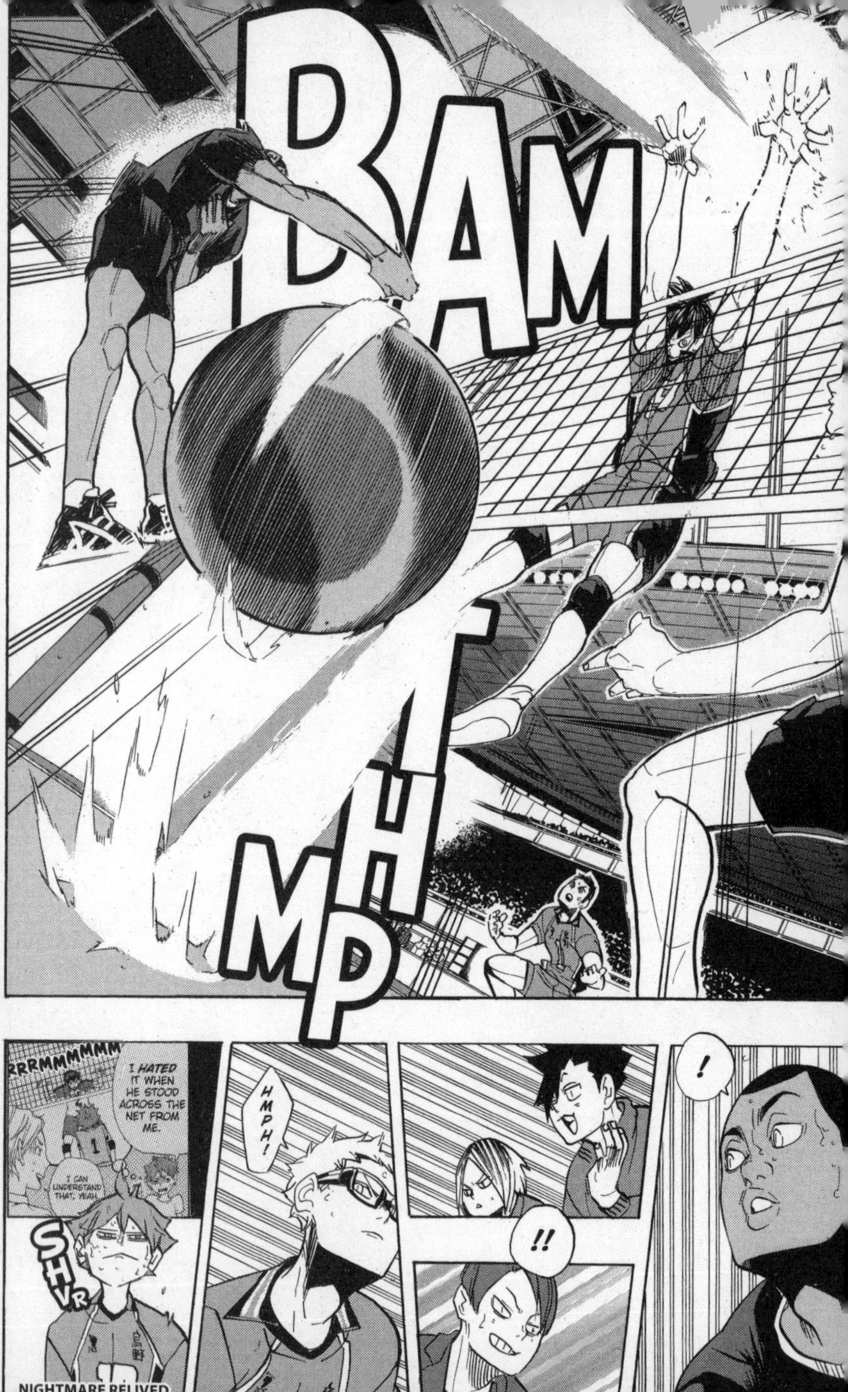
BAM
THUMP
!
!!
HMPH!
RRRMMMMMM
I HATED IT WHEN HE STOOD ACROSS THE NET FROM ME.
I CAN UNDERSTAND THAT, YEAH
SHVR

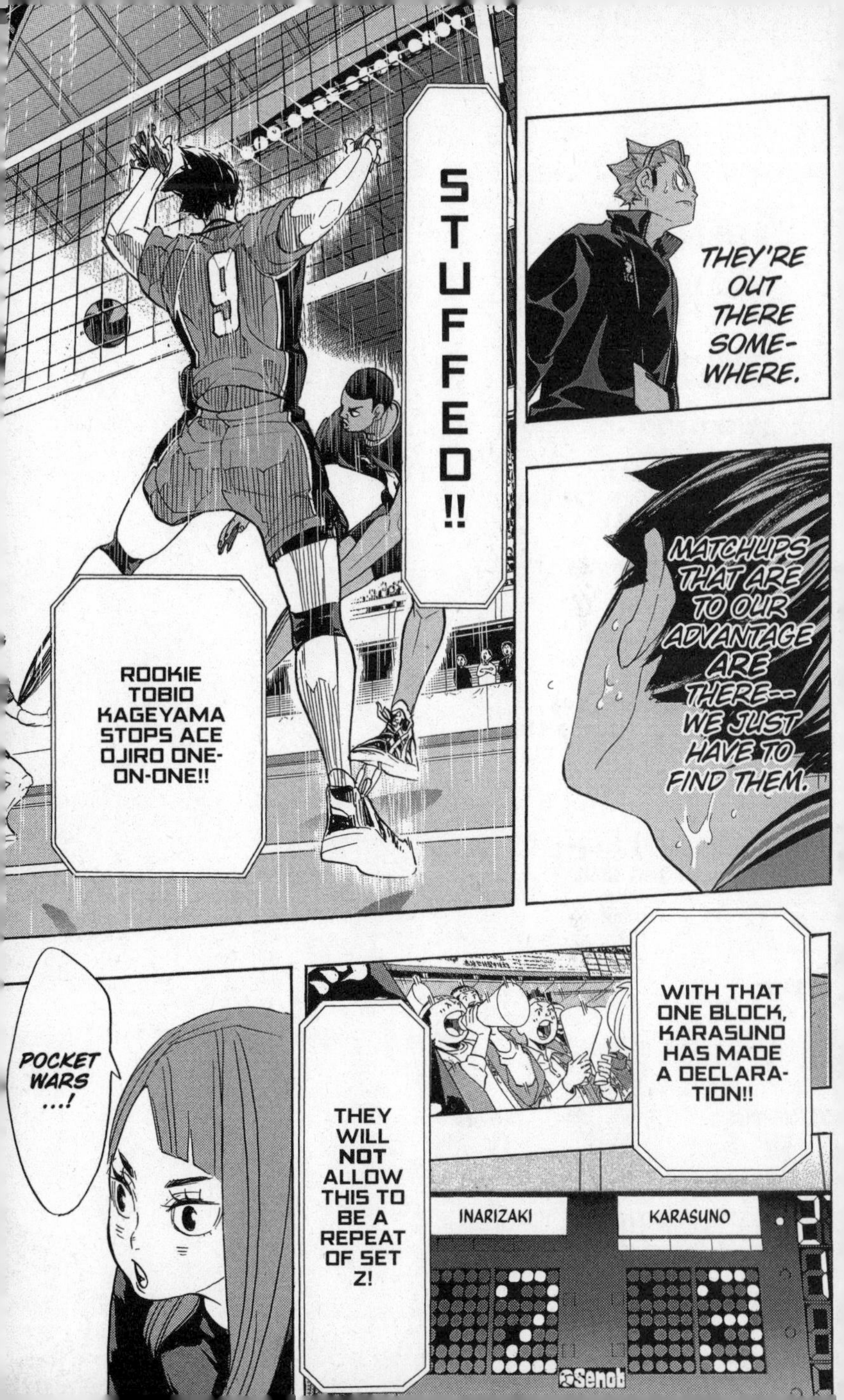
THEY'RE OUT THERE SOME-WHERE.
MATCHUPS THAT ARE TO OUR ADVANTAGE ARE THERE-- WE JUST HAVE TO FIND THEM.
STUFFED!!
ROOKIE TOBIO KAGEYAMA STOPS ACE OJIRO ONE-ON-ONE!!
WITH THAT ONE BLOCK, KARASUNO HAS MADE A DECLARA-TION!!
THEY WILL NOT ALLOW THIS TO BE A REPEAT OF SET 2!
INARIZAKI
KARASUNO
POCKET WARS ...!

REN OHMIMI

**INARIZAKI HIGH SCHOOL
CLASS 3-7**

**POSITION:
MIDDLE BLOCKER**

HEIGHT: 6'3"

**WEIGHT: 178 LBS.
(AS OF JANUARY, 3RD YEAR
OF HIGH SCHOOL)**

BIRTHDAY: FEBRUARY 17

**FAVORITE FOOD:
WHITEFISH SASHIMI**

**CURRENT WORRY:
ATSUMU SAW HIM AND
KITA HAVING TEA AND SAID
THEY LOOKED LIKE AN OLD
MARRIED COUPLE.**

**ABILITY PARAMETERS
(5-POINT SCALE)**

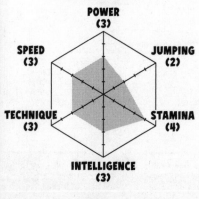

POWER
(3)

JUMPING
(2)

SPEED
(3)

STAMINA
(4)

TECHNIQUE
(3)

INTELLIGENCE
(3)

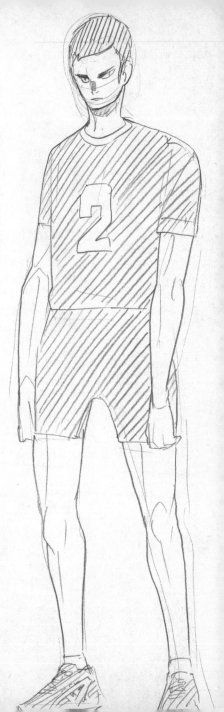

CHAPTER 277: Many vs. One

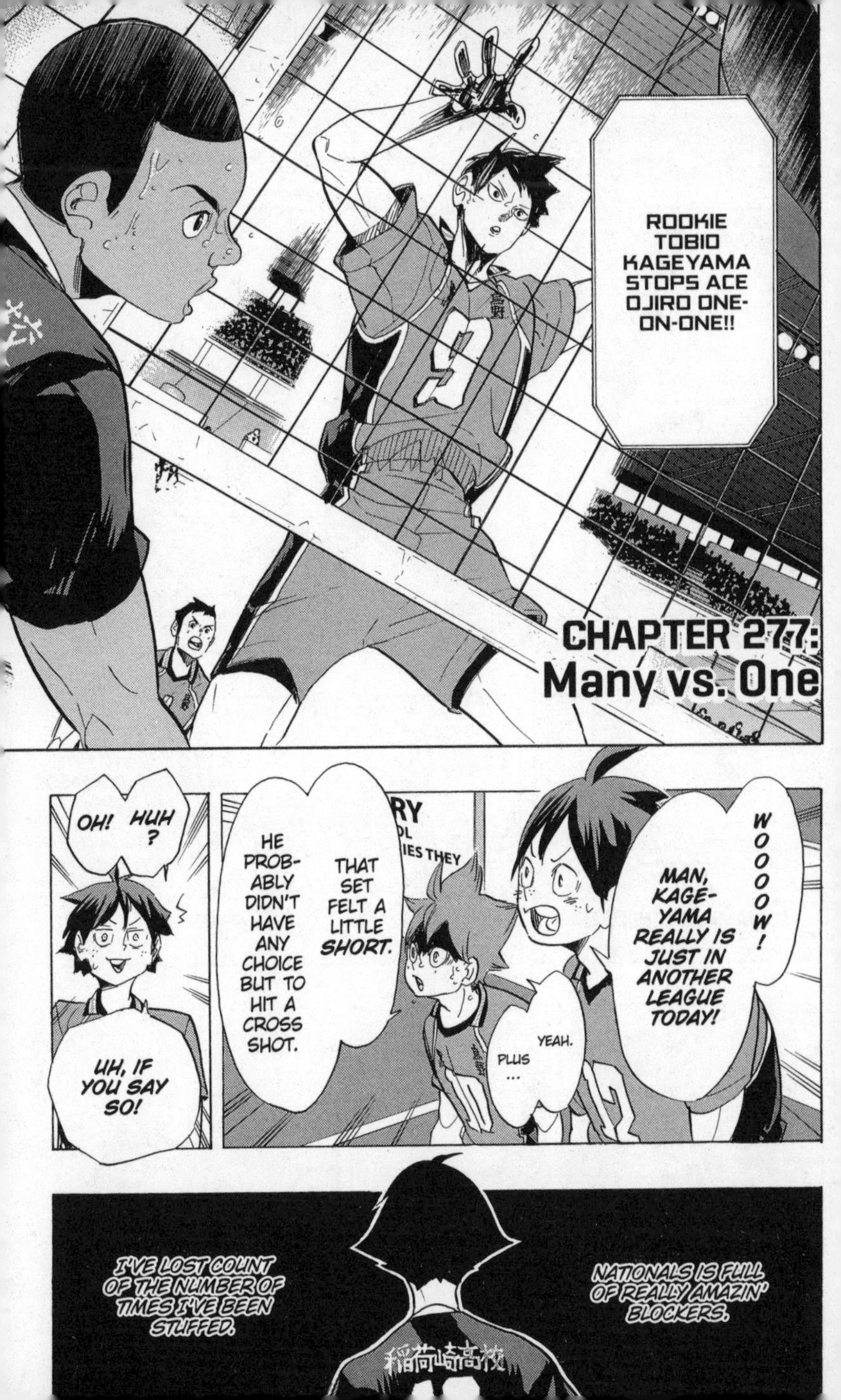
ROOKIE TOBIO KAGEYAMA STOPS ACE OJIRO ONE-ON-ONE!!
CHAPTER 277: Many vs. One
WOOOOOW!
MAN, KAGEYAMA REALLY IS JUST IN ANOTHER LEAGUE TODAY!
YEAH.
PLUS...
THAT SET FELT A LITTLE SHORT.
HE PROBABLY DIDN'T HAVE ANY CHOICE BUT TO HIT A CROSS SHOT.
OH!
HUH?
UH, IF YOU SAY SO!
NATIONALS IS FULL OF REALLY AMAZIN' BLOCKERS.
I'VE LOST COUNT OF THE NUMBER OF TIMES I'VE BEEN STUFFED.
稲荷崎高校

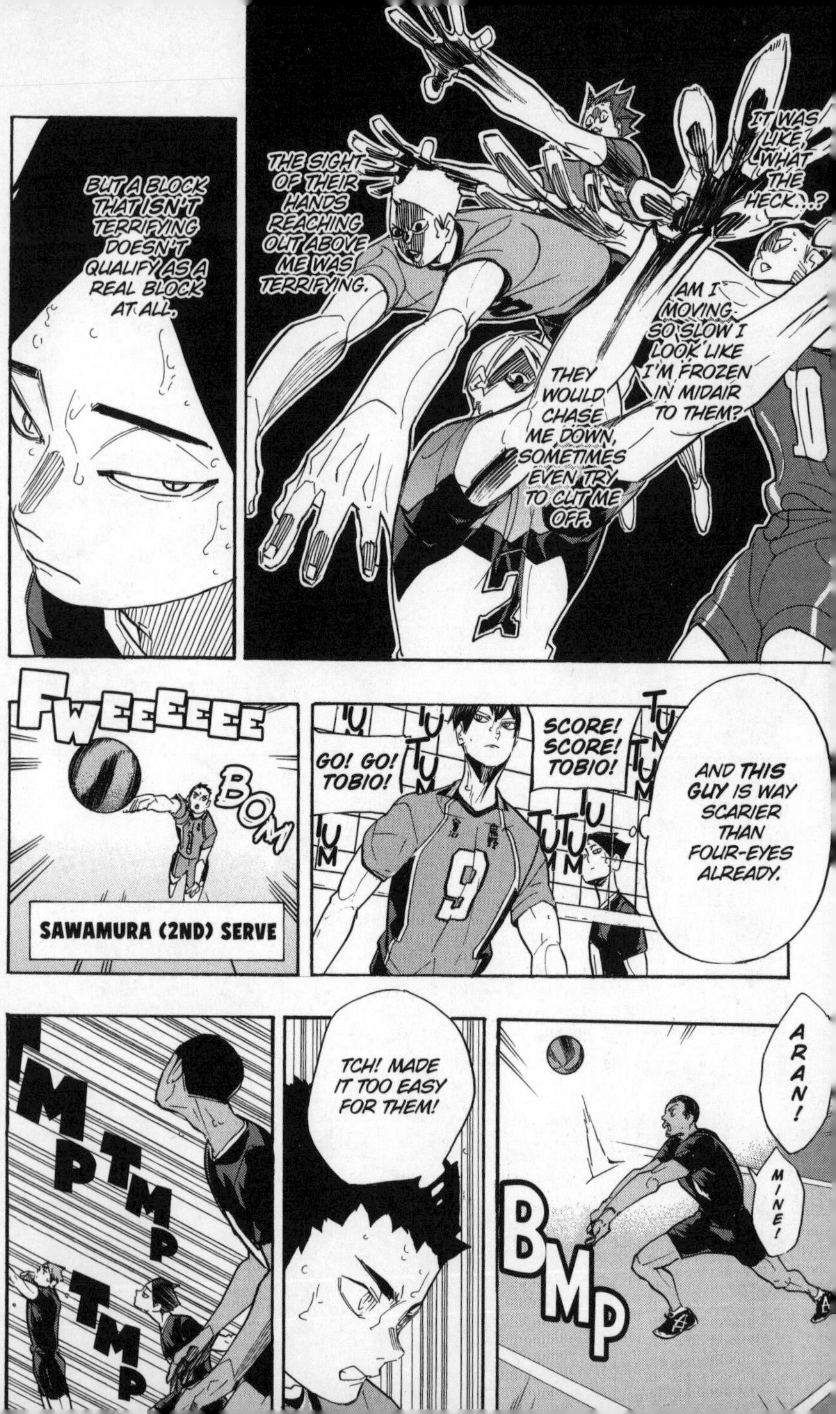
IT WAS LIKE, WHAT THE HECK...?
THE SIGHT OF THEIR HANDS REACHING OUT ABOVE ME WAS TERRIFYING.
AM I MOVING SO SLOW I LOOK LIKE I'M FROZEN IN MIDAIR TO THEM?
THEY WOULD CHASE ME DOWN, SOMETIMES EVEN TRY TO CUT ME OFF.
BUT A BLOCK THAT ISN'T TERRIFYING DOESN'T QUALIFY AS A REAL BLOCK AT ALL.
AND THIS GUY IS WAY SCARIER THAN FOUR-EYES ALREADY.
SCORE! SCORE! TOBIO!
GO! GO! TOBIO!
FWEEEEEE
BOM
SAWAMURA (2ND) SERVE
ARAN!
MINE!
BMP
TCH! MADE IT TOO EASY FOR THEM!
TMP TMP TMP

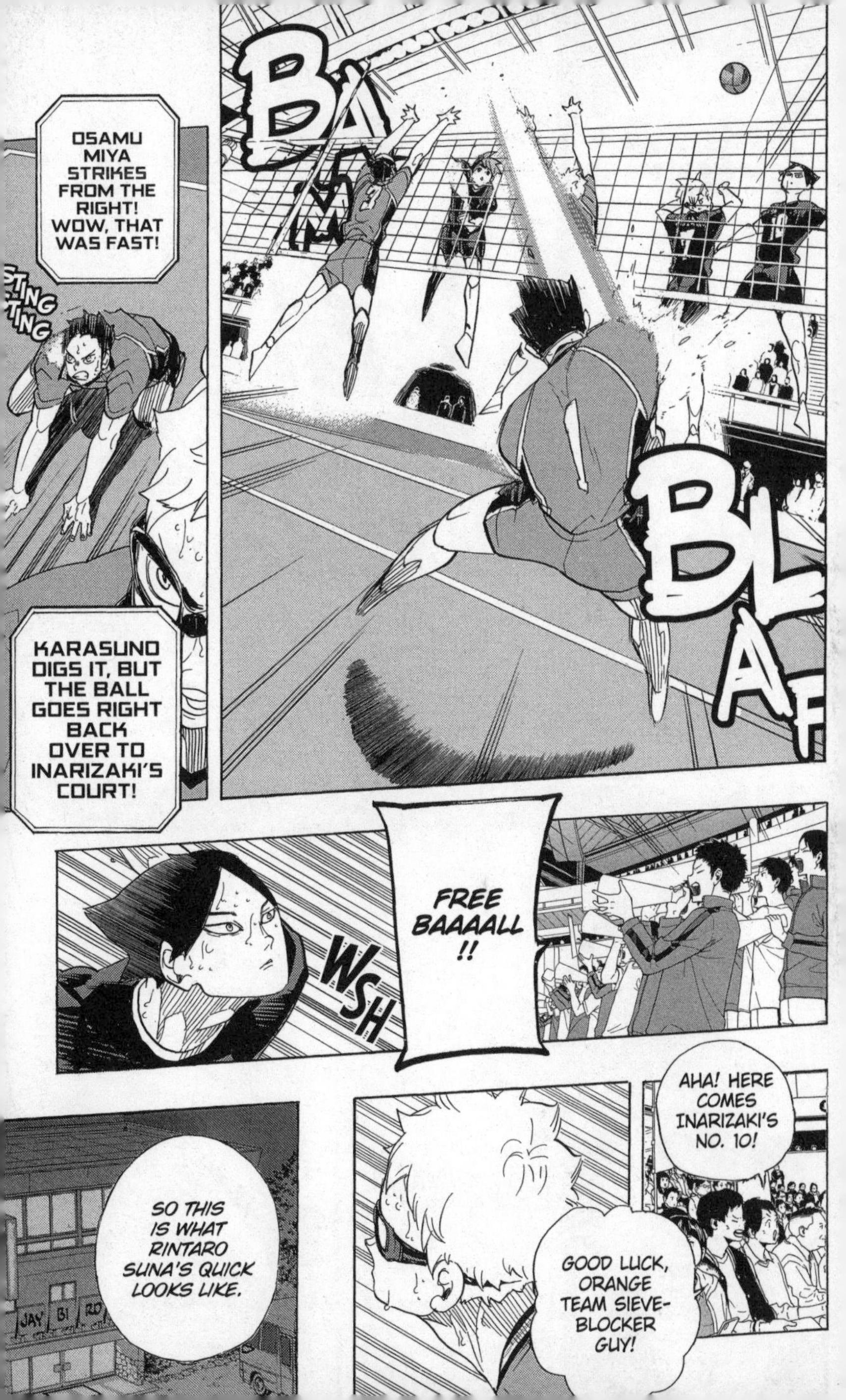
OSAMU MIYA STRIKES FROM THE RIGHT! WOW, THAT WAS FAST!
STING STING
KARASUNO DIGS IT, BUT THE BALL GOES RIGHT BACK OVER TO INARIZAKI'S COURT!
FREE BAAAAALL!!
WSH
AHA! HERE COMES INARIZAKI'S NO. 10!
GOOD LUCK, ORANGE TEAM SIEVE-BLOCKER GUY!
SO THIS IS WHAT RINTARO SUNA'S QUICK LOOKS LIKE.
JAY BI RD

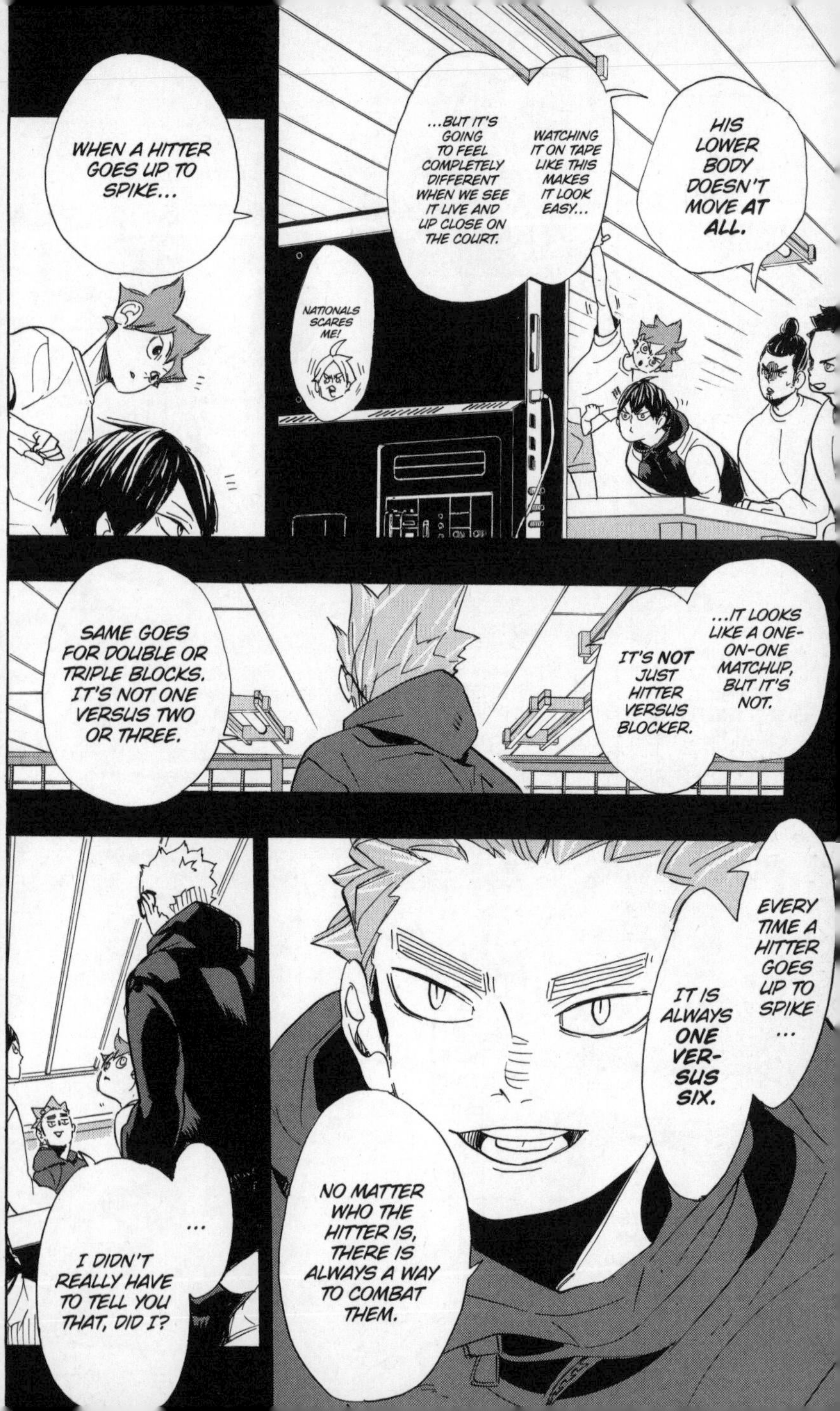
HIS LOWER BODY DOESN'T MOVE AT ALL.
WATCHING IT ON TAPE LIKE THIS MAKES IT LOOK EASY...
...BUT IT'S GOING TO FEEL COMPLETELY DIFFERENT WHEN WE SEE IT LIVE AND UP CLOSE ON THE COURT.
NATIONALS SCARES ME!
WHEN A HITTER GOES UP TO SPIKE...
...IT LOOKS LIKE A ONE-ON-ONE MATCHUP, BUT IT'S NOT.
IT'S NOT JUST HITTER VERSUS BLOCKER.
SAME GOES FOR DOUBLE OR TRIPLE BLOCKS. IT'S NOT ONE VERSUS TWO OR THREE.
EVERY TIME A HITTER GOES UP TO SPIKE...
IT IS ALWAYS ONE VERSUS SIX.
NO MATTER WHO THE HITTER IS, THERE IS ALWAYS A WAY TO COMBAT THEM.
...
I DIDN'T REALLY HAVE TO TELL YOU THAT, DID I?

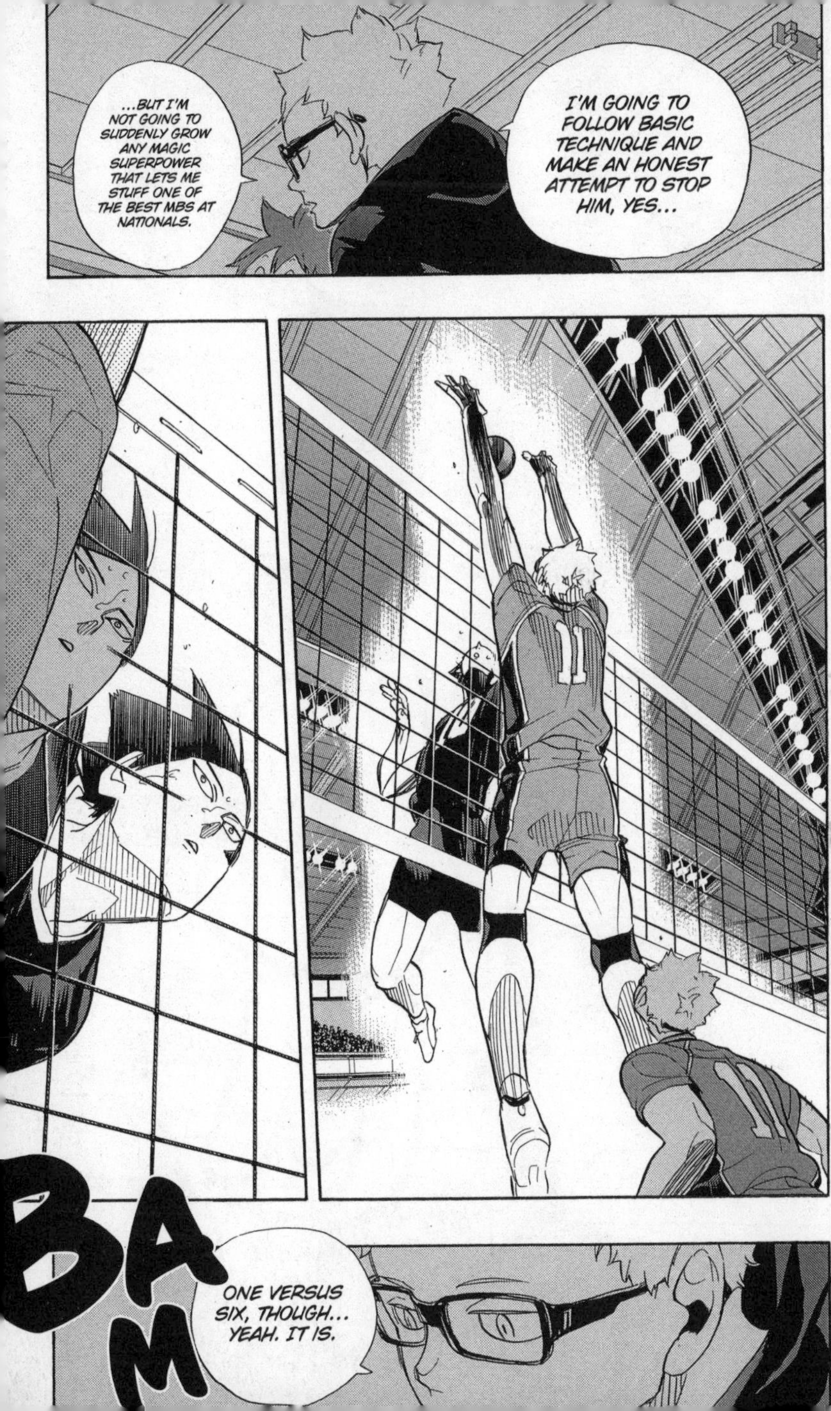
I'M GOING TO FOLLOW BASIC TECHNIQUE AND MAKE AN HONEST ATTEMPT TO STOP HIM, YES...
...BUT I'M NOT GOING TO SUDDENLY GROW ANY MAGIC SUPERPOWER THAT LETS ME STUFF ONE OF THE BEST MBS AT NATIONALS.
BAM
ONE VERSUS SIX, THOUGH... YEAH. IT IS.

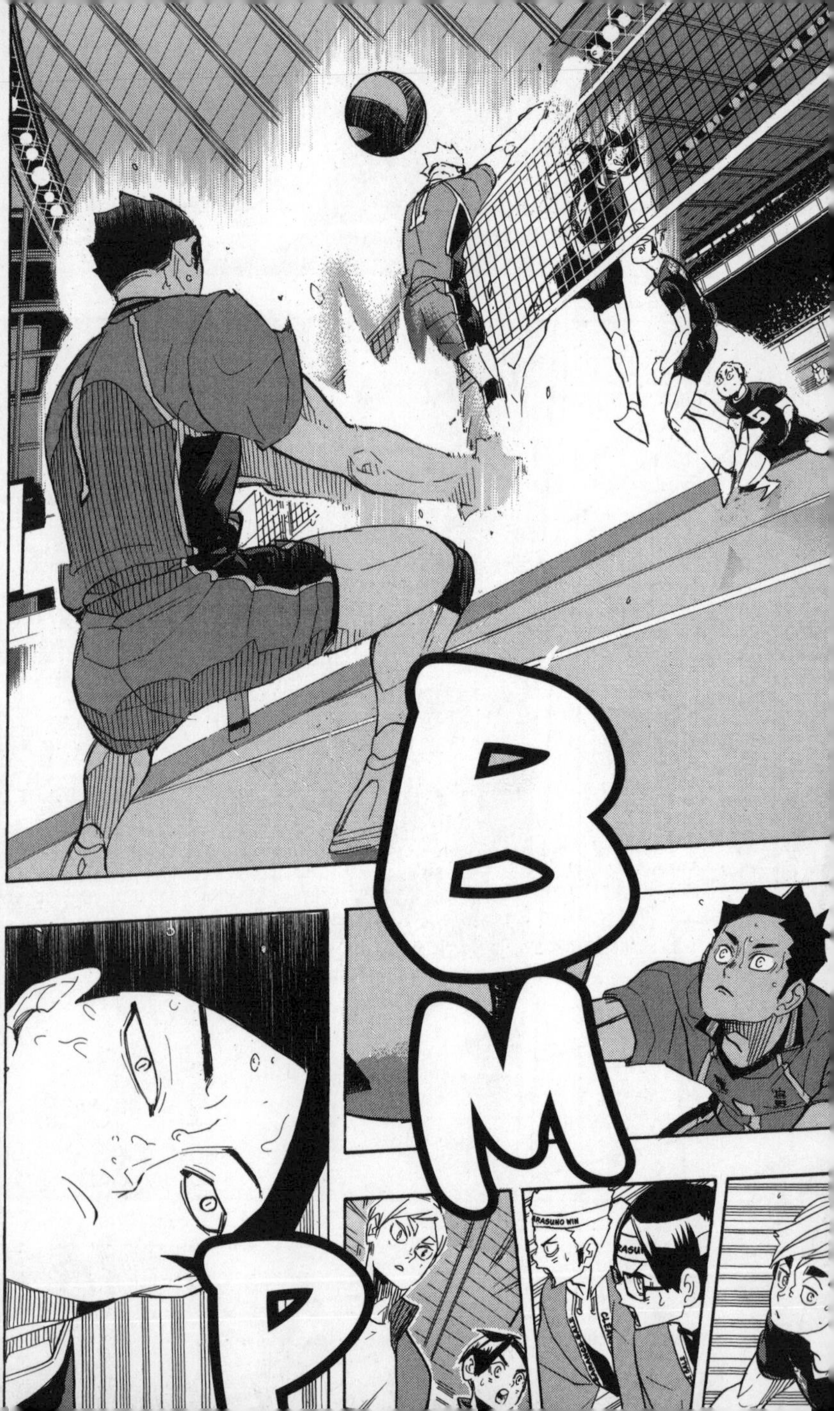
BMP

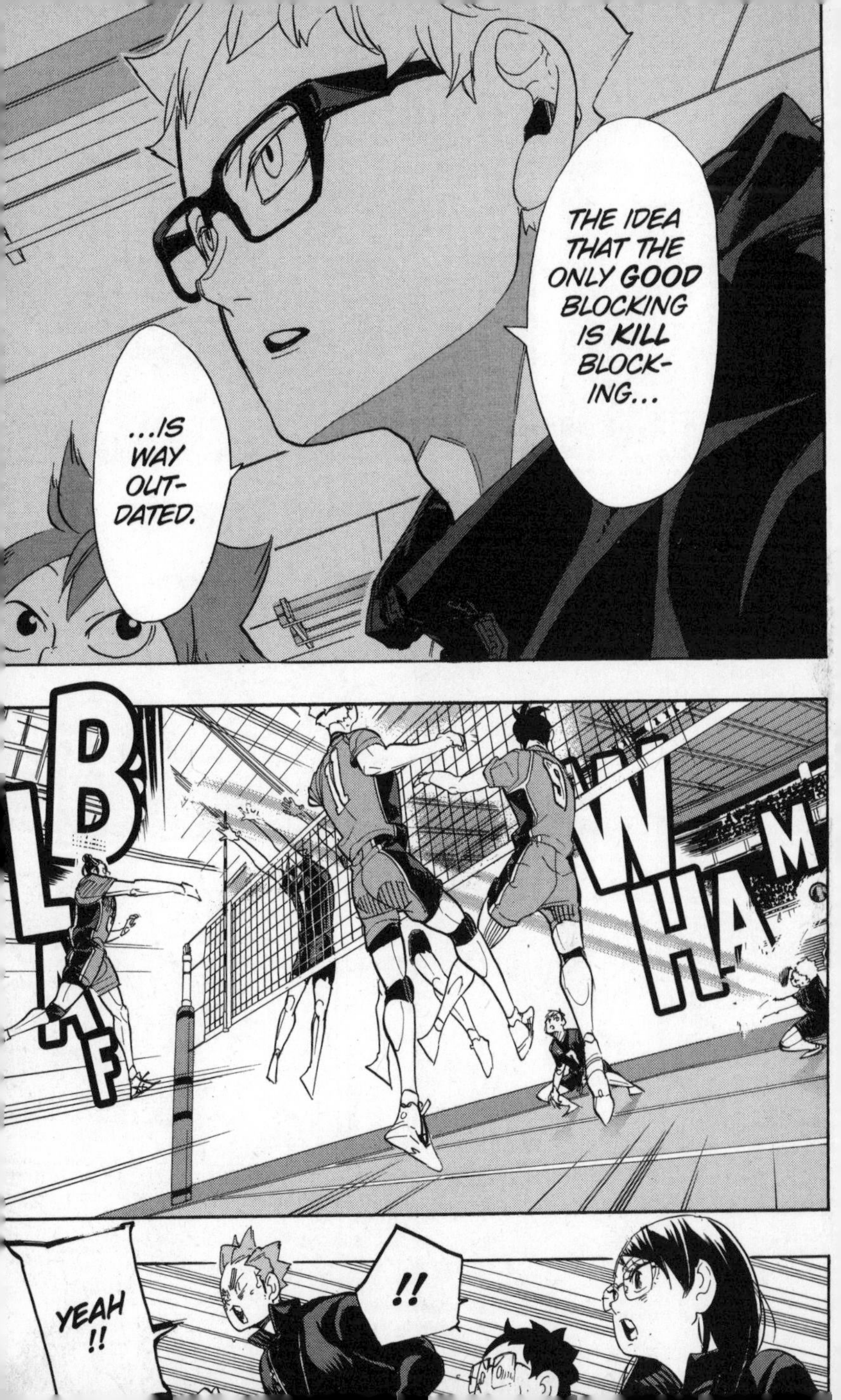

THE IDEA THAT THE ONLY GOOD BLOCKING IS KILL BLOCK-ING...
...IS WAY OUT-DATED.
WHAM
BLUFF
!!
YEAH !!

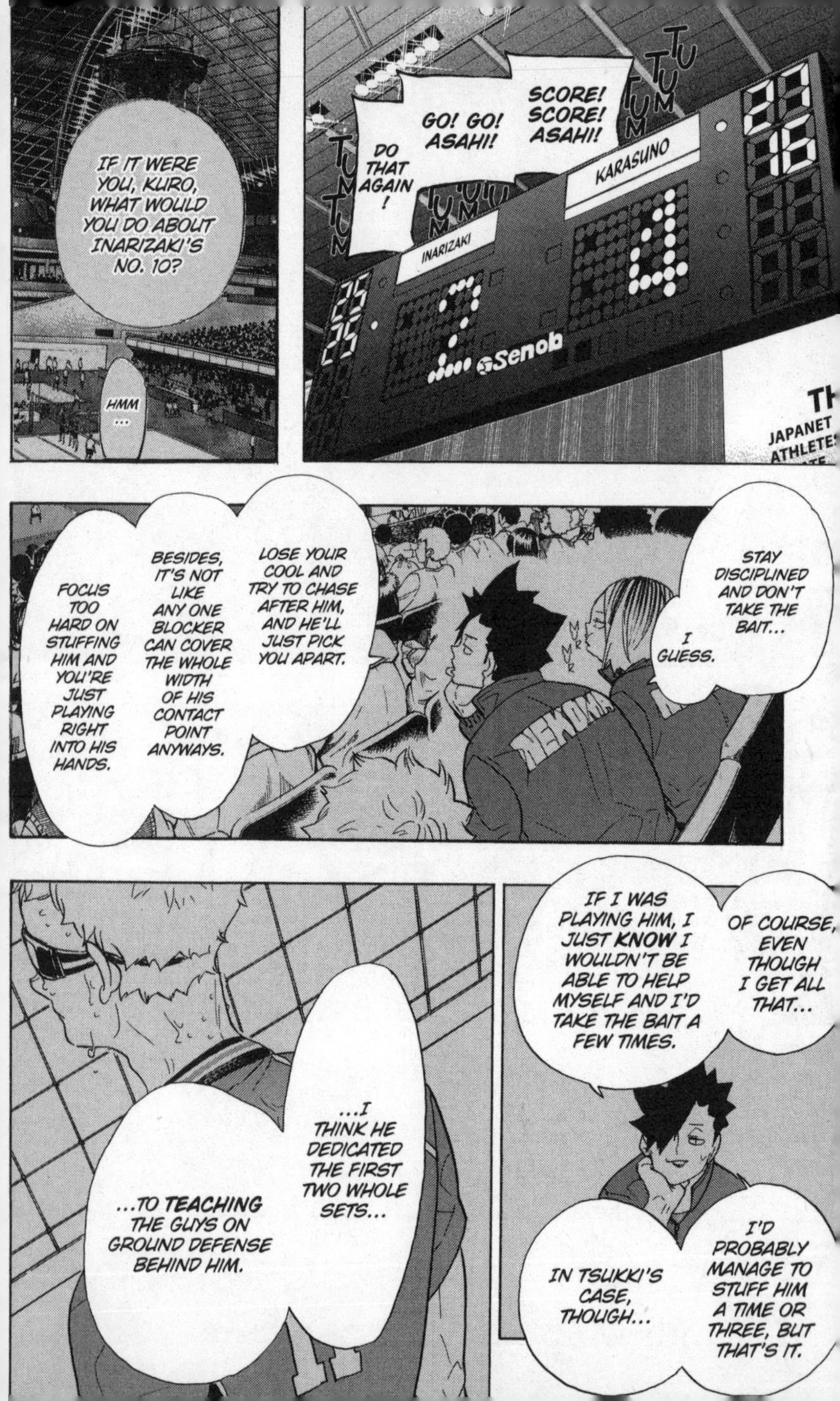
TUTUM
SCORE! SCORE! ASAHI!
GO! GO! ASAHI!
DO THAT AGAIN!
TUMTUM
KARASUNO
INARIZAKI
Senob
JAPANET
IF IT WERE YOU, KURO, WHAT WOULD YOU DO ABOUT INARIZAKI'S NO. 10?
HMM...
STAY DISCIPLINED AND DON'T TAKE THE BAIT...
I GUESS.
LOSE YOUR COOL AND TRY TO CHASE AFTER HIM, AND HE'LL JUST PICK YOU APART.
BESIDES, IT'S NOT LIKE ANY ONE BLOCKER CAN COVER THE WHOLE WIDTH OF HIS CONTACT POINT ANYWAYS.
FOCUS TOO HARD ON STUFFING HIM AND YOU'RE JUST PLAYING RIGHT INTO HIS HANDS.
OF COURSE, EVEN THOUGH I GET ALL THAT...
IF I WAS PLAYING HIM, I JUST **KNOW** I WOULDN'T BE ABLE TO HELP MYSELF AND I'D TAKE THE BAIT A FEW TIMES.
I'D PROBABLY MANAGE TO STUFF HIM A TIME OR THREE, BUT THAT'S IT.
IN TSUKKI'S CASE, THOUGH...
...I THINK HE DEDICATED THE FIRST TWO WHOLE SETS...
...TO **TEACHING** THE GUYS ON GROUND DEFENSE BEHIND HIM.

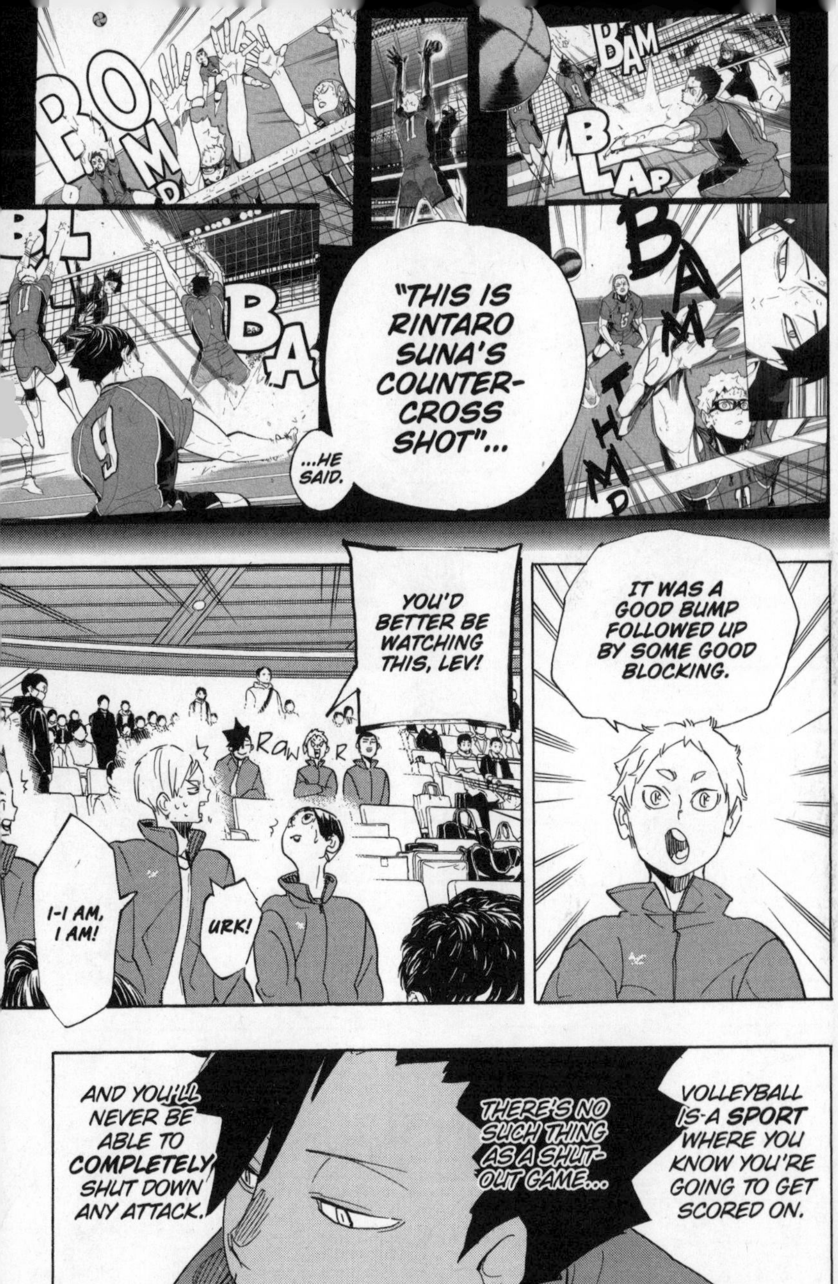
BAM
BLAP
BOMD
BAM
THMD
"THIS IS RINTARO SUNA'S COUNTER-CROSS SHOT"...
...HE SAID.
BA
IT WAS A GOOD BUMP FOLLOWED UP BY SOME GOOD BLOCKING.
YOU'D BETTER BE WATCHING THIS, LEV!
RAWR
URK!
I-I AM, I AM!
VOLLEYBALL IS A SPORT WHERE YOU KNOW YOU'RE GOING TO GET SCORED ON.
THERE'S NO SUCH THING AS A SHUT-OUT GAME...
AND YOU'LL NEVER BE ABLE TO COMPLETELY SHUT DOWN ANY ATTACK.

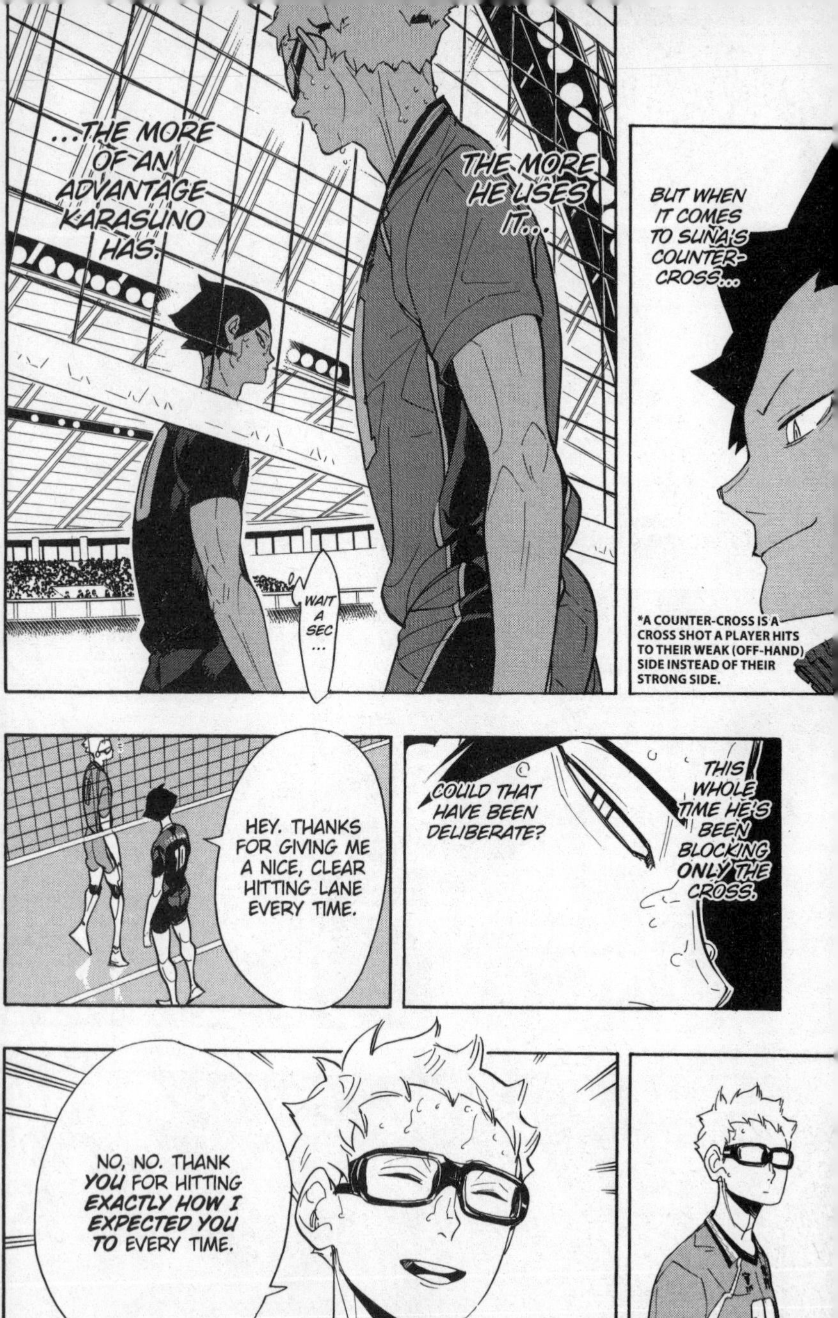

BUT WHEN IT COMES TO SUNA'S COUNTER-CROSS...
*A COUNTER-CROSS IS A CROSS SHOT A PLAYER HITS TO THEIR WEAK (OFF-HAND) SIDE INSTEAD OF THEIR STRONG SIDE.
THE MORE HE USES IT...
...THE MORE OF AN ADVANTAGE KARASUNO HAS.
WAIT A SEC...
THIS WHOLE TIME HE'S BEEN BLOCKING ONLY THE CROSS.
COULD THAT HAVE BEEN DELIBERATE?
HEY. THANKS FOR GIVING ME A NICE, CLEAR HITTING LANE EVERY TIME.
NO, NO. THANK YOU FOR HITTING EXACTLY HOW I EXPECTED YOU TO EVERY TIME.

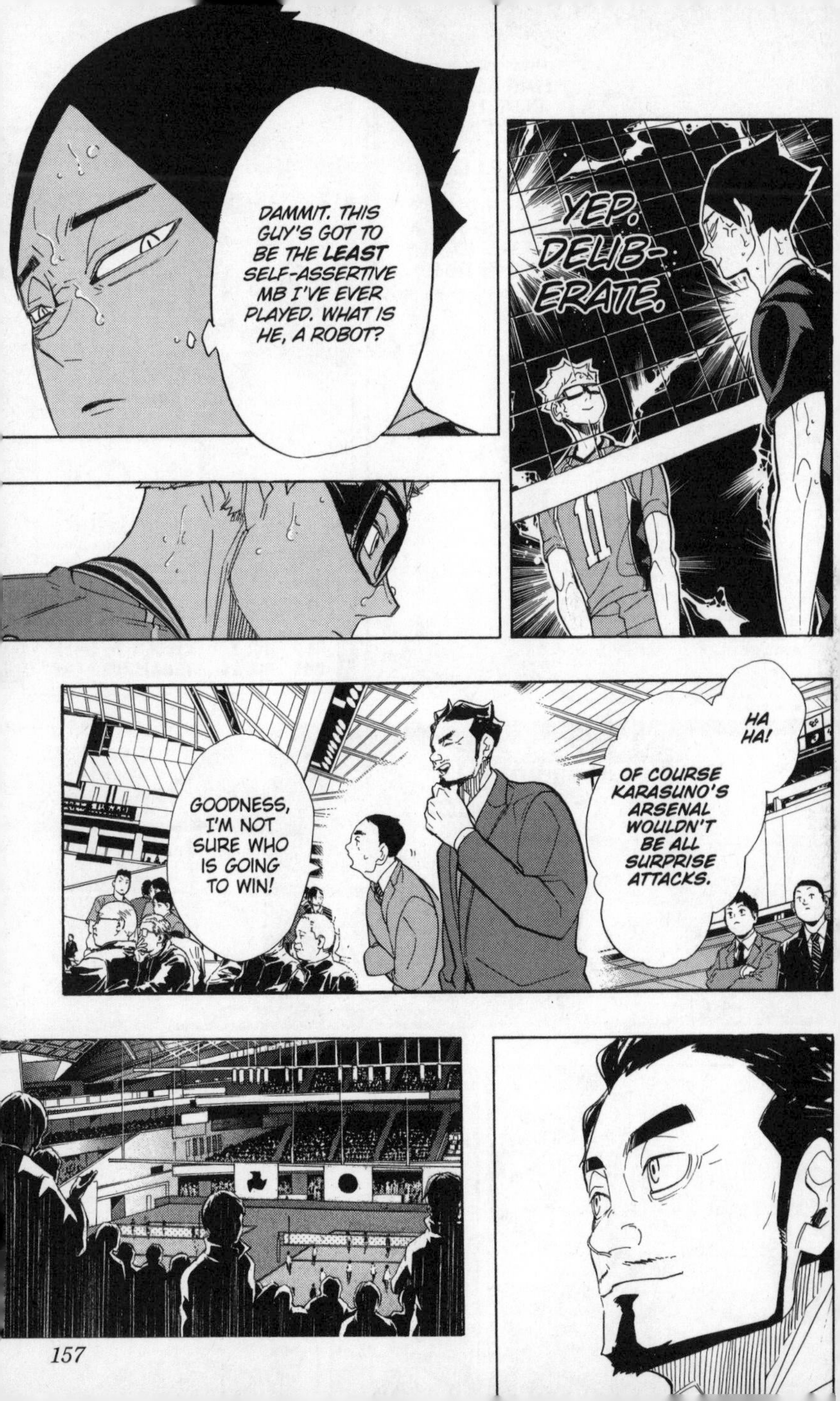
YEP. DELIB-ERATE.
DAMMIT. THIS GUY'S GOT TO BE THE **LEAST** SELF-ASSERTIVE MB I'VE EVER PLAYED. WHAT IS HE, A ROBOT?
HA HA!
OF COURSE KARASUNO'S ARSENAL WOULDN'T BE ALL SURPRISE ATTACKS.
GOODNESS, I'M NOT SURE WHO IS GOING TO WIN!

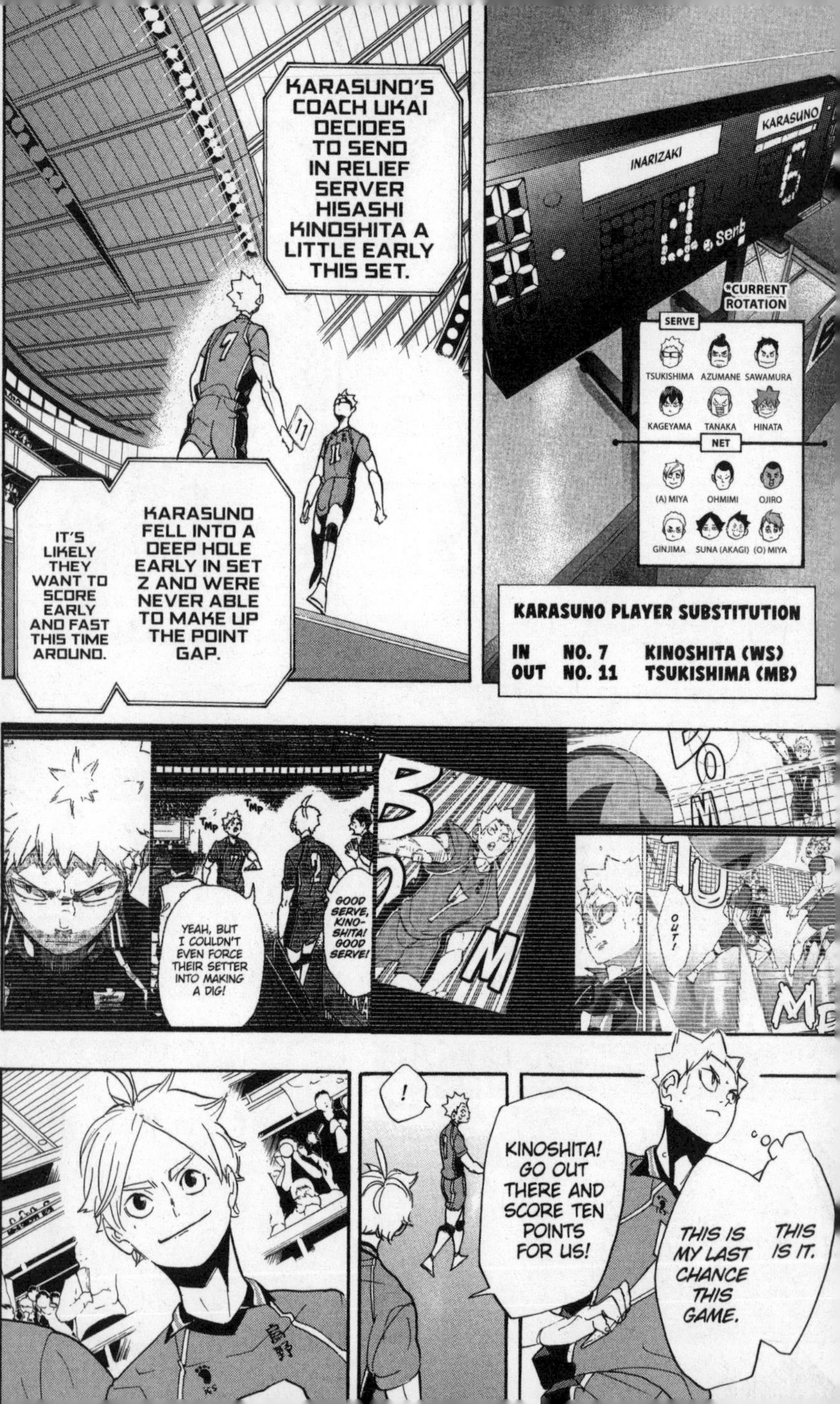
KARASUNO
INARIZAKI
*CURRENT ROTATION
SERVE
TSUKISHIMA
AZUMANE
SAWAMURA
KAGEYAMA
TANAKA
HINATA
NET
(A) MIYA
OHMIMI
OJIRO
GINJIMA
SUNA (AKAGI)
(O) MIYA
KARASUNO PLAYER SUBSTITUTION
IN NO. 7 KINOSHITA (WS)
OUT NO. 11 TSUKISHIMA (MB)
KARASUNO'S COACH UKAI DECIDES TO SEND IN RELIEF SERVER HISASHI KINOSHITA A LITTLE EARLY THIS SET.
KARASUNO FELL INTO A DEEP HOLE EARLY IN SET 2 AND WERE NEVER ABLE TO MAKE UP THE POINT GAP.
IT'S LIKELY THEY WANT TO SCORE EARLY AND FAST THIS TIME AROUND.
OUT!
GOOD SERVE, KINOSHITA! GOOD SERVE!
TMP
TMP
YEAH, BUT I COULDN'T EVEN FORCE THEIR SETTER INTO MAKING A DIG!
THIS IS IT.
THIS IS MY LAST CHANCE THIS GAME.
KINOSHITA! GO OUT THERE AND SCORE TEN POINTS FOR US!
!

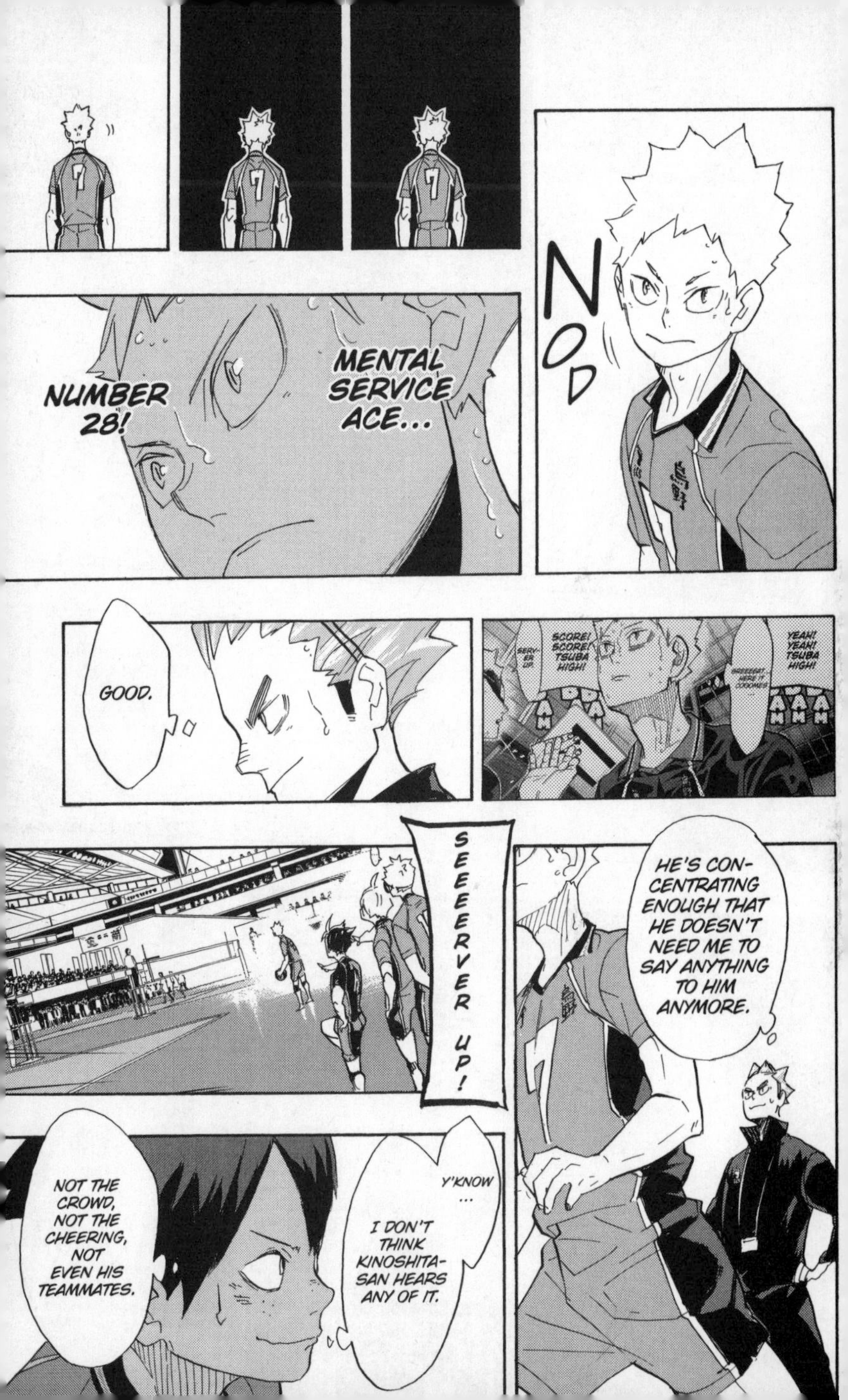
NOD
MENTAL SERVICE ACE...
NUMBER 28!
YEAH! YEAH! TSUBA HIGH!
HERE IT COOOMES
SCORE! SCORE! TSUBA HIGH!
SERV-ER UP.
GOOD.
HE'S CON-CENTRATING ENOUGH THAT HE DOESN'T NEED ME TO SAY ANYTHING TO HIM ANYMORE.
SEEEERVER UP!
Y'KNOW...
I DON'T THINK KINOSHITA-SAN HEARS ANY OF IT.
NOT THE CROWD, NOT THE CHEERING, NOT EVEN HIS TEAMMATES.

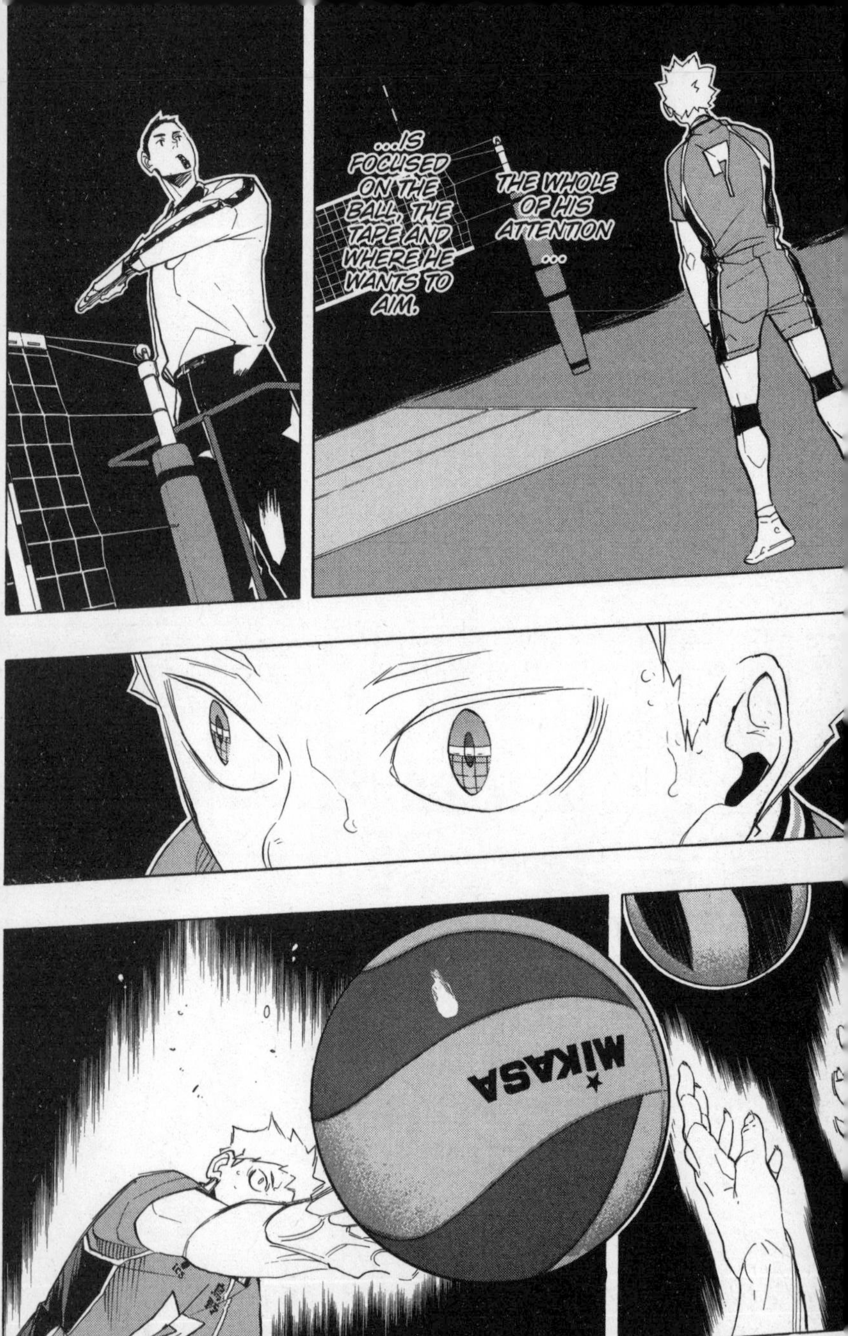
THE WHOLE OF HIS ATTENTION ...
...IS FOCUSED ON THE BALL, THE TAPE AND WHERE HE WANTS TO AIM.

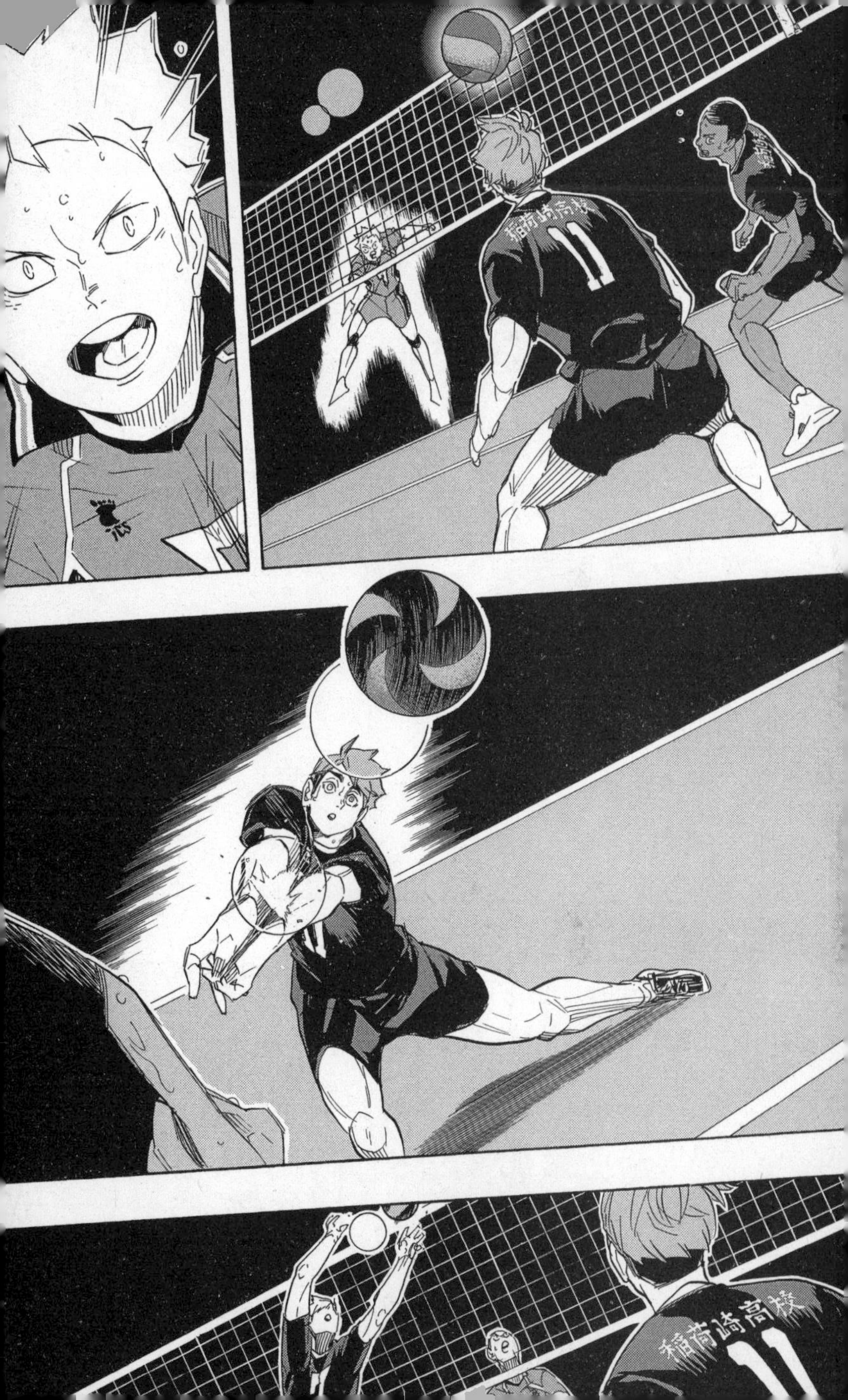
稲荷崎高校
11
稲荷崎高校
11

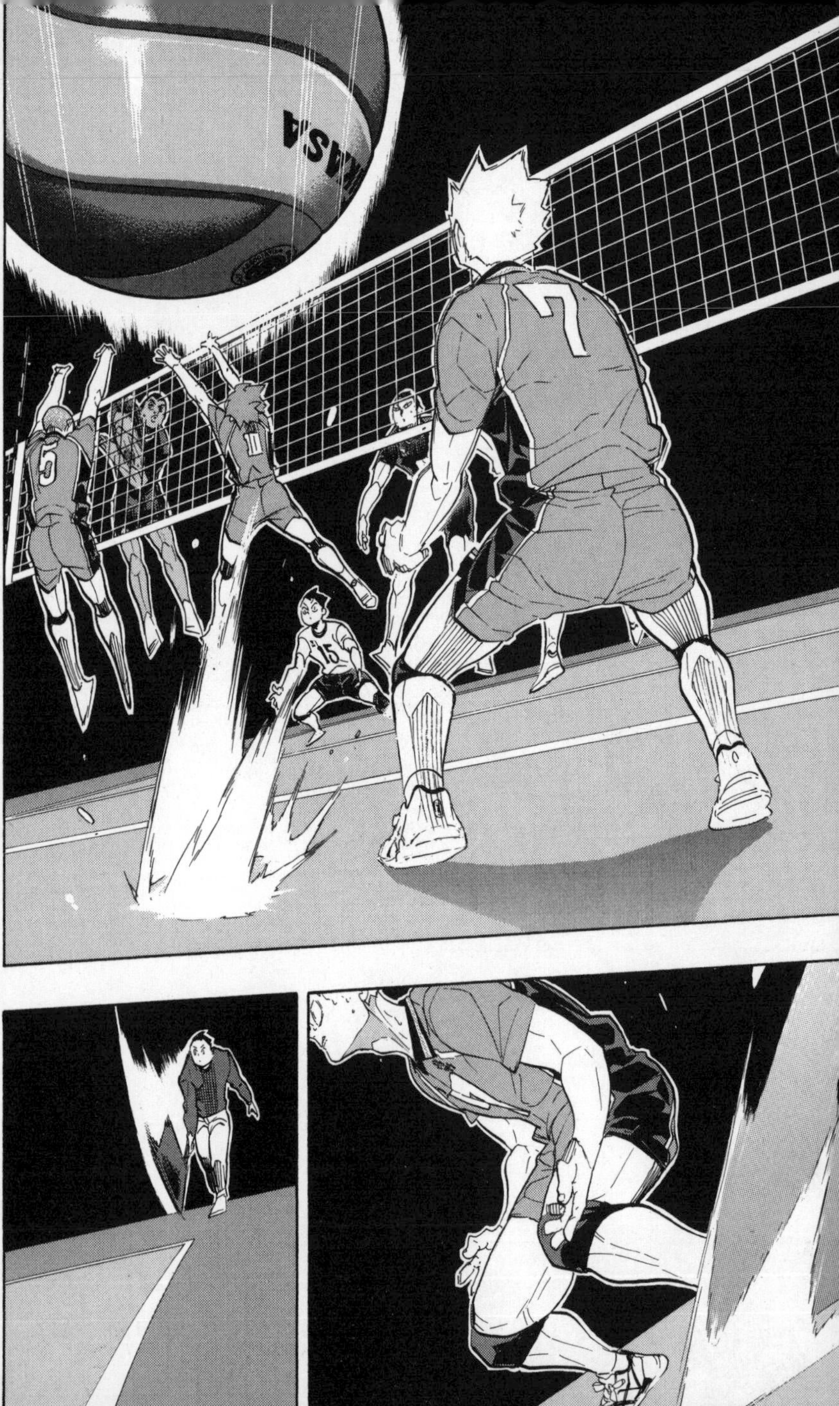

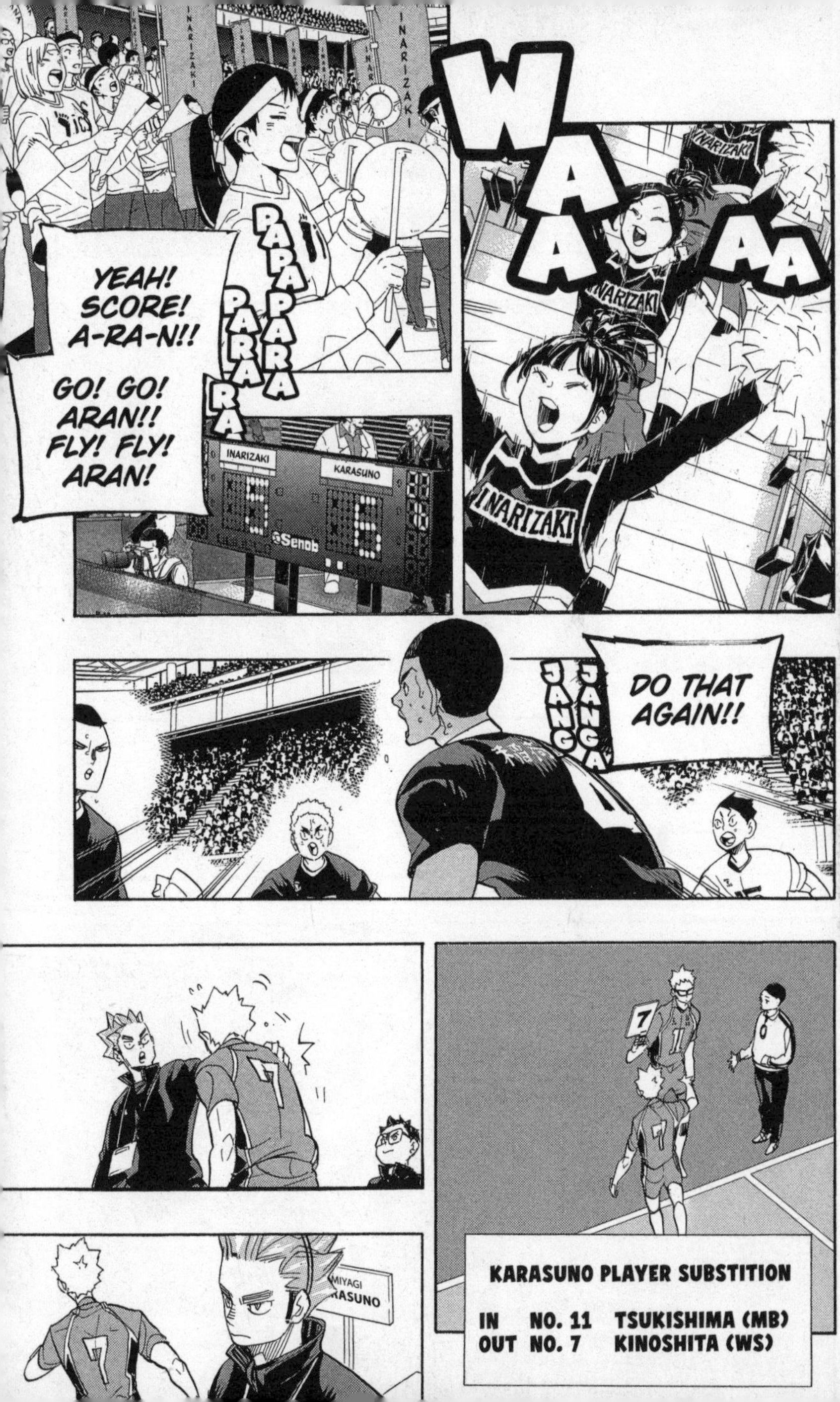
WAAAA
INARIZAKI
PAPAPARA
PARARA
YEAH! SCORE! A-RA-N!!
GO! GO! ARAN!! FLY! FLY! ARAN!
INARIZAKI
KARASUNO
DO THAT AGAIN!!
JANGA
JANG
KARASUNO PLAYER SUBSTITION
IN NO. 11 TSUKISHIMA (MB)
OUT NO. 7 KINOSHITA (WS)
MIYAGI

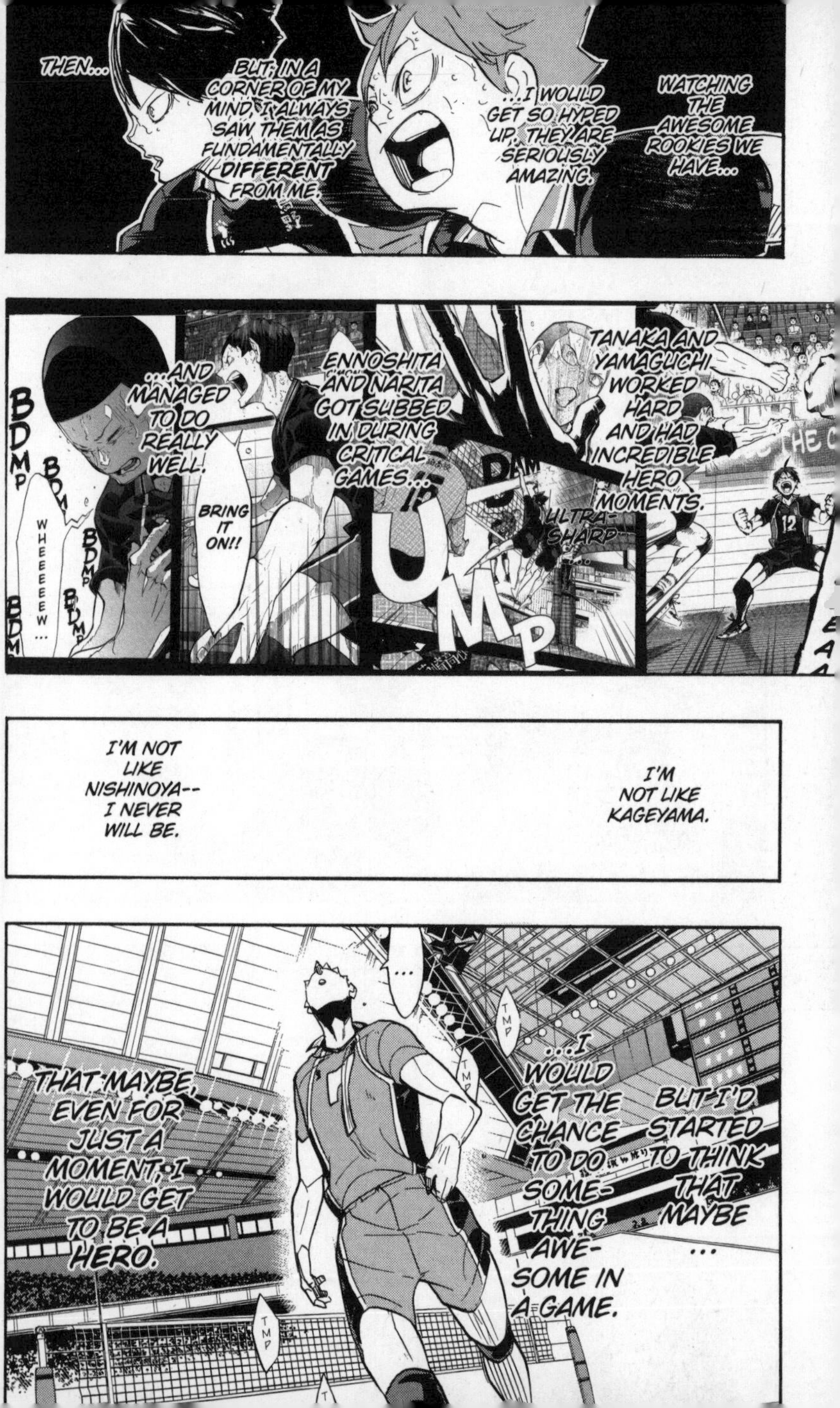
WATCHING THE AWESOME ROOKIES WE HAVE...
...I WOULD GET SO HYPED UP. THEY ARE SERIOUSLY AMAZING.
BUT, IN A CORNER OF MY MIND, I ALWAYS SAW THEM AS FUNDAMENTALLY DIFFERENT FROM ME.
THEN...
TANAKA AND YAMAGUCHI WORKED HARD AND HAD INCREDIBLE HERO MOMENTS.
ULTRA-SHARP...
UMP
ENNOSHITA AND NARITA GOT SUBBED IN DURING CRITICAL GAMES...
BRING IT ON!!
...AND MANAGED TO DO REALLY WELL.
BDMP
BDMP
BDMP
BDMP
BDMP
WHEEEEEEW...
I'M NOT LIKE KAGEYAMA.
I'M NOT LIKE NISHINOYA-- I NEVER WILL BE.
...
TMP
TMP
BUT I'D STARTED TO THINK THAT MAYBE...
...I WOULD GET THE CHANCE TO DO SOMETHING AWESOME IN A GAME.
THAT MAYBE, EVEN FOR JUST A MOMENT, I WOULD GET TO BE A HERO.
TMP

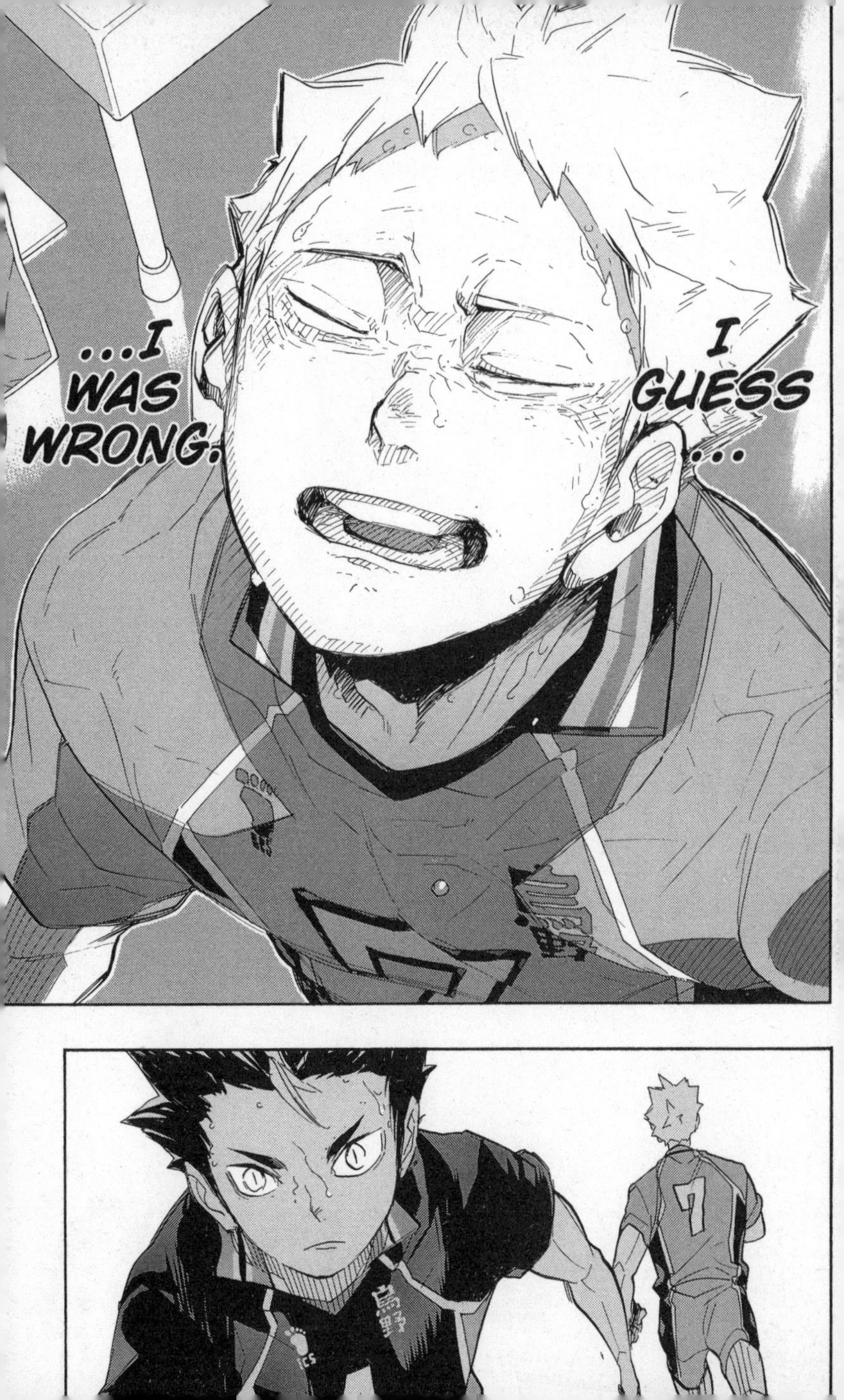
I GUESS...
...I WAS WRONG.

HAIKYU!!

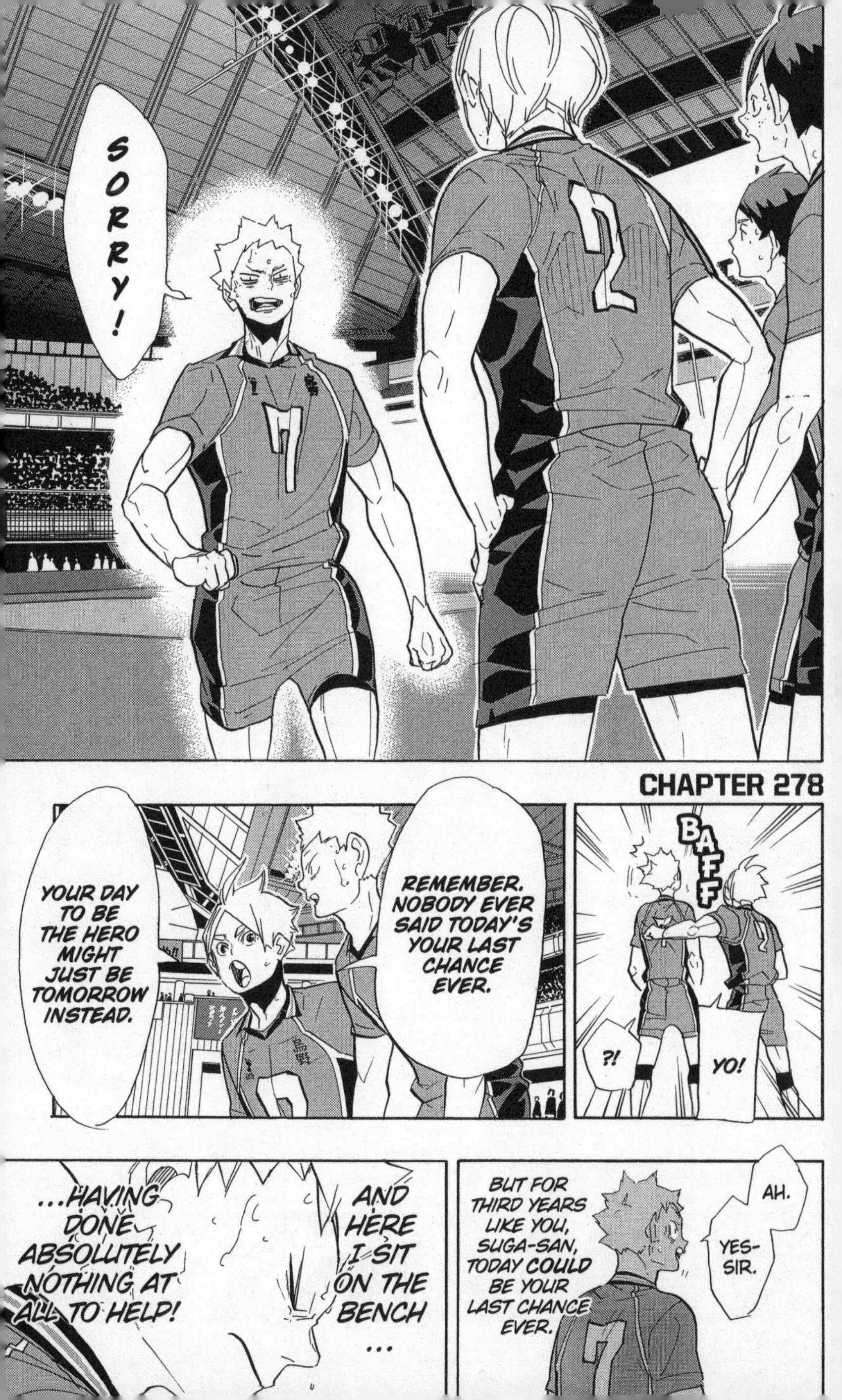
SORRY!
CHAPTER 278
BAFF
YO!
?!
REMEMBER. NOBODY EVER SAID TODAY'S YOUR LAST CHANCE EVER.
YOUR DAY TO BE THE HERO MIGHT JUST BE TOMORROW INSTEAD.
AH.
YES-SIR.
BUT FOR THIRD YEARS LIKE YOU, SUGA-SAN, TODAY COULD BE YOUR LAST CHANCE EVER.
AND HERE I SIT ON THE BENCH...
...HAVING DONE ABSOLUTELY NOTHING AT ALL TO HELP!

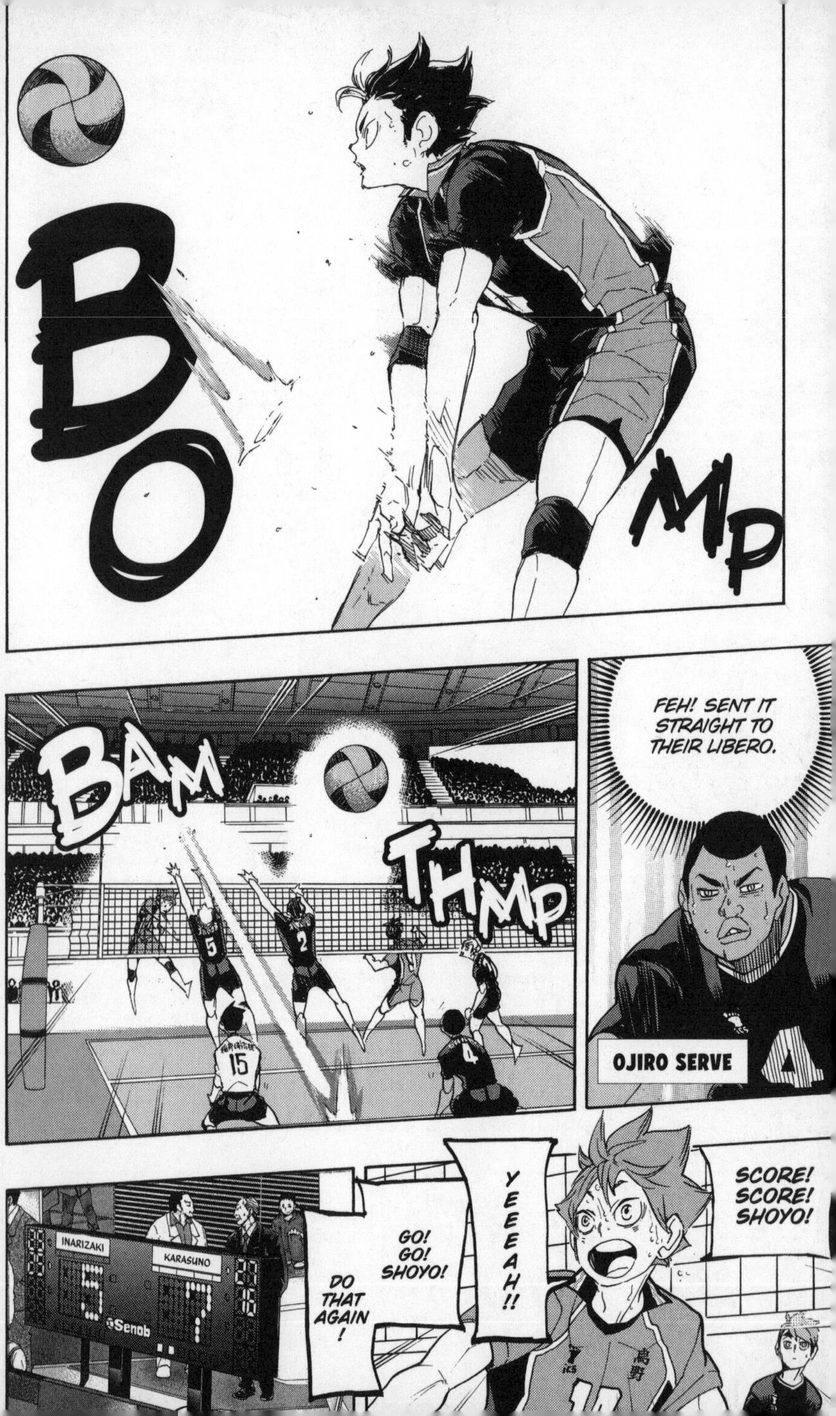
BOMP
FEH! SENT IT STRAIGHT TO THEIR LIBERO.
OJIRO SERVE
BAM
THMP
SCORE! SCORE! SHOYO!
YEEEAH!!
GO! GO! SHOYO!
DO THAT AGAIN!
INARIZAKI
KARASUNO
Senob

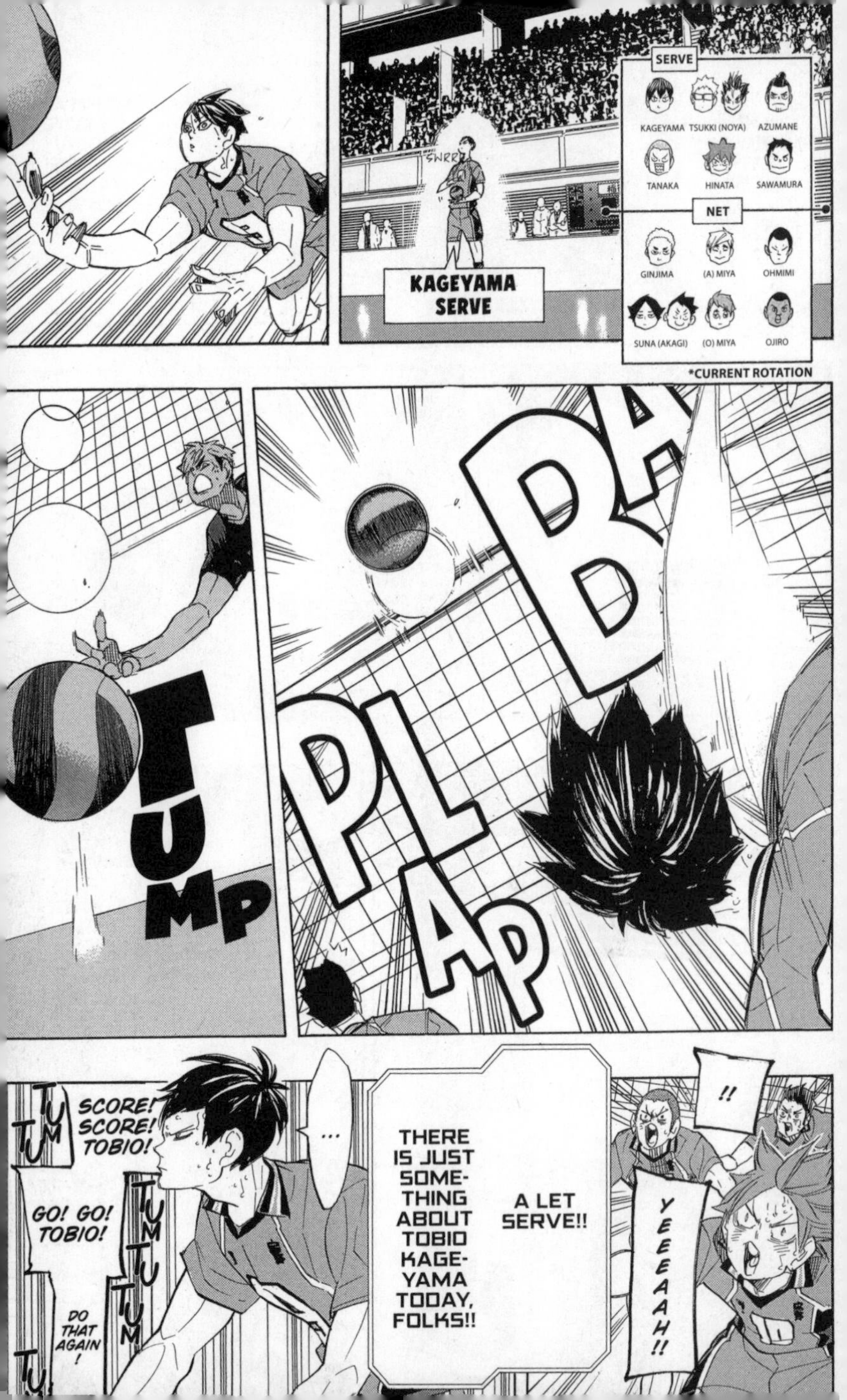
SWRR
KAGEYAMA SERVE
SERVE
KAGEYAMA
TSUKKI (NOYA)
AZUMANE
TANAKA
HINATA
SAWAMURA
NET
GINJIMA
(A) MIYA
OHMIMI
SUNA (AKAGI)
(O) MIYA
OJIRO
*CURRENT ROTATION
BA
PLAP
JUMP
!!
YEEEAAAH!!
A LET SERVE!!
THERE IS JUST SOMETHING ABOUT TOBIO KAGEYAMA TODAY, FOLKS!!
...
TUM TUM
SCORE! SCORE! TOBIO!
GO! GO! TOBIO!
TUM TUM TUM TUM
DO THAT AGAIN!
TU

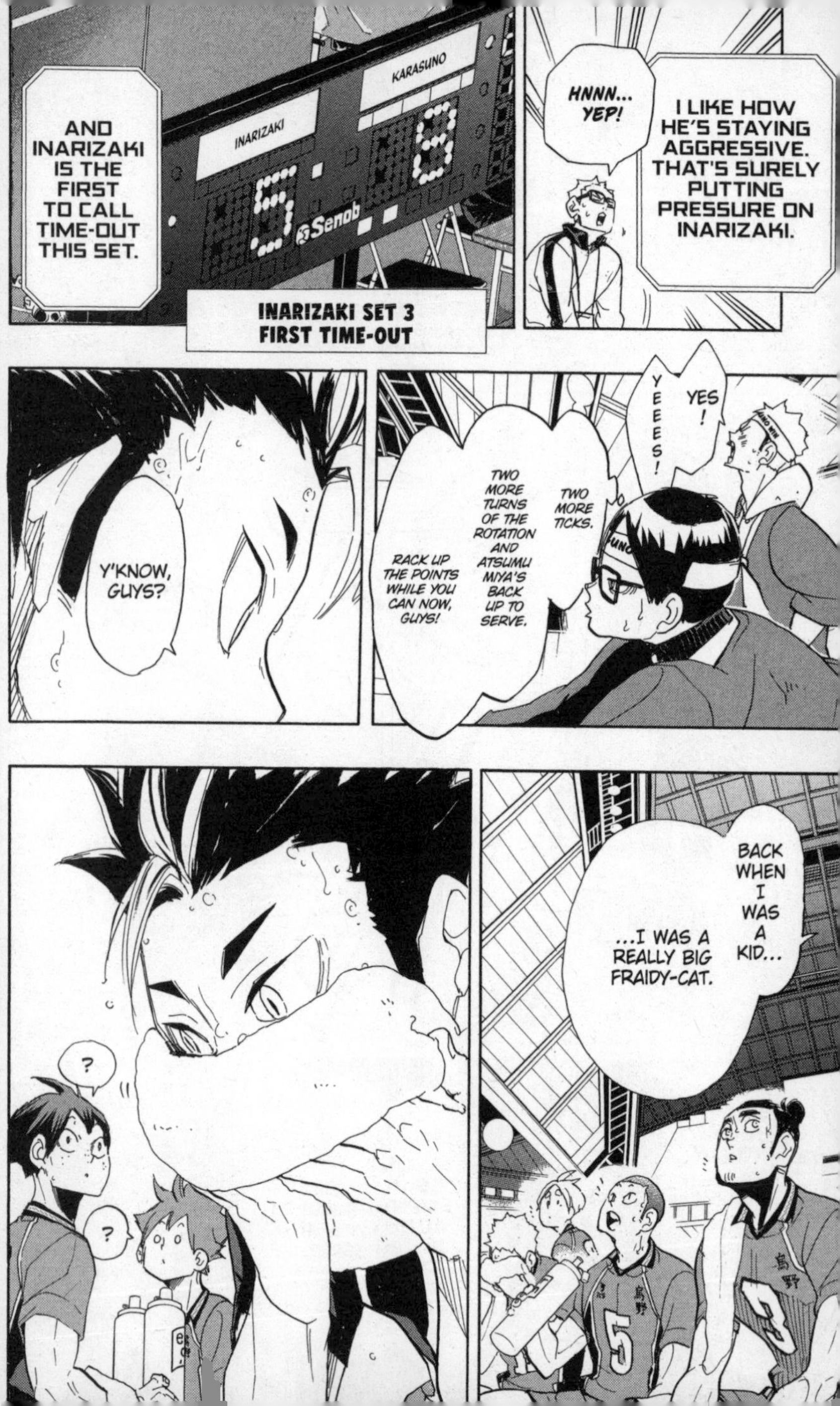

I LIKE HOW HE'S STAYING AGGRESSIVE. THAT'S SURELY PUTTING PRESSURE ON INARIZAKI.
HNNN... YEP!
KARASUNO
INARIZAKI
Senob
AND INARIZAKI IS THE FIRST TO CALL TIME-OUT THIS SET.
INARIZAKI SET 3 FIRST TIME-OUT
YES!
YEEEES!
TWO MORE TICKS.
TWO MORE TURNS OF THE ROTATION AND ATSUMU MIYA'S BACK UP TO SERVE.
RACK UP THE POINTS WHILE YOU CAN NOW, GUYS!
Y'KNOW, GUYS?
BACK WHEN I WAS A KID...
...I WAS A REALLY BIG FRAIDY-CAT.
?
...
?

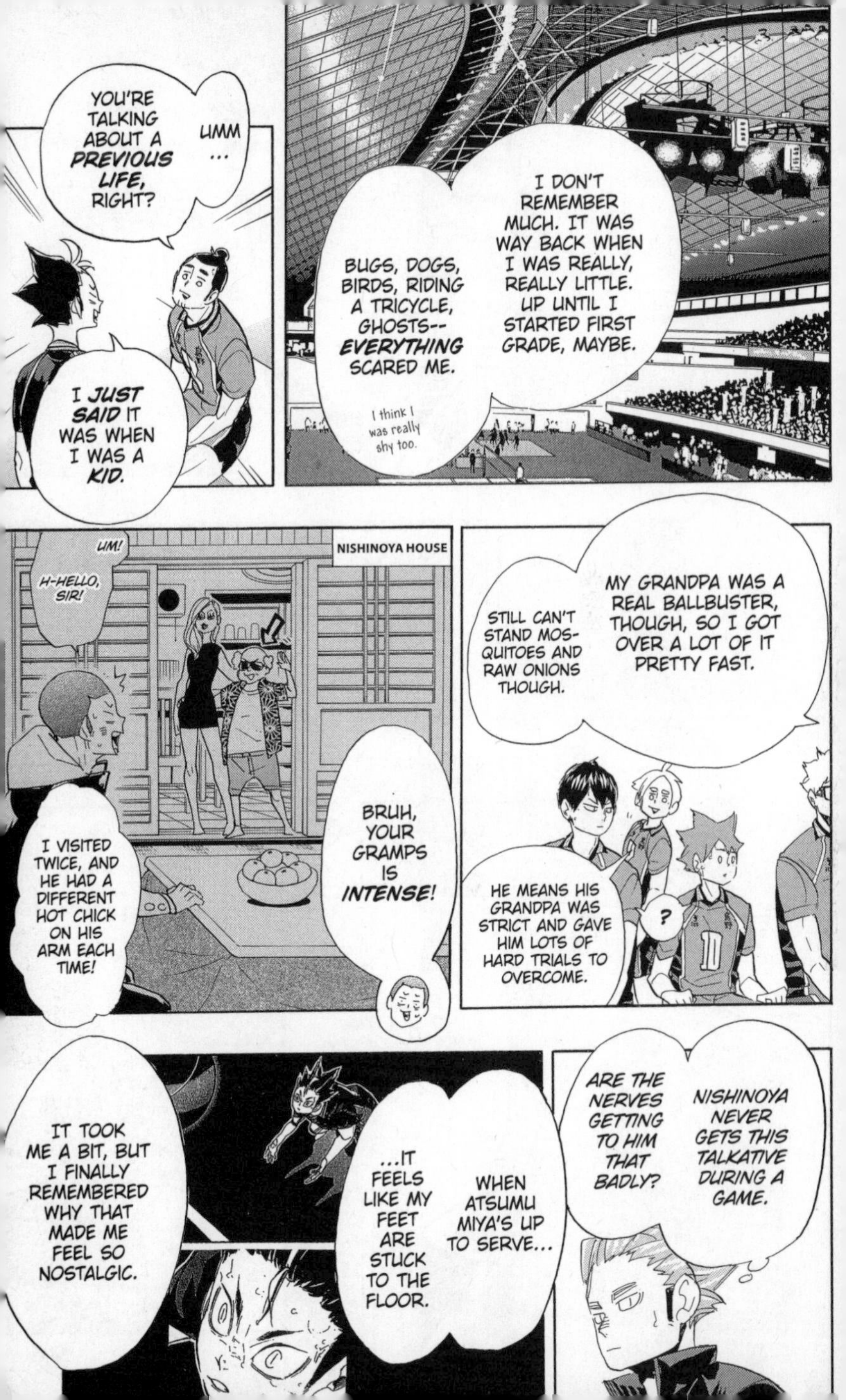
I DON'T REMEMBER MUCH. IT WAS WAY BACK WHEN I WAS REALLY, REALLY LITTLE. UP UNTIL I STARTED FIRST GRADE, MAYBE.
BUGS, DOGS, BIRDS, RIDING A TRICYCLE, GHOSTS-- EVERYTHING SCARED ME.
I think I was really shy too.
YOU'RE TALKING ABOUT A PREVIOUS LIFE, RIGHT?
UMM ...
I JUST SAID IT WAS WHEN I WAS A KID.
MY GRANDPA WAS A REAL BALLBUSTER, THOUGH, SO I GOT OVER A LOT OF IT PRETTY FAST.
STILL CAN'T STAND MOS-QUITOES AND RAW ONIONS THOUGH.
HE MEANS HIS GRANDPA WAS STRICT AND GAVE HIM LOTS OF HARD TRIALS TO OVERCOME.
?
NISHINOYA HOUSE
UM!
H-HELLO, SIR!
BRUH, YOUR GRAMPS IS INTENSE!
I VISITED TWICE, AND HE HAD A DIFFERENT HOT CHICK ON HIS ARM EACH TIME!
NISHINOYA NEVER GETS THIS TALKATIVE DURING A GAME.
ARE THE NERVES GETTING TO HIM THAT BADLY?
WHEN ATSUMU MIYA'S UP TO SERVE...
...IT FEELS LIKE MY FEET ARE STUCK TO THE FLOOR.
IT TOOK ME A BIT, BUT I FINALLY REMEMBERED WHY THAT MADE ME FEEL SO NOSTALGIC.

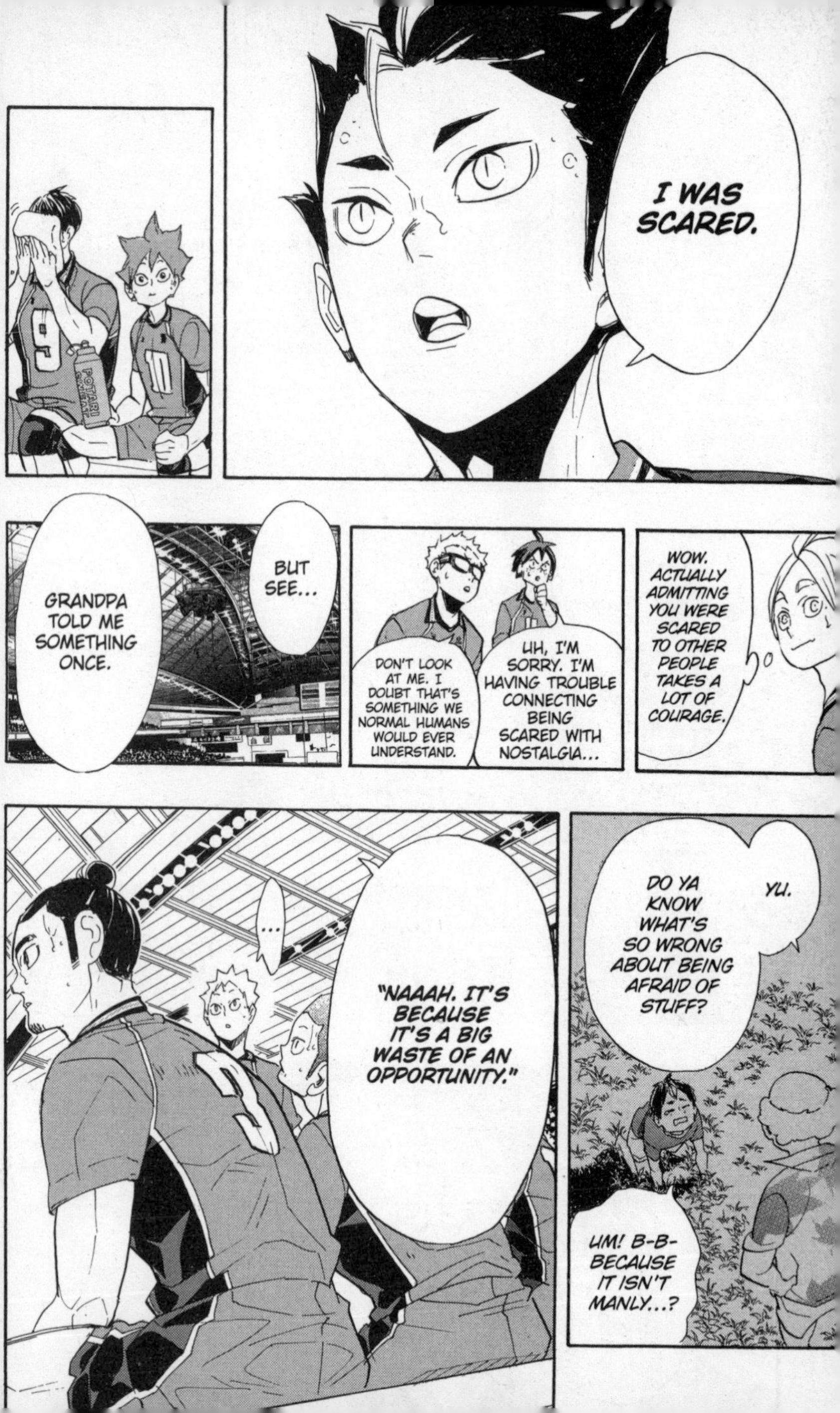
I WAS SCARED.
WOW. ACTUALLY ADMITTING YOU WERE SCARED TO OTHER PEOPLE TAKES A LOT OF COURAGE.
UH, I'M SORRY. I'M HAVING TROUBLE CONNECTING BEING SCARED WITH NOSTALGIA...
DON'T LOOK AT ME. I DOUBT THAT'S SOMETHING WE NORMAL HUMANS WOULD EVER UNDERSTAND.
BUT SEE...
GRANDPA TOLD ME SOMETHING ONCE.
YU.
DO YA KNOW WHAT'S SO WRONG ABOUT BEING AFRAID OF STUFF?
UM! B-B-BECAUSE IT ISN'T MANLY...?
"NAAAH. IT'S BECAUSE IT'S A BIG WASTE OF AN OPPORTUNITY."
...

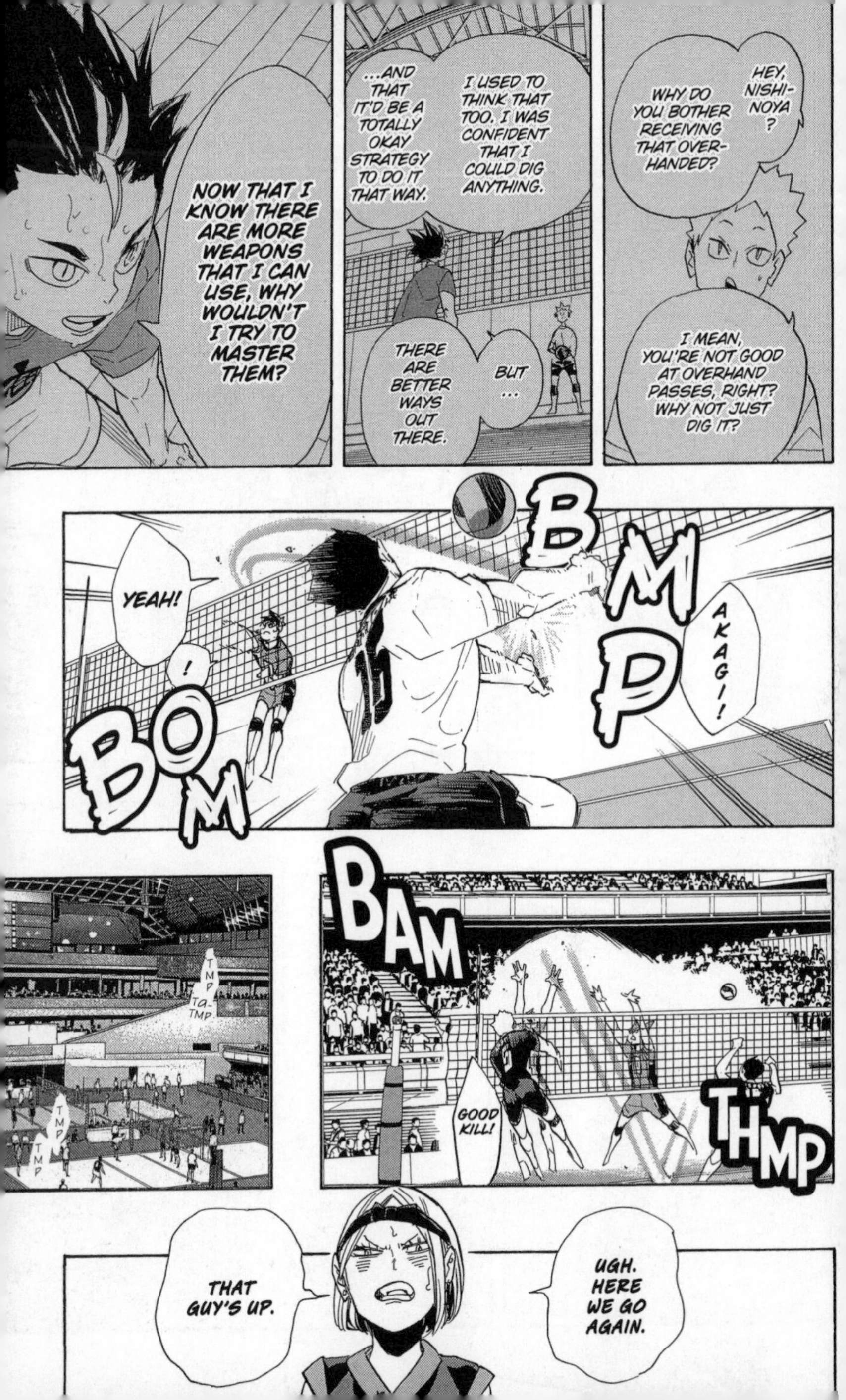
HEY, NISHINOYA?
WHY DO YOU BOTHER RECEIVING THAT OVERHANDED?
I MEAN, YOU'RE NOT GOOD AT OVERHAND PASSES, RIGHT? WHY NOT JUST DIG IT?
I USED TO THINK THAT TOO. I WAS CONFIDENT THAT I COULD DIG ANYTHING.
...AND THAT IT'D BE A TOTALLY OKAY STRATEGY TO DO IT THAT WAY.
BUT...
THERE ARE BETTER WAYS OUT THERE.
NOW THAT I KNOW THERE ARE MORE WEAPONS THAT I CAN USE, WHY WOULDN'T I TRY TO MASTER THEM?
BMP
AKAGI!
YEAH!
!
BOM
BAM
GOOD KILL!
THMP
TMP TA-TMP
TMP TMP
UGH. HERE WE GO AGAIN.
THAT GUY'S UP.

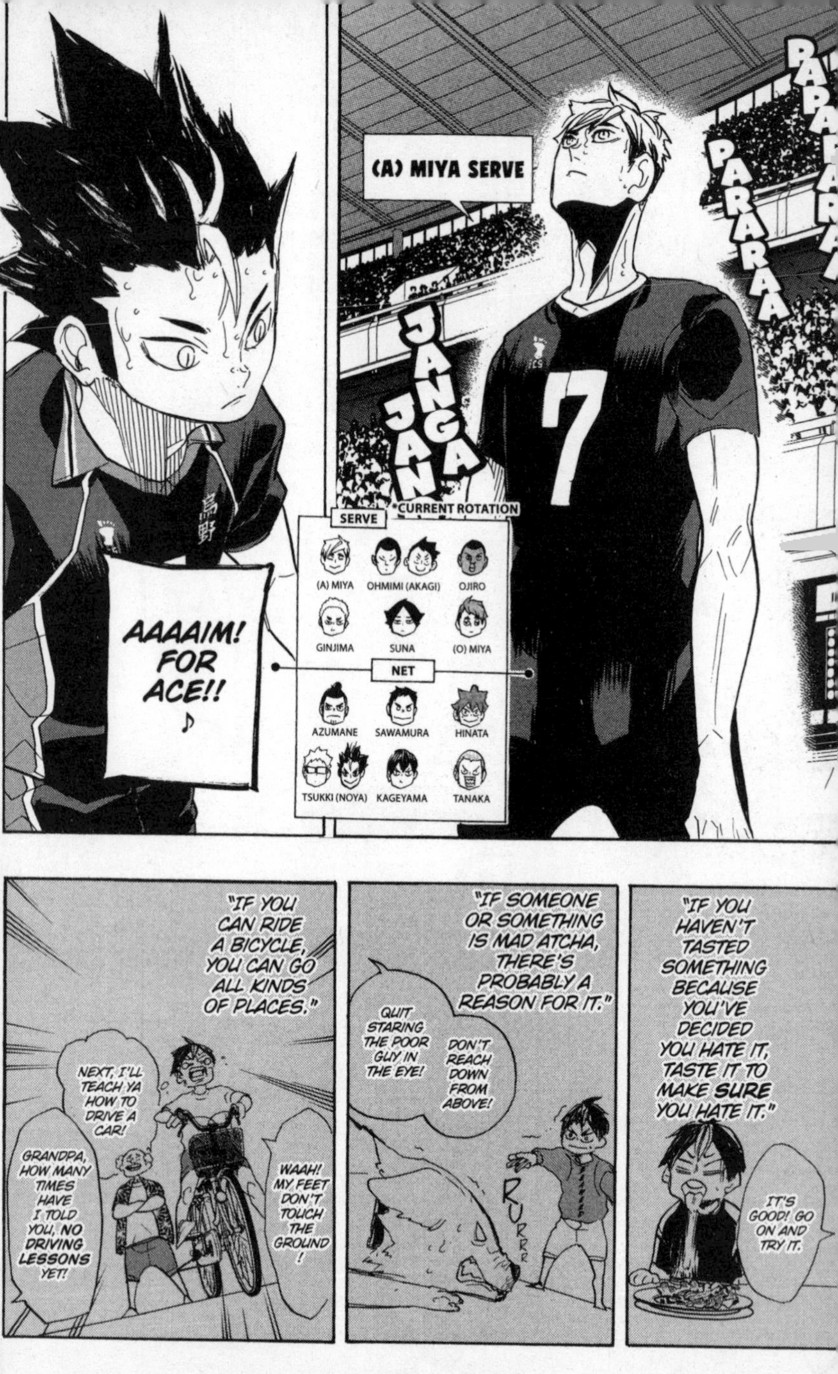
PAPAPARA
PARARAA
(A) MIYA SERVE
JANGA JANGAN
*CURRENT ROTATION
SERVE
(A) MIYA
OHMIMI (AKAGI)
OJIRO
GINJIMA
SUNA
(O) MIYA
NET
AZUMANE
SAWAMURA
HINATA
TSUKKI (NOYA)
KAGEYAMA
TANAKA
AAAAIM! FOR ACE!! ♪
"IF YOU HAVEN'T TASTED SOMETHING BECAUSE YOU'VE DECIDED YOU HATE IT, TASTE IT TO MAKE SURE YOU HATE IT."
IT'S GOOD! GO ON AND TRY IT.
"IF SOMEONE OR SOMETHING IS MAD ATCHA, THERE'S PROBABLY A REASON FOR IT."
DON'T REACH DOWN FROM ABOVE!
QUIT STARING THE POOR GUY IN THE EYE!
RURRR
"IF YOU CAN RIDE A BICYCLE, YOU CAN GO ALL KINDS OF PLACES."
WAAH! MY FEET DON'T TOUCH THE GROUND!
NEXT, I'LL TEACH YA HOW TO DRIVE A CAR!
GRANDPA, HOW MANY TIMES HAVE I TOLD YOU, NO DRIVING LESSONS YET!

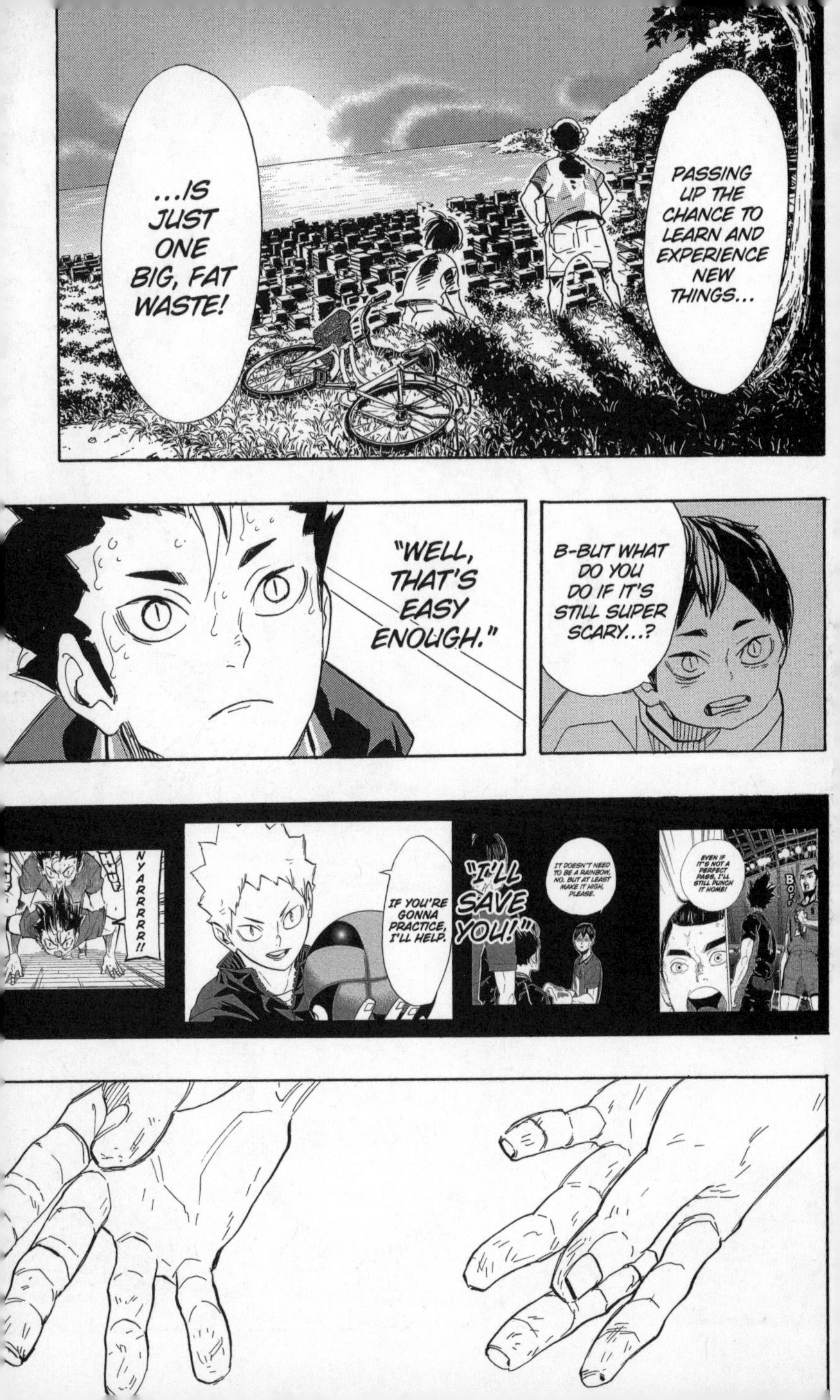
PASSING UP THE CHANCE TO LEARN AND EXPERIENCE NEW THINGS...
...IS JUST ONE BIG, FAT WASTE!
B-BUT WHAT DO YOU DO IF IT'S STILL SUPER SCARY...?
"WELL, THAT'S EASY ENOUGH."
EVEN IF IT'S NOT A PERFECT PASS, I'LL STILL PUNCH IT HOME!
IT DOESN'T NEED TO BE A RAINBOW, NO. BUT AT LEAST MAKE IT HIGH, PLEASE.
"I'LL SAVE YOU!"
IF YOU'RE GONNA PRACTICE, I'LL HELP.
NYARRRRR!!

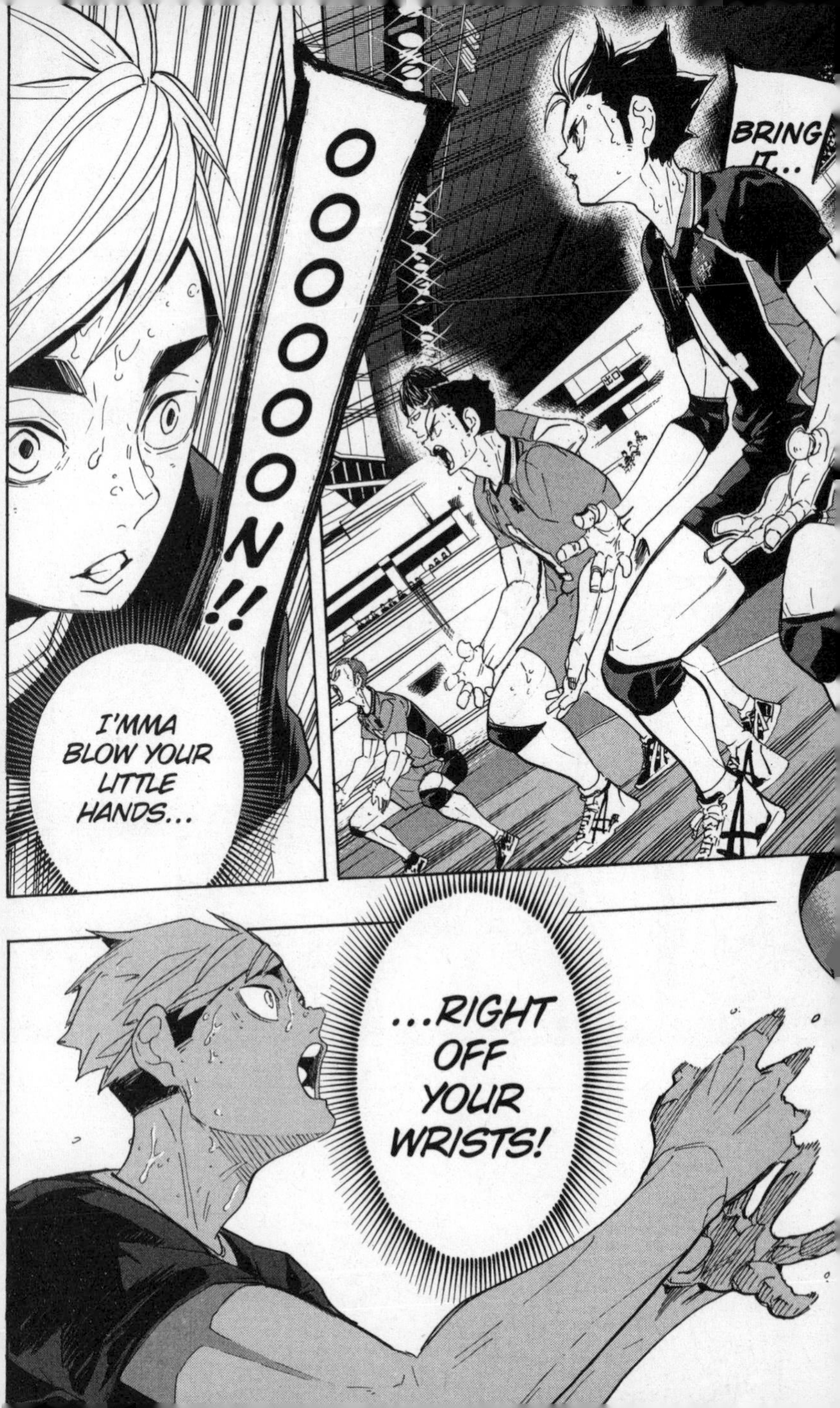
BRING IT...
OOOOOON!!
I'MMA BLOW YOUR LITTLE HANDS...
...RIGHT OFF YOUR WRISTS!

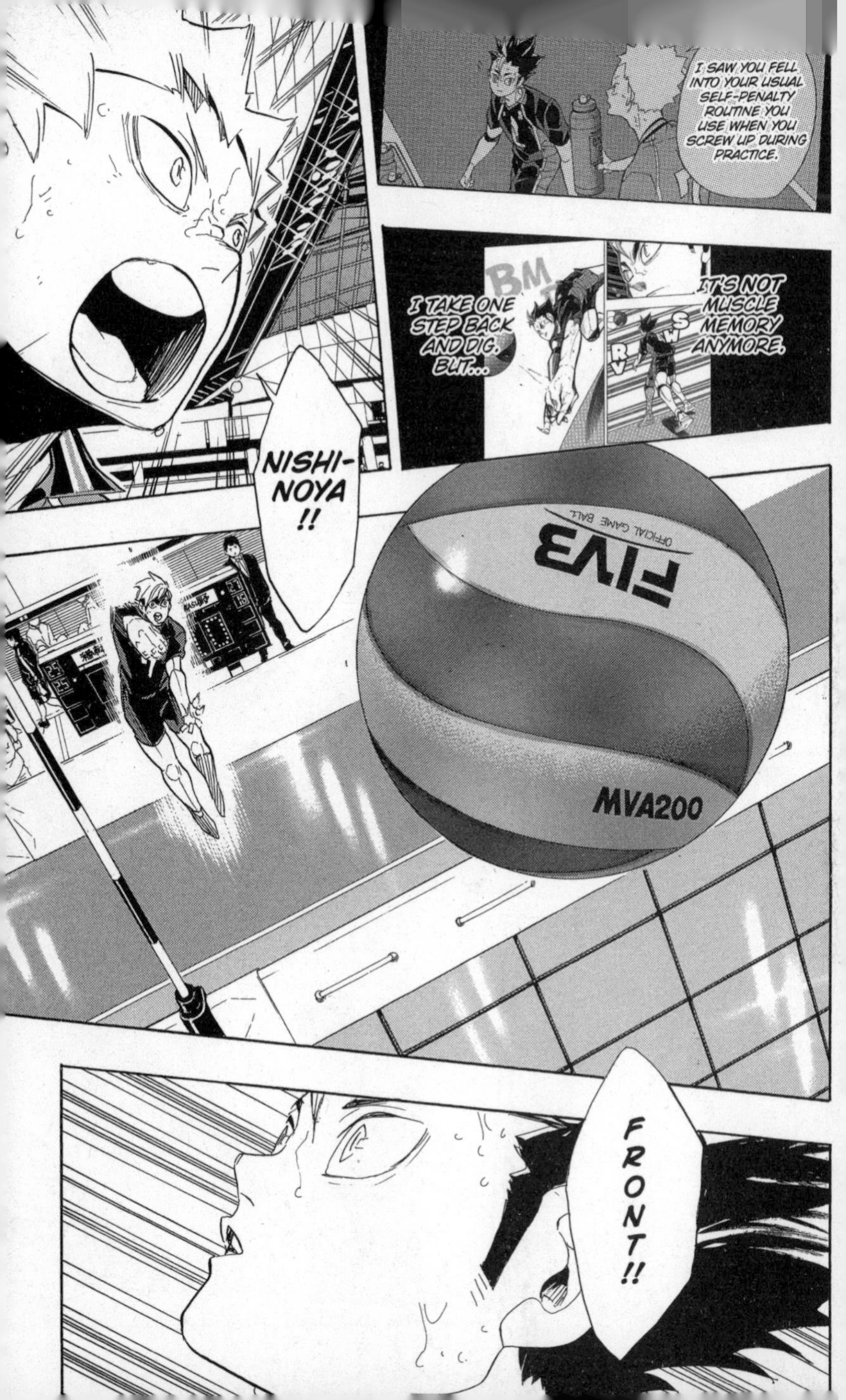
I SAW YOU FELL INTO YOUR USUAL SELF-PENALTY ROUTINE YOU USE WHEN YOU SCREW UP DURING PRACTICE.
IT'S NOT MUSCLE MEMORY ANYMORE.
I TAKE ONE STEP BACK AND DIG. BUT...
NISHI-NOYA!!
MVA200
FRONT!!

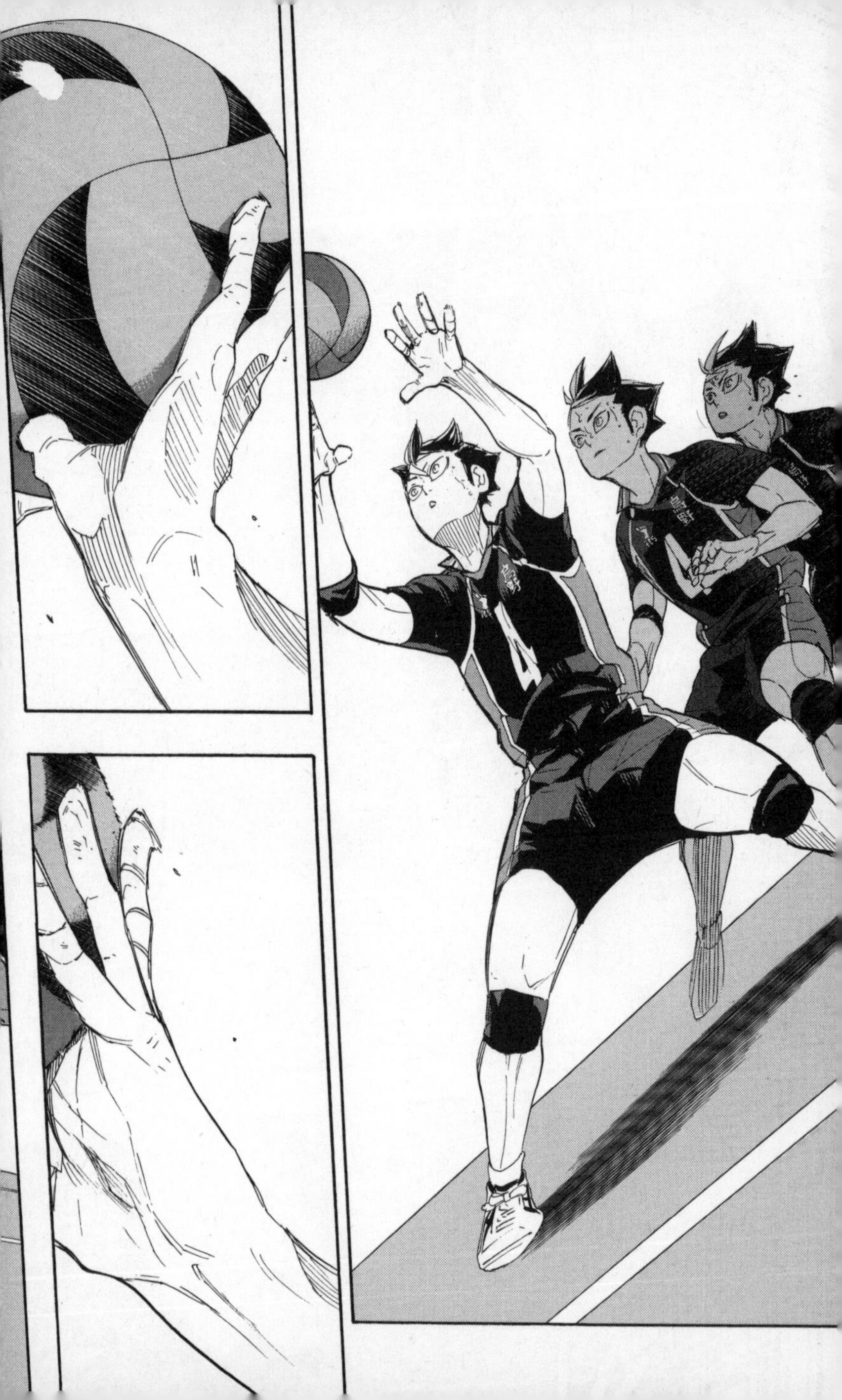

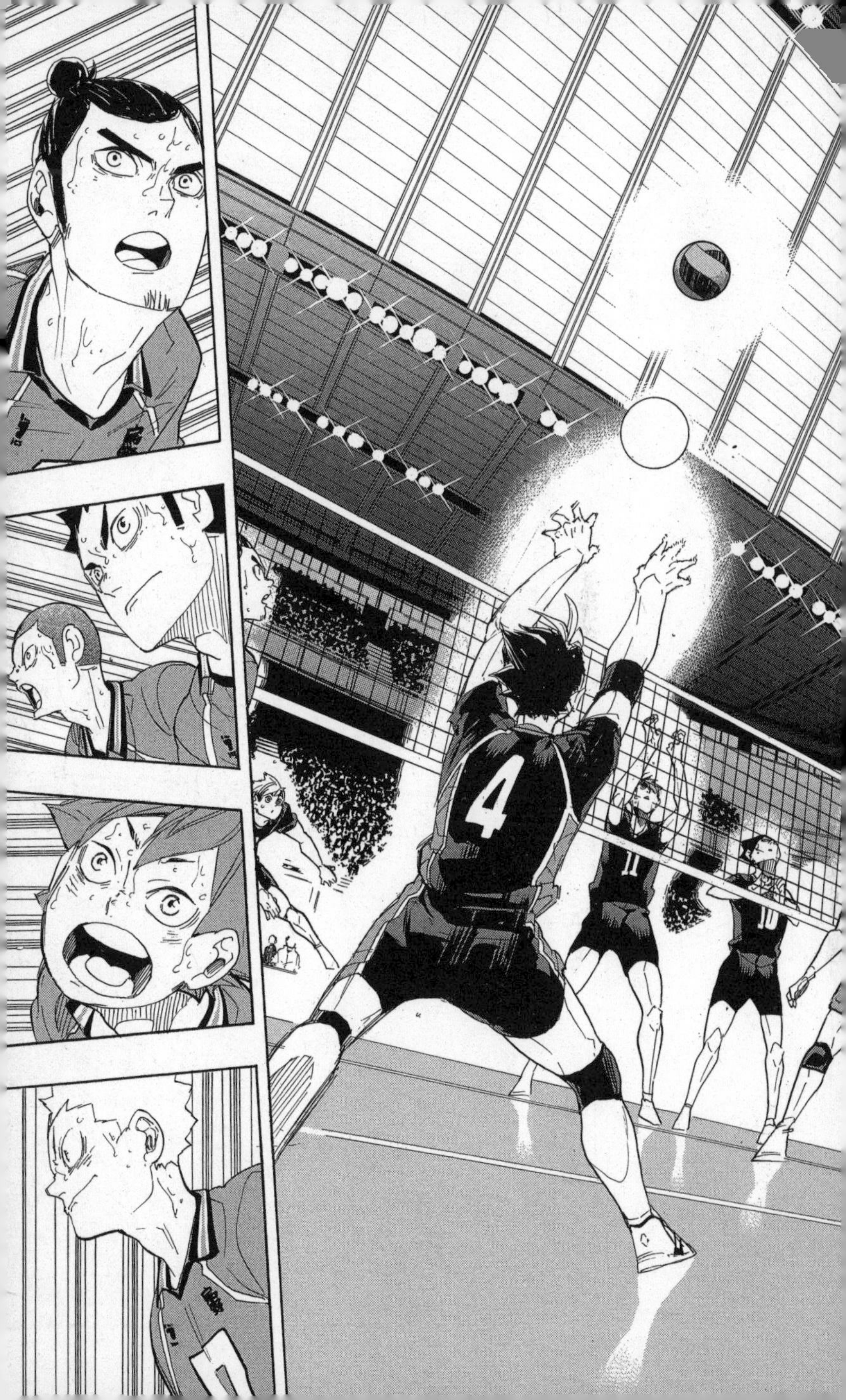

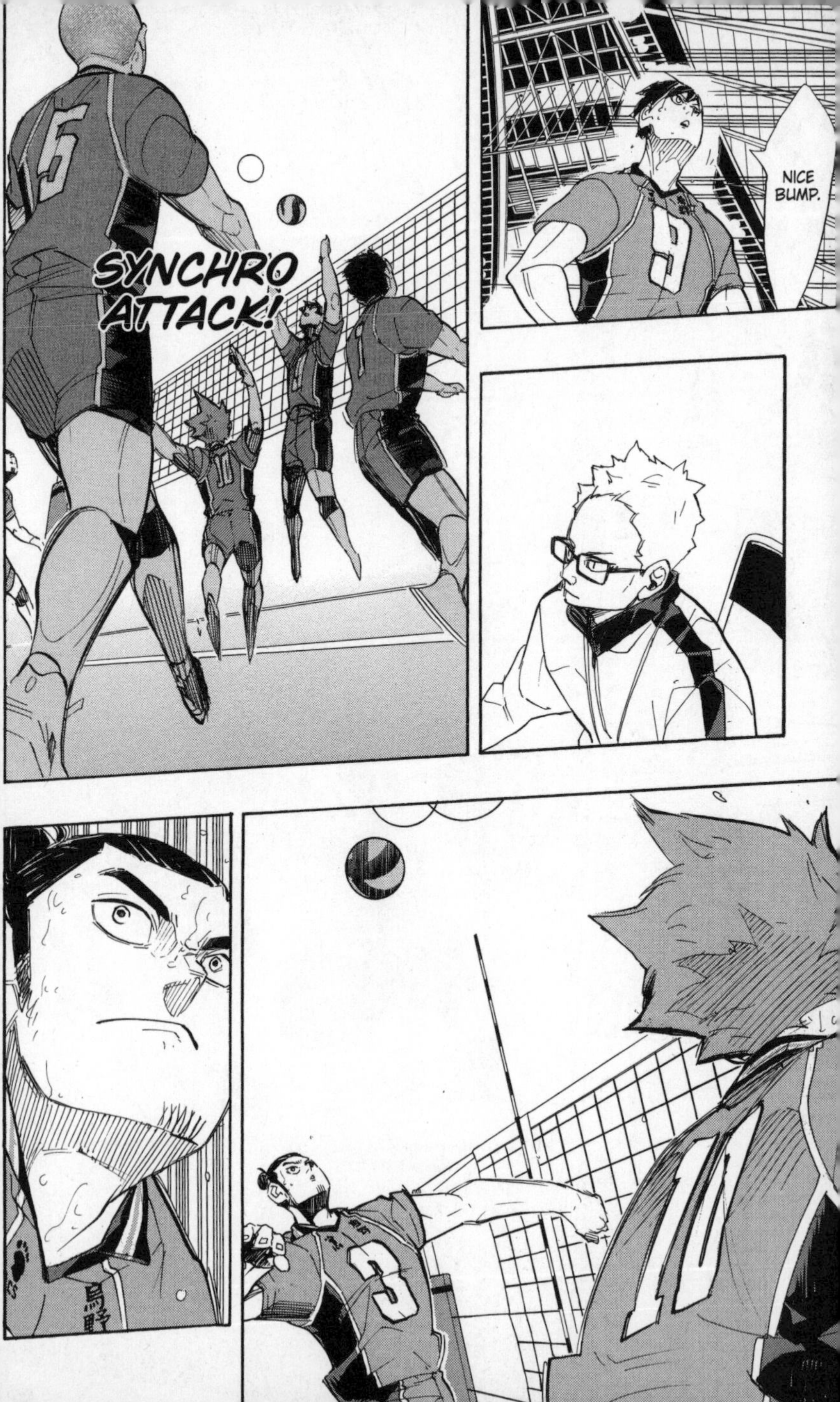
NICE BUMP.
SYNCHRO ATTACK!

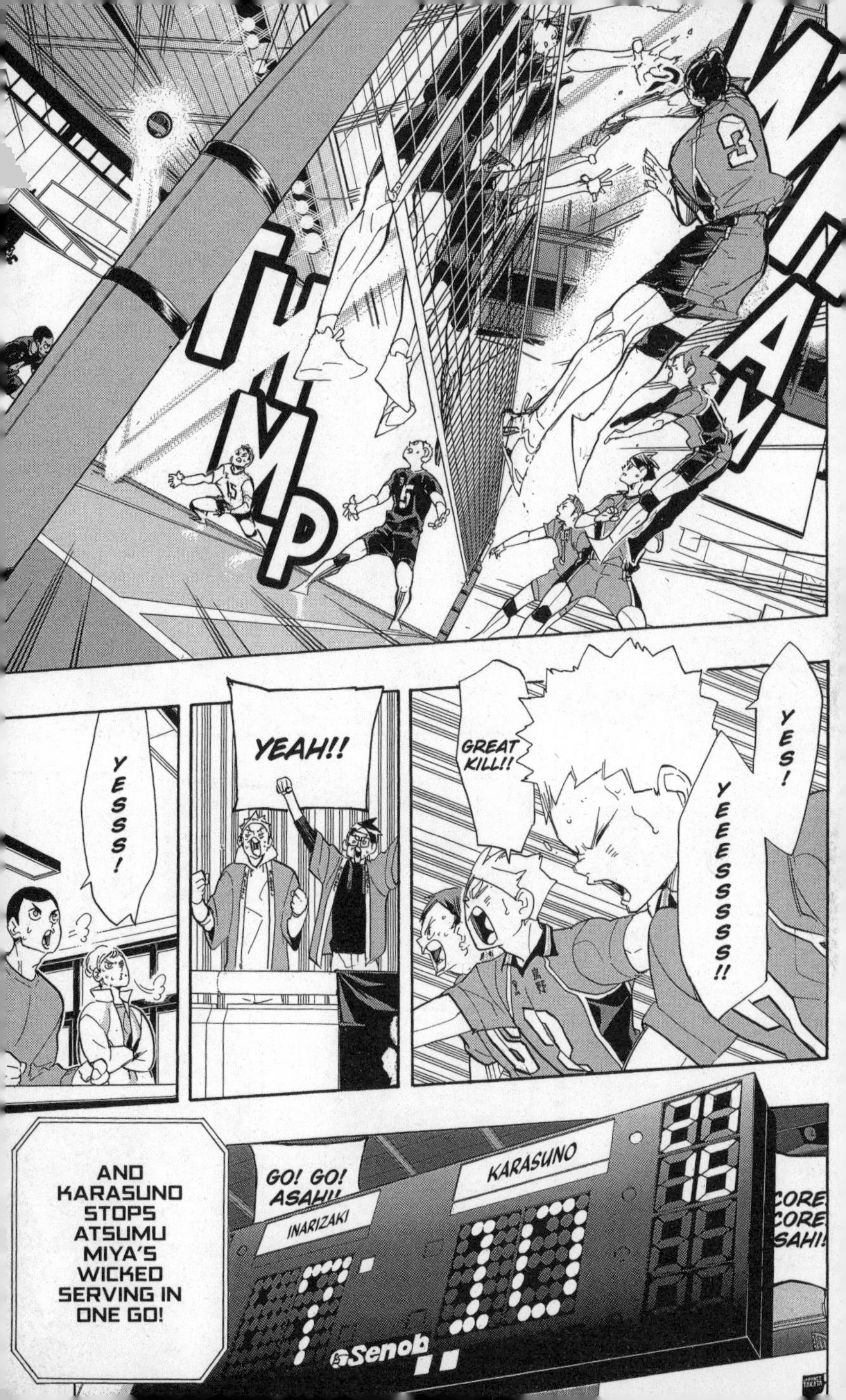
WHAM
THUMP
YES! YEEEESSSSS!!
GREAT KILL!!
YEAH!!
YESSS!
KARASUNO
GO! GO! ASAHI!!
INARIZAKI
AND KARASUNO STOPS ATSUMU MIYA'S WICKED SERVING IN ONE GO!

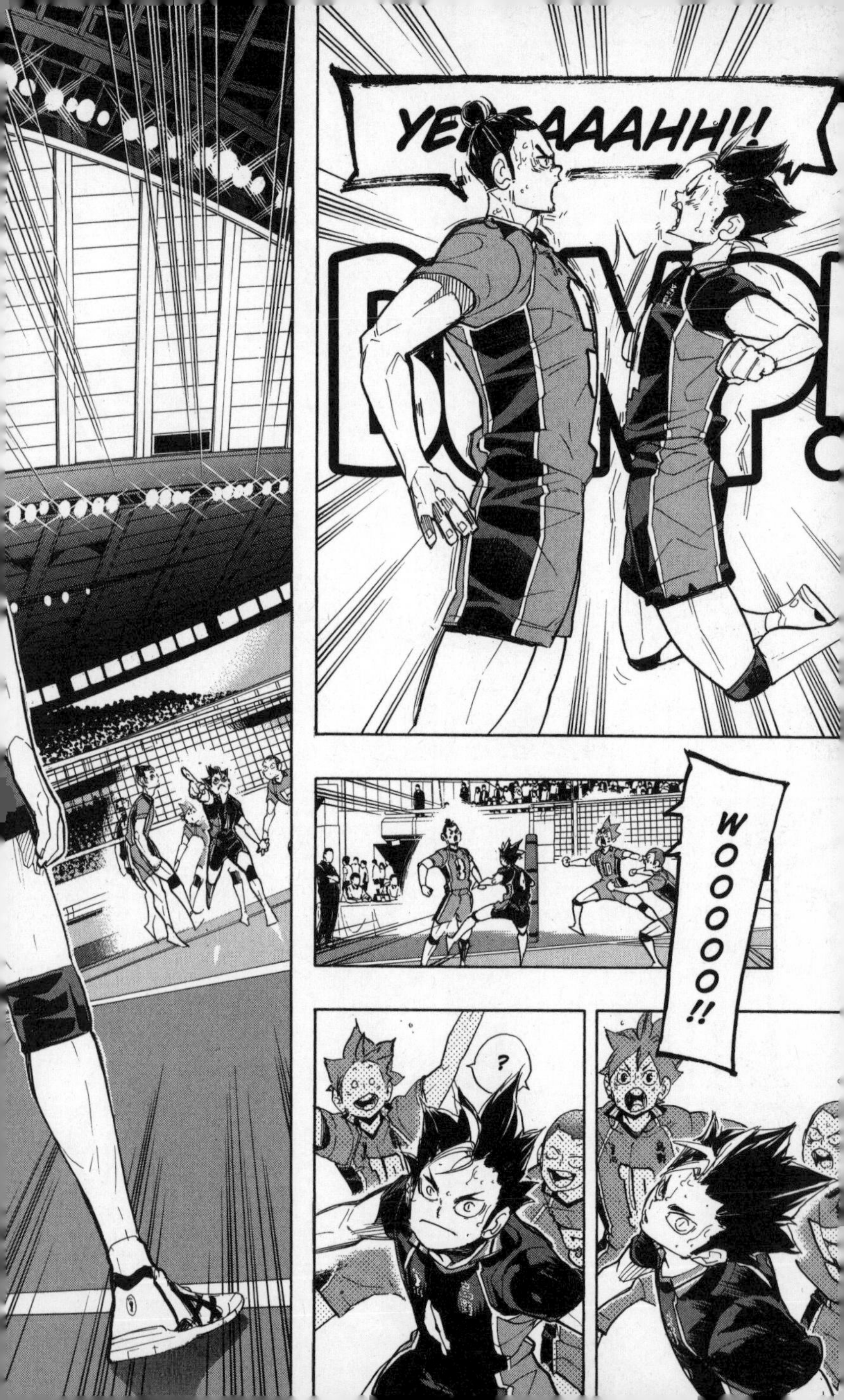
YEAAAAHH!!
WOOOOOOO!!
?

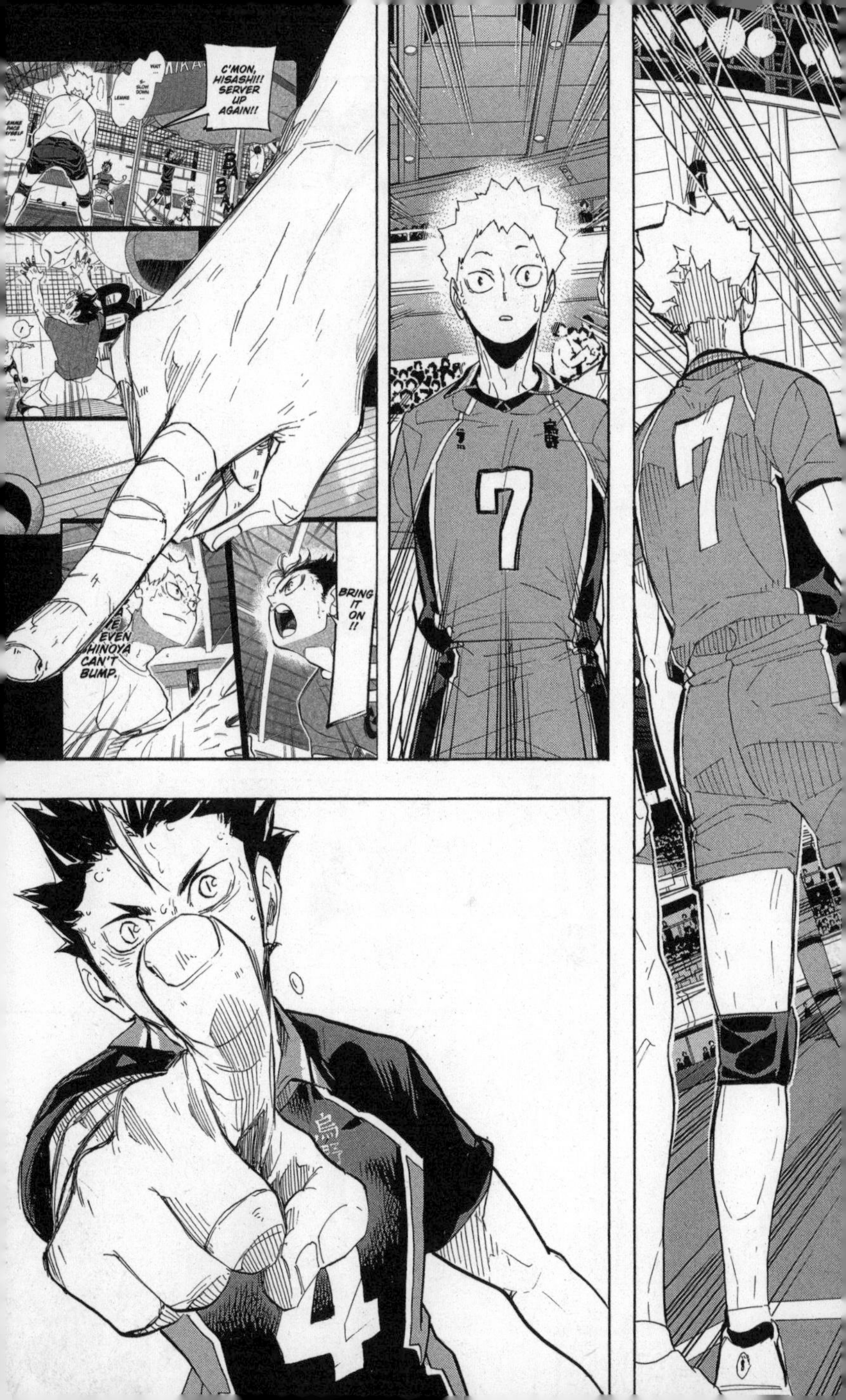
C'MON, HISASHI!!! SERVER UP AGAIN!!
WAIT ...
S-SLOW DOWN ...
LEMME ...
BA BAM
BRING IT ON !!
CAN'T BUMP.

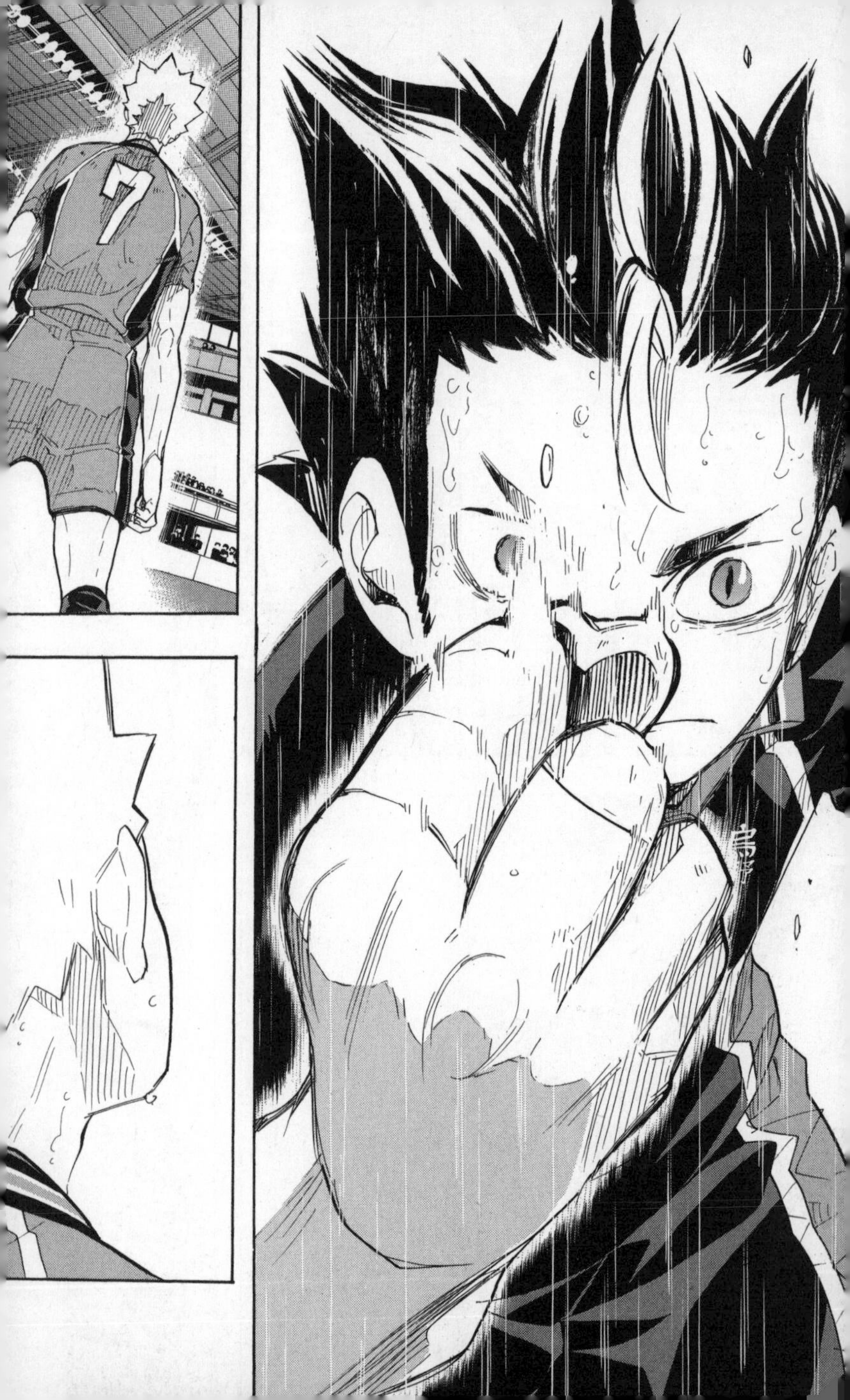

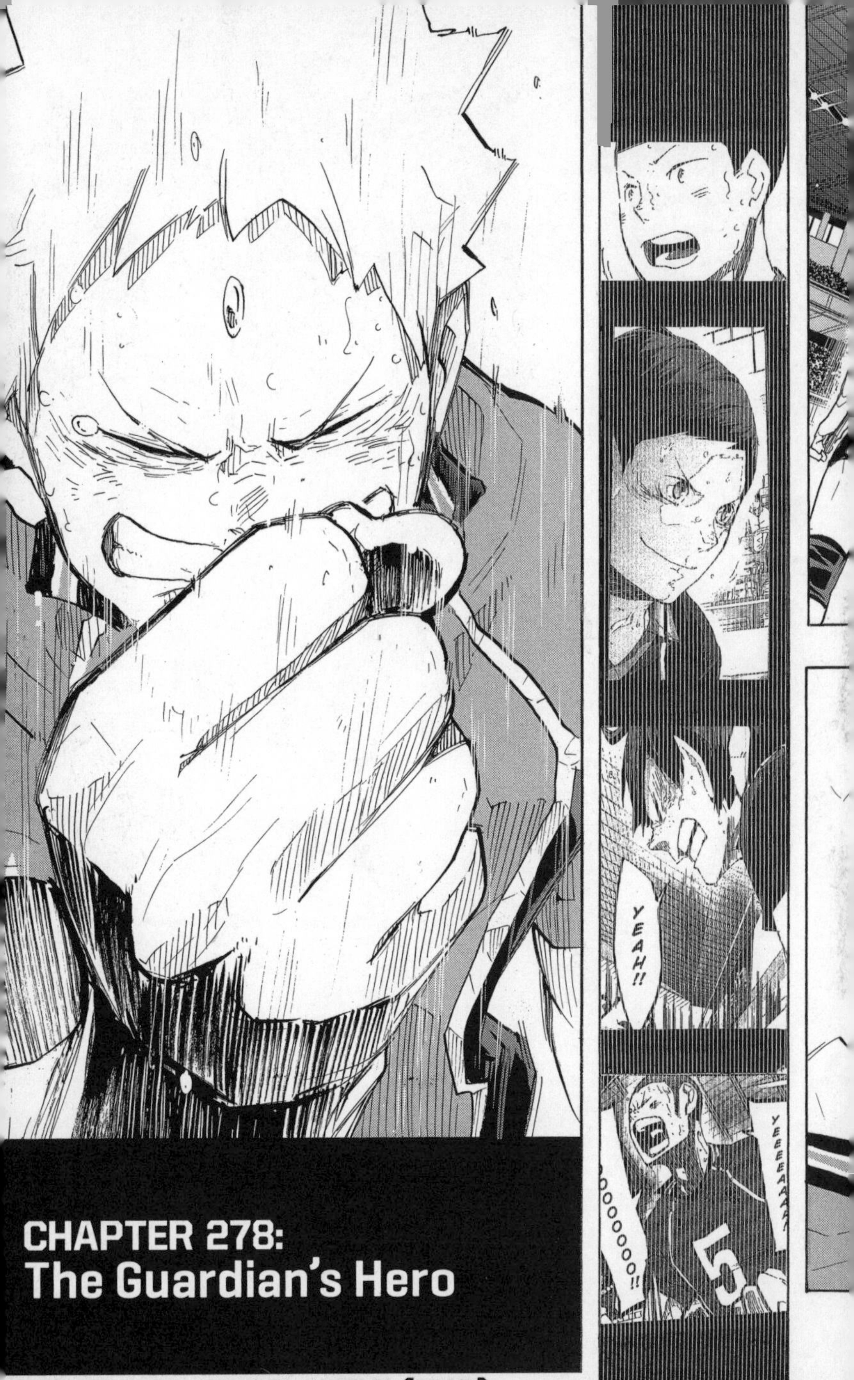
YEAH!!
YEEEEAAA!
OOOOOOOO!!
CHAPTER 278:
The Guardian's Hero

HAIKYU!! VOL 31: HERO (END)

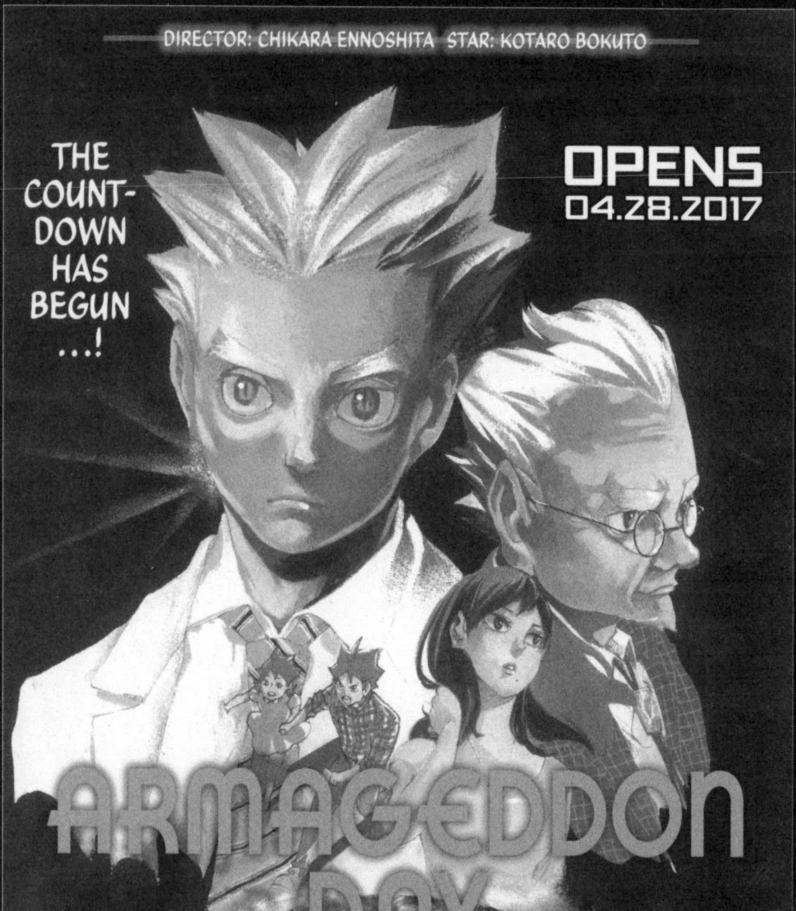

DIRECTOR: CHIKARA ENNOSHITA STAR: KOTARO BOKUTO
THE COUNT-DOWN HAS BEGUN ...!
OPENS 04.28.2017
ARMAGEDDON DAY
DIRECTOR / SCREENPLAY: CHIKARA ENNOSHITA
KOTARO BOKUTO
TANJI WASHIJO
SHOYO HINATA
NATSU HINATA
FILMING: KEIJI AKAASHI
ART DIRECTION: KANAME MONIWA
SOUND DIRECTION: SATORU TENDO
www.j-haikyu.com
"ARMAGEDDON DAY" PROJECT GROUP

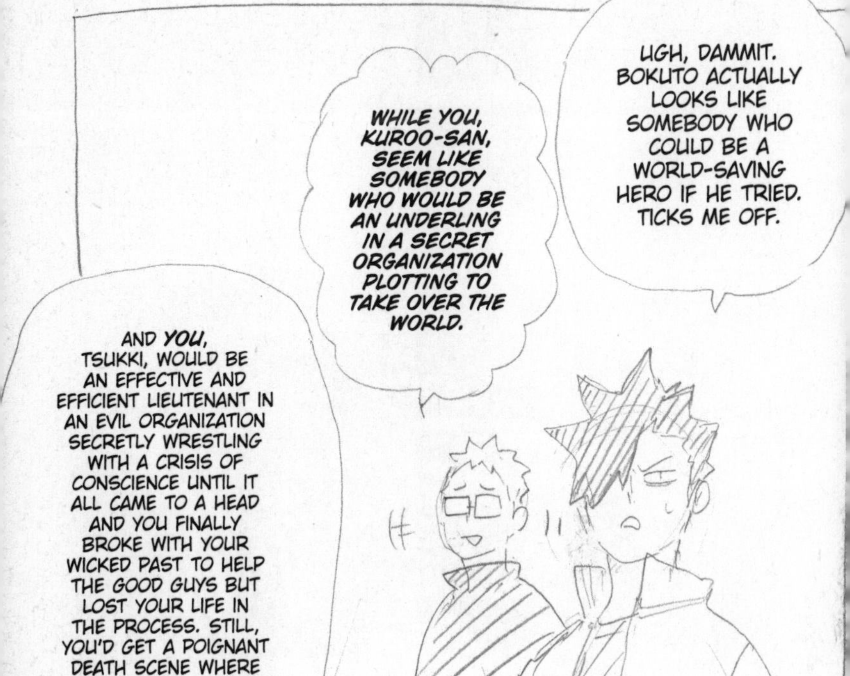
UGH, DAMMIT. BOKUTO ACTUALLY LOOKS LIKE SOMEBODY WHO COULD BE A WORLD-SAVING HERO IF HE TRIED. TICKS ME OFF.
WHILE YOU, KUROO-SAN, SEEM LIKE SOMEBODY WHO WOULD BE AN UNDERLING IN A SECRET ORGANIZATION PLOTTING TO TAKE OVER THE WORLD.
AND YOU, TSUKKI, WOULD BE AN EFFECTIVE AND EFFICIENT LIEUTENANT IN AN EVIL ORGANIZATION SECRETLY WRESTLING WITH A CRISIS OF CONSCIENCE UNTIL IT ALL CAME TO A HEAD AND YOU FINALLY BROKE WITH YOUR WICKED PAST TO HELP THE GOOD GUYS BUT LOST YOUR LIFE IN THE PROCESS. STILL, YOU'D GET A POIGNANT DEATH SCENE WHERE YOU'D QUIETLY DIE WITH A SATISFIED SMILE ON YOUR FACE.
EXCUSE ME?!
WANNA SHOOT THAT NEXT?
ENNOSHITA

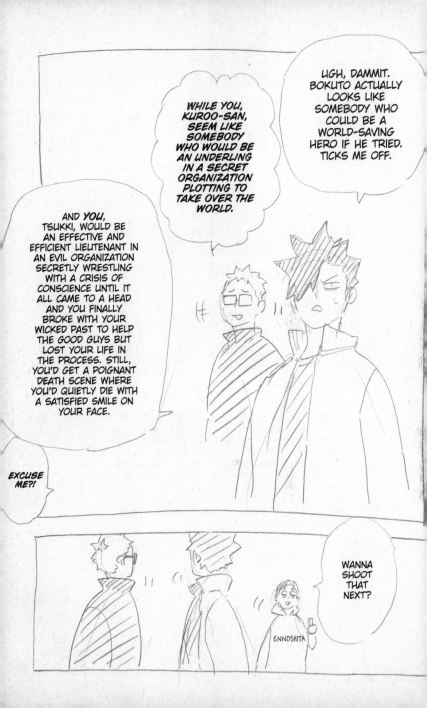

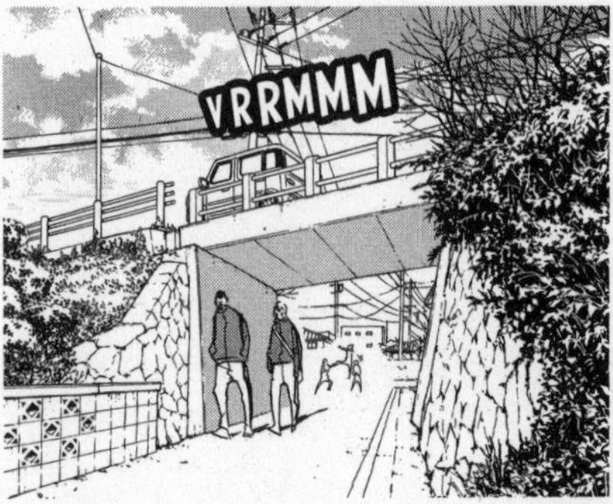
VRRMMM

INARIZAKI IS A HIGH SCHOOL SET IN HYOGO PREFECTURE, BUT THIS PANEL FROM CHAPTER 274 IS ACTUALLY BASED ON A PLACE IN OITA PREFECTURE. ONE SUMMER I WENT ON A (COMPLETELY UNPLANNED) "HECK WITH IT! POST-ALL-NIGHTER OITA PREFECTURE EXPLORATION TREK." ONE OF THE PHOTOS I TOOK FROM IT LOOKED PRETTY GOOD, SO I USED IT AS A REFERENCE FOR THIS PANEL. OH, AND THE SEA BREAM *CHAZUKE* I HAD AT A PLACE NEAR THERE WAS AMAZING.

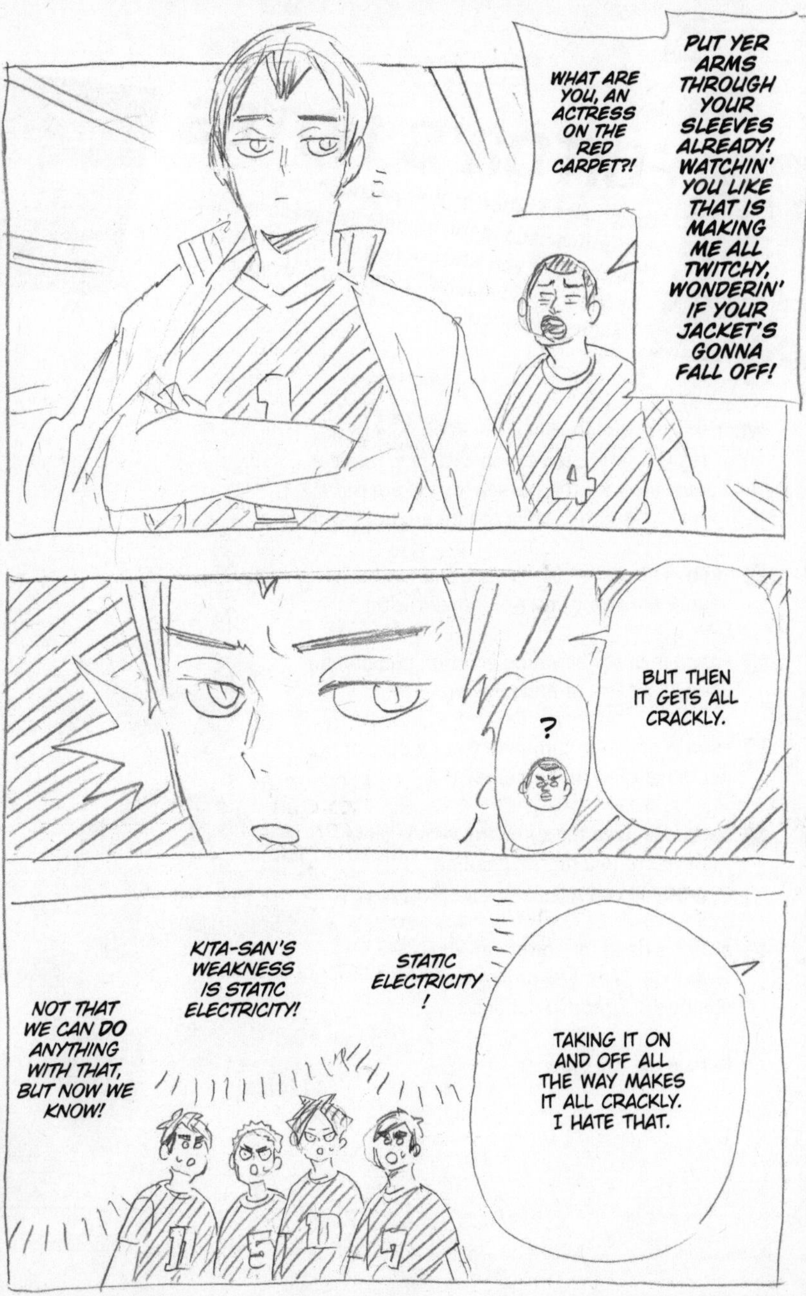

PUT YER ARMS THROUGH YOUR SLEEVES ALREADY! WATCHIN' YOU LIKE THAT IS MAKING ME ALL TWITCHY, WONDERIN' IF YOUR JACKET'S GONNA FALL OFF!
WHAT ARE YOU, AN ACTRESS ON THE RED CARPET?!
BUT THEN IT GETS ALL CRACKLY.
?
TAKING IT ON AND OFF ALL THE WAY MAKES IT ALL CRACKLY. I HATE THAT.
STATIC ELECTRICITY!
KITA-SAN'S WEAKNESS IS STATIC ELECTRICITY!
NOT THAT WE CAN DO ANYTHING WITH THAT, BUT NOW WE KNOW!

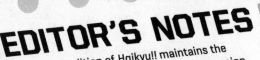

EDITOR'S NOTES

The English edition of Haikyu!! maintains the honorifics used in the original Japanese version. For those of you who are new to these terms, here's a brief explanation to help with your reading experience!

When saying someone's name in Japanese, a suffix is often attached to indicate how familiar the speaker is with the person. Some are more polite and respectful, while others are endearing.

1. **-kun** is often used for young men or boys, usually someone you are familiar with.

2. **-chan** is used for young children and can be used as a term of endearment.

3. **-san** is used for someone you respect or are not close to, or to be polite.

4. **Senpai** is used for someone who is older than you or in a higher position or grade in school.

5. **Kohai** is used for someone who is younger than you or in a lower position or grade in school.

6. **Sensei** means teacher.

You're Reading the
WRONG WAY!

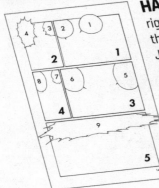

HAIKYU!! reads from right to left, starting in the upper-right corner. Japanese is read from right to left, meaning that action, sound effects and word-balloon order are completely reversed from English order.